THE
PENINSULAR
JOURNAL,
1808-1817

NAPOLEONIC LIBRARY

THE PENINSULAR JOURNAL, 1808–1817

Major-General Sir Benjamin D'Urban

Edited, With An Introduction By
I. J. ROUSSEAU, M.A.

Greenhill Books

Greenhill
Books

This edition of *The Peninsular Journal, 1808–1817*
first published 1988 by Greenhill Books, Lionel Leventhal Limited,
Park House, 1 Russell Garden, London NW11 9NN

British Library Cataloguing in Publication Data
[Journal of Major-General Sir Benjamin D'Urban . . . 1808–1817]
The Peninsular Journal, 1808–1817
(Napoleonic Library, v.8)
1. Napoleonic Wars. Peninsular Campaign.
Army, operations by Great Britain.
I. [Journal of Major-General Sir Benjamin D'Urban . . . 1808–1817]
II. Title   III. Series   940.2'7

ISBN 0-947898-87-5

Publishing History
This edition of *The Peninsular Journal, 1808–1817* was first
published in 1930 as *The Peninsular Journal of Major-General
Sir Benjamin D'Urban, 1808–1817*, and is reproduced now
exactly as the original edition, complete and unabridged.

Greenhill Books
welcome readers' suggestions for books that might be
added to this series. Please write to us if there are
titles which you would like to recommend.

Printed by Antony Rowe Limited,
Chippenham, Wiltshire.

PREFACE

During my leave of absence from the Rhodes University College, Grahamstown, South Africa, I communicated with Sir Benjamin D'Urban's grandson, W. S. M. D'Urban, Esq., of Newport House, Countess Wear, near Exeter, to inquire whether he had retained copies of his grandfather's private papers and letters which he had so generously presented in 1911 to the Union of South Africa, through the late Dr. McCall Theal. None, unfortunately, existed, but Mr. D'Urban informed me that he possessed the original Peninsular 'Journal,' of which he had made a typed copy some thirty years before. This at the time he had lent to Colonel Henderson of the Military Staff College, but the outbreak of the Boer War and subsequent ill-health prevented the latter from preparing it for the press.

Some years later Sir Charles Oman undertook his monumental work on the Peninsular War, and after the appearance of the second volume Mr. D'Urban informed him of the existence of the 'Journal' and supplied him with his copy. How helpful this proved may be gathered from Sir Charles's testimony in the successive prefaces and the constant references in the later volumes. It was, in fact, on his advice, after consultation with Professor Clapham, that I suggested to Mr. D'Urban the publication of the 'Journal.' Agreeing to this, he kindly sent the original MS. to King's College Library, so that I could edit it. In addition Mr. D'Urban, in spite of his advanced years—he was ninety-three last July—set to work to supply me with data of family history, making copies of a large number of private letters. Indeed, without his help I could not have undertaken the task.

It may well be asked why Sir Benjamin never published his 'Journal' himself, especially when after his

return from the war he printed for private circulation a
' Report of the Operations . ., . under Sir W. C. Beresford
. . . during the Campaign of 1811 . . .,' a pamphlet which
Napier used for his famous history and which subsequently appeared as an appendix to ' Further Strictures
on those Parts of Colonel Napier's History . . . which
relate to Viscount Beresford. . . .'

The answer may well be that Sir Benjamin was of
too modest and retiring a nature, as is proved by the
rigorous suppression of all personal reference to himself
in the Diary, a fact which enhances the value of the document as a record of the war.   More likely the reason was
the one given by Lord Pauncefote, the first Ambassador
to the United States of America, who, when approached
on the subject of a biography, observed, ' No, I have
worked too hard all my life to be a sufficiently interesting
subject for any biographer.'   Certainly this was the case
when Sir Benjamin embarked on his successive governor-
ships, first in the West Indies, then in British Guiana, and
lastly at the Cape, whence in 1837, after years of devoted
service, he was recalled because of his disagreement with
the then Secretary of State, Lord Glenelg, on the question
of Native policy.

From letters to former friends during his retirement to
Wynberg, near Cape Town, it would appear that he was
revising his notes and papers, but what has not been known
before is that he was in constant correspondence with his
successor, Sir George Napier, who invariably sought and
obtained his advice during those troublous years in South
Africa.   Nor is it known that Sir Benjamin sent his
private papers (the same subsequently presented to the
Union of South Africa) to John Centlivres Chase while he
was compiling his ' Natal Papers' (published 1843), a rare
and valuable contemporary authority.   It was not till 1846
that he was appointed Commander-in-Chief of the British
Forces in British North America.   Three years later he sup-
pressed the 'Montreal Riots.' He died in the same year, 1849.

It should be remarked that no part of Sir Benjamin's
' Journal ' has been omitted except ' Movement of Troops '
during the latter part of the campaign and the return
to Portugal of the Portuguese army.   The Post War
Journal till 1817 is also included as giving an insight into
the troubles of Beresford and his British officers with the

Regents in Portugal, the Royal Family being still absent
in Brazil. The voluminous enclosures, some in Portuguese
and Spanish, during and after the war, should prove of
great value for a study of the period, especially for a Life of
Sir William Carr Beresford, whose own private papers have
unfortunately been lost and whose biography remains a
desideratum in British military history.

Besides these there are original sketch maps (one of
Salamanca prepared by D'Urban's D.Q.M.G., Henry
(afterwards Lord) Hardinge) and some forty contemporary
maps, some of them the same, and therefore as unreliable,
as those used by Masséna, except that from the first extensive reconnaissances were undertaken by the British,
as shown by the ' Journal.' It is interesting, further, that
the two maps of Salamanca (' second part comprising the
battlefield and the country around the city of Cuenca ')
missing from the Irish collection are to be found enclosed
with the D'Urban papers (*vide infra*, p. 187).

The very pleasant task remains of thanking Mr. D'Urban
once more for his constant interest and valuable assistance ;
Sir Charles Oman for revising the typescript and checking
the spelling of the proper names, also for the ready permission to use the map of Spain and Portugal which
appears at the end of this volume ; Major Carey Curtis,
La Cotte, Fort Road, Guernsey, for the loan of MS. letters,
copies, and photographs ; Mrs. Christobel Wheatley of
Berkswell Hall, Coventry, for Sir Henry Watson's correspondence with Sir Benjamin about Salamanca ; and lastly,
one nearer home, for encouragement and help throughout
the whole course of preparation as well as the correction
of the proofs and compiling the index.

I. J. R.

King's College,
  Cambridge,
    23rd November 1929.

P.S.—I have just received from Sir Henry Beresford-
Peirse, Bart., Melcombe House, Weybridge, great-grand-
nephew of Lord Beresford, two batches of private letters
dealing with the events of the period. It almost appears
as if he were on the track of the long-lost Beresford correspondence. It is hoped that further search among the
family archives may prove successful.

I. J. R.

IN MEMORIAM

ANNIE HELENA ('BABY')

OBIIT 23 NOVEMBER 1915.

———

' *Majorem hac dilectionem nemo habet . . .*'

CONTENTS

MAPS

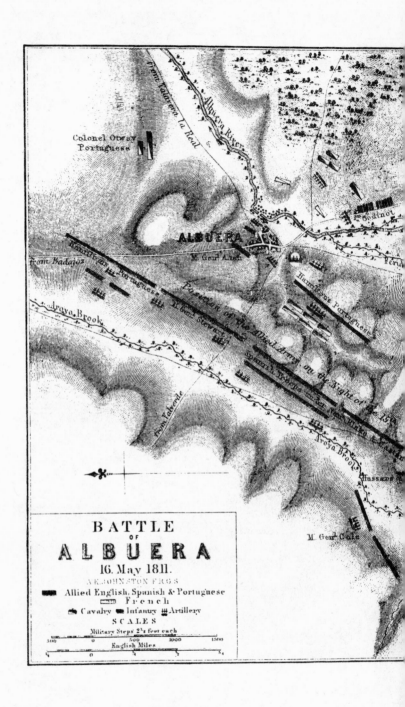

BATTLE
OF
ALBUERA
16. May 1811.
A.K. JOHNSTON F.R.G.S
Allied English, Spanish & Portuguese
French
Cavalry Infantry Artillery
SCALES
Military Steps 2½ feet each
500   0   500   1000   1500
English Miles
¼   0   ½   ¾

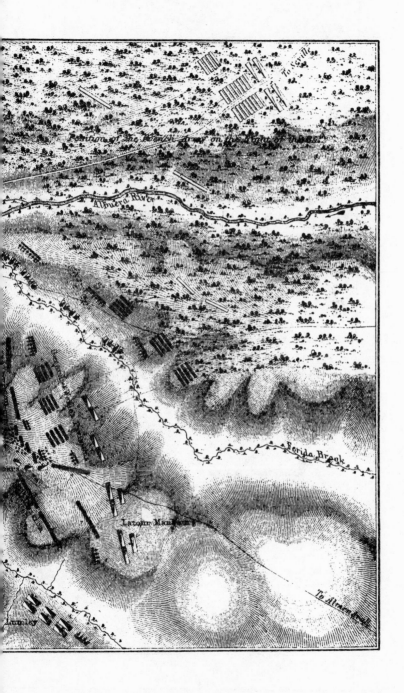

Position of the French Army on the Night of the 15th...

Albuera River

To Seville

Forida Break

Latour Maubourg

To Almendral

Lumley

THE ROADS OF THE SA

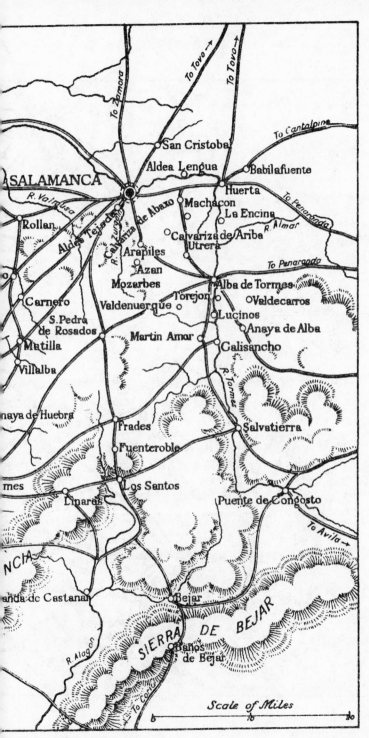

SALAMANCA ALMEIDA REGION

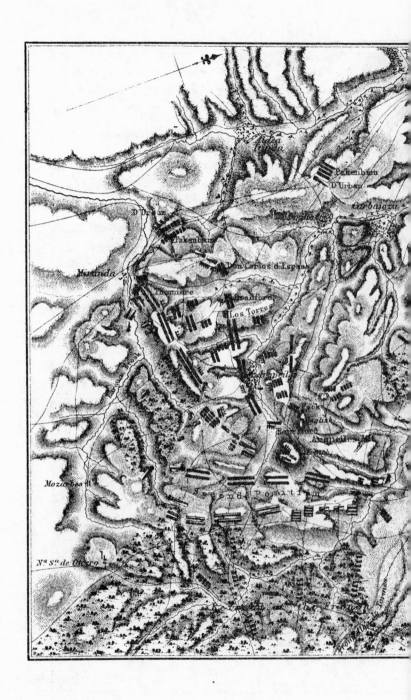

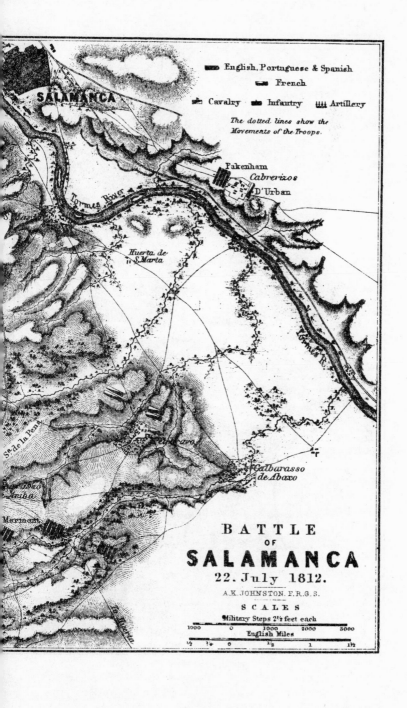

English, Portuguese & Spanish

French

Cavalry   Infantry   Artillery

The dotted lines show the Movements of the Troops.

SALAMANCA

Pakenham
Cabrerizos
D'Urban

Tormes River

Huerta de S.Marta

Sª de la Peña

...asso Ariba

Mozarbes?

Calbarasso de Abaxo

Tormes R.

BATTLE
OF
SALAMANCA
22. July 1812.
A.K.JOHNSTON. F.R.G.S.

SCALES
Military Steps 2½ feet each

| 1000 | 0 | 1000 | 2000 | 3000 |

English Miles

| ½ | ¾ | 0 | ½ | 1 | 1½ |

Scale of English Miles.

MAP

OF

SPAIN & PORTUGAL

to Illustrate the

CAMPAIGNS OF 1808 ETC.

A.K.JOHNSTON,F.R.G.S.

EXPLANATION.

	TOWNS of upwards of 50.000 inhabitants
	Towns of 30..50.000 inhabitants
	Towns of 10..30.000 inhabitants
	Places below 10.000 inhabitants

2 Longitude West from Greenwich 0 Longitude East from Greenwich 2

INTRODUCTION

A. The D'Urban Family

ACCORDING to a family tradition, one which Sir Benjamin
shared, the D'Urbans were French Protestant refugees, but
in the parish register of Brockley in Somersetshire, there is
recorded as early as 1598 the christening, on June 7, of a RICHARD
DURBAN, while in 1514, JOHN DURBAINE—the name also occurs
as DURBIN—was presented by Sir James Percival to the
benefice of Weston-in-Gordano, hundred of Portbury, county
Somerset, these three names appearing in the registers of Cheddar,
Wrington, Chelsey, Nailsea and Axbridge. This last church
also contains a monument to ' Elizabeth and her child, wife
and daughter of Richard Durban, deceased 25th of December
1665 '—dates all prior to the Revocation of the Edict of
Nantes and the consequent Huguenot emigration.

It would seem that in this century a son of the Richard
just mentioned moved to Norfolk, for a Walter Durban is
described as being ' born in Somersetshire on the 8th of October,
1640, but now of Long Stratton,' a village due south of Norwich,
where he died on January 15, 1724 (his wife, Bridget, pre-
deceasing him on April 27, 1714). Their son Richard [1] (born
September 24, 1681) became the father of John (born February 4, 1721), who at the age of twenty entered the Navy and
served as surgeon's mate on board H.M.S. *Royal Sovereign*
during the war of the Austrian Succession. After the Peace
of Aix-la-Chapelle, he returned to London to study medicine,
ultimately becoming a Doctor [2] of Physic of Edinburgh. Shortly

---

[1] Richard would seem to be a family name, for another of the Somerset
branch is commemorated in 1753 by a tablet in Brockley Church for
the gift of . . . 'twenty five pounds, the interest thereof to be given in
bread to the poor of the said parish . . . the Sunday after Christmas Day
and the Sunday after New Years Day, yearly, and for ever." See
Collinson's *Somersetshire*, ii, p. 121.

[2] ' I do not remember what office (almost a nominal one, I fancy) my
father held about the court of King George II, but in virtue of it this
mourning ring was sent to him at His Majesty's death.' Note signed
B(enjamin) D(Urban).

afterwards he married in St. Margaret's Church, Westminster, Elizabeth,[1] only daughter and heiress of Benjamin Gooch, a celebrated surgeon and writer of the time, who was, moreover, prominently connected with the founding of the first cottage hospital in England, namely, at Norwich. Dr. D'Urban[2] must have settled at Halesworth, for here was born on February 16, 1777, the youngest and only surviving son, Benjamin, the writer of ' The Peninsular Journal.'

Nothing is known of D'Urban's childhood, except that at the age of five he lost his father, so that his early training must have fallen entirely to his mother. The next event is his entry, at the age of fifteen, into the Army as Cornet in the 2nd (or Queen's Bays) Dragoons, the year that war broke out between England and Revolutionary France.

There was a prospect of active military service abroad when his regiment was under orders to proceed to the Continent, but the instructions were countermanded. D'Urban was more fortunate in the beginning of 1795, when he embarked, in charge of a detachment, and joined his regiment in Westphalia after the disastrous retreat of the British Army from Holland. The close of that year he exchanged into the 29th (afterwards the 25th Light Dragoons), in order to accompany Sir Ralph Abercromby to the West Indies, where he remained for eighteen months. On his return in 1797 he married, on August 7, in St. James's Church, Piccadilly, London, Anna, only surviving daughter of William and Mary Wilcocks, of the parish of St. Swithin in the city of Norwich. For some months he stayed in England and was on the point of rejoining his regiment in Jamaica when he was placed on the staff of the Earl of Pembroke, with whom and the Honourable General

---

[1] It is interesting that Lord Chancellor Thurlow courted the young lady, ' but she would not have him, for she was positively afraid of him.' It is said that this rebuff caused him to forswear matrimony. See *Lives of the Lord Chancellors*, by Lord Campbell, v, p. 656.

[2] ' It is not known,' so writes Mr. W. S. M. D'Urban, ' when the name Durban was changed to D'Urban, but Benjamin Gooch in his works published in 1792 uses the latter form, while Dr. D'Urban signed his name thus as early as 1777.'

Mr. D'Urban goes on to say that his great-grandfather visited Italy about this time and met a Duke D'Urban, which may have influenced the alteration. There is also a town of Durban near Carcassone and another, with the apostrophe inserted, to the south of Toulouse—the latter obviously connected with the French family of that name. Strangely enough, after the Battle of Toulouse, the Marquis D'Urban, the head of the Languedoc branch, made himself known to General D'Urban and, claiming relationship, asked for a petition to be sent to the King, Louis XVIII, through the British ambassador ; ' At that period,' adds the General, ' English auspices were considered the most availing of all others for the promotion of any suit to Louis 18th, hence it came that the Marquis made this request to me.'

St. John he continued to serve until the end of 1799, the date of his appointment as Major of the Warwickshire Fencible Cavalry, with permanent rank in the Army. The next year he studied at the Royal Military College, High Wycombe, received promotion early in 1805, and joining the 89th Regiment at Cork, soon afterwards proceeded to North Germany with the expeditionary force under Lord Cathcart.

In the following year, appointed to the 9th Garrison Battalion, he returned to Ireland and joined the staff of the Quartermaster-General's Department, training that was to prove of inestimable value in his future career.

B. HISTORICAL [1]

In the year 1808 it would seem Napoleon had reached the zenith of his power, with the annexation of Spain and Portugal—at least their crowns—to his Empire. He had, however, reckoned without the Spanish people, who thereupon rose in revolt—the first of those national risings destined ultimately to lead to his downfall—a chance, moreover, ' so unexpected and fortunate ' for Great Britain that she immediately answered the appeal for help by sending in July an expeditionary force, in temporary charge of Wellesley, to the Peninsula. The troops and their commander had meanwhile heard, previous to their disembarkation in Mondego Bay, the encouraging news of the Spanish patriots' capture of a whole French army at Baylen, a feat no continental nation had accomplished since the remarkable Italian victories. At the same time, by an irony of fate, Wellesley learnt that as the junior Lieutenant-General he had been superseded, but in spite of his bitter disappointment, he completed the arrangements for the landing of his men and spent the time while awaiting his successor, in a much-needed organisation of his commissariat, preparatory to his march upon Lisbon.

On August 15 [2] the first shot was fired in the campaign ever since known as the Peninsular War, which was to rehabilitate the reputation of the British Army, so low and mean at

[1] For the better understanding of the ' Journal ' the reader is referred to vol. ix, chap. xv, of the *Cambridge Modern History*, by Sir Charles Oman, whose monumental *History of the Peninsular War* is just about to be completed. It will, in future, be referred to merely under his name.

[2] The day before, Wellesley's successor, Sir Harry Burrard, had arrived. Wellesley duly reported himself, but ' being, as it seems, a leisurely sort of man, the new commander resolved to sleep on board for one night more and to come ashore next morning, a resolve that cost him that chance of commanding a British Army in a pitched battle which so many generals have in vain desired '—for on the following day (August 21) Junot made his attack. See Oman, i, p. 250.

the time as to explain Napoleon's contempt for it throughout the war, a miscalculation that proved a further factor in his final overthrow. The victory of Wellesley at Vimiero was, in fact, the first step in that process, which might have been considerably hastened, but for his supersession by slow and unenterprising generals who counselled awaiting Sir John Moore's division before renewing the attack upon Junot, in the meantime accepting the latter's offer of an armistice of forty-eight hours. There followed the Convention of Cintra and the evacuation of Portugal by the French, while the British generals were recalled to face a public inquiry in connexion with recent events.

Fortunately for the Peninsular campaign, Wellesley was completely exonerated, but it was not till April of 1809 that he returned in command of the British army, re-established at last as a fighting force in the eyes of Europe and able to face the French.

With Junot's departure from Lisbon and the retreat of Jourdan's army together with the ' Intrusive King,' Joseph, the close of the first Peninsular War is reached, and if the Supreme Junta, that was established at Madrid, had acted with energy and despatch instead of wrangling among themselves, Napoleon might have desisted from a second invasion. Instead, he was given all the time he wanted to deliver his counterstroke, and though he profoundly despised the Spaniards, he was determined that this attempt was not to end like the first, massing an army of more than a quarter of a million good troops against ' the tumultuous levies of the Junta.'

Initial and instantaneous success blinded Napoleon to the unique difficulties of the campaign that began to develop with the incidence of guerilla warfare and the kind of resistance that could be offered by a determined nation in arms, proud and revengeful.

Meanwhile the British forces were still concentrated around Lisbon, in spite of the fact that Wellington's second successor, Sir Hew Dalrymple, had been promised heavy reinforcements as soon as the news of Vimiero reached England. Nor had he made any attempt, first, to explore the roads leading from Portugal into Spain, reconnaissance, as we shall see, which D'Urban undertook immediately on his arrival ; and secondly, to continue Wellesley's good work, ' the formation of a proper divisional and regimental transport for the army,' lacking 'because of England's long abstention from continental warfare on a large scale,' as Sir Charles Oman points out, ' and not due to the Ministry, the permanent officials in London or the executive officials on the spot.'

' The art of war in this as in its other branches,' he continues, ' had to be learnt; it was not possible to pick it up by intuition. . . . Nothing can be more interesting than to look through the long series of orders and directions drawn up by the Quarter Master General's department between 1809 and 1813, in which the gradual evolution of order out of chaos by dint of practical experience can be traced.' It is indeed in this department that D'Urban rendered such excellent service, making his ' Journal ' so valuable a document for British military history.

Such was the situation when, on October 6, Sir John Moore succeeded to the command, aggravated further by the fact that the Spanish Junta would appoint no Generalissimo, while the Portuguese were averse to contracting their animals, mostly mules, for places beyond the frontier.

Under very grave difficulties, therefore, Moore began his march from Lisbon with a view to joining up with the rein-forcements expected from England. On October 13 these arrived off Corunna under Sir David Baird,[1] with Lieut.-Colonel D'Urban as Assistant Quartermaster-General.

The opposition to Baird's landing by the Galician Junta, his money difficulties, entailing the loss of all-important time in linking up with Moore's forces and so checking Napoleon, in the meantime carrying everything before him on his march to Madrid, must be told by the ' Journal.'

[1] Previously in command of the troops who captured the Cape in 1806.

MAJOR-GENERAL SIR BENJAMIN D'URBAN

Knight Commander of the Most Honourable Military Order of the Bath,
Knight Commander of the Royal Military Guelphic Order,
Knight Commander of the Ancient and Most Noble Order
of the Tower and Sword,
Major-General in the Portuguese Service,
Colonel in the Spanish Army.
Later Governor of Antigua, Montserrat and Barbuda;
of Demerara and Essequibo
(afterwards with Berbice, British Guiana;
and of the Cape of Good Hope;
and Commander-in-Chief of the British Forces in Canada).

From a miniature painted after his return in 1817 from the Peninsular War.

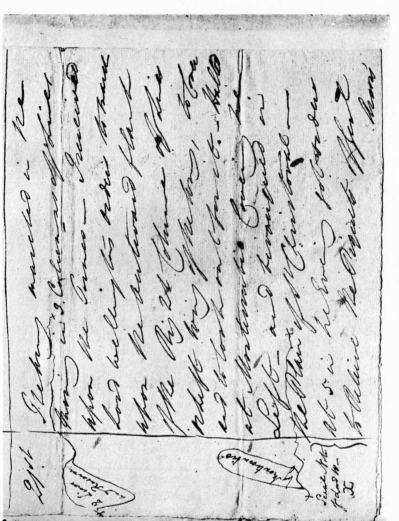

Facsimile from the *Journal*, describing the day before Salamanca (July 22, 1812).

(1) The "Pencil note of Lord W——", is printed along with other letters from Wellington in the *Cambridge Historical Journal*, Vol. iii. No. 1, 1929.

THE
PENINSULAR
JOURNAL,
1808-1817

NAPOLEONIC LIBRARY

D'URBAN'S PENINSULAR JOURNAL

JOURNAL I

ARMY OF SIR DAVID BAIRD

1808, *Sept.* 21. Received an order [1] appointing me Assistant-Quarter-Master-General to the Army assembling at Falmouth for foreign service. . . .

Sept. 24. In the evening left for London for Falmouth.

Sept. 27. Arrived and reported myself to M(ajor) G(eneral) W(arde).

Sept. 28. Sir David Baird arrived with the Cork Division. Reported myself and received his orders.

Sept. 29. The Army now assembling consists of . . . 13,000 men [2] nearly.

Sept. 30–*Oct.* 1–5. During these days, through the whole of which the wind was decidedly foul, every preparation was made for sailing, both by the Army and Navy. The Convoy consisted of H.M. ships *Loire, Amelia,* and *Champion,* and the *Sybilla* was expected. The troops were equalised in the transports. 6 empty ships, arrived from the Eastward, enabled us to make this arrangement. The provisions reported complete to 6 weeks by the Principal Agent of Transports, Capt. Bower. The General Officers and Staff were allotted to the different Men-of-War, and Lt. Gen. Sir David Baird officially reported to Captain Schomberg of the *Loire* (Senior Captain) that the Army was in readiness to proceed.

Oct. 6. The Commodore made a signal to prepare for sea and orders were given for all to repair on board. Wind in the afternoon became fair, but with so large a fleet it

---

[1] At this time I was an A.Q.M.G. on the staff of Ireland, but for the moment in London on a short leave of absence.—B. D.

[2] See Oman, i, p. 501, footnote, which agrees substantially with the analysis given by D'Urban.

would have been impracticable to work out and clear the land before the night fell; we were to sail at daybreak. N.B. arrived 60th Regiment and detachment of the 52nd from Jersey and Plymouth. . . .

Oct. 7. The wind became unfavourable in the night. No hope of sailing.

Oct. 9. The wind being fair, the *Loire* made the signal for sailing at daybreak and by 12 o'clock the whole fleet of 150 sail had cleared the harbour.

Oct. 13. *Corunna.* Made Cape Ortegal at daybreak and by 2 o'clock the Fleet anchored in the Harbour. . . .

(On the 12th we fell in with a division of Junot's Army returning to France,[1] spoke and passed.)

Sir David Baird immediately waited upon the Junta of the Province. It was here learned that the Junta of Madrid had been declared supreme and Count Florida Blanca vice-president of it, and Regent of the Kingdom.

This perhaps is fortunate, as hitherto the Spaniards have had no supreme head but each province has been directed by its own Junta. Castaños is declared Commander-in-chief, Palafox commands the Advanced Guard, and the Marquis of [La] Romana (not yet arrived from England)[2] and General Blake have each a wing of the Great Patriotic Army.

It does not appear that the British Army was expected here even if it were looked for more to the Eastward. The Junta of the Province had received no intimation about it, nor had they any authority to permit it to land; an Express was despatched to Madrid for orders upon this head, the return of which cannot be expected in less than six days. In the meantime Sir David sent an Express to Sir John Moore at Lisbon, who instead of meeting this division at Corunna, as had been rather expected, will not be able to do so till the ships that have brought it to Spain proceed to the Tagus to convey his Army. A small Ship of War was ordered to England to convey despatches. Can it be that the Ministry of the

---

[1] 'Evacuating Portugal in terms of the Convention of Cintra.'

[2] 'With 7,000 Spanish troops, who, having deserted from Napoleon's army in Denmark, were returning to Spain in British ships to aid in the war of Independence.

'*Note.*—This and all other information collected only from report.—B. D.' A pretty shrewd guess! *Cf.* Oman, i, pp. 498 *et seq.*

Spanish Government were not perfectly agreed as to a British Force being received with open arms ? Or even as to the plan of its arrival ? Above all, would they expect a combined movement of Sir John Moore's by sea to Corunna, and be ignorant that his Transports are employed in carrying home the Army of Junot ? It would be premature to judge of the feelings of the Spanish Government or the Body of the People from what is exhibited in an extreme Seaport like this, otherwise it would not appear that the arrival of 13,000 English inspires much joy . . . *Mais nous verrons.*

Oct. 15. Sir David Baird sent an aide-de-camp (Capt. Gordon) in the *Champion* to Lisbon. The Junta are anxious that this Division should upon disembarking move forward considerably.

Sir David Baird having determined to disembark the horses and three of the waggons, altogether 850 empty wood houses were inspected and approved of. The necessary communications made with the Agent of Transports, landing places fixed upon and a report made to Sir David that everything was ready, when he should order the disembarkation. The Junta proposed an advance of the Army in several columns upon a *point d'assemblement* at Benavente in the Kingdom of Leon there to re-unite. Sir David Baird's orders, however, confined him to Galicia for the present. This, therefore, fell to the ground and they proposed a cantonment from Lugo to Orense. This, however, would appear too far (24 Spanish Leagues, equal to 96 English miles) unless it were the intention to advance which it evidently is not, as this Army is only considered a part of Sir John Moore's and waits his orders, perhaps his arrival.

Oct. 17. It is impracticable to procure money for the use of the Army. No provision having been made to its arrival here. A courier therefore sets out for Lisbon, by Oporto, where the Consul may perhaps have it in his power to be of use in this exigency. He carries to Lisbon duplicates of Capt. Gordon's despatches, and also pressing representations to Sir John Moore about the want of money.

Oct. 18. The Army held in readiness to disembark in light marching order with a half allowance of Tents.

Returns therefore ordered of the weight of Baggage

of the respective Corps and of camp equipage in possession
and wanting. Packet made up for England.

Oct. 19. Arrived the *Semiramis* frigate from England
with the Marquis of La Romana and Mr. Frere, Plenipo-
tentiary to the Spanish Government at Madrid. (Supreme
Junta.) This Ship also brought a considerable sum of
money. Strange to say it did not appear to have been
intended for the Army, a part of it, however, must be
made use of. Orders received from Sir David Baird to
lay before him returns of Bat and Forage Allowances.
This was done without loss of time and orders given for
the payment of it and a Month's pay to the 24th October.

Oct. 20. It was apparent that great difficulties existed, and much perplexity prevailed at Head Quarters,
many unexpected disappointments were probably experienced, and no little confusion reigned ; Orders and
Countermands succeeded each other rapidly. From the
beginning I had known nothing but by report, by casual
observation, and by judging of causes by their effects, for
the General did not communicate with me upon the state
of things, (wherefore I know not) any further than giving
me as Senior Assistant of the Quarter Master General's
Department such orders as related thereto. I was not
in his confidence and as my opinion was never asked, of
course I never ventured to obtrude it—once only after a
conversation that had passed in my presence by chance,
when Don Tomas de Morla had (I fancy) proposed on the
part of the Junta an advance (upon disembarking) as far
as Benavente, I suggested to the Military Secretary, as I
thought it a positive duty, although I had not been called
upon, that it was, I thought, too advanced a position as I
understood the General's Orders were not to act *per se*
but to consider himself under Sir John Moore's orders,
and wait for a combination with him. For if the Army
moved to Benavente, and the Enemy made a forward
demonstration, Sir David would be committed and obliged
to act. Here I was informed by the General himself that
he had no power *yet* to quit Galicia. I further suggested
the necessity (before the Army disembarked) of ensuring
sufficient depôts, upon the different routes, agreeable to
the established rules of War, so that the General might
feel his movements perfectly independent of the promises
f the Junta, which I should myself feel no inclination to

confide in. I added that I could not presume to make any proposal to Sir David, as he had not at any time spoken to me on the subject, but that it was my wish to send forward some officers of the Department to reconnoitre the routes, and estimate the probable resources for the Army, if he would be pleased to give me timely notice when and how he intended to move. Afterwards of course I attempted to suggest nothing further, merely attending for Orders at the times appointed for the Heads of the different Departments.

Oct. 22. Orders from Lisbon arrived and announced to me, to my infinite surprise and mortification, that I had been from the first, at the Horse Guards, intended for Sir Harry Burrard's Army in Portugal, and Col. Murray said in addition, that he should send Col. Bathurst to take charge of the Department immediately.

There is no help for this disappointment, not a disappointment for the being removed from the Head of a Staff which must soon cease to be separate, and of which I never considered myself anything more than a casual holder, and which had become in an especial degree irksome to me from the instant I could no longer avoid feeling that the General did not treat me as a Confidential Staff Officer. It was not this, therefore, that I repined at, it was the being removed from an active to an inactive Army, and at losing the prospect of seeing Service when I had considered myself secure of it, and after having given up my Staff Situation at home with that view and expectation, and with that alone. Wrote Genl. Anstruther and Col. Murray to endeavour to get my destination changed . . . [obliterated] . . .

Oct. 25. Colonel Bathurst arrived. Gave up everything (scarcely anything), indeed, because as no steps had been taken to disembark, this not having yet been practicable, from a variety of causes, such as want of provisions etc. which I had predicted). Signified to Sir David Baird my intention to go to Portugal by land and received his permission. My reason follows :—I was determined of course, to make every effort not to lose the Campaign, and therefore chose to go by the route of Salamanca and Ciudad Rodrigo, to meet Sir John Moore's Head Quarters, and try to remain in some shape with the active Army.

Oct. 26–28. Sir David Baird signified to me (who had

not told him that I intended to diverge from the direct
Road to Portugal) his desire (or order) that I should proceed to the Head Quarters of Sir John Moore, wherever
they might be, to explain some circumstances of *delay*;
these I was supposed to know, but as I could not but by
inspiration, I explained so much, and desired to be informed, for otherwise of course I should have but ill-
answered any questions of Sir John Moore.

Conversation with the Military Secretary :—M.S. You
are referred to Sir D. Baird's letter for explanation.   B.D.
What have been the obstacles ?   M.S. You know of course.
B.D. No.—'Tis easy for me, in common with others, to
judge generally what—but particulars and detail I *cannot*
know as I have *never been told*.

Upon receiving the requisite instructions (CX)[1] I
found, I am sorry to say, my predictions verified, my
suspicions confirmed as to the fulfilling of the Junta's
promises.   No means *had* been taken, relying upon these,
to form independent Magazines, and all stood still.

On the last day of October, my credentials being ready,
I took leave of Sir David Baird.

Nov. 1.   Set out for Salamanca by Betanzos.   The
road good, the Country not apparently rich, but if a judgment might be formed from the Fair of Betanzos, very
populous.   Great resemblance to Ireland both in the dress
and manners of the lower orders as well as in the face of
the Country.   Thus far, Fish probably forms a great part
of the subsistence of the Country.   Supplies for an Army
in this part of Galicia and indeed, perhaps as far as Villa
Franca del Viergo, will at all times be difficult to procure,
and in the event of an English Force landing at any period
at Corunna, it will always be a necessary measure to form
Magazines of Provisions in advance, independent of the
resources of the Country.   (I rode all this journey at
about 15 Spanish Leagues, equal to 60 English Miles a
day, therefore any observations made so perfectly *in
transitu* must be short, and perhaps incorrect.)   As far as
Villa Franca ;   from thence the Country becomes rich
and fertile and can contribute a sufficiency for the wants
of 15,000 Men, marching through it, having a few days'

---

[1] These are enclosed along with letters, orders, despatches, reports
(referred to under letters) throughout the Journal, which are too voluminous
for printing.

notice, and the Columns consisting of not more than 2,000 Men, following each other with two days' interval. Bread and Wine and Meat here, and these excellent of their kinds, but meat in sufficient quantity for a regular supply must not be expected. Abundance, however, for Hospital and Convalescents daily, and if properly regulated perhaps about 2 Meat days in a week for the whole Force.

To Montesegreyo (2½ Leagues) a Mountain Road which though good in substance is steep, and will much retard the passage of Artillery. No passage for Troops as far as may be judged but by the high road, and a few Jägers and very light Artillery might defend these Mountains for a long time, and indeed render them, I should think, impassable.

Valleys narrow, with streams and pasture; the lower falls covered with vines and all the channels of the Mountain Streams lined with Chestnut Trees, a great part of the Food of the People.

To Gitteritz (2½ Leagues), flat Country, good road. Not very abundant. Room for a march in several parallel Columns.

To Valdomar (3 Leagues) and Lugo (3 Leagues). Tracts of cultivated Country, a very few spots of which are almost equal to Essex and Kildare, but they do not extend far enough to afford any considerable means of subsistence for an Army. Room for several Columns, but there are two Rivers whose banks, steep and *escarpés*, probably furnish strong positions. Lugo is a good Cantonment for 2,000 Men, and ought to be rich from its being a thoroughfare to Corunna and Ferrol, thus being afforded a great facility of procuring the Produce of the Interior and Sea Ports. No strength—Old Moorish Town. Detained here one day by several duties.

Nov. 3. To Sobrado—the features of the Country unequal—and so on to Benevrea—good roads, however, and nothing to impede a march in two Columns, the Country rich too, in grain and vines, but so small a distance, although it might much assist, cannot furnish a secure dependence for provision of an Army *per se*. From Benevrea commenced a chain of splendid Mountains, picturesque beyond description, covered with Chestnut Trees, beautifully interspersed with villages. Admirable Bridges crossing the Gorges and torrent crevices, and the *ensemble* furnished a scenery not easily to be forgotten. This Chain forms the Mountains of Cabrera which extended over many leagues beyond Villa Franca, but there diverged to the South and then inclined Eastwards, their tops covered with snow. The Roads made with the greatest judgment, and every advantage that could be derived from each *douce piste* most promptly taken. No passage for an Army but in one Column by the high roads, and the Country, however beautiful, affords no subsistence to be depended upon.

Hitherto there did not appear any great enthusiasm amongst the people, either of hatred to the French, or love for the English, who were coming to assist them, but the French had not penetrated beyond Villa Franca, and this may account for it ;—what a Nation does not feel, but only hears, rarely rouses it to vengeance against its foes, or gratitude to its Friends.

Nov. 4. To Ponteferrada, a rich and fertile Country, and for 2 L. from Villa Franca a perfect Garden ; to Bembibre fertile also, to Manzaial a short extent of Mountain road, from thence to Astorga little descent and plain. Good subsistence, it would strike me, for an Army all the way, and nothing bad about the roads ; if any opposition were looked for between Bembibre and Manzaial, some loss must be expected, but the Mountains' extent is so short that the passage could be easily forced. At and from Villa Franca, which had been occupied by the French, the popular hatred against them began and increased, the appearance of an English Man was hailed with joy, and the reception even of a simple individual of that Nation was quite gratifying.

Astorga is an old Moorish Town, may well hold two Regiments of Infantry and one of Cavalry, and appears, as one looks from its tottering walls, to be the Queen of a most extensive and fertile plain, nothing but Corn-fields meet the eye, and from hence, I imagine, commences the promised fertility of the Province of Leon. Don Eugenio McCrohan, a Colonel in the Spanish Service, his Father an Irishman, has here forwarded the interests of the English Army, with all the enthusiasm of a Friend and a Countryman. The Junta of Leon assembled at Cabillos have appointed a Committee of three of their number to attend exclusively to the Provisions of the British Army, and this is the fairest promise of a speedy and uninterrupted advance I have yet met with—*Gracias a McCrohan*.

Wrote to General Craufurd at Villa Franca to say that he must expect no Mules at Astorga for that the Governor had been obliged to lay hands on all that were sent to the Fair of Leon for their Armies.

Nov. 5.   Detained by duty at Astorga.

Nov. 6.   Banega (4 L.), Bisara (3 L.), Benavente (3 L.). This Country fertile beyond measure, uninterrupted Plain, the roads good, and in a Circle of about 20 English Miles in diameter, or about 60 English Miles in circumference there are so many Villages (probably 40), that I imagined the whole British Force might be Cantonned here, disentangled from the mountains, Provisions easily drawn together, the Roads good, and the Army thus in readiness to move without any obstacle or delay at the first orders. As I knew, or had reason to suppose, that Sir David Baird was in ignorance of this, and as before I left Corunna he had received advices of the Army from Portugal being on its march, and orders from Sir John Moore to move on as far as this point, I wrote from Banega to him (B. Y.) to state what I had observed, and to say that if it accorded with his views, a most desirable Cantonment might be here obtained, making Astorga Head Quarters, and putting the two Light Regiments (43rd and 1 and 2, 95th, equal to 1,800 Men) of the Advanced Corps with General Craufurd in Banega.

Near Bisana, an immense estate of the Duc del Infantado and Palace.   The Puerta del Bisana an excellent Bridge. The Town of Benavente of beautiful approach, and the Country richly wooded.

Benavente will hold two Regiments.   The greatest loyalty amongst all the people through this day's journey, hatred to the French, Love and extreme kindness to everything English.

Nov. 7.   Niego (4 L.), Pedrieta (3 L.);   could proceed no further, no Horses being to be had by any means whatever.   The country still flat and fertile and admirably calculated for the movements and subsistence of an Army.

Nov. 8.   Procured Horses and proceeded by Zamora (5 L.), Corzales (8 L.), Carova (3 L.) and Tarasa (4 L.) to Salamanca (3 L.);   Zamora is a large and beautiful Town upon the Douro. The loyalty of the People enthusiastic. The Country from Zamora to Cuovo, perfectly a Garden, at once the Granary and Vineyard of Old Castile. Along the whole extent of Country from Astorga to Salamanca, Cavalry and Flying Artillery must carry everything before them, not the slightest impediment exists to their combined movements in any direction, but in the district within a circle of about 6 Leagues diameter round Zamora, Jägers will be necessary for the Vinefields especially when the Vines are in foliage. Within this circle is made the best Wine in Spain, and here, as well as along the whole extent from Villa Franca del Vierzo (immediately upon quitting the mountains of Galicia) the Bread, even of many of the Peasants, is of a superior quality to any I have ever met with in England; it has a whiteness and flavour unknown there, and requires nothing to be eaten with it to render it excellent. Many of the Farmers produced samples of Wheat much heavier, thinner skinned, and fuller of flour than that of England. In short, the Vin du Pays and the Bread alone furnish a repast for an Epicure.

Arrived very late at Salamanca. The incessant Rains, which indeed had continued night and day almost without interruption, of course prevented the Horses from getting on so well as they would otherwise have done, but the Specimens I have had of Spanish Horses, in thus riding above 300 English miles, convinces me that, though small, they are excellent, and admirably calculated for Hussars.

Note :—These Rains which continue like a Monsoon in Spain, from October to March, render those Months very unfit to take the Field in, ill health among the Troops must be the certain effect, and Military operations should certainly be avoided at this season, unless called for (as is probably now the case) by the most urgent and pressing necessity.

Nov. 9–10. At Salamanca.—I have found Major Montalabert and Capt. Gomme of the Qr. Mr. General's Staff of the Army of Portugal; they had come forward to establish Cantonments for that Army which marches in several Columns and here reunites to rest for a few days.

General Anstruther is at Almeida, thither therefore I go upon the morning of the 11th. He will afford me some clue by which I may find Sir John Moore and fulfil

Sir David Baird's orders, and he also will tell me what chance I have of remaining with the active army   Sir John Moore has not passed Salamanca, and from all I can learn he will come by Almeida and Ciudad Rodrigo, where I shall be before him.   I wrote to General Anstruther by a Courier of Montalabert's on the morning of the 9th.

Note :—Salamanca is a magnificent City and fully equal to all that has been written or said of it.   The Great Square surpasses anything I have seen, and being entirely surrounded by Piazzas, is equally convenient for the wet and hot Months of this Country.

Nov. 12.   Left Salamanca for Ciudad Rodrigo (16 L.), met Sir John Moore and Col. Murray at St. Martin del Rio.   Delivered my despatches, and fulfilled Sir David Baird's orders.

In a long conversation with Col. Murray urged everything I could suggest to effect my desire of remaining with the Army as a Volunteer or in any way, to no purpose. ' It was all arranged in England,' he said, ' and could not here be altered.'

Nov. 13.   To Almeida (6 L.)—My fears too true ; General Anstruther received both my letters from Corunna and Salamanca, while Sir John Moore and Col. Murray were at Almeida, and said everything to retain me,—'twas all to no purpose. . . . [obliterated] . . .

Nov. 14–17.   Almeida.—Having now remained four days at Almeida, I signified to General Anstruther my intention of proceeding to Lisbon.   He expressed a wish that I should remain for a time, as he might have occasion for me, and independent of my real desire to do anything he wishes (a desire which this kindness to me justly calls for) I am but too happy in any event that prolongs my stay, even for a few days, with this Army, for with the adage ' while there's Life, etc.'   Of course I expressed my willingness to be of use in any way, and on the

Nov. 18.   Some intelligence from the Spanish Army in Biscay arrived.   The General told me he wished me to reconnoitre the Country for some distance in front and rear of the Coa ; 'tis just possible that this may become the Winter Quarters of the Army, and 'tis right therefore that its resources, Roads of communication both with Portugal and Spain, and its natural features of defence should be at least generally known to him.

Nov. 20.   I prepared to set out and Capt. Pierrepoint,
Dp. Ast. Qr. Mr. Genl. being casually at Almeida, the
General directed him to accompany me, and we set out
from Almeida, and crossing the River Coa proceeded to
Aldea Nova and Ansul.   Here we separated, Capt. Pierrepoint to reconnoitre the Country along the River Pinhel.
. . . Myself proposing to proceed along the Western bank
of the Coa. . . . Thus Capt. Pierrepoint will ascertain
the resources of the Country Forming this Frontier Position, and communication with Guarda on the Interior,
and Salamanca and Ciudad Rodrigo on the exterior side,
and I shall have become acquainted with the Resources,
Communications, and general capability of Defence of the
Line of the Coa, a combination of which Intelligence will
form such a Report as the General desires.   I inspected
the Country South. . . . The summit of the range of
Hills, and the falls and banks of the Coa, the Bridge and
Passages of the River, and arrived at Castello Mendo (?)
in the evening.   Remained there for the night.

Nov. 21.   Inspected Castello Mendo and the Valley
or Ravine in which it stands, and proceeded along the
course of the Coa Southward, and along the summit of
the Hills, thence to Villa Mayor.   Evening.

Nov. 22.   At Villa Mayor.   So impenetrable a Fog
that to proceed would be useless.   The Country is well
cultivated and very productive, but this was to its Inhabitants little labour; it requires no manure and the scratching
the surface is sufficient tillage.   Grapes and Rye in abundance;   some Wheat and Indian Corn.

The Line of the Coa furnishes the front of a very strong
position from Almeida, the key and *appui* of its Left (as
far at least as Punte de Sequeiros from whence I came here).

This place has the square Tower of the Keep of its
Ancient Castle remaining very perfect, its construction and
shape exactly like the Old Irish Square Tower, excepting
that the stairs instead of being spiral and revolving within
one of its angles are a straight oblique, and carried in
succession along its sides.

Nov. 23.   The Fog clearing a little in the middle of the
day, inspected Villa Mayor and proceeded to Valdomalos
(see Field book P. 4) to the Coa, crossed it at Punte [de]
Sequeiros, and proceeded along the Western bank of the
heights rising from thence to Sabugal;   there I found

letters from Genl. Anstruther wishing amongst other
things a Report upon the Roads between that place and
Penamacor as connected with the Transport of Convoys
from Portugal to Spain. Answered it and sent off a
Courier to Almeida. Letter and Answer DW.

Nov. 24–25. Inspected every Road and Pass ; returned
to Sabugal, Report (EV) for General Anstruther.

The People certainly improve a little as one advances.
At Penamacor a most intelligent and gentlemanlike
Priest. The Country exceedingly beautiful and the
valley, hill, and Town of Penamacor very picturesque.

Nov. 26. Inspected Sabugal and all the Eastern line
of the Coa to Villa Mayor. Great cordiality and kindness
from the People. (Field Book P. 5). . . .

Nov. 27. Continued to inspect the Passages and
Eastern bank of the Coa (see Field Book P. 6) and proceeded to Freynada. Fell in with on the road a very
intelligent Pilgrim returning from St. Jago de Compostella.
Olive Harvest—great gaiety.

Nov. 28. Finished the proposed Reconnaissance and
arrived at Almeida.

Dec. 3. Gave in to General Anstruther a Report and
Sketch of which the Field Book and Rough Sketch are
the basis. (Of this he was kind enough to express his
approbation.)

The three Spanish Armies have been successively
beaten by the French who are in great force, and have,
since the last Action at Tudela (Nov. 28) in which the Army
of Castaños was totally dispersed, advanced by the Pass
of Samosierra, and proceeded as far as Segovia ; this has
determined Sir John Moore to fall back upon Portugal,
sending orders to Sir David Baird to retire to Corunna and
re-embark. Orders have in consequence been given to
stop all the Convoys advancing, and to make (as covertly
as possible) every preparation for a Retreat. The General
directed me in consequence to mark out Cantonments for
the whole Army within the line of the Coa. . . .

Here I cannot help asking myself, Why is this British
Army, from which so much has been expected, so much
hoped, to fall back upon the first reverse and incur the
contempt of the Enemy and a diffidence and distrust on
the part of our Allies which nothing will ever efface ?
It had better not to have advanced at all, since perceiving

what has happened was to be expected.   Every Military
Man has long predicted that if the Spaniards ventured
upon a Battle with the regular Columns of the French
Army before they were joined by the British, they would
infallibly be beaten.   But are 40,000 English therefore
to fall back, desert Spain at its utmost need, give the
People we came to assist just cause to say that we only
advanced while they were between us and the Enemy,
and above all justify the arrogant boast of Bonaparte,
who it seems is with his Army, ' That the English would
not wait to face him ' ? . . . [obliterated] . . .

The Armies of Portugal and Corunna are not joined,
it may be said, but Why are they not so ?   The Junction
might have been formed before the 20th of last month ; [1]
the reinforcements only reached the French Army in
Biscay on the 16th, and all would have been in time . . .
(obliterated).   What will come of it all I am ashamed to
think.   Come what will, should some miracle intervene,
should the Spanish reassemble and some success of theirs
induce the C. in C. again to advance, 'twill be the Spaniards
and not the British who have turned the scale.   [Obliter-
ated but legible : ' Never was such a moment for setting
the name of England as high as heaven.']   One evil will
inevitably result ; the Spaniards are a keen, a penetrating,
and now more than ever, a suspicious People, they already
suspect us, in spite of all our caution, and they will never
forget that in their greatest pressure, when the danger
was most urgent, we intended at least, to leave them to
their fate. . . . [obliterated].

Here let me pay a tribute of respect and just praise to
the firm and comprehensive mind of General Anstruther.
When no human being thought of the possibility of a retreat,[2] when conquest and success were in every mouth,
he alone looked forward to a reverse, he provided for
falling back, though it was a thing almost out of the question, and when he sent me to reconnoitre the Frontier
Line of the Coa, he said to me ' No one can say how soon
this knowledge may be necessary.   A Retreat to Portugal
may yet be upon the Cards, and as we have leisure, we
will be prepared.'   Now, although evidently loathing the
measure of retiring, and condemning the doing so without
a Battle as a loss of National Honour, he has so effectually

---

[1] See Oman, i, p. 492.   [2] See Oman, i, p. 494.

exerted himself that in a few hours every preparation is made, the Convoys all turned back, orders for provisions given, and all this with so much finesse that whatever the Spaniards may imagine from the unguarded steps nearer to Head Quarters, the Portuguese at least believe that these measures are in a part a feint to deceive the Enemy, in part a provision for reinforcements from Lisbon and Oporto, to countenance which the Garrison of the latter place in March for Lamega.

Dec. 4. The suspicions of the Spaniards are aroused, and no wonder. Independent of all the appearances which indicate retreat, our indiscretion at Ciudad Rodrigo has divulged, in part, the secret which should have been preserved till the last. No supplies can be procured. The Spanish Magistrates have orders ' to assist the British advancing, but not retiring.' . . . [They are right . . . rest obliterated.]

Dec. 5–7. Nothing new—Everything retrograde. Silence, Melancholy and Depression.

Dec. 8. 'Tis the wish of the Commander-in-Chief that a Cantonment and Position along the Agueda, from San Felices to Ciudad Rodrigo, should be reconnoitred as (probably) an intermediate Stand between Salamanca and Portugal. In this he is possibly right, for as the French have arrived at Valladolid, approached Madrid and pushed their Posts almost within sight of Salamanca (as far as Arevalo) they will scarcely permit an uninterrupted retreat to the Line of the Coa.

I have received the General's order therefore to proceed instantly along the left Bank of the Agueda, and ascertain the Resources and Cantonments of the Country, and on arriving at Ciudad Rodrigo, I shall for expedition sake, make my Report direct to Col. Murray at Head Quarters by express and then return along the course of the River to San Felices, and from there Report upon its features of defence and local fitness for the Line of a Position.

Dec. 9–10. Finished the proposed Reconnaissance, arrived at Ciudad Rodrigo, and despatched the Report (GS) to Col. Murray.

All the way the minds of the People in a state of ferment and suspicion. Put the best possible face upon the matter, but a retreat is evidently expected by them.

Official accounts of a Victory gained by the Spaniards at Madrid, our measures are all changed, the retiring Convoys ordered forward. A Despatch has been sent to stop Sir David Baird, and the Armies are to join upon Zamora. Our fatal and hasty determination to retire has not, however, escaped the penetration of the Spaniards, and an Ecclesiastic [1] high in Office has imprudently let fall in my presence, what I have no doubt is the general opinion of us throughout Spain. 'The English [2] will advance,' he said, ' now that there are no Frenchmen in the way.' ' Great Heaven ' . . . (rest obliterated).

I have learned that the Spaniards had determined in case of a Retreat to seize upon the money (16,000 Dollars) and the Military Stores worth £100,000 : this they might well have done, for by some chance or other, not 50 British were in the Town, the three Companies of the Buffs having been quartered without the Town, and the Gates actually shut upon them.

There is now no use in returning along the Agueda. I shall set off to the General.

Dec. 11. Arrived at Almeida. Reported to General Anstruther what had been contemplated by the Spaniards at Ciudad Rodrigo, in order that if we still continue to make it a Depôt for valuable Stores, we may never again be without a sufficient force there to command their safety.

Dec. 12. The faces of all the world are changed, and every one looks gay, and all are advancing. The General has set out for the Army. . . . (obliterated). Before setting out for the Army the General communicated to me his ideas that if the French got possession of Madrid [3] (a very possible event, especially if they bombard it), they would endeavour to put a Corps along the Tagus and alarm us at once for Portugal and for our own supplies, and therefore signified to me his wish that I should proceed to Castello Branco, and make myself well acquainted with the Country from thence directly in front to Alcantara, and Spain, and also to the right along the course of the Tagus, from Alcantara to Abrantes, in the

---

[1] Treasurer to the Bishop of Ciudad Rodrigo.
[2] Because Moore had countermanded his orders and determined on an advance.
[3] Napoleon had already entered it eight days before.

course of this reconnaissance I am to order a strong working
Party of the Companies of the Buffs at C. Branco to repair
such parts of the Road to Villa Velha as I shall think
necessary ; and when I have finished, I am to Report
in duplicate to Colonel Murray, Sir John Moore's Qr.
Mr. Genl., and to the Commander of the Forces at
Lisbon.

[A page of the Note Book cut out and part obliterated.]

Dec. 14–20. Proceeded by Guarda, Belmonté, Alcaide,
and Alcaes to Castello Branco ; the Valley between the
Sierra d'Estrella and the Sierra de Val Precisa, is the most
beautiful Garden imagination can conceive, every inch of it
is covered with Vineyards, Corn-fields, Groves of Chestnut,
Olive, Cork and Oak, intersected by streams, interspersed
with beautiful Villages, and as it were shut out from the
rest of the World by two arcs of most beautiful, picturesque
and splendid Mountains whose Tops are in the Clouds.
'Tis very like a fairy land, or the scenery of an Arabian
Tale.

'Tis impossible I should ever forget the hospitality
and kindness of my Hosts through the greater part of
this journey [100 English miles]. The Names of three of
them I must record as People to whom if it ever fall in
my way I must shew every kindness in my power—At
Guarda—Diego Dias Preto Jacanha, Chantre de la Cath-
edral. At Alcaide—Silvestre Praizo. At Alcaes—Padre
Jacinto Pero Goulao, and his Brother.

Before I left Almeida I reported myself to the Commander of the Forces, and the Dep. Qr. Mr. Genl. at Lisbon,
and said their Orders would reach me at C. Branco.

At Castello Branco I have met with Col. Donkin,[1] Dep.
Qr. Mr. Genl. of the Army of Portugal who, with many
Staff Officers, is engaged in making a very extensive
reconnaissance of the Tagus and its Banks, and of the
Country in General, and this he commenced with a view
of our Spanish Army retreating, which he had expected
from a letter from Colonel Murray from Salamanca. I of
course reported myself and explained the views of Colonel
Anstruther.

I have received the orders of Col. Donkin to reconnoitre
to Rosmaninhal and along the Tagus to Villa Velha, as a

[1] Afterwards Sir Rufane Donkin, Acting Governor of the Cape during
the arrival of the 1820 British settlers.

C

portion of the General Reconnaissance upon the tapis. Wrote General Anstruther to this effect.

Dec. 21–25. Reconnoitred the Communication to Rosmaninhal . . . Returned to Castello Branco. Colonel Donkin gone. Wait here to make my Report and to afford the last chance for a letter of recall to the Army in Spain to reach me.

Dec. 26–29. Made my Reports and Sketches of the preceding Reconnaissances. The 29th and 31st Regts. arrived from Lisbon. In the evening of the 29th, I learned that a letter (B 40) had been received by Colonel Campbell commanding the latter (and the Senior Officer) from the Junta of Alcantara, announcing a French Corps having crossed the Tagus at the Punte del Arzobispo (driving back the Spanish General Galluzzo who was charged with the defence of that Passage), advanced to Placencia, and was probably proceeding towards Alcantara. I therefore waited upon him, and on finding it true, suggested the propriety of his sending me forward to the frontier to communicate with the Spanish General commanding at Alcantara and the Portuguese General Silveira de Fran-cesca, who had gone forward in the morning to Sequeira ; and to observe, and give him certain intelligence of the motions of the Enemy. I also enquired if the Lt. Col. had received any orders ; he had, and they were, *if the Enemy appeared in force* to fall back upon Abrantes. He acqui-esced in my idea that falling back should not be resorted to but in the last extremity, agreed in the propriety of sending me to reconnoitre and gave me orders accordingly. I wrote to Col. Donkin (X60).

Dec. 30. I recommended to Colonel Campbell to establish Posts d'Advertisement at the Chapel on the hill near the bridge over the Poncal on the road to Monforte, and also near Idanha Nova, provided I should report to him that the Enemy was actually upon the frontier, and set out for Segura, accompanied by Major L'Estrange of the 31st Regt., and Lt. L'Estrange of the 71st Regt. who had very kindly asked leave of the Lt. Col. to go with me.

Dec. 31. Arrived at Segura, and there found the Portuguese B. General Silveira de Francesca occupied in assembling a force to oppose the Enemy who have advanced to Placencia and Coria according to reports he has received. The Spanish General Galluzzo fell back after a short

resistance upon Puente de Mirabete. Wrote to Col.
Campbell (Z61). Proceeded to Alcantara, found the
people in much apparent consternation, this probably
arises from the conduct of the Governor, a Spanish brigadier named Gabrielle,—very little doubt of his being in
the French interest, if not, he is himself frightened to a
degree almost beyond belief, and seeks to communicate
his own fears to the people. He was, I find, a creature of
the 'Prince of Peace.'[1] Promised the Junta British
assistance, and they at length seemed to lose a part of
their alarm. They have 8 guns, and plenty of ammunition, their bridge may be defended till doomsday. Nothing
to be expected from the exertions of the Governor. Agreed
to meet him and the Portuguese General Fonseca at
Pedres Elvas to-morrow,—'tis necessary that I should
be present at this conference.

1809, *Jan.* 1.   Met the Portuguese and Spanish B.
Generals at Pedras Elvas; after a long conference the latter
promised to arm to the number of 500 peasants, and to
exert himself to the utmost. Genl. Fonseca appears a
very intelligent man, and determined to do his duty. 'Tis
his intention while his Corps is weak to defend the Points
of Zarza, Salvatierra, Alfayates, and Penamacor, at which-
ever the Enemy may attempt to penetrate, and when he
becomes stronger, if the French Corps still remains upon
the Tagus, to march and attack it. Accompanied him
to Zarza. Despatched (Z62) to B. Genl. Stewart who I
learn has arrived at Castello Branco. I am sure that this
French Corps, reported to be 7,000 men, can never be
intended for Portugal. Bonaparte would never detach
so largely to attack that country now that he is playing
for so great a stake in Spain. Its real intention must be
to march by Ciudad Rodrigo and Almeida and not only
place itself between Sir John Moore and Almeida, the gate
by which all his supplies arrive, but perhaps, marching
by Ledesma upon Zamora turn the right of his position,
which is supposed to be near Benevente. Pressed this
upon Genl. Stewart and urged his marching by Sabugal
(or Belmonte) and forming a Corps of observation in the
left and rear of the Enemy. Report that the Enemy are
at Coria.

Jan. 2. Promised to report everything interesting

[1] Godoy, the notorious minister of King Charles IV of Spain.

to Genl. Fonseca and set out in the direction of Coria. At Moraleja found that the Enemy had a detachment there yesterday but were withdrawn, proceeded to Coria. The Enemy are in force at Placencia; according to report 6,000 infantry and 2,000 cavalry. The Spanish General Galluzzo made no resistance at the Bridge of Almaraz and Arzobispo and has never ceased to retreat till he has reached Dom Benito on the southern bank of the Guadiana, where he ventures to think himself in safety. All hope of co-operation with him is of course at an end. Enemy's advanced posts at Galisteal (4 leagues) and Montermosa (3 leagues) from Coria. Wrote (Z63) to B. Genl. Stewart.

Jan. 3. Received certain intelligence (Z64) that the whole Corps of the Enemy had marched from Placencia taking the route of Ciudad Rodrigo, on Salamanca. This movement they masqued by continuing their outposts at Galisted (?) and Montermosa till the whole of the main body had moved off, these then followed and formed the rear-guard. This Corps was commanded by Marshal Lefebvre. Wrote so to Genl. Stewart, to Genl. Fonseca, to Sir John Cradock and to Col. Donkin. . . .

Jan. 4–6. Proceeded along the left of the French line of march (which they pursued by Puerto de Baños, and the Bridge of Cor Ginto over the Tormes, to Avila) by the mountains of Geta and Penaparda (?) to Ciudad Rodrigo. Here I found that Sir John Moore's advance guard had been attacked by the Enemy, near Benavente. A corps of their cavalry 900 strong were cut in pieces by ours—all this is mere report, nothing certain has been received from the Army since the 27th December, when it was in its position near Benavente, where some partial skirmishing had taken place.

Jan. 7. Sir Robert Wilson arrived with part of the Portuguese Legion; he has advanced from Almeida upon hearing of the French march. He is very deficient in Staff Officers, and has requested me to remain with him for a time. I have complied, and hereby consulting my own inclinations, for here at least is a chance of something being done, at least one is near the Enemy. I have written to Sir John Cradock and to Col. Donkin for permission to do this.

Jan. 8. God knows for what reason, but the whole British Corps at Castello Branco have retreated to Abrantes,

and this day a French officer, Aide-de-Camp to Marshal
Berthier, has been brought in, and his arrival opens our
eyes to events so unforeseen, and so unexpected, that if his
account were not perfectly connected and circumstantial
I should refuse all credit to it. The British Army has
retreated to beyond Astorga, even beyond the Plain of El
Vierzo, for the French advance posts were at Ponteferrada
upon the 3rd of this month ! Great Heavens ! . . .

This man who is an Italian (his name is Marnot, and he
speaks English, French, Spanish and his own language)
and whom we have taken under our protection, that he
may not be ill treated, was on his way to Madrid. At
2 o'clock on the morning of the 3rd Bonaparte himself
delivered to him, at Astorga, a letter for his brother Joseph,
written by his orders by Marshal Berthier (Prince de
Neufchatel) expressive of his (Bonaparte's) dissatisfaction
at and diffidence of the conduct and indecision of his
brother in his advance (especially in the Market Place of
Aranjuez), complaining also of the march of Marshal
Lefebvre (Duke of Dantzic) to Placencia ; and concluding
that all these blunders had determined Bonaparte to
return to the centre of operations, and give up the idea of
following the British to their ships, which had been his
intention, and that he would be at Valladolid by the time
Joseph received that letter. This Aide-de-Camp is so
clear in his story, that however reluctantly, I am compelled to give credit to the general tenor of it. This throws
light upon the unaccountable retreat of Lefebvre, after
his march down the Tagus.

Jan. 9. A report that a French Corps has been seen
at Zapedas. The Junta as usual in consternation. Zapedas is in the road from Placencia to Avila, and 'tis just
possible that some stragglers of their rearguard have
occasioned this alarm. Proposed to Sir Robert Wilson
that I should go and reconnoitre ; received his permission,
and set off, accompanied by Lt. L'Estrange. On reaching
Alversa, near Zapedas, the whole report turns out to be a
fable. Wrote to Sir Robert to set the minds of the Junta
and people at rest, and proceeded to Miranda del Castañar
in the Sierra de Francis. These are a range of mountains
splendid and beautiful beyond description, the moun-
taineers their inhabitants, a fine loyal people, active and
vigorous, hating the French. The Corregidor of Miranda,

Don Estevan Abad, a most excellent man and magistrate, having great influence with the people. He contrives to have excellent intelligence of all the French movements. I have established therefore a correspondence with him ; and on the 10th in the evening returned to Ciudad Rodrigo.

Jan. 12.   The Junta again frightened by a report of Zamora being occupied by the French and of their having advanced to Ledesma upon the Tormes; this is a point so important, that independent of my wish to keep these good people at rest, if it be possible, I am very anxious to see with my own eyes all that relates to it, requested, therefore, of Sir Robert to be allowed to proceed to Ledesma. Received his permission, and set out with my friend Lt. L'Estrange.

Jan. 13.   We used every possible means with the Junta of Ledesma to induce them to defend their town. I inspected their bridge and gave our true opinion that it might be maintained against 10,000 men ; offered them, in the name of the General, 500 men, and some guns and pledged ourselves to remain with them while one stone stood upon another. All would not do, they determined not to defend themselves, prepared to receive the French with open arms, and are in short in the French interest. Our small Force won't admit of our defending people who don't wish to be defended ; however important, therefore, this place must be left to its fate.

Jan. 14–15.   Returned by Martin del Rio where we expected to find Sir Robert Wilson, but Salamanca having opened its gates to the French altered his direction, and he established his Head Quarters at Banovares. A very well chosen post *pro tempore*, and till his Corps crosses the Agueda, upon the Northern bank of which his position is secure and good at this period of the year, when the river is not fordable. The guns sent round by Ciudad Rodrigo very much to the discontent of that most foolishly jealous people. . . .

Jan. 16–17.   The Corps moved across the Agueda and stationed at Barba de Puerco, Villa de Ceivos and Villa de la Yegua ; the people or rather the Junta of Ciudad Rodrigo dissatisfied. Sent in by Sir Robert to give things the requisite turn. Proceeded thither, my friend L'Estrange accompanying me. A conference with the Junta has placed things on a better footing ; they won't give their Battalion out of the Town, but are convinced, at length, that it is Sir Robert's intention loyally to defend them, and desire a conference. I have therefore written to advise it.

Received His Majesty's Declaration of December 15, 1808 (from Sir Robert Wilson), translated it, and gave it to the Junta (of Ciudad Rodrigo).

Jan. 18. Sir Robert entered. All smooth and fair in appearance on the part of the Junta. Major Grant of the Legion, and Capt. Ruman of the 97th Regt. have for many days continued to observe the motions of the Enemy, with an intrepidity, zeal, and ability beyond all praise.

Jan. 19. It becomes necessary both to give confidence to the people here—(The Governor, Don Ramon Blanco, appears a good man, but an invalid and ill supported. The engineer and artillery officers ignorant and obstinate. The place is splendidly appointed with artillery and ammunition, and might in 4 or 5 days be put in a state to resist 10,000 men, but there is so much laziness and unwillingness that 'tis requisite by feints and reconnaissance to keep the Enemy as long as possible confined close to Salamanca and the Tormes, hence the determination of looking forward now to keep the flame of resistance alive)—as well as to know really what the French are about. Sir Robert therefore having ordered the Portuguese Dragoons of the Regt. of Almeida (30) at St. Felices to meet him at Martin del Rio, and having left directions for 80 men more of the same regiment, promised him by the Officer commanding at Almeida, to join him, set out for Martin del Rio. I accompanied him. In common prudence it would perhaps have been right for us to have fallen back upon Abrantes and given up the thing, on the night of the 16th, when he learned certainly that there was every appearance of embarkation both in Galicia and Portugal. Sir Robert resolved upon taking the risk of an opposite line of proceeding, and I am glad that he has done so. After all he cannot be very wrong, though his means are small, in employing them in acting up to the spirit of His Majesty's Declaration.

Jan. 20. Proceeded to Martin del Rio, where at length 13 Dragoons of the Regt. of Almeida under Capt. Piralugi of the Legion (Loyal Lusitanian) joined us. Went on to

Guardella ; met there Major Grant, and from him learned
that the Enemy had a Post of Cavalry at Calcidella, 1½
league from Salamanca, of an officer and 30 men. If
these could be carried off without much loss, a great effect
would be produced ; the French alarmed, would imagine
us in force, and act with slowness and caution ; we should
learn the real strength of the Enemy now not at all known
with accuracy, and probably get some news from the other
side the Douro, which would now be infinitely desirable.
The country is woody, and this enterprise may certainly
be undertaken with every chance of success.   To-morrow
night will be the time.   Moved forward in the night to an
isolated house on the skirts of a wood which extends to
the French Post (Tazamula).   Sir Robert left orders for
the two detachments of Dragoons to follow with as little
observation as possible.

Jan. 21.   Neither of the detachments have joined, but
it is necessary to do something immediately, the confidence
of the people as well as other ends, are to be gained by it,
as suggested above, and we cannot remain longer undis-
covered, which with our small force is everything.   Early
in the morning therefore resolved to move by the wood
towards the Enemy's outposts and be guided by events.
Evening.—We have this day done as follows :—On proceeding about half way to the Enemy's Post at Calcidella,
we were joined by a peasant who told us that the Enemy
occupied two Posts—at Calcidella and Torre—that the
former was the officer's Post and that what was doing at
the one could not be seen from the other ; Sir Robert
determined therefore instantly to attack it, this he did
in the most gallant manner, and it was carried in an
instant, but with the loss of Capt. Piralugi who was shot.
We saved the prisoners with some difficulty from the rage
of the Portuguese Dragoons and now found that this was
only a small post with a Sergeant commanding it.

There is a break in the ' Journal ' till March 6—' carried
on upon loose sheets which were lost '—but the correspondence
is preserved, from which extracts follow.

This is also a convenient point to summarise the distances
D'Urban travelled since he left Corunna on November 1 :

(*a*) To Marten del Rio, where he met Sir John
     Moore on the 12th   .   .   .   .   360 miles.

(*b*) The reconnaissance of the Coa (Nov. 20–28) 240 ,,

(c) The reconnaissance of the Aqueda (Dec.
6–13) . . . . 120 miles
(d) From Castello Branco to observe the movements of Lefebvre (Dec. 28–Jan. 6) . 360 „
(travelling on an average 40 miles in a
day of ten hours)
(e) Lastly, posting from Ciudad Rodrigo to
Miranda del Castaña (Jan. 9–10) . . 80 „

—a total of 1,160 English miles, a remarkable feat accomplished
in an entirely strange country. The last ride on horseback,
it should be noted, was at the request of Sir Robert Wilson [1]—
that intrepid and gallant officer who organised the Loyal
Lusitanian Legion, and whose conduct was in such striking
contrast to that of the over-cautious, almost dilatory, Sir John
Cradock, who, succeeding Sir John Moore, practically locked
himself up in Lisbon, expecting at any moment to embark his
troops for England.

D'Urban's correspondence opens with a letter to Anstruther
(subsequently returned to him, for Anstruther died from ex-
haustion seven days before, after the completion of that heroic
retreat to Corunna, Jan. 16, 1809).

Jan. 23. Ciudad Rodrigo. . . . ' . . . On my return
from following the French line of march I found here Sir
Robert Wilson, who had posted his corps behind the Agueda
with a view to afford all the protection in his power to
Ciudad Rodrigo and to stimulate the inhabitants of this
place to defend it. Sir Robert was induced to adopt this
resolution instead of retiring, because being in total
ignorance of the intention with which Sir John Moore had
fallen back (all communications with the Army having been
cut off since December 27) having letters from Mr. Frere
at Seville which announced the determination of England
to continue the contest ; and having beside received His
Majesty's Declaration expressing his resolution still to
support the Spanish cause, he could not imagine that an
actual retreat was decided upon and therefore conceived
it his duty to prolong the struggle here to the last.

' His exertions have succeeded in rousing the Junta and
People and from a state of depression and dependence,

[1] Enclosed in the correspondence are several letters in connexion with
a subsequent controversy which arose between Beresford and Wilson.
D'Urban being appealed to, wrote a lengthy comment in a pamphlet
(copy enclosed).—*Letter from Sir Robert Wilson to his Constituents* . . .
advanced in the *Quarterly Review*, September 1818, London.

they are now become full of confidence and determined
to defend themselves. The enemy successively occupied
Toro, Zamora, Salamanca, and the Line of the Tormes,
and as it was impracticable to procure good intelligence
of their probable subsequent movements or real strength
by any other means, as well as to give confidence to the
Town, and by occasioning alarm, delay (perhaps), the
appearance of any detachment before it, Sir Robert
patrolled on the 19th, 20th, 21st, and 22nd with a few
Dragoons of the Regiment of Almeida, along the French
advanced posts at Calcidella, Torre, and La Rude; the
first of these (1½ league from Salamanca) favoured by the
wood which abounds in that direction, he succeeded in
carrying off. From one of the prisoners he learned that
the Corps in Salamanca which had been represented as in
great force, consisted only of 1,600 infantry, 400 cavalry,
and 2 small guns, and from several circumstances it appeared likely even, that they were about to retire from it
altogether, having during their stay levied a very heavy
contribution. . . .

'Sir Robert, however, has derived from this trifling
affair all the advantages he proposed, certain information
of the Enemy's strength, has impressed them with an idea
of his being in some force (for on the succeeding day they
reinforced the posts with 300 cavalry), and has given great
additional confidence to the Junta and the people here.
He retired gradually having been joined by a small reinforcement of Dragoons, and established an advanced post
at Martin del Rio, with one of observation at Guardilla,
and then returned (to-day) to this place.

'Sir Robert Wilson, being very deficient in Staff Officers,
and having had the kindness to express a wish that I
should remain with him for a time, I have done so, though
I am aware I can be of very little use, and I have informed
Sir John Cradock (and Col. Donkin) of my doing so. . . .

'(P.S.).—Morning, 24th.—I am sorry beyond measure,
to add that letters have just arrived from Sir John Cradock,
which announce his total ignorance, except from report,
of the movements of Sir John Moore, his belief that he is
going to re-embark, and his consequent determination to
call back the British Brigade which was advancing to
Almeida, and whose approach had inspired the greatest
confidence and hope through the whole of this district.

I trust, however, that a few days will convince him his
suspicions are unfounded and will induce him to alter his
determination of so suddenly and abruptly falling back,
which cannot but be pregnant with the most disastrous
consequences, and which no present appearances warrant,
because the Enemy are exceedingly weak upon the Portuguese Frontier (if the Tormes can be so called), and because
(from whatever cause) they are evidently obliged to withdraw large detachments from all their armies, having not
only retired a Corps from Zamora towards Valladolid, but
actually detached 10,000 men from the siege of Saragossa.'

'Towards the end of January' (to continue with a memorandum of D'Urban's) finding that the French were
increasing at Salamanca, and feeling certain that they
would soon reconnoitre us in force, in the direction of
Ciudad Rodrigo and the Agueda, at once discovering the
secret of Sir Robert Wilson's utter weakness in efficient
troops, and perhaps destroying his handful of a Corps, being
as it was, completely in the air, and isolated from any combination with other Forces, bearing in mind too what I had
observed during my short visit to the Sierra de Francia
on the 9th and 10th January, that by posting his Infantry
at Miranda del Castañar it would be in comparative
security for the present, while it would be equally *rapportée*
of Ciudad Rodrigo for all practical purposes, while it could
by extending itself to the Sierra de Bejar, defend the Pass
of the Puerte de Baños, leading from Salamanca to Cuesta's
left upon the Tagus and co-operate with him upon the
Tietar, and have its retreat into Portugal, by the Gata,
more secure than in any other position,—reflecting upon
all this, I say,—I became thoroughly convinced of the
expediency of the measure, and accordingly proposed to
Sir Robert Wilson that he should send me immediately,
1st—to examine the Sierra Francia more precisely with
a view to his making it his main post and pivot.

' 2nd.—Examine the Bejar—the Puerto de Baños—and
their communications as to Placencia—the Tietar and
Cuesta's left.

' 3rd.—Communicate with Cuesta as to Sir Robert's
acting in concert with him.

' Sir Robert was so kind after due consideration, as to
concur with me, and hence I passed all February in the
different missions and reconnaissances (riding some 450

miles), and the Infantry of the (Loyal Lusitanian) Legion
occupied Miranda del Castañar first, and then Baños and
the Bejar, in the course of which, (D'Urban informs
Donkin about Wilson's daring) ' attack upon the Enemy's
post at Calcidella,' (with) ' but 14 Dragoons, the effect
of which was precisely what he desired and intended,[1] as
from an intercepted letter of the French Commandant
of Salamanca to the General of Division at Zamora,
demanding reinforcements which fell since into our hands,
it appears that the carrying of a post within $1\frac{1}{2}$ leagues of
his Corps impressed him with an idea of our strength,
which has made him very cautious, and deterred him from
attempting anything till he could receive the support he
had asked for.   Time has thus, and by constant demonstrations since, been gained for the arrival of the Marquis of
(La) Romana for whom Ciudad Rodrigo and the country
in its front, extending to the Tormes, is now open, instead
of being in the hands of the Enemy, while his communications with Cuesta, and means of acting upon the right flank
of Lefebvre, will be assured by the movement of Sir Robert
Wilson[2] into the Sierra Francia.'

---

[1] See Oman, ii, pp. 257 *et seq.*

[2] To give some idea of the kind of man Sir Robert Wilson was, we give
one of his letters to D'Urban from Fuente St. Estevan, February 17, 1809.
It is unfortunate as Sir Charles Oman remarks, that for this interesting
period of Wilson's life there is no published record.

' I return you my sincere thanks for all the measures you have taken
altho' I grumble with Mayne at the rate of the premium for our means are
on the wane and twelve guineas will startle the auditors for a prize which
was public property *de jure et facto.* He will moreover tell you what we
have been about now the sun shines in our Hemisphere.

' I have some thoughts of moving away myself for a few days, in which
case the *Command of this Province,* as far as my jurisdiction extends,
devolves on you, with certain preliminary conditions, such as the continued
occupation of the place with the present Force and a secession only by the
necessity of Superior Force.

' I am only awaiting tidings from Oporto to determine. Unless the
Enemy crosses the Minho, I will not attend to that Quarter, but my post is
wherever I can, by example or service in any way oppose the progress of
the Enemy. Sometimes Salamanca invites me but *utrumque paratus* will
enable me to choose either.

' Like a prudent Officer I will prepare for reverses and shall order my
spare ammunition to Alcantara, and the seizure of the Puerto de Baños
appears prudent altho' I have not sufficient local knowledge to decide the
merit of the movement. It appears, however, that if so important,
Ruman must remain there, no Portuguese Officer can be trusted, nor will he
inspire confidence or friendship among the Spaniards.

' I have sent to Frere the French papers, to the Junta for the Supreme
Government the Returns, but I could not make out the strength of the
Army, or the number of the sick either. I suppose some are mislaid.

The narrative may be resumed by giving a letter from

D'Urban to Donkin.

Miranda del Castañar, *Feb.* 27, 1809.

(I set out) . . . to observe the Tietar, and the French posts upon it. . . . The Tietar is at present impassable and will continue so for a few days longer, when if the Enemy be not opposed upon that point, he will have it in his power to advance along the north bank of the Tagus, and turn the position of General Cuesta. Sir Robert Wilson's Force, even if there were no necessity for his holding the Pass of Baños, or of attending to the movements of the French at Salamanca, is too weak to render any essential service in that quarter, but he has applied to General Cuesta to spare him 2 or 3 Battalions, which he may very well do, and with which, if he does, the Enemy's passage may be disputed with advantage between Malpartida and the Tietar, as well as a very efficient Corps of observation formed upon his right, the use of which, in case of a combined attack upon the Spanish position I need not comment.

The French have within these three days, assembled a force of 7,000 men and 10 pieces of cannon at Salamanca, and are, I know, making preparations for an immediate march, but whether that will be upon Puerta de Baños, with a view of moving towards Placencia, or whether it will be diverted upon Ciudad Rodrigo, I cannot yet ascertain, but if I might venture an opinion, the former measure is their real intention, because they are well aware that the defeat of the Army of Estremadura ensures (almost) the fall of the latter place, and will scarcely therefore, divert such a Corps from their operations upon the Tagus, to employ it detached.

' There is no doubt of an Austrian War, and indeed Russian, for the King always assured me that he would when he feared a rupture remove his family to Petersburg, and this he has done.

' Resource will bring us handsomely thro' the struggle and retrieve I hope England's honor.

' We hear that 4 Kings are at Paris, Bavaria, Westphalia, Holland and Naples. This is further confirmation. At Salamanca I believe the advices from France are more recent than those you intercepted and a Council of Officers was held at m¹dnight relating to them.

' Adieu, and believe me your faithful and obliged Friend,

'R. Wilson.'

Notwithstanding, the Enemy will very probably, availing himself of his superiority, especially in Cavalry, attempt to drive in Sir Robert Wilson's outposts, and approach the town, in the hope of the gates being opened to them, but in this, I am sure, they will be disappointed, for there exists among the people a very determined spirit of resistance.

Sir Robert Wilson is doing everything to rouse and animate the Junta and the inhabitants, and as his conduct in defence of the country in their front for so long a time, against such an extraordinary superiority, has very justly acquired their confidence, there is good reason to believe his exertions will have all the effect they deserve. In the meantime he has strengthened the Puerta de Baños to the utmost of his means so that in the event of the Enemy bending his course that way, the attempt to pass must be attended with very heavy loss to him, and will be I trust ineffectual.

While preparing for the march which he meditates the Enemy has strengthened his advanced posts in front of Salamanca, and having added to them a Corps of 600 Infantry, has pushed them as far as Vitigurdo on his right and in front of Calsada on his left; this, however, is very likely only a feint, or the prelude to a partial attempt upon Ciudad Rodrigo to which I have before adverted.

In consequence of the Manifestoes sent into the French posts there are abundance of deserters.

Why they are sending away Artillery if they are meditating a forward movement I am at a loss to conceive; in the meantime they still remain at Salamanca, but two days ago they reconnoitred with 170 horse the road by Vitigurde to the Bridge of Yesla, which is in the line of direction to St. Felices and Almeida, and upon the 2nd soon after daybreak with a view, it would seem, of looking forward upon the high road to Ciudad Rodrigo, considerable detachments of their Cavalry drove in our Videttes and approached this place. They were ultimately, however, driven back by Sir Robert Wilson, and pursued for several leagues, with loss of a few people killed, wounded, and taken on their side—none on ours; they retreated to Calsada which is their principal advanced post.

These reconnaissances would appear to indicate an advance in this direction and it is possible are preparatory to it, in which case the Enemy may have in view one of the following projects for an attack upon Portugal :—

1. He calculates upon the speedy fall of Ciudad Rodrigo, and then intends to proceed with its guns upon Almeida (which would reduce it in a very few days), and enter by that avenue.

2. Or, he means to cross the Agueda at the Fore Villa de la Yeagua, and proceed by Gallegos, Espeija, Sabugal, and Penamacor.

3. Or, he designs to pass Ciudad Rodrigo and then taking the route of Perales, advance upon Zarza, and Salvatierra. . . .

. . . I am now procceding without delay to the Head Quarters of General Cuesta, as well to observe, for the information of the Commander-in-Chief whatever may be passing there, as to endeavour to persuade him to spare Sir Robert Wilson 2 or 3 Battalions immediately for the defence of the position behind the Tietar which he must feel to be the last interest to his own security and the occupying of which will at the same time be a strong support to the post at Baños.

March 6. Set out from Ciudad Rodrigo to the Head Quarters of General Cuesta, Captain General and Commander-in-Chief to the Army of Estremadura.

March 7. Found him at Jaraicejo (a distance of 112 miles), proposed that he should put a certain force under the command of Sir Robert Wilson, for the defence of the position behind the Tietar ; he considers any detachment under present circumstances a great sacrifice, but at the same time is much gratified by Sir Robert's offer, and evidently pleased at the idea of having an Officer, whose reputation stands so deservedly high, in some measure under his orders. He is impressed with the necessity of attending to the very important point in question, and upon my assuring him that there is no intention of employing the troops destined by him for its defence in any purpose more remote, he offers 2 complete Battalions equal to 1,700 men and a small detachment of Horse, provided Sir Robert brings with him 400 men ; if the latter consents to this proposal the General Cuesta will consider him as commanding a Division of his Army, will support him by every possible means, will send General O'Donaju to assemble the Acaldes, and order, under pain of immediate punishment, the Armed Peasantry (whom he will furnish with powder and ball) to join Sir Robert, to whom he will send also three Troops of the Portuguese Cavalry Regiment of Chaves, and 2 Regiments of Portuguese Chasseurs (Caçadores) now at Zibeira and Salvatierra, whom he expects to join him in a few days.

In consequence of my communication of the intended treachery at Ciudad Rodrigo, General Cuesta orders the immediate removal of the Commandant of Artillery and Chief of Engineers, and replaced the Militia Regiment of the place by a Regular Battalion from Badajoz; the Governor has been changed in consequence of some previous information.

Wrote the result of these conferences to Sir Robert Wilson to whom I said that although I thought the ground required 3,000 men even in a defensive view, yet with 2,000 I thought much might be done. I took care, however, to say nothing that might bias him to undertake the defence of the Tietar with a force that he might think too small, but if he undertakes it, which I am inclined to think he will, I am convinced that General Cuesta, seeing more and more every day the importance of the thing, will reinforce him with Spaniards if the Portuguese don't arrive; for upon my suggesting it would be of infinite advantage if the Corps on the Tietar could be sufficiently strong to assume an offensive attitude upon Marshal Victor's right and rear, he was aware, he said, of the great effect of such an aspect, and that it was his wish, if he had the means, to see Sir Robert Wilson on the Tietar with 5,000 men. I despatched my letter to Sir Robert Wilson by express, and urged that whatever he resolved on, might be immediate, as an interesting moment was fast approaching which if he came at all, I should wish him not to lose. Every appearance indicating a speedy general attack upon the Spanish position.

I wait here Sir Robert's answer, because General Cuesta has requested that I will do so, that in case Sir Robert should accept the proposed force, I may immediately proceed to post the Battalions, so that no time may be lost. As, moreover, the Spanish General intimated that in the occupying the Tietar, my remaining there would have considerable weight with him, I told him candidly that my present duty upon the Staff of the Army of Portugal required me to watch the Enemy upon the Eastern Frontier, that I was exceedingly happy that duty was, from circumstances, perfectly compatible, at present, with my being on the Tietar, and that while it was so, I would certainly consider it my post and not quit it.

Visited the Spanish advanced Guard at the Bridge of Almaraz,—2 Regiments of Cavalry, 3 of Infantry equal to 4,000 men. In good order, lively, alert, and in high spirits. Commanded by Don John Henestrosa. This vanguard, under this Officer, drove the French from Mirabete, and across the river, and took three guns, in the end of January, 2 Batteries commanding the passable part of the river ; in each a howitzer of 6, and three guns of 8 lbs. The bridge had two arches, the northern one is destroyed. Jaraicejo is 3 leagues from the bridge.

If the French pass the river the vanguard after an obstinate resistance falls back upon the Puerto de Mirabete, 1 league, and there the Spanish General means to make the struggle. In this point if the Spaniards do their duty, the French can't penetrate, their real attack must be elsewhere, further eastward ; that ground I have not yet seen. Great kindness, politeness, and ability in General O'Donaju.

March 8. Wrote to Mr. Frere (No. 1) at Seville, all that had passed, suggested the expediency of Spanish rank for Sir Robert Wilson, as giving him more power and influence, very necessary in the position he now stands. Urged the necessity of a supply of money being ready for him, and gave him whatever local observations the present state of things suggested.

Wrote to Col. Donkin (No. 2), official Report for the information of Sir J. Cradock. Stated as much of the Tietar plan as was necessary, pointed out strongly the particular bearing any French force penetrating here would have upon Portugal ; endeavoured to shew that a small assistance given to the Spaniards upon the Tietar now, would do more than a whole Portuguese Army afterwards upon the Elgas ; and hence begged that the C.-in-C. would instantly make it a point with the Regency that the

Chasseurs at Zebreira and Salvatierra should be instantly put under the orders of Sir Robert Wilson. Added all the local information.

Wrote a note to General O'Donaju to beg that if General Cuesta thought I could be of the slightest use now, in going to his detachments of 350 men upon the Tietar (about which he seemed rather anxious, and who had shown some timidity, not knowing the real advantages of their ground) he would say so, and that I would instantly repair thither, and to assure the Spanish General that either there, or elsewhere, I should be most happy to execute any orders which he might think fit to honour me.

March 9. General Cuesta received intelligence that the French had removed their barricade at the Bridge of Arzobispo ; this indicated an intention to pass, and the General therefore proposes to move nearer to the point of attack. His Head Quarters will be tonight at Deleytosa, 2 leagues on the direct route to Arzobispo. Requested permission to accompany him. He granted this in the most polite and flattering manner. Arrived at Deleytosa.

March 10. Morning.—The Enemy have not as yet attempted to pass at Arzobispo ; all remains as it was. No official account has arrived (but that which General Cuesta has received is of a nature that induces him to give it full credit) of the fall of Saragossa (Feb. 27), by famine. The defence of this place has been protracted beyond all human expectation. This event lets loose a large reinforcement for the French Army (they are said to be in march for Madrid) whether it will be directed towards the Andalusian Army under the Conde del Castoajal, now at Valdepenas in La Mancha, in case of the defeat of which this Army would be very critically situated ; or whether it will be thrown into the scale of Marshal Victor, and then attack General Cuesta, cannot yet be conjectured. At all events it would be a good measure to attack the French Army on the other side of the Tagus without delay. The pontoon bridge, however, which would be necessary for that purpose has not yet arrived from Badajoz, indeed I fear it hasn't yet left that place, in which case it cannot reach the Tagus before the 17th. This is much to be regretted, for the moment will pass away. If the Andalusian Army would advance upon Toledo, and all that is disposable of that of Cuesta attack by the Tietar, and if these attacks be well combined, the Army of Marshal Victor must retire upon Madrid, or be cut off. I shall suggest this idea to General O'Donaju this evening. It is certainly not by waiting in detached positions for the Enemy's concentrated attacks that the Spanish Armies can hope to succeed, or the cause of the Spaniards be prosperous. If these two Armies would but instantly and cordially combine for the destruction of Victor, the Corps from Saragossa, if it continued its march, would only arrive to find itself in the presence of a superior force strongly posted and flushed with victory.

Evening.—Suggested the above idea to Genl. O'Donaju, he replied that it had been the wish of Genl. Cuesta, but that he had no power over the other Army. Hence a radical evil which, till it be rooted out, must ever paralyse all the efforts of Spain. Instead of being combined under one Chief and all their means directed to one point, and directed by one head, they are split into independent Armies, and their struggles are without ensemble, feeble, partial, capricious and disjointed. Not so the Enemy, wherever he turns he brings his whole force to bear, and this beats these Captains General in detail, because they will not unite.

This Army of Marshal Victor, I imagine, never intended to attack till Saragossa should fall and reinforcements from thence be at hand. If it had he would not have been so long inactive,—that is not the fault of the French— in the mean time, he has employed for these 6 weeks both the Armies of Estremadura and Andalusia to watch him, and prevented all diversion in favour of Palafox. Now, in a short time, his hands will be strengthened, by the Troops that the defeat of the latter will have left at liberty. He will attack first one, and then the other and very possibly beat them both in detail.

Wrote to Mr. Frere (No. 3) what I think upon this subject. If he can sway the Central Junta to give positive orders for a combined and immediate attack upon Victor, a blow fatal to the French may yet be struck upon the Tagus.

March 11. 'Tis difficult to determine the precise strength of the French Corps under Marshal Victor, because all that part of it concentrated round his Head Quarters of Ocralada de Mata, is quartered in the huts which stand in the woods, and round these a cordon is drawn and no one allowed to enter or go out, but from the bread and meat which is daily sent to this Circle, there is reason to suppose that the force within it amounts to 7,000 and as 11,000 beside can be accounted for, his aggregate force is probably about 18,000 men, of these about 3,500 Horse. This Corps occupies the position of a Circle fronting the Tagus, of which the left extremity of the arc is at Talavera, the right at Toril and the centre about Oropesa. The Head Quarters Peralada de Meta and 1,500 men with a General of Division at Navalmoral. A small detachment of Cavalry is pushed over the Tietar at the Salsbral, to collect provisions at Jaraiz.

His position is well chosen for attack if he had the means of passing the river, because whatever point he chose to bear upon he would approach by a chord, while his antagonist to meet him must proceed by an arc of the same circle, but the features of the ground do away with the general advantages of this, for Cuesta's two advanced Guards are so strong, so well composed and so powerfully posted near Almaraz, and Meza de Ibor, that there will be full time in any case to support either or both of them. The Spanish General can concentrate 12,000 Infantry, 2,500 Horse and an excellent Artillery, independent of the two Advanced Guards, upon either of these points, centrically between both in a very short time, and he is establishing a Corps upon the Tietar which, if augmented, as I trust it will be, to 5,000 men under Sir Robert Wilson, will not only be an infinite embarrassment and dread to the Enemy in case of his intending to attack, but in case of his being (as he will shortly I trust be) attacked, it will advance not only upon the right but actually upon the rear of the Enemy, by ' Z Z ' (see map).[1] Upon this subject and to strengthen this important point, wrote to Sir J. Cradock (No. 4).

From the apprehension of the Spanish General making a movement to get between the Corps at Toledo and his Corps on the Tagus, Victor has destroyed the Bridge of Montalva, near Malpica, and thereby deprived himself of a flank approach, as well as of a means of combining readily in an attack upon the Conde de Castoajal. Cuesta promulgated this report for the very purpose which it has effected.

[1] Enclosed with MS.

The French Cavalry are dying by hundreds of famine and some villages abandoned by their inhabitants on account of the stench of unburied carcases. The Enemy too are in great distress for bread, for although they have corn, they can't grind it, all the water mills being under the fire of Cuesta's Chasseurs who suffer no one to approach them.

General Cuesta receives to-morrow the Dragoons of Almaraz. He will then have 3,500 Cavalry and 25,000 Infantry, not more, however, than 18,000 of the latter armed. He has 26 guns (3 of them taken from the French) of these 14 are at the advanced Guards, the remaining 12 disposable, and he has effected a road through the mountains never before practicable, by which he can readily approach them to his centre and right.

The Conde del Castoajal is at Val de Penes, with 30,000 Infantry, 2,000 Horse and 2 Brigades of Artillerie à Cheval.

The French General of Division Sebastiani is at Toledo, Yeltes and Aranjuez with 12,000 men and 10,000 from Saragossa are in march to join him. If Victor can be beaten, before they arrive the united Corps of Cuesta and Andalusia will act against him. The seasonable occupation of the passes in the mountains of Bejar (Baños and Tornavejos) prevents any diversion or assistance from the 7,000 men at Salamanca, who would else, past all doubt, be now at Placencia.

Suggested to General O'Donaju the making an arrangement for a direct communication with Col. Mayne and Capt. Ruman at Baños, and Tornavejos.

Now if the British Brigade that, in my report of the 3rd from Fuente St. Estevan to Col. Donkin, I have so strongly urged the necessity of being sent to Penamacor, be but in motion, and if Sir J. Cradock will but listen to my repeated suggestion of the Portuguese moving from Idanha, Zibreira, and Salvatierra to the Tietar, we shall have a strong Corps upon Victor's right and rear, the British Brigade even may advance for a momentary exertion. The Pontoon Bridge now on its way shall afford a passage for a front attack near Almaraz with 12,000 Foot, 2,500 Horse and 12 pieces of cannon, and the result has every prospect of being brilliant. If it succeed, then advance the British and the Tietar Corps to keep in check the French at Salamanca, and the combined Armies of Andalusia and

Estremadura cannot fail of destroying Sebastiani. Then the Tormes Corps must fall or retreat, and if the latter, the greater part of the Spanish Army may follow at their heels to Madrid and the remainder reinforce Romana in Galicia where Soult must fall too if the British Army in Portugal lends its aid and wipes off the recollection of the late disastrous retreat.

March 12. The French have held a Council of War at Talavera, at which assisted the Generals Lasalle, Cesar, Alto and some others (but not Marshal Victor); it was given out that this was to determine upon the feasibility of an attack by Almaraz, and that the making such an attempt was negatived. Meanwhile they have strengthened again the barricade at the Bridge of Arzobispo and destroyed a boat which used to pass the river near it. This of course is to prevent the possibility of discovering what they are about; they meditate something and the information hitherto received here does not enable one to judge what. Their tone of arrogance, however, to the people at Talavera is much altered, and this is generally an indication upon the part of the French of their foreseeing, or knowing of, some disaster. Either they meditate a retreat or a march by their right. Scarcely I think the latter, for they would not wish to leave Sebastiani at Toledo, in the air. No movement has taken place. But yesterday, the detachment of Spanish Infantry fired upon 40 of their Horse near Jaraiz, of whom only 17 escaped, the rest being killed or taken prisoners, and this has drawn over today a strong detachment of their Cavalry who remain on the Placencia side of the Tietar, and probably will do so, to ensure the supplies which they must draw from the Val de Placencia.

March 13. Great anxiety at receiving no answer from Sir Robert Wilson. The mystery is solved, General Cuesta has this morning discovered that the person he entrusted with establishing the Post from Merida to Ciudad Rodrigo and who reported that he had done so, has not, but has pocketed the money which the being charged with that service put into his hands and absconded. By that channel it was that General O'Donaju sent my letter to Sir Robert, and although it has certainly gone, yet this arrangement not having been made will occasion it to be two additional days in going.

Infinite rascalities are practised under the cloak of these times. The other day some villains who had the charge of furnishing forage for all Cuesta's Cavalry, either from being his enemies, or treacherous, or both, so managed matters that the horses had no subsistence for 6 or 7 days.

Wrote to Mr, Frere (No. 5).

March 14. Visited the advanced Posts at Mesa de Ibor, commanded by the Marquis of Portago, in very good order. Cuesta's line is amazingly strong as to country, 'tis the range of mountains extending from Almaraz in the direction of Guadalupe, the Puertas of which are occupied. The Head Quarters of this 2nd advanced Division is at Fresnedose, and advanced Guard from it at Mesa de hor, and a Post d'Avertisement at Arzobispo. All these consist of about 3,000 men. About the Head Quarters of Deleytosa he can concentrate 12,000 Infantry, 2,500 Horse and 12 guns to advance either upon his right towards Arzobispo, or his left towards Almaraz to meet the Enemy if he attacks, or to cross the river when the bridge shall arrive, and attack him. The Enemy have put 150 men into the two towers upon the Puerta de Arzobispo to defend it, in addition to the barricade. Constant fire upon the mills, the Enemy can grind no corn. They are certainly in movement for some purpose. Cuesta's defensive position is admirable.

March 15. The French are certainly in movement and they have some boats upon wheels, but I do not think they intend to attack this Army ; they either mean to retreat, for all their measures tend towards their left, or they will march upon Toledo, unite with the Corps of Sebastiani and fall upon the Conde de Castoajal. In this latter case if they are not very rapid, Cuesta will be able to pass the river, and fall upon them on their march. The pontoon bridge will be here tomorrow night, or the following morning—but at all events, if they move off everything but a detachment to guard the Bridge of Arzobispo, a party must be pushed over the river to take it, and the Dutch who occupy it will not make much resistance. Then there will be a passage for this Army.

Sir Robert Wilson's answer (No. 6) has at length arrived. He has had his hands full in the Plain. I wish he were out of it. His activity, his gallantry and that of the British officers with him, have once more done wonders,

but this must end—at every nearer approach the Enemy
becomes better acquainted with our history and will at
length dive into the whole secret. We are but a paper
currency, and I would not have 'em examine too narrowly
our means to support it.

Communicated with General Cuesta and wrote to Sir
Robert Wilson (No. 7); at 2 in the morning received
(No. 8) from General Don F. O'Donaju—unsealed my
packet to Sir Robert and inserted the news (that the
Enemy will attack us very soon however extraordinary
you may find it after the news we had until this day).
Sent by express to Baños. I intended to go to-morrow
to the Tietar, of course I shall remain to see if the Enemy
do really attack ; I scarcely think even yet that he will.
There is no doubt but that the French would have ere now
retired everything from Castile and Estremadura, and
concentrated behind the Ebro as before, for they feel their
weakness, and there having beside been serious quarrels
between the French and Germans at Madrid, Sir Robert
Wilson's proclamations too having caused the foreigners
to desert in great abundance, they have deliberated upon
this point, but O'Farril [1] has dissuaded them from such a
step, and urged their attacking the Spanish Armies,
assuring them that they will not stand. This man is the
real King of Spain of infinite ability, both as a statesman
and a soldier, well versed in European politics, and most
intimately with all the resources of Spain, of which he has
so perfect a local and geographical knowledge that he has
maps (by far the best extant) of the greater part of the
Kingdom, made under his own inspection and from surveys
in which he himself has assisted. He speaks every European language, and is of the most determined courage
both personal and political. He strenuously opposed the
entrance of the French into Spain ; when, however, they
were admitted, it was his decided opinion that they would
subjugate it, and he determined to take care of himself
in the New Government, when he conceived the old one
gone past redemption ; a hasty and ill-advised decree of
the Junta while he might still have been reclaimed,
declaring him a traitor, by the mouth of the Public Exe-
cutioner through all the streets of Madrid, completely
decided him; he felt that he had thrown away the scabbard,

---

[1] Marginal note. This account of O'Farril from Cuesta himself.—B. D.

that he had no longer any safety but in the success of the French, and for that he has most effectually exerted himself ever since. Joseph Bonaparte moves by his tuition, and he is the only Spanish traitor that the French treat with any degree of respect; they know his value, he is worth a host to them, and if Spain be subdued by France, it is O'Farril that bows the neck of his country to the Corsican yoke. Infinitely great talents, thus prostituted to the purpose of treason, powers which might have saved a nation exerted to destroy it, make one give a sigh to the frailty of humanity, while one laments that an O'Farril should have tarnished his great acquirements, his splendid abilities, his acknowledged personal virtues by being the betrayer of his Country. He was born at Havannah, and his wife is a most able and intelligent woman, devoted to the French, and very dangerous, since her masculine understanding and her feminine fascinations well qualify her to make proselytes to the Cause she favours.

March 16. It was this morning intended to move the Head Quarters to the Puerta de Mirabete, for the General expected an attack by Almaraz; they don't move, however, till to-morrow morning. Great activity as the crisis approaches.

Wrote to Col. Donkin (No. 9) and Mr. Frere (No. 10). Towards afternoon finding that there was no change and that the Head Quarters do actually move to-morrow morning early to Mirabete, retained the letters in order to send them tomorrow night, and insert in them whatever tomorrow may produce.

March 17. The Head Quarters moved to the Puerta de Mirabete. On arriving there General Cuesta received a report from the Junta of Placencia that grieves me much,—'tis that Ruman is driven from Tornavejos, by 300 Infantry and 100 Horse; as there is no report direct from him, I doubt it, for General O'Donaju promised to establish a direct communication, yet the Portuguese are such troops that I should not be surprised to hear that they had deserted him. I fear this Post has been too weakly occupied; time will shew. Baños however will hold out, and by Tornavejos they can bring no guns, scarcely even Cavalry in single file. Everything indicates a real attack and Cuesta seems confident. *Nous verrons.*

The French must of necessity lose abundance of people—
so many—that I still think that the French General takes
a dangerous measure for himself. If the Tietra plan had
been acted upon when I first recommended it on the
16th February, that position would have been now occupied
and Tornavejos might have been too strong to be carried
de vive force at least. Ruman's letter makes me fear he
thought his force too weak, and what he had was bad, 50
Portuguese and 50 Germans—too little—I thought he was
much stronger.

The Marquis of Portago arrived in the night. The
French demonstrations near Almaraz, which induced the
Spanish General to believe the attack was intended there,
were a feint, their real attack is by the Puerta de Arzobispo,
and they have commenced it. They attacked the whole
line of the advance on the right from Fresnedoso to Mesa
del Ibor, at 8 o'clock this morning in force ; they employed
in this attack 15,000 Infantry, in five columns, they succeeded at 3 o'clock after an obstinate resistance in getting
possession of Mesa del Ibor, and the Puerta de la Mesa,
where they have their advance while that of the Spaniards
is at Capillos.   The French have, it appears, lost abundance
of men, and when they have a little taken breath, they will
probably proceed to attack the Spanish advanced position
between Fresnedoso and Delertoso, in aid of which, 'tis
most likely they will push on a Corps from Mesa del Ibor,
by the road of Valderaches (a very bad one) in order to
threaten the cutting off the advanced Guard at Almaraz
(such a movement at all events would oblige it to retire),
by advancing upon Ronagardo, and afterwards of pre-
senting themselves in front of Mirabete, which, if they can
succeed in carrying the position in front of Delertoso and
Fresnedoso, they will have taken very good steps to turn it.

The Enemy has united everything for this attack, even
the Corps of Sebastiani at Toledo, which has been so completely called in, that there are not 4,000 men left from
Aranjuez to Talavera. The Duke of Albuquerque who
commands the advanced Guard of the Conde del Castagal,
at Villa Real (18 leagues from Toledo) will 'tis to be supposed, take advantage of this movement by which the
Enemy has exposed his left and rear so decidedly, and if
the Conde del Castagal supports him by moving his whole
Army instantly, the French will be in a very critical

situation. By the junction of Sebastiani their numbers
probably amount to from 26 to 28,000 men.

What they have gained, however, is only an advanced
post, and the strongest part of the Spanish position is
yet to be taken. The Duke del Parque commands the
Advance of the Spaniards, and the 2nd in command of the
whole is a Lt. Genl. de Aguia, a member of the Council
of War, and a man whose talents are highly spoken of.

March 18. Morning.—With no small degree of astonishment I find that not a measure has been taken to concentrate upon the right, which is the real attack and
vulnerable point. If the Enemy penetrate to Deleytoso
the position is turned. With almost equal surprise I am
aware that not only the Passes of Valderaches road have
not been originally occupied, but ever since the Enemy
got possession of Mesa del Ibor this step has been neglected,
till 'tis probably useless, the detachment under the Baron
de la Buria only marched this morning for the purpose.
It is not possible but that with such an Enemy as the
French, such negligence, imbecility and delay must lead
to bad consequences.

2 o'clock.—My predictions are fast verifying. The
Baron de la Buria has met a French column of 8,000
Infantry advancing by the Valderaches road ; he has
retired before it without fighting. It has in consequence
come to Romanguda, and Don John Henestrosa, having
his flank turned, and his retreat endangered by so superior
a force, has, of necessity, withdrawn his guns from the
Batteries commanding the passage of the Tagus, burned
his Camp, and fallen back upon Mirabete. Thus the
advance upon the left which might have to cost Victor
5,000 men, is lost without a blow. Meanwhile the Duke
del Parque and the Marquis of Portago who commands the
right, still remain *here*, and no effort has yet been made to
check the Enemy there. If that were done the left is
still invulnerable, and 'tis the highest of all possible wonders
to me that General Cuesta don't move by Deleytoso with
10,000 men and support his right which is strong naturally,
but now very weakly defended. This can never do. The
position and all its advantages are I doubt lost.

March 19. Morning.—Truxillo. All my predictions
have been but too quickly followed by their fulfilment.
A report was received in the evening of yesterday, that a

French Corps was at Deleytoso, and the Spanish General, upon the instant, withdrew every post and retreated upon Truxillo. The Army is halting for a few hours' rest and will then march 3 leagues further on the road to Merida and take up for the night (I know not if for longer) the strong post of la Puerta de Sta. Cruz. Thus in a day, almost without fighting, has a position been abandoned which might have held out till Doomsday, and with it all the advantages which depended upon its being maintained ; the salvation of all the rich country between the Tagus and the Douro, the rising spirit of the people, which promised everything good, public opinion, public hope, all has been sacrificed in four-and-twenty hours, and almost without an attempt to prevent it. Indeed not one measure for the defence of this position (since the French passed the river) has been taken, omission has succeeded to omission, and so very glaring has been the imbecility, so beyond all telling the neglect, that nothing but madness, or a specious determination to abandon it, can account for it. The Enemy too had drawn in his whole Toledo Army for his attack, and if he had but been held in check for a few days, the Conde del Castagal with 45,000 men might have fallen upon his rear while his front could not advance, and his right was open by the Tietar and the Tagus. All this too has happened upon the part of the people who have a hundred times confidently assured me that they would even attack themselves, so soon as the pontoon bridge arrived. We met the bridge on the road to Truxillo, so near was it. One is lost in astonishment and indignation ! If Spain be thus defended, notwithstanding her admirable peasantry, she must fall beneath the all destroying grasp of Napoleon for her resources are collected and concentrated but to be thrown away at once, and treachery, or imbecility, paralyse all her energies.

Wrote No. 11 to Col. Donkin, a hasty letter to Mr. Frere, and another to Sir Robert Wilson.

March 20. Puerta de Sta. Cruz.—This position is strong, but its left can be turned, and the French will turn it if Cuesta remains, which I don't think he will. Skirmishing between the French Cavalry and that of Don John Henestrosa's advanced Guard. An officer or two, of rank, killed on both sides. A Colonel of the French Cavalry, by Manuel Henestrosa, the General's nephew, and the Spanish Colonel of the Voluntarios d'Espagna (Hussars).

Received Sir Robert Wilson's packet, forwarded all to Mr. Frere.

March 21. Medellin.—Early this morning the Army got orders to march and retreated to the Plain of Miajadas, there it halted to refresh during the heat of mid-day. The French advanced Guard shewed itself on the heights, Cuesta made a disposition, and indeed a very good one, but it was not to be supposed, from many circumstances, that a serious attack was intended; it proved only a strong reconnaissance, which very foolishly descending from the heights, was enveloped and cut off by the Regiments of Almanza and Infanta and all perished. A Colonel of Cavalry, and 70 men, the Spaniards making no prisoners (the Colonel was killed by Jeronimo Henestrosa, the General's other nephew). Lt. Col. Cox here met the Army; he came on the part of Genl. Beresford, lately appointed F. Marshal and C. in C. of the Portuguese Army, to complement Genl. Cuesta, and brought me No. 12. All my plans were succeeding thus for the occupation of the Tietar, but for this strange and unaccountable retreat. Lt. Col. Cox is gone express to Idanha, of course tostop the march of the Portuguese Corps, and I have written again by that channel to Sir Robert Wilson for security's sake.

Put Col. Munro (who I met at Truxillo) in possession of the detail of everything, and my opinion as to measures, and consequences, and sent him express to Lisbon, with a letter to Colonel Donkin, for the information of Sir J. Cradock, and another for General Beresford, these were merely notes, and Capt. M. will supply the rest. The substance of what he will say is the same as these observations.

The Army marched again at nightfall and reached Medellin at 2 in the morning. The birth-place of Herman Cortez,—would he have retired thus?

March 22. Here Cuesta has for the first time attempted to give a reason for all that has happened—time will shew (if indeed it be his real one) whether he has reasoned rightly. He says that he has fallen back, and he means to continue to do so upon Badajoz, thus to draw off the Army of Victor, and leave the Conde del Castãojal and the

Duke of Albuquerque at leisure to march to Madrid, the whole Country is thus abandoned for the Capital. Time will shew—I don't augur well of this measure, nor *can* bring myself to believe it the real motive of the retreat.

March 23–24. Quintana and Valle.

March 25. Quintana—Head Quarters at Valle. The rearguard having again this morning got orders to march, and the French not having pursued, the whole thing looks so like a retreat upon the Sierra Morena, that I shall remain with the Army no longer; even if the retreat be upon Badajoz, as the Enemy remain behind the Guadiana, 'tis necessary for me to be nearer to him, lest he move upon the Tagus without my knowing it. Hitherto nothing can have occurred near Alcantara without being known to Lt. Col. Cox who has been on his way to Idanha, having passed by Merida before the French advanced to Miajades, so that I am not at present uneasy upon that head, but I must keep them in view a little nearer. With the rearguard, to this moment, I have known all their movements well and speedily enough. I shall go to the Head Quarters, demand a passport and get towards the Tagus, somewhere by Badajoz, probably, for the French occupy the line by Montanchos, Careeres and along there to the Tagus.

Valle.—All is changed,—the General must have got a sudden order from the Junta to put a stop to his retrograde movement. He has signified to me that he moves instantly back to the Guadiana, and has charged me with the order to Don J. Henestrosa to march at daybreak for Medellin, and then to patrol towards Miajades. This because of course I laid aside my intention of going by a circuitous route to observe the Enemy, when with the advanced Guard I shall get near them by a shorter one, and with more power to look closely to them. Whatever has occasioned this change I rejoice in it, first as it is good upon the instant for Portugal and then because the Enemy will not at his leisure pillage the south bank of the Guadiana, which is as rich as the best cultivated part of England and indeed may be called a magazine of corn and forage. The Duke of Albuquerque's reinforcement of 7,000 men is arrived at Castvera (2 leagues off), and I trust that now this Army will at length act upon the offensive,—for now it must or never. . . .

Cuesta is very anxious still to have Sir Robert Wilson,

and will give him the same Spanish force, which is all well
when the Spanish Army arrives again upon the Tagus ;
for the present I have therefore begged that the Corps may
be placed under Sir Robert Wilson to be in readiness, and
to move upon the north, in proportion as Cuesta moves
upon the south bank of the Tagus.

March 26.   Marched to Don Benito.   Enemy close
to Medellin.   Advanced Guard arrived at Don Benito.
From the report of the advance and of peasants, the Enemy
were 5,000, near Medellin, on the other side of the Guadiana.
An advance sent to Medellin, another to the Fords on the
right.   Report made to the General-in-Chief at Guardia.

March 27.   Answer from the C. in C. that he would be
by the middle of the day with the whole Army between
Villaneueva de Serena and Don Benito.   Advanced Guard
marched from Don Benito about ½ a league in front towards Medellin.   Captain Boroni of the Regiment of
Almanza, commanding the advance, returned from the
ford on the right and reported that the Enemy in *two
columns* were approaching the ford.   Don John's orders
were to maintain his post in front of Don Benito and
secure the line from it to Serena till the arrival of the
Army.   A disposition made of the advanced Guard along
the crest of the little heights in front of the village, fronting
the roads from the ford, Light Infantry *en tirailleur* in
the brushwood extending to the Front ; Infantry (Valencia, Badajoz, Merida) in the border of the Olive Grove ;
2 guns on their right, 2 guns on their left ; Cavalry
(Horse Carbineers—Almaza, Infante ; Hussars-Estrema-
dura, Voluntarios d'Espagna) closing the left of the Infantry where the trees and hedges ceased and the Plain
commenced.

The report of the Captain was groundless, the Enemy
occupied Medellin and pushed some Cavalry and guns
across the river towards the evening.   The Caçadores de
Toledo (Cavalry) and the Grenadiers of Colonel Zaya,
arrived to support the advanced Guard.   Fire from a few
howitzers on each side—Captain of Almaza killed—evening
closed.   Quiet through the night.

BATTLE OF MEDELLIN

March 28.   At daybreak two Squadrons of the Enemy
were in the plain at the foot of the little hill in front, and

to the right of Medellin. About ten, guns and Infantry followed; at 11 the C. in C. arrived and the heads of the columns of the Army reached the summit of the range of hills between Don Benito and Medellin. At ½ past 12 the Enemy arrived on the line of the right of the Castle Hill in 3 close columns and began to deploy to his left, his rear to the river; at one cannonade commenced, at about ½ past was pretty hot, at about ¼ before 2 General Cuesta gave orders to advance. The Army did so and formed one line as it advanced. The Grenadiers under Colonel Zaya were to turn the Enemy's right. The Cavalry to support. Everything possible was done by the Grenadiers, who lost twelve officers, but the Cavalry ran away when they approached the Enemy (The Hussars of Estremadura and the Voluntarios d'Espagna are to be excepted, they were elsewhere employed and behaved well). The Grenadiers after the most gallant and unavailing efforts were obliged to fall back. The Enemy turned the Spanish left. The centre and right, who had hitherto behaved well, lost confidence and fled; complete dispersion was the consequence and at 4 o'clock not a Spanish Corps remained in the field. Don John Henestrosa made every effort to rally the Cavalry but in vain, and was the last to leave this fatal field, where the hopes of Spain have been so disappointed and its just and excellent cause trodden under foot.

The Commander-in-Chief who behaved with the fire of five-and-twenty, ridden down by his own Cavalry, was with difficulty preserved and got off.

Note.—His nephew and I pulled him out from under the horses' feet, bruised and nearly senseless, remounted him, and sent him off under the charge of a Sergeant and some half-dozen of the Carbineers.—B. D.

Don John and myself found him at Guardia, 2 leagues from the field with the principal General Officers about him. There he passed the night, heart-broken and wretched. Unfortunate old man that not one ball should have prevented his outliving his blasted hopes, and the ruin of the last Army of his Country!

The French Artillery, heavier, more numerous and better served, was severely felt; but they committed several glaring faults and if we had had a good reserve might still have been defeated.

Col. Campbell arrived from Seville in the night. He brought me letters from Mr. Frere.

March 29.   Retreated to Campillo in the heights of the Sierra Morena.   The greater part of three Regiments of Cavalry, Almaza, Carabineers Infante, stragglers from the Caçadores e Caballos, came in.   Scarcely any Infantry. Wrote Mr. Frere and Col. Donkin—the facts shortly and made no comments.

March 30.   Dispositions made for cantoning the Divisions and Generals to receive the Army as its stragglers may arrive.

March 31.   Enemy at Merida.   Very few Infantry arrived.   Marched to Berlarga.

April 1.   At Berlarga.   Letter from Mr. Frere dated 31st—he had not received mine.   Wrote him that I had written, that my duty and my orders obliged me to set out for Portugal now threatened from three quarters, that the French were advanced to Almendralejo.   That this Army must not be expected to give any opposition, that it was quite dispersed, that I would go close to the Enemy's posts and send him all possible information. That if it was necessary to expend any greater sum than I could charge in my contingents, I would do so, in consequence of his letter.

April 2.   Llerena.—Received directions from Sir John Cradock to repair to Lisbon as soon as it may be practicable.

Finding that Mr. Frere, our Ambassador at Seville, was very ill-informed upon much relating to this Army which was very necessary for him to know, resolved to have a conference with him, before repairing to Lisbon, where I am ordered to go and whither it is now, on every account, my duty to go without loss of time.   Wrote therefore to Col. Donkin to say so and

April 3.   rode to Seville.

April 4.   Seville.

April 5.   Had several conferences with Mr. Frere. Stated to him unreservedly my opinion of the Spanish Army with which I had been for the last month, and of the conduct of the Spanish Affairs as far as they had gone under my judgement.   I found that I had made him acquainted with much that he had been hitherto utterly ignorant of, and I hope therefore my coming hither has not been altogether useless.

E

April 6.   To Monasterio on my way to Lisbon.   Head Quarters of Genl. Cuesta.

April 8.   Set out for Lisbon.

April 9.   In the night reached Sir John Cradock's Head Quarters at Lisbon.

April 10.   Lisbon.—Sir John Cradock has received me in the kindest and most gratifying manner that can be conceived.   He informs me that Marshal Beresford has asked for me to be Quarter Master General of the Portuguese Army, which he has just commenced the task of re-organizing, and says that he (Sir J. C.) thinks I may render good service to the Cause by accepting the Marshal's offer, retaining always my appointment in the English Quarter Master General's Department, leaving it, however, entirely to my option to do so or not.   I have answered him at once that wherever I can be most useful I shall be best pleased to go, and therefore that I accepted it at once.

April 11–12.   Making preparations, etc.

April 13.   At night set out for Marshal's Head Quarters at Thomar.

April 14.   Joined the Marshal at Thomar.[1]   He has received me in a very agreeable and flattering manner, and appointed me Colonel and Quarter-Master-General of the Portuguese Army.

B. D'Urban.

[1] Further reconnaissances from March 6 to April 14—a distance of 560 miles—and D'Urban adds : 'this was the distance travelled upon post horses and mules, exclusive of all the country upon which I went upon my own horses which I used whenever I could avail myself of them, and embracing the movements and operations of Sir Robert Wilson's corps in January and February with those of Cuesta's Army from March 7 to April 14, in a word, the total since the first of November amounted to some 2,168 English miles ! '

JOURNAL II

1809, *April to August*

BERESFORD COMMANDER-IN-CHIEF OF THE PORTUGUESE ARMY, D'URBAN QUARTERMASTER-GENERAL

INTRODUCTION

WHAT was the situation at this juncture ? The timid and cautious Cradock had at last been persuaded by Hill and Beresford [1] to make a forward move against Soult, so that Wellesley on his return, April 22—just eight months since his recall—'found the greater part of the disposable force already well advanced in the direction of Oporto. During this time British Officers were with the advanced corps upon the most important points : Sir Robert Wilson and Colonel Wilson on the Upper Tagus, Colonel Trant and Majors Campbell and Douglas on the Vouga, Colonel Cox at Almeida and Major Patrick on the Tamega.' [2]

Wellesley believing 'the best defensive to be a vigorous local offensive,' planned ' to push forward his main body upon Oporto with all possible speed while sending a flanking column under Beresford to cross the Douro near Lamego, join Silveira and intercept Soult's line of retreat. . . .' [3]

Unfortunately news arrived shortly afterwards (May 3) that the bridge had been forced at Amarante, its gallant defender being killed in the attempt. As a result, Silveira had retired behind the Douro with the wreck of his army, but this did not deter Wellesley from advancing—it merely made him more cautious.

In the meantime, from April 14 to the beginning of May,

[1] Appointed to the command of the native Portuguese Army, and since his arrival in March organising with the aid of British officers, including D'Urban, as many regiments as he had been able to assemble at Lisbon upon the Zezere, and principally at Thomar, where he established his headquarters.

[2] Annotation of D'Urban in Jones's *Account of the War in Spain and Portugal*. The whole volume is profusely commented upon, with maps and illustrations added, and on the fly-leaf . . . 'the best and most faithful history of the war which has yet been published. . . . Written April 1845, viz. in retirement at the Cape after his recall as Governor.

[3] See Oman, ii, p. 316.

D'Urban worked 'to get some sort of order, and beginning with his own department, which did not exist at all,' a statement that speaks for itself! How well he succeeded and the splendid services he rendered with his remarkable powers of organisation and abundant energy, the following pages of the Journal will show.

May 6.   Upon this day Marshal Beresford left Coimbra.

May 7.   Head Quarters at Vizeu.

May 8.   Lamego. The Brigade of M. Genl. Baccelar was already there, and the 4th Regt. of Dragoons arrived.

May 9.   The 6th Chasseurs were posted at Peso de Regoa with an advance at Cidadella. The Division of Loisson pushed an advanced Corps to Mezamfrio. The British Brigade, the Cavalry and the guns were to arrive at Lamego on the 11th.

May 10.   Loisson's Division arrived at Mezamfrio, and marched upon Peso de Regoa, its advanced Guard was at Serguda and Fontellas, its Force about 6,000 Infantry and 1,000 Horse with 4 guns. Marshal Beresford crossed the Douro in boats with the Brigade of M. Genl. Baccelar and 4 3-pounders, and occupied the position of Peso de Regoa to defend the approach to the passage of the river. At this demonstration the French immediately retired upon Mezamfrio, suffering some loss from the fire of the peasantry on the southern bank of the Douro. Their advanced Guard remained for the night at Cidadella, and they had pickets at Serguda and Fontellas.

May 11.   Head Quarters at Peso de Regoa, the Brigade of Lopez de Souza and the 4th Chasseurs crossed the river. The French pickets were withdrawn. They set fire to Mezamfrio and retired. The 4th Chasseurs advanced to Mezamfrio. The Enemy had retired in the direction of Amarante and their rearguard was at Pedroces de Texeira. The guns and Cavalry arrived at Lamego, but not the British Brigade.

May 12.   Head Quarters at Pedroces de Texeira. The Enemy at Amarante, a strong picket within about a league of the town. The Army with the exception of the British Brigade and Infantry, bivouacked at Pedroces. The British Brigade of Infantry arrived at Lamego this evening and crossed to Peso de Regoa.

Note.—During these events I had the good fortune to become acquainted with Major Hardinge (afterwards Lord), of the English officers brought out by the Marshal to organize and discipline the Portuguese Army. He was at the Marshal's Head Quarters waiting to be appointed to a Regt. or otherwise employed. I requested him to reconnoitre Mezamfrio, a dangerous and delicate service which he performed so much to my satisfaction, that I wished him to belong to my Department as Deputy-Quarter-Master-General of the Army. He acceded, and the Marshal appointed him accordingly.

May 13. The Enemy withdrew his pickets and left Amarante at 4 o'clock in the morning. The Army marched to Amarante and arrived about 11. The French marched for Guimaraens. Halted for the night at Pombeiro. No Intelligence from Sir Arthur Wellesley. Head Quarters Amarante.

May 14. Still no intelligence from Sir Arthur. A patrol pushed forward to Pombeiro, the Enemy marched to Guimaraens. A French Commissary sent in by the patrol. From his account the French are evacuating Oporto and there is indeed reason to suppose that Sir Arthur is already there. The probable retreat is Chaves. The Marshal sent an Aide-de-Camp to break the Bridge of Ruivaes and gave orders for Silveira with his Division and the 4th Chasseurs to proceed to Chaves. The Brigades of Baccellar and de Souza to march for Chaves, the first by Mondin, the last by Villa Real. The British and the Cavalry to march at 3 to-morrow morning, the whole to arrive on the 16th. Orders sent to Sir R. Wilson, now at Lamego, to march to Chaves.

May 15. In the morning, letter from British Head Quarters. Oporto taken. Sir Arthur in full pursuit.

May 16. Arrived at Chaves, Enemy reported at Ruivaes, took a position for the night in front for the bivouac of the Army; it did not, however, arrive.

May 17. Reconnoitred the Enemy at Montalegre. Army arrived; Lopez much scattered. British without shoes.[1]

May 18. Sir Arthur at Salamonde. Marched for Ginzo. Bivouacked at St. Mellor. British not up.

[1] See Oman, ii, p. 353, where in a footnote he quotes a letter of Lord Gough: ' The men were without a shoe to their feet—the result of their forced marching with incessant rain that swelled the rivulets into rivers.' In view of this it is hardly fair of Napier (see vol. ii, p. 302) when he blames Beresford for not marching on Salamonde and intercepting Soult.

May 19. Marched to Ginzo. French picket retired out of the town. Woods and hills cleared by the 60th. Enemy retired upon Alariz. Letter from Sir Arthur to say he had ceased the pursuit [1] for want of bread and was anxious to return to the Tagus. Of course pursuit alone was useless. Pushed on a patrol in front ; took up outposts ; Bivouacked Sir Robert and Lopez ; British in town ; Cavalry in advance ; Baccelar not arrived.

May 20. Rested the Army and pushed on a patrol of Lt. Col. T. (Talbot ?) and the Dragoons. They advanced beyond Alariz (?). Made 54 prisoners. Saw the French near Orense.

May 21. The Army marched on its return and arrived at Chaves, where Baccelar and Lopez remained.

May 22. Sir Robert, the British and Cavalry marched to Villa Pouca.

May 23. Villa Real.

May 24. Lamego.

May 27. The British marched to Guarda on their way to Abrantes according to Sir A. W.'s orders.

(End of May and beginning of June with the Marshal to Lisbon.)

June 13. Abrantes (from Lisbon).

The Marshal in the end of May, had ridden post from Lamego to Lisbon, upon indispensable public business with the Regency, and rejoined Sir Arthur Wellesley at Abrantes June 13.

Three Brigades (10,000 men) under B. Generals Sir Robert Wilson and Campbell and Colonel Lecor, with four Brigades of 6 and 9-pounders, and four Squadrons of Cavalry were assembled at Castello Branco to proceed with the British Force under Sir Arthur Wellesley against the Corps of Marshal Victor, whose Head Quarters had been at Merida, but were now at Truxillo. Marshal Beresford was detained at Abrantes by Sir Arthur Wellesley. The British Division could not move for want of money and shoes both for the men and horses. Sir Arthur seems adverse to the advancing of M. Beresford's Division, to occupy the line of the Tietar, and the strongholds and

---

[1] See Oman, ii, p. 360, footnote. The corroboration for Napier's statement is found in an annotation of D'Urban on Jones' History: ' The pursuit was continued many leagues, where he took a considerable number of prisoners and where he discontinued it by Sir Arthur's orders.'

passes of the Sierra de Placencia and the Bejar. It would
be a good measure to do this, and the Marshal has urged
it strongly. It would deprive the Enemy of almost his
only present resource for provisions, cut off his communications with Castile, confine him to one route in his retreat,
and expose his left flank to great danger in crossing the
Tagus at Almaraz. Indeed, with Cuesta in his rear, either
Victor (the proposed movement by Beresford's Division
being made) will not venture to pass the Tagus, but
remain where he is and must be delayed till (the British
Army having time to arrive in the plain between the
Tietar and Tagus) his discomfiture will be certain, or if
he venture to proceed by Almaraz (his only route) towards
Toledo and Madrid, I for one can't see how he can effect
his escape between Cuesta and Beresford and Sir Arthur.
The latter, however, does not appear to regard the
occupation of those passes and that fertile country as of
sufficient importance for the advance of the Marshal's
Division.

June 14–16. Abrantes. Things in the same position ;
our reports from the advance confirm more and prove
my opinion of Victor's retiring altogether on Madrid. I
have felt certain of this since the 10th and have indeed
always supposed that he would do so when the British
Army was known to be in march, hence it was that upon
Sir Arthur Wellesley's doing me the honour to ask my
opinion before I left Coimbra, I urged the expediency of
marching direct upon Almaraz, while Cuesta occupied
the Enemy's attention on the side of Merida and Medellin
and thus cutting off his retreat and ensuring the total
. . . [page cut out] . . . we might at least secure its
produce for ourselves.

June 17. Abrantes. There is no longer any pretext
for delaying the departure of Marshal Beresford for his
Division, he is at length to be permitted to set out tomorrow for Castello Branco. I still fear some obstacle,
however, for I think I can see that it is determined
otherwise. Hardinge set out to fix upon a hutted camp
on the road from Castello Branco to Idanha Nova.

June 18. My conjectures are just, a very foolish and
vague report from two officers, who are always frightened
at their shadows, Romana and Silveira, of Soult's Corps
reapproaching the Northern Frontier, has furnished the

requisite plea, and Sir Arthur Wellesley has ordered the Marshal to repair thither with his Division. So end all hopes of seeing this Campaign, doubly galling to me, because from my intimate knowledge of the country and the people, I might have hoped to render good service in my humble way, as well as from the credit in which I have the good fortune to stand, however undeservedly, with the Spanish Army with which we are to co-operate . . . [obliterated] . . . The two Battalions the Loyal Lusitanian Legion, and the 5th Chasseurs (about 1,800 men) remain and become a Brigade for Sir Robert Wilson. The 9th of the Line and the 3rd and 4th Chasseurs form a Brigade (2,000) for Col. Lecor, and with that (2,200) of B. Genl. Campbell (3rd, 13th, 15th Regts.) march by Guarda and Lamego to Braga ; the 23rd Regt. (1,300) from Almeida to Braga also, replaced by the 12th from Viseu. The Grenadiers of Oporto meet at Guarda, form one Regiment (1,100), and proceed by Lamego to Braga. The 1st Chasseurs and 4th of the Line (1,800) under Colonel Campbell by Coimbra to Oporto.   B. Genl. Blunt's Brigade (2,000) 7th and 19th from Lisbon to Braga ; the 10th and 16th (2,000) from Coimbra to Braga.   Thus with what is already in the North, there will be assembled in a few days 20,000 men.   Hardinge ordered to set out by Lamego for the Tras os Montes, take up a camp at Villa Real, another at Chaves, a third near Braga, send Intelligence, and meet the Marshal at Oporto.   Belson sent off by Guarda and Lamego to ensure supplies, Leite ordered to arrange them on the other roads.   The Brigades of Guns to Thomar, and all the Squadrons back to Galgao.   The Bureau to Coimbra. The Marshal goes by Lisbon where his presence is necessary and will yet reach Braga before the Troops.

June 19–20.   Lisbon.—By the reports from the north it is pretty evident that the Enemy's movements in Galicia only tend to a retreat upon Castile, by Braganza and Zamora.   This we felt quite sure of long ago.

June 23–24.   Lisbon.—Reports from the north confirm the above supposition.   Part of the Troops in march therefore halt, as follows—B. Genl. Blunt's Brigade at Coimbra ;   Campbell's, Le Cor's, and the 18th at Guarda, 23rd at Lamego.   These Troops are conveniently placed to march upon Almeida and the Agueda, and take up a camp in front of Ciudad Rodrigo between the Tormes and the Sierra Francia.   Excellent ground for manœuvre and discipline and a good position (supposing the Enemy to retreat from Galicia) to support and communicate with Sir Arthur Wellesley.   Orders sent to Belson and Leite to provide accordingly at Guarda, Pinhel, and Almeida and instructions given to B. Genl. Cox, Governor of Almeida, to communicate with the Duke del Parque at Ciudad Rodrigo upon the subject, and arrange for provisions etc., for a force of 20,000 men.   Colonel Trant's desire to retain the 10th Regt. in consequence of the possibility of the people being unquiet acquiesced in. Silveira has had the effrontery to send to the Regency what he calls an Official Diary of his operations in the Tras os Montes, including the whole of the late Campaign against Soult, in which with the most intrepid falsehood he states himself to have been the sole Chief, and altogether forgot the Commander-in-Chief who commanded in person, while Silveira was not even present either at the crossing the Douro, the driving back of Loisson, or our subsequent pursuit of the French across the Minho. This man though a perfect charlatan is nevertheless very dangerous.   I have long suspected him.   I trust the Marshal's eyes are opened now.

The Regency either from folly, or intrigue, or both, have published this diary in their official Gazette.   The intention to me is clear.

June 25–27.   Nothing new from the north.   Victor in full retreat;   Cuesta's advanced guard at Almaraz. The British still at Abrantes.

June 28.   Lisbon.   The Marquis de Romana and Silveira having taken fright once more, the former has retired to Baltar, and the latter writes that Ney and Soult united threaten to enter Portugal by Monterey.   If they had intended to invade Portugal again they would have scarcely passed the great road from Orense.   A day or two will bring a report from Hardinge.   It is absolutely necessary, however, that the Marshal should not at present quit Lisbon, unless the Enemy is actually and decidedly advancing into Portugal, for nothing can be effected with this Regency, but by personal conference, and much yet remains to be arranged.

For precaution, however, the 23rd Regt. at Lamego are ordered to Villa Real, if there be any demonstration upon Chaves, Col. Campbell with the 4th and 1st Chasseurs and 2 Guns to Guimaraens, and Col. Trant to watch carefully over the passes from Salamonde to Melgaco. Brig. Genl. Blunt to proceed to the line from Melgaco to Amarante, and take charge of the operations.

June 29–30. Lisbon.—Reports from the north indicate still more strongly the going off by Braganza.

July 1. Lisbon.—Marshal Beresford wrote the Marquis of Romana, who (with a force, which he himself admits he cannot depend upon, and which he states to be without arms, clothing, or provisions) is perpetually complaining of want of co-operation, stating explicitly his own views, and his unwillingness to enter into any fruitless combination in Galicia which would only tend to obstruct the necessary organisation of the Portuguese Army, and to prevent the movement he meditates to support Sir Arthur Wellesley, and cover the district of Salamanca, but at the same time declaring his readiness to combine with the Marquis and co-operate in any feasible scheme, and calling upon him to state his views and means.

July 2–3. The reports from the north confirm beyond a doubt the decided going off of the Enemy in the direction of Benavente and Zamora ; Ferrol and Corunna evacuated ; guns spiked ; ammunition blown up. Blunt's Brigade ordered to march to Viseu. Duke del Parque's answer of acquiescence to our plan received. Every preparation made for taking the field.

July 4–11. Preparations continue for the field. 5 Brigades of 9 and 6-pounders ordered to march. Intercepted letters from Soult to Joseph Bonaparte. His Army arrived at Zamora, in the worst condition—very sickly, much diminished, no money, medicines, stores or arms—quite unfit for service—complains of his Generals and admits that his people are murdered by the peasantry wherever they can take that advantage. The position in front of Ciudad Rodrigo becomes more and more and more important, and the Marshal will immediately move to take it up. Orders for the accelerating provisions in the frontier, moving stores, ammunition, etc. All in readiness. The British Army only commenced its march from Abrantes the 27th and will therefore not be on the Tietar before the 11th.

The British Government, as if anxious to do all the

harm possible to the measure of forming the Portuguese
Army, have sent out as Brigadiers a . . .

[Page cut out.]

July 13-14. The Field Marshal set out for the Frontier,
—Santarem-Punhete—from Galgao orders repeated to
Genl. Miranda to march the Artillery Brigades.

July 15. Coroicada.

July 16. Castello Branco. Brigade of 6-pounders
there ordered to Sabugal.

July 17. Fundao.—Orders to B. Genl. Blunt to march
with his Brigade to Celorico and report his march enclosing
his route.

July 18. Guarda. Letters from Cox; the Duke del
Parque does not disapprove of the retired line upon the
Yeltes, but seems to wish that cantonment should extend
from Tamames to St. Felices for the benefit of provisions.
This is a powerful inducement, no doubt, but with such
troops as the Portuguese, unformed and undisciplined, the
cantonment is too extensive.

July 19. The Field Marshal reviewed B. Genl. Campbell's Brigade ; their movements excellent and everything
bespeaks the greatest attention, zeal and ability upon the
part of him and his officers. The late restrictions as to
rank, the English Government rescinding their promise of
a step of English rank, which will strike at the root of
procuring efficient officers, have naturally occasioned
much anxiety and discontent among them.

Orders to Le Cor to march the 13th Grenadiers to
Guarda to join their Corps, to Stubbs to march with the
23rd Regt. from Lamego to Pinhel ; and for Trant to
march the Coimbra Students to Almeida. In reply to
his representations of Oporto being too crowded to admit
the detachment of the 6th, 9th, and 18th, orders sent to
him to send out an equal number to make room for them,
their speedy move to the eastward being most important.
Orders to Silveira to march the 11th from Chaves and
Monervo and to hold the 2nd and 14th in readiness.

July 20. The Marshal proposed to visit the Troops at
Pinhel ; I received his orders to proceed to Ciudad Rod-
rigo and candidly and explicitly state to the Duke del
Parque his views and intentions and the state of his means.
In the doiñg this it appears necessary that I should :—

1st. Assure the Duke of the esteem the Marshal

entertains for his character, the inclination he has to make his acquaintance, and his consequent desire to meet the Duke's wish by paying him a visit at Ciudad Rodrigo.

2nd. That I should state strongly that the Field Marshal has no isolated or selfish ideas of confining himself to the protection of Portugal, that independent of his cordial affection for the Spanish Cause, it is evident to him that of Portugal can only be benefited by the success and triumph of that of Spain, hence the Peninsula, the *whole* Peninsula, enters into his views of being useful upon every account, and his actions shall correspond with his assertion.

3rd. The Duke del Parque, however, must be aware that the Field Marshal cannot do all that he would, he must understand that the Portuguese Military was in the most wretched state when the Field Marshal accepted the Command of the Army, and that the circumstances of the times, which have ever since required incessant marching, have so militated against any real improvement that the Troops he brings with him require a few days working together before they can effectually serve any purpose against the Enemy, a few days of manœuvre also under the Field Marshal's immediate eye is requisite because there will, as may be well conceived, exist among the Portuguese officers, a certain degree of jealousy with regard to the English officers who have been placed at the head of Regiments and Companies to assist in the labour so much wanted ; a camp of manœuvre under the Marshal's inspection would immediately put this matter to rest ; such a camp therefore it is his desire to establish in the first instance. Hence, although he cannot but approve highly of the line of position chosen by the Duke, which is indeed excellent, yet from the foregoing reasons he would prefer to concentrate his whole force near the centre of the proposed line at, or about, Martin del Rio; in the doing this he would of course have small Corps of observation upon his flanks and an advance in front, but still the main body of his Corps would be constantly under his eye ; and would, he conceives, in 10 days or a fortnight be fit for any service.

4th.—While in this position the Army would have every effect in point of demonstration, as far as regards Cuesta and Wellesley, and be ready to act upon a short line of operations should the movement of the French make such a step necessary.

5th.—The Field Marshal proposes to hut the Troops in the position, by which means although the villages will be at a somewhat greater distance, and the transport of provisions of course rather more difficult, yet on the other side, the people in the villages will not be embarrassed by the crowd and inconvenience of Troops quartered in their houses and will therefore with more ease bake and make the requisite arrangements for preparing and expediting the Provisions. The concentration of the Troops in this way will also keep them in perfect readiness to move, which will be very desirable, because although the F. Marshal would wish for the reasons above adduced to have a few days for instruction and formation in order afterwards to act with more effect, yet he by no means would let slip any favourable occasion of acting whenever it might present itself.

6th.—With regard to money, it was the determination to arrange this point so as to preclude all uncertainty that detained the Field Marshal at Lisbon so long beyond the time he wished to set out for Ciudad Rodrigo. A sufficiency to pay for everything is therefore on its way from Lisbon; it is not indeed actually arrived, but its speedy arrival is certain. Can the Troops enter Spain and begin to receive supplies for a few days upon this assurance? Or must they wait till it is actually here?

7th.—He wishes, however, to state explicitly to the Duke del Parque, that the finances of Portugal are by no means in the most flourishing state. The money coming will be sufficient in all probability for six weeks or longer, but after that period of regular payments, should there be an interval of a few days before a fresh supply arrives, he trusts he may depend upon sufficient credit, to be certain of not starving. He has been in this, as he wishes to be on all points, explicit to the Duke that no mistake may be hereafter owing to him.

8th.—The F. Marshal is himself very weak in Cavalry. Not more than 800. The Regiments were all so bad that he considered the bringing any more till they were somewhat more efficient, a mere useless consumption of forage. The Duke can probably assist him in this particular, by affording him a few Horse in addition, for his outposts,

and also by using his influence for the immediate con-
veyance of Intelligence from the loyal peasants in the
villages in front.

9th.—The Field Marshal's first line of about 12,000
Infantry and the Cavalry and part of the Guns, can take
up its ground in three days if required, being at present
in Almeida, Pinhel, Guarda, Sabugal, and Celorico.

10th.—The second line of 6,000 men is on its march
and will arrive in due succession.

11th.—So incessant has been the marching of the
Troops that they are in a great measure unclothed; their
clothing is pursuing them now, and the Duke must have
the goodness not to be astonished at seeing them ragged.

12th.—It would be very desirable that the Marquis of
Romana should be induced to co-operate by moving up
in the direction of Carvajales. The F. Marshal would
then establish a Corps of communication with him; but
it is necessary to observe that if the notions of the Marquis
do not become a little less desultory than they have
hitherto been, it will be utterly impossible to act in conjunction with him, or consider him as a part of the combined Army.

Arrived at Almeida and conversed with B. Genl. Cox.

July 21. Arrived at Ciudad Rodrigo. Great cordiality
on the part of the Duke. Very much occupied with
French prisoners just arrived from his outposts, and other
affairs. He has fixed my audience for tomorrow morning.

July 22. Discussed all the above points in a conversation with the Duke del Parque,—he seems perfectly satisfied
upon every point, and entered fully into the necessity of
devoting a few days to the putting the Troops together
under the Marshal's own eye; that this purpose may not
be interrupted, he has promised to push forward an advanced Guard and flanking posts and to take all the out
duties. He seems to think that there will be a difficulty
in finding transport for the provisions if the Troops are
concentrated at, or about, Martin del Rio. He has just
learned by letter from Estrevania that Romana is at
Astorga and marching upon Fermoselle.

Wrote the Marshal the result of my conference with the
Duke and strongly advised his coming to visit him to
arrange finally, especially as the Duke seems to wish it
much, and to take it for granted that he will come. Sent

instructions to two officers of my Staff to reconnoitre
without loss of time the line from St. Felices to St. Espiritus
and the banks of the Yeltes to Martin del Rio.

July 23. Went from Ciudad Rodrigo to Miranda del
Castanar, saw Abad and arranged my communication with
him and Romana at Barco d'Avila.

Sir Arthur Wellesley's advanced Guard was two days
ago at Talavera de la Reyna. Joseph Bonaparte has
returned from Toledo to Madrid.

July 24. Proceeded by Careceda and Aldea Nueva de
la Sierra to reconnoitre the right of the proposed line ;
found near Tamames a most excellent position, upon the
chain of heights formed by the falls of the Sierra Francia.
This position possesses great advantages, watching the
probable march of Soult and Mortier, whether they proceed by Perales or Baños to fall upon Sir Arthur's rear,
and is admirably calculated for our purpose. It is quite
secure, being appuyed upon the Sierra, and from the nature
of the ground the superiority of the Enemy's Cavalry
will avail him nothing. As a post of demonstration it is
excellent, and the occupying it will not fail to create great
perplexity [1] in the French Generals. It commands two
high roads to Salamanca, one, by Alba de Tormes to
Peñaranda on the route from Salamanca to Madrid,
protects the left rear of Sir Arthur and covers Ciudad
Rodrigo. Many villages and abundant wood and water.

Martin del Rio.—Advanced post of the Regiment of
the Queen.

July 25. Returned to Ciudad Rodrigo, and met the
Marshal who had arrived yesterday. Explained to him
the nature of the position of Tamames ; he agrees in its
advantages, and if nothing arises to prevent it in his
conference with the Duke del Parque, he will probably
occupy it immediately.

The vexation of having to do with such Troops as we
have is beyond description. Our first line which false
returns made amount to 13,000 falls short of 9,000.

July 26. At Almeida. The Duke del Parque will do
nothing positive as to assistance in point of Troops, notwithstanding his promise at my first conversation. I

---

[1] D'Urban bears out the contention of Sir Charles Oman in regard to
Cradock. A remarkable coincidence, for Sir Charles did not see this Journal
until after his second volume which tells of these events had appeared.

foresee that what we do, we must do ourselves. Whether
the Duke has found out the deficiency in our first line,
or the bad description of people we have, I know not,
both perhaps, and this accounts for the change so visible
in him. All, however, is perfectly smooth and apparently
cordial, but I foresee we shan't get a man from him.

July 27. The Duke del Parque has informed the
Marshal that French detachments—each of 2,000 men—
have proceeded to Ledesma and Tamames. He considers
them to be of consequence and indicating the march of the
Corps at Salamanca. In the direction perhaps of Ciudad
Rodrigo; The Duke does not dislike to give it this appearance because he wishes to avoid furnishing any assistance in men and this affords an excuse. The Marshal
seems inclined to give the French credit for some movement of this kind. I can't think so and am persuaded
the whole will turn out a party of contribution, plunder and
pillage. This intelligence has made the Marshal defer
his march upon Tamames.

Algave Brigade and 6th Chasseurs from Chaves to
Torre de Moncorve. 1st Chasseurs and 10th Regt. from
Oporto to Almeida.

July 28. Marshal Beresford will occupy the position
behind the Agueda. There he will wait events, concentrate his Corps in security and be ready to act according
to circumstances. I go to choose a position in the direction the Marshal wishes.

The passage of the Agueda at Barba de Porco is quite
impracticable for anything but Infantry; horses may
be led down the Zig-Zag, and the bridge when arrived at
is a good one. St. Felices will make a very good left for
the intended position; to be occupied with light Troops,
holding too the passage of the bridge.

Proceeded from St. Felices, ascertained that the French
have quitted both Tamames and Ledesma; they were as
I imagined, Detachments to enforce requisitions.

July 29. Finished the reconnaissance of the position.
The Agueda impassable from Barba de Porco to the ford
opposite Villa de la Yegua.

Returned to Almeida. Gave the Marshal memoranda
of a position—A Corps of the Army with a 6-pounder
Brigade to be hutted on the woody heights between Villa
de la Yegua and the Agueda, on the left of the road leading

to the ford. 2 Squadrons of Cavalry and a 6-pounder Brigade at Villa de la Yegua. Head Quarters at Villa de Ciervo with a Reserve of the 23rd Regt., a Brigade of 9-pounders and 2 Squadrons of Cavalry.

Detachment of Infantry and 20 Horse at Mastillar or Martiveriego to communicate with Ciudad Rodrigo. On the right Le Cor's Brigade at St. Felices, occupying Barba de Porco and 50 Horse. Outposts from Lombrales by Benavares to Aldea Nuova de Parta Nobis.

Communication between the Camp and Barba de Porco. This arrangement I think secures all and we are in readiness to move. The Marshal is good enough to approve of this position. The Troops ordered to move; General Campbell from Guarda to Almeida. General Blunt by Pinhal; Col. Le Cor to St. Felices.

July 30–31.—Intelligence of the French of the 29th and 30th. Mortier marched from Salamanca upon Alba de Tormes with 10,000 men.—Soult followed with the main body. They have collected from 26 to 30,000 men, 18 guns and 4 howitzers.—Independent it would appear of Ney, who has not arrived. If they moved upon Baños which is likely, they will place themselves upon the rear or left of Sir Arthur. He was repeatedly urged to occupy the Bejar before he moved forward. If circumstances have permitted him, however, to bring Victor to action, the other Army will only arrive to learn the news, and to fall in detail. The French had spread a report of a victory over the Austrians, and of the Emperor's having asked an armistice of 2 months giving Gratz and Brunn as securities.

The Marshal despatched an officer to the Marquis of Romana, urging him to co-operate instantly—this is the moment upon which much depends, and we must do all we can however bad our means.

I go to Villa de Cierve, to prepare for the arrival of the Troops to take up the position and then establish the chain and look to the front.

Aug. 1–2. Proceeded to Villa de Cierve, fixed upon the position, left Hardinge to take it up, and went on to establish the chain on the other side of the Agueda, from the ford of Serranillo on the right, to St. Felices and Lombales on the left. Established the chain, and sent back the orders for its formation to Hardinge for Benovaes.

Proceeded forward again to gain certain intelligence of
the Enemy at Salamanca, by St. Espiritus, Martin del
Rio, Fuerto, St. Estevan, and Garcirey. Here I met Don
Francisca Gracia, a most excellent Priest whom I had
often had occasion to prove while I was with Sir R. Wilson.
Hitherto I had sent to him in vain, for he was obliged to
fly from the French, but he had this day (2nd) returned to
his house. From him I had certain intelligence that the
whole French Army had removed from Salamanca (united
Divisions of Soult, Ney, and Mortier) 32,000 Foot, 4,000
Horse, 18 guns, 4 howitzers, by the road of Baños for
Estremadura. There has been a battle however, certainly,
upon the Tagus ; the result is of course in favour of Sir
Arthur and if it has been decisive this Corps will arrive
too late.

August 3. Arrived at Villa de Cierve. The Marshal
had not fixed his Head Quarters here as he had previously
determined, but was gone back to Almeida—followed—
found him with Sewell who had returned from Sir Arthur.
There has been a battle as I learned yesterday. It has
been bloody and obstinate. Began the 26th, continued
27th and ended the night of the 28th in the complete
defeat of the French after a series of the most furious
and determined attacks. The battle was fought near
Talavera del Reyna.

The Marshal determines upon moving immediately
forward, and I am very glad that he does so. Pity we
had not moved before. Had the position of Tamames
been occupied, we might have moved by the mountains,
and much impeded the march of Soult.

There are here two Spaniards, an Aide-de-Camp of the
Duke del Parque and the Corrijedor of Salamanca sent to
propose a movement occupying a line extending from
Baños to the Puerta del Piro, 18 leagues ! How he could
ever suppose we could attempt to occupy such an extent
I am at a loss to conceive. These gentlemen propose on
the part of the Duke, that to accelerate and facilitate our
march in the direction he wishes, two Spanish officers
shall be attached to each of our Columns, to smooth the
way to our getting provisions, and serve as guides. This
offer it is well to close with, and therefore I have done so,
because we can make two days' marches by the route he
wishes, deriving the advantages offered by the assistance

of these Spanish officers, and we can afterwards concentrate to the right, centre, or left, according to what may be most expedient. This Spaniard never gives help but for some private view, and its therefore fair to avail ourselves of this aid and turn it to our own purpose in the present instance.

The Troops ordered to march ; Le Cor from St. Felices to Fuente de St. Estevan ; Campbell to St. Espiritus ; McLeith, Sepulveda ; Blunt, Gallegos ; Dixon and Arentschilde 6 and 9-pounder Brigades, Gallegos and Alameda, tomorrow the 4th St. Payo, Benovares.

Aug. 4. Sent off Harvey to the Bejar by Miranda to ascertain if the Enemy occupied the Puerta, or if they had all passed. Sent off two officers of the Engineers to reconnoitre the Perales, the road to Coria, the communications with Portugal by Zarga and Penamacor and with the Tagus, and to send intelligence of the Enemy towards Placencia.

Proceeded to St. Espiritus to meet the Spanish officers, found them there. Sent two to each of the columns of Blunt, Campbell and Le Cor. Put McLeith's Brigade into the Division of Campbell. Each column also a guide, one of the Spanish officers always to stay with it, the other to precede it and have provisions ready. The Duke del Parque has altered his mind with regard to the route of the columns, and writes me to say so enclosing the routes upon which the provisions will be most plentiful. The first march of men from their present posts will not interfere with anything we may afterwards wish to do, and as the Marshal has promised to meet me very early tomorrow morning (the 5th) at Ciudad Rodrigo, there will be abundance of time to prevent their going further, and to make our after arrangements. I shall order the Troops to move therefore by the routes proposed, still to preserve the assistance of the Duke to the last. Despatched the orders of march. Campbell, Monsagro (having McLeith at Serradilla) ; Le Cor to Puebla de Yeltes, Maguoroz, and Baños ; Blunt to Guinaldo and Perales and Gata. I have not moved Arentschilde or Dixon or St. Payo till I see the Marshal, as it is better that the Artillery and Cavalry should not be concentrated till he determines whether to act by Baños or the Perales.

Aug. 5. Arrived very early at Ciudad Rodrigo. At

3 o'clock P.M. the Marshal not being arrived sent orders for Dixon and Arentschilde to march to Guinaldo. There is no waiting longer and leaving the Artillery further behind. I know too that the Marshal rather inclines to Perales, and at all events this move to the left from Guinaldo will be easy. The Cavalry I will still leave. Ordered couriers to be ready to send to stop the further march of the columns. If Marshal Beresford does not arrive by 5 o'clock I shall take upon myself to halt them. The Marshal arrived between 3 and 4. I urged the importance of halting the Troops where they now are, if only to let them have one day of plenty after three days of starving. At Lisbon I remonstrated against the having a Portuguese Commissary General, I have been continually remonstrating since to no effect. The want of food notwithstanding the exertions of the Brigadiers and the British officers attached to the Regiments, as well as of the officers of my Staff who have acted as Commissaries, has been shocking.

Night.—As I predicted it is too late to ensure the sending the orders, what with the delay of the Governor (probably intentional) and the want of energy in the Duke del Parque, everything wanted for the public service of the Auxiliary Force is slowly and unwillingly furnished.

Orders sent to St. Payo to march with the Cavalry from Benavares to Trasbon and Mores Verdas. Blunt to halt at Peraparda. Le Cor to halt at Puebla de Yeltes. Dixon to march to Cuidad Rodrigo. Arentschilde to halt at Guinaldo. These orders must reach the Regiments late, too late probably to stop them. And St. Payo also will have scarcely time to make his whole march to-morrow. It would appear from the studious difficulties thrown in our way that the Spaniards wish to thwart us.

Aug. 6. Letters from Sir Arthur Wellesley have decided the Marshal to move upon the passes of Perales. These letters are written at Oropesa. Sir Arthur hearing of Soult's passage through the Baños, had determined to attack him without delay, and engaging therefore, the Spaniards to look at the beaten Enemy for as many days (two or three probably) as would have sufficed for the march he meditated, he proceeded on his way to Placentia. To his astonishment, however, Cuesta broke up from Talavera and followed him, leaving the British Hospital to the Enemy. With such Allies it is impossible to act—

Treachery or panic ?—Sir Arthur wishes Marshal Beresford
to be at the passes of Perales where he can move to stop
Soult if he be beaten, or fall back upon Castello Branco
if Sir Arthur crosses the Tagus. Blunt's Brigade, and
Arentschilde's Artillery to Payo holding the passes.
Dixon's Artillery to Guinaldo. St. Payo's Cavalry to El
Bodon. Campbell and McLeith to Martiago, Le Cor to
Monsagro. 4th Regt. and 6th Chasseurs on march from
Pinhel to Alfayates. A demand made for the British
biscuit at Ciudad Rodrigo evaded by the Duke del Parque.
The Troops are starving. I shall advise their helping
themselves.

Aug. 7. Guinaldo.—Proposed to the Marshal to be in
readiness to concentrate all his Corps between Perales and
Cilleros, and to send to Sir Arthur Wellesley to say so, and
that if he wished to attack Soult at Placentia, the Marshal
would and could move by his left and fall upon his rear or
flank. The British (Lighthouse and Catlin Crawfurd) may in
the proposed position join us from Zarza and upon their arrival there or at Salvatierra we ought to move. The Marshal
approved of this. Hardinge is despatched to Sir Arthur.
Now we might be of infinite use. . . . [obliterated] . . .
Nightingale ordered to march immediately ; by the 12th
we shall be ready to act all together. Sir Arthur can't
be ready before. Fusquini and Chapuzet to ascertain
distances and resources within the triangle ' Z.'

Aug. 8. Went to the front by Moraleja with Col.
Wilson, and to the left to ascertain the communications
towards Valdo Bispo, etc. by which route we must move
if Sir Arthur will have us.

Good communications,—Superior Cavalry will afford
the Enemy no advantage. Ordered Fusquini and Chapuzet to make a reconnaissance upon the road to Val do
Bispo and Oliva, thus to the Baños of Placentia.

Aug. 9. Head Quarters at Arebo. Blunt and
Arentschilde, Perales; Campbell, Arebo; MᶜL—— (?), Gata;
Dixon, Payo; St. Payo, Perales and Moraleja. Spanish
Commissary arrived. Every effort made to get provisions
for the Troops who have been hitherto, from the shameful
inattention of the Spanish authorities, almost starved.

Aug. 10. Le Cor arrived at Valverde del Fresne.
4th Regt. and 6th Chasseurs will arrive tomorrow. By
the 12th all will be ready to move. On the 14th both

Crawfurd and Nightingale will shake hands with us, and then with 15,000 men of which 5,000 will be English, we may, if Sir Arthur will allow us, turn the scale of an action at Placentia.

2nd and 3rd Chasseurs and 300 Lusitanian Legion given to Col. Wilson; his outpost established at Villa Buenas. Upon enquiry for this Lusitanian Legion Detachment, the Marshal informed me to my utter astonishment, that he had ordered it to march to Placentia. These people will be cut off. I have sent Capt. Harvey to stop and turn them (if possible) to Herelaga, where they will form the advance of Wilson. Harvey will afterwards proceed to get intelligence. Fusquini and Chapuset ordered to reconnoitre from Perales to Cilleros and from thence to Zarza.

Aug. 11. In the night the Marshal suddenly ordered the march of the Army upon Cilleros, this is somewhat of the earliest, and will I apprehend cause some difficulty as to provisions. However all possible means are taken to bring down the resources to Cilleros ; Blunt, Campbell, and McL——(?), and Arentschilde will be there by 12 o'clock ; in the night Le Cor and the 4th Regt. will arrive.

Cilleros 12 o'clock.—Near Cilleros an excellent and safe position, commanding the Zarza road with a good road in the rear of the Gata to Penamacor, 5 leagues. While taking up the position the Marshal, giving credit to the report of a man of Cilleros, imagined himself in a cul-de-sac, and thinking there was danger of being cut off, though the Enemy were 45 English miles from us, ordered the Troops to march to Venta dos Cavallos, three long leagues upon the road to Zarza. This is lamentable ! The Troops will be jaded to death, will have out-marched their provisions and will have swerved so much to their right as to lose the communication with the left, and the consequent ability of acting with Sir Arthur Wellesley, should Hardinge's return announce his wish for their doing so. . . . The Marshal persists. . . . Head Quarters for the night at Moraleja. Immediately on arriving there, the Marshal directed the march of all the Troops at Venta dos Cavallos to their old quarters in the mountains.

These Troops will be killed—14 leagues without rest.

Arentschilde to Zarza under orders of B. Genl. Craufurd.

Aug. 12. By Vallas Buenas to Los Heyos. Wilson's

post of course in high order. The French have a post
at Galisted. Hardinge arrived in the evening from Sir
Arthur Wellesley. He fancies that the Enemy are collecting at Placentia to march upon Portugal, and gives
orders accordingly that we shall fall back upon Castello
Branco. Reports make it certain to us that the Enemy
is marching upon Baños. This Sir Arthur does not know.
Arbuthnot despatched to tell him, and to urge his not
quitting his position of Mirabete for a more backward one.
Sir Robert Wilson at Bejar having been of the greatest
use by remaining in the rear of the French Army. Letter
from him.

Aug. 13. Los Hayos.—Troops rested but ordered to
march tomorrow to Moraleja. The General's reason that
if Sir Arthur still persists in thinking Portugal the Enemy's
object, we can go thence by Zarza,—if he will move upon
Placentia we can do so too. French Cavalry approached
Coria. Hardinge set out with a Squadron to look at them.
Hervey sent to take up a bivouac for the 2nd line at Venta
de Cavallos. Wrote B. Genl. Craufurd to meet the General
at Moraleja tomorrow.

Aug. 14. Moraleja.—Troops all arrived. Hardinge
returned,—the French Cavalry retired from Coria at his
approach,—he fixed his outposts . . .

Set out in the evening with 40 Horse to . . .

Aug. 15. Returned in the morning. Found that
the General had suddenly determined to fall back on
Zarza. Letters from Sir Arthur order to that effect.
Army marched at 12 o'clock at night. The French by
numbers and Artillery of which we had none, have forced
Baños, and are passing to Castile. Sir Arthur Wellesley
fought against every disadvantage for 9 hours at Baños.

Aug. 16. At Zarza.

Aug. 17. At Salvatierra. Arbuthnot returned—
nothing but to retire.

Aug. 18. Dixon and Le Cor, and Algarve marched
for Castello Branco by Zibreira and Lodino.

Aug. 19. Campbell, Blunt, McL——(?) to Lodino.

Aug. 20–21. The whole Army to Castello Branco.
Count St. Payo, Salvatierra and Zarza—Poste d'Adver-
tissement.

Aug. 30–31. To Lisbon leaving the charge of the
Frontier to Sir R. Wilson stationed at Castello Branco.

JOURNAL III[1]

Sept. 1809–*June* 1810.

INTRODUCTION

D'URBAN's last entry may be said to have closed with the Talavera campaign, which had for its object the capture of Madrid. In this the Allies failed, owing in large part to the lack of Spanish co-operation with Wellington, an experience that definitely determined him to leave them to their own devices and defend Portugal. In addition, Napoleon's victory over the Austrians at Wagram (June 1809) made it very probable that he in person would conduct another offensive in the Peninsula.

The task before Wellington was, therefore, a most arduous one, rendered more difficult by the stern opposition amongst his own officers, D'Urban being the outstanding exception, thus rendering his Journal for this period of unique interest and importance.

The preparations made during the winter of 1809–10 and the ensuing spring—embracing as they do the central crisis of the whole war—may be summed up as follows :—

(*a*) [2] The complete re-organisation of the Portuguese military forces, Beresford being put in charge of them with D'Urban as his Quartermaster-General, in which capacity he rendered such excellent service.

(*b*) The arrangement for the great scheme of devastating the countryside in front of the invader and so fight him with the weapon of starvation.

(*c*) And most important of all, the construction of the 'Lines' of Torres Vedras, in Wellington's mind as early as September 1809, but definitely taking shape in his famous memorandum of a month later, after a flying visit to Lisbon

---

[1] In another neat little book bound in white leather, most probably made by D'Urban himself. The latter Journals are for the most part on loose sheets of foolscap paper, but all carefully numbered, and each tied in a bundle with despatches and reports sent and received.

[2] See Oman, iii, p. 171.

with D'Urban in attendance.[1] ' In that document the whole
project for defending the Portuguese capital by a series of
concentric fortifications is set forth. . . . In short the Lines
which were to check Masséna had been thought out in the
British General's provident mind exactly twelve months
before the French army appeared in front of them.' [2]

D'Urban has no entries for the months of September,
October, November and early December, taken up, it would
seem, with routine work as chief of staff in connexion with the
cantonment of Beresford's army, but not of sufficient interest
for entry into his Journal.

1809. *Dec.* 7. Field Marshal Beresford having it in contemplation to make a Tour of Inspection of different Posts
and Corps, left Lisbon, where his Head Quarters had
been from the beginning of September.

TORRES VEDRAS.—7 Leagues. The heights to the
Northward of this Town are naturally so strong, and so
peculiarly well situated for defending the approaches on
that side, that when the Works, constructing under the
orders of Lieut. Colonel Fletcher of the Engineers, shall
be completed, the advance of anything by the High Road
from Caldas, would appear impracticable, but the ridge
passing the *Right* must be carefully attended to, for there
seems to be a possibility of a Route, covered by its summit,
turning the Works altogether, and entering the High Road
in their Rear.

Dec. 8. VIMIERO.—2 Leagues. The Ground upon
which Sir Arthur Wellesley fought in the August of 1808,
was very well adapted to the force with which he occupied
it, but had he been beaten, it is difficult to imagine how
he would have retreated; fortunately the never-failing
gallantry of the British rendered this unnecessary. The
French combined their attacks badly. Their Column of
the Right which attacked General Ferguson, did not arrive
at its point till those of the Centre and Left had already
been defeated, and was routed instantly by the brilliant
Advance of his Brigade (36th and 71st Regts. supported
by the 82nd), the conduct of which was as excellent as
anything in the annals of our Military History. It can

---

[1] With the papers are enclosed : Memoranda—Positions upon the right
bank of the Tagus, after attending Lord Wellington upon his reconnaissance
of the ground afterwards known by the denomination of the ' Lines,'
October 1809, by B. D'Urban.

[2] Oman, ii, p. 610.

never be sufficiently lamented that the British Army did
not immediately march upon Torres Vedras,—they would
have infallibly preceded the Enemy, would have placed
themselves between him and Lisbon, upon most favourable
Ground, and from the confusion and dismay which prevailed in his Army, would have, without doubt, completed
his destruction. The want of Cavalry alone appears to have
saved the Right Column of the French from annihilation.
Peniche, 3 leagues from Vimiero ; 5 from Torres Vedras.

   Dec. 9. PENICHE.—Inspected.[1] The Isthmus over
which the peninsula of Peniche is approached, is covered
with water at High Tides, and from the Line of the Works
describing a sort of arc, very powerful cross-fires may be
established upon every part of it. Indeed all approach
may be rendered impracticable if the Left flank be attended
to, and a trifling repair given to the Centre. There are
nearly 100 heavy Guns upon the different Works, most
of them very good, the Brass ones especially. The Range
proved very long. This Peninsula is the most favourable
position that can be conceived for the Embarking the
British Army, should it ever be necessary to do so in the
Face of the Enemy. Its circumference abounds with
Creeks, or clefts in the Rocks, in which there is always
smooth water, and an easy egress and regress for Boats,
and if a certain number of the Fishing Vessels of the
Country be kept in these Creeks, the Troops can always
be embarked out of the reach of the fire from the side
of the Isthmus. And indeed there is sufficient ground to
encamp a large Force perfectly beyond the range of the
Enemy. If it should be necessary provisions can be sent
on shore from the Ships. If it should be thought worth
while this Peninsula might be held by England, even if
Portugal otherwise was in possession of the Enemy, a
very little pains might make it impregnable towards the
Isthmus, its only approach, and it produces within itself
abundance of wine and no inconsiderable quantity of
Corn. There is abundance of water. The position is
perfectly healthy, and certainly a very interesting one for
England to turn its attention to, as connected with Portugal. It becomes the more important for the Commander-
in-Chief to consider of, as there is actually no other place
of embarkation between it and the mouth of the Guadiana,

[1] See Oman, iii, p. 188 *et seq.*

where the Troops could be either safely got on board or
the Ships sure of getting away when they were so. If it
be the wish of Lord Wellington, he can still retire upon
Lisbon, give battle before it, and then, should the day be
against him, retreat upon Peniche through a difficult
Country, and ultimately, if the state of the pursuing
Enemy should warrant, the putting of everything to the
hazard of another Battle, the Peninsula itself offers a most
advantageous Field,—let the Centre of the Line of Works
be thrown down, the extreme flanks preserved, let the
Enemy enter, and let the issue be tried to the uttermost,
I scarcely can conceive any odds that a French Corps
could have, that would preserve it from destruction then.

By Rorissa (2 leagues), and Obidos (3 leagues) to
Caldas (4 leagues) Rorissa (ROLIÇA).—Here Sir Arthur
Wellesley's advance forced the heights of Columbeira and
drove back the Corps of Laborde on the 17th August 1808.
That this Position should be carried in front, as it was by
the British, is almost beyond credibility, and is another
proof, if that were wanting, that no obstacle whatever
can stop the Troops in the execution of their Orders.
The part of the heights which was carried by the 9th
and 29th Regts. especially is so difficult of ascent, and
affords so much advantage to the defenders that how they
suffered a man to reach the summit must astonish every
Soldier who looks at the Ground. Lt. Col. Lake who led
the 29th up the Gorge on the Enemy's Left was killed and
is there buried. In attacking this position in front Sir
Arthur certainly appears to have taken the Bull by the
horns, and as the Enemy's Corps did not exceed from
4 to 5,000 Men, he might easily have turned both its flanks,
and its retreat would have been the natural consequence ;
it is however to be considered that this would have required
time ; and that time would have allowed the Corps of
Loison (which had already marched from Rio Mayor, and
which then could not have been more than 2 Leagues
from that of Laborde) to arrive. This it was, of course,
which determined the Commander-in-Chief to go straight
forward and carry the Position without delay, whatever
might be the loss.

OBIDOS.—Here the first Action took place after the
landing of Sir Arthur's Army, the French Light Troops
being driven out of the Town and Groves by the 95th

Regt., who pursuing too far suffered severely. This is a Post of much importance, 'tis the point from whence the Roads to Peniche and Vimiero diverge, and might be made very strong with a little labour. The old Walls of the Town, which stands upon an isolated Rock, would facilitate this, and there is water within them, independently of the Aqueduct. The forcing this Post ought to cost the Enemy a serious loss.

Caldas.—Hot Baths—Mineral Spring.

Dec. 10. ALCOBAÇA.—4 Leagues.—Difficult Country. —Two or three defensive Positions. The most magnificent Convent in Portugal, founded by Alfonso 1st, stands between the Alcoa and the Baza. Pedro and Inez de Castro are buried here. A most splendid Library.

Dec. 11. LEIRIA.—5 Leagues.—The road to Caldas falls into the High Road from Coimbra to Lisbon at about 3 leagues from Alcobaça. It strikes me that the former might be without much difficulty rendered impracticable, in which case the Enemy coming from the North would be confined to the High Road. This, independent of the advantage of confining him to one Line of operations, and one Column of March, would compel him to pass through a very sterile Country.

Received Col. Murray's Letter of the 7th asking the best Route from Sabugal to Pinhel, and Cantonments at Guarda, Pinhel, and Viseu.

Dec. 12. LEIRIA.—Marshal inspected General Colman's Brigade (11th, 13th, 23rd Regts.) Leiria by taking advantage of the Ground upon which the remains of the Castle stand, and two or three other arrangements, should be made to cost the Enemy dear in the passing. In short every strong Post upon his line of March should be made the grave of some of his people, and if 30,000 more stand of Arms are sent from England according to Marshal Beresford's request, the Militia will be well armed, and any French Corps ought to reach the place where the real stand is intended to be made in a state not quite so fit for Combat as when it set out. There is a good Cistern within the Castle Walls, having a spring of excellent water rising in it.

Dec. 13. THOMAR.—7 Leagues.—The whole of this road easily rendered impracticable, and every inch of it affording means for a vigorous defence.

Dec. 14. Received Col. Murray's communications as to the Route of the British Army. Made all the necessary arrangements for the passage of the first Corps, according to his orders.

Lord Wellington has at length determined to move. It can never be enough lamented that he did not adopt this resolution 2 Months earlier. His Army would have answered every possible purpose between the Tagus and the Mondego, as well as upon the Guadiana and he would have saved the lives of 3,000 Men at least, that the pestilential swamps of Spanish Estremadura and the Alemtejo have destroyed. One ought not however to venture an opinion. Nobody can appreciate all the motives that sway a Commander-in-Chief, but himself.

The Marshal inspected the 4th and 10th Regts. of Portuguese Infantry. Col. Campbell and Lt. Col. Oliver— these Officers deserve the highest credit. I have never seen an English Brigade move with more steadiness and precision.

Dec. 15–17. THOMAR.—Marshal received the letter 139 from D.M. Forjaz. Correspondence in consequence.

Lt. Col. Canler ordered to reconnoitre Leiria. Plan and Estimate of Post there. Instructions given.

Dec. 18–19. ABRANTES.[1]—Inspected the Works carrying on under the direction of Capt. Patton of the R. Engineers. The hill upon which Abrantes stands from the great extent of its base and the Ravines that close in it, forming knolls in their lower falls, and a good deal *escarpé* in the sides, requires much time and labour to fortify it for a protracted Siege. Its weak point is upon the height of the Windmill upon the road to Punhete. The soil is generally in its first and second strata unfavourable for working, being a dry and gravelly sand which cannot be made to adhere. Water tolerably abundant.

The Marshal inspected the 1st, 2nd and 3rd Regiments of Chasseurs between Turcos and Punhete. The progress of Lt. Col. Elder in forming and training the 3rd is perfectly wonderful. Certainly no Regimental Officer has yet done so much in so short a time, since the British Officers began to act with the Portuguese Army.

Dec. 20. GOLEGÃO. Inspected Major Dickson's Division of Artillery and the 4th and 6th Regiments of

---

[1] See Oman, iii, p. 190, footnote.

Chasseurs. The Artillery in a most excellent state, working rapidly and correctly.

Col. Murray's letter of the 18th relative to the Cantonments of the British. Answered by Courier.

Dec. 21. TORRES NOVAS.—Inspected the Brigade of Algarve, 2nd and 14th Regts.

Dec. 22–29. THOMAR.

Dec. 30. Lord Wellington arrived from Badajoz ; the Marshal met him at Punhete. His Lordship inspected the Chasseurs at Tancos,—the Villa Real Regiment by the exertions of Lt. Col. Elder are in a state of discipline altogether excellent.

Dec. 31. Lord Wellington inspected the Algarve Brigade at Torres Novas. Perfectly pleased.

1810. *Jan.* 1. LEIRIA.—Lord Wellington inspected the 4th and 10th Regts. under Col. Campbell,—perfectly pleased,—marked his approbation by making Col. Campbell (to the great satisfaction of all people) a Colonel on the Staff.

Jan. 2. LEIRIA.—Inspected the 13th, 11th, and 23rd under Genl. Colman—fine Regts., but certainly not equal to those previously seen. Lord Wellington to Coimbra.

Jan. 3. FIGUERIAS.—8 Leagues. Marshal Beresford inspected the 7th and 19th Regts. Brigade of B. Gen. Blunt. These Regiments admirably well drilled, especially the 19th, Lt. Col. McBean. In this Bay, the mouth of the Mondego, Sir Arthur Wellesley landed in the August of 1808 ; even in moderate weather the landing place is a bad one, in blowing weather I should think impracticable. The High Road to Leiria in part excellent, but from Gerias to Figueira so heavy as to be quite impassable for Guns in Winter, from the nature of the soil, however, temporary routes on each side, if there be time, may be made parallel to the Road.

COIMBRA.—7 Leagues.—Both banks of the Mondego from Figueiras to Coimbra are exceedingly rich and fertile, producing (or capable of producing) more Corn than any other space of the same extent that one meets with in Portugal,—several excellent Villages, and the whole furnishing admirable cantonments for Troops. The Road on both sides heavy and either sandy or muddy and subject to the overflowings of the River or its ditches. Lt. Col. Canler having finished his Reconnaissance in the environs

of Leiria, received instructions to examine and report
upon all the Roads within the space bounded by a line
from the sea at Pederneira by Alcobaça, Moliero, Rio
Mayor and Obidos to the sea at Peniche.

Jan. 5. COIMBRA.—Lord Wellington and the British
Head Quarters here. His Lordship and Marshal Beresford
inspected Brigadier Genl. Campbell's Brigade (6th, 9th,
16th Regts.); these Regiments are excellently disciplined
and their Field Day did the highest possible credit to Genl.
Campbell. The French have not advanced much upon
the Castilian frontier. The Duke del Parque is in the
Cantonments of the Gata and Perales that were occupied
by Marshal Beresford in the August of last year, but he
appears to be intending, and perhaps very properly, to
get into Galicia. Perhaps the knowledge of the British
Army having left the Guadiana and the Tagus, to place
itself upon the Mondego and the Douro has occasioned
this wish in the Duke ; at all events he has nothing to eat
where he is. This is one of the best Armies that Spain
has assembled for the present struggle and it has been
ruined (as well as Old Castile lost) by the incapacity of
its General. The gallantry and steadiness of its Vanguard
and 1st and 3rd Divisions of Infantry at Alba [de Tormes]
in the end of November ought never to be forgotten.
After the Duke del Parque's retreat across the Tormes
in the end of November 1809, these Divisions, all very
weak, were left upon the right bank of the Tormes to
protect and cover the passage of the Bridge of Alba, for
the rest of the Army. While they performed this duty
the whole of the French Army 30,000 strong under Kellerman arrived. They had with their advance 4,000 Cavalry
and after ineffectually offering terms they attacked this
isolated infantry successively for several hours, during
which their Cavalry made 3 ineffectual charges and lost
nearly 2,000 Men.

Jan. 6–9. COIMBRA. The last Division of the British
Army passed under Genl. Cole [1] on its way to Guarda,
having its front at Pinhel, and its rear at Coimbra, with
a Division on the Tagus, and all the British Cavalry in the
Villages upon the right bank for the facility of subsistence.
Marshal Ney has returned to Spain, and has gone the other

---

[1] Sir Lowry Cole, afterwards D'Urban's predecessor as Governor of
the Cape.

day from Salamanca to Segovia. The French advance at Ledesma have plundered Vitigudino, Yerle, and several Towns upon the Yeltes.

Jan. 10.   Lord Wellington left Coimbra for Viseu.

Jan. 11.   COIMBRA.—1 Brigade of 3-pounders ordered from the Tras os Montes (2 Brigades of 3 and 1 of 6-pounders will still remain with Silveira) to Castello Branco, and the 6-pounder Brigade now there, on the arrival of the other, to Chamusca to Major Dickson.

Jan. 12.   To SARDÃO.—7 Leagues upon the High Road to Oporto, to Mealhada 3 Leagues, (which also is the commencement of the road to Viseu) the Road is good and practicable for everything, from thence to Sardão, for the greater part very bad, and without much repair, especially in winter, very difficult for Guns.[1]   At Sardão a very good Regiment of Militia 1,100 strong, that of Maia.   There are several Positions apparently of considerable strength between Coimbra and Mealhada and Mealhada and Sardão ; and between Mealhada and Sardão several tolerable Villages of Cantonment in the Valleys, which are, for Portugal, very fertile, and ought to furnish good subsistence for the passage of 3 or 4 Divisions of 5 or 6,000 Men.   The Agueda runs through Sardão, and joins the Vouga near the Lake of Aveiro.

Jan. 13.   OLIVEIRA.—6 Leagues.—The Road from Sardão to the Bridge of the Vouga is for the most part very bad and almost impracticable for Guns in bad weather. Several strong positions, especially that upon the Vouga. This River was between the French Out Posts and those of the Portuguese at the arrival of the British Army under Sir Arthur Wellesley from Lisbon, in the beginning of May 1809. The Valleys and slopes of the hills from Sardão to the Vouga are fertile, and generally well cultivated, furnishing considerable subsistence. The Bridge over the Vouga is a good one, that stream no trifling barrier, more by the nature of its banks than by the depth or rapidity of the River itself. From the Vouga to Bemposta is an excellent Cavalry country, for the first half league sprinkled with Fir Groves, affording a good line of Posts for Light Troops. Barren, hot and little subsistence. Here especially between Albergaria Velha and Albergaria Nova, the first skirmishes took place between the British

[1] Quoted Oman, iii, p. 178, footnote.

and French advanced Posts, in May 1809, when those of
the latter were driven in and retired upon Oporto.   Genl.
Franeschi who commanded them had his Head Quarters
at Oliveira.   From Bemposta to Oliveira is less favourable
for Cavalry, being a strong Country a good deal intersected,—the roads bad,—several considerable positions,—
very fertile and well-cultivated.

Jan. 14–18.   OPORTO.—6 Leagues—from Oliveira to
Avifana the Road bad,—a good Position in rear of the
latter, and in its front also, several Positions in succession,
running at right angles to and crossing the High Oporto
Road, parallel to, and a little in the rear of a line from the
hill above Feira on the left to the Mountains of Moilleros
de Payares on the right,—between that line and Avifana
there are few intersections, and many places well adapted
to Cavalry and Flying Artillery.   From the rear of Avifana
to Oliveira, the Country is more intersected and less
favourable for these arms.   Fertile and much cultivated,
especially upon the nearer approach to Oporto.   Over
all this District and especially in the Town of Feira (the
principal one), the French in April 1809, while Soult's
Head Quarters were at Oporto, committed the most
unheard of barbarities, and followed a system of cruelty
and murder for the purpose of striking terror, altogether
unworthy of a civilised Nation.   Attila might have blushed
at having ordered the atrocities perpetrated by the Command of Soult and of his Generals.

The Marshal inspected the 1st and 21st Regiments.

Lord Wellington writes that the Head of Junot's
Division [Corps] passed Paris in the middle of December
on its way to Spain, and conjectures an Attack upon
Portugal to be probable immediately on its arrival, or as
soon after as the necessary preparations can be completed ;
—it may be doubted whether the Enemy will dare to do
this leaving Spain (certainly anything but subdued, notwithstanding all her misfortunes) in his Rear ;—yet it is
possible that the inveteracy of Napoleon may prompt him
to lay aside all other objects, and risk everything to fulfil
his promise to the Senate of driving the ' Leopards ' into
the Sea, especially as he of course imagines that on getting
rid of them he cuts out by the root the opposition of the
Peninsula.   Be this as it may, His Lordship, looking
forward to the expected attack, wishes the Militia to be

immediately assembled especially those for the Minho,
Tras Os Montes, Almeida, Abrantes and Elvas. It may
be doubted whether the increased scarcity of Provisions
(already so great from the poverty and imbecility of the
Government, that the Troops of the Line are half-starved),
caused by assembling these Troops, will not more than
counter-balance the advantages of embodying them. It
strikes me that their mouths will embarrass more than
their hands assist us. A very small portion of them are
at present armed. Two Regts. (Louzão 1,035, Soure 1,035,
Firelocks 2,070) at Abrantes ordered to be completed, these
two are all armed. All that are armed of three Regiments
(Viseu 867 ; Arganil 600 ; Trancozo 505 ; Total 2,052
Firelocks) ordered to be immediately assembled at Almeida ;
upon their arrival there, it being the intention to concentrate all the Portuguese Regular Troops in second line
upon the Mondego and Douro, the 12th and 24th Regts.
will march from that Fortress upon Alveiro. The 8th
Regt. will remain at Almeida and its strength will then be
as follows :—Militia 2,052 ; 8th Regt. 1,500 ; Artillery
300 ; Total, 3,852. The Numbers tolerably competent,
the Description of Troops of the very worst, and, if besieged, it will require all the steadiness, ability and gallant
soldiership of Cox to do his duty to his own satisfaction. . . .

Various orders sent . . .

. . . (including one) to send an Officer to inspect the
Batteries of the Passes in front of the Zezere, and
the progress of the respective Corps of Ordnance in the
Gun Practice. 'Tis almost impossible to spare Artillery
Detachments for permanent duty in these Batteries.

By our accounts from Spain it would appear that all
the French disposable force is concentrating for Valenza
and the South of Spain. Augereau advances upon Valenza.
Victor joined by Sebastiani is at Almagro. Areyzaga
in the Passes of the Sierra Morena, Albuquerque at its
base. Del Parque in the Perales.

Gerona [1] has, I fear, certainly fallen to Augereau, and
possibly this has given rise to the hope among the French
Marshals that they can present their Master with the South
of Spain upon his Arrival on this side of the Pyrenees, or
at all events, so occupy the Spaniards that they may give
no interruption to his attack upon Portugal and the British.

[1] Marginal note : Fell December 11.

The Armies of the Duke d'Albuquerque and Areyzaga, in and about the Morena, are strongly and centrically placed as a Corps of Observation, and the South of Spain may still be the grave of the Enemy now assembling to attack it. I trust, at least, that when Portugal falls, he will pay us the full value for it.

Every Soldier must look with astonishment at the place where General Hill crossed the Douro with his Brigade (Buffs, 48th, 66th), which formed Sir Arthur Wellesley's advance upon the 12th May 1809, when he attacked Oporto. The Passage of this River is without a parallel in point of daring and good fortune. I don't think that any Military History records a River so passed.

Jan. 19. VIANA. Nominally 10 Leagues,—actually 13.

The Road from Oporto to Villa da Conde, very bad and in its present state quite impracticable for Guns; there is, however, a better close to the sea. Along this extent are several strong Positions. A good Stone Bridge over the Ave from Azurar to Villa de Conde, and the Country between the River and Cavado is rich and well cultivated to a degree that makes it unlike any of the more Southern parts of Portugal. Much intersected by stone walls and enclosures.

The Country offers no strong features, excepting the descent to the Cavado. After crossing the Cavado at Barca de Lavos, the cultivation is less perfect and the Soil more barren, rocky and covered with Fir Trees. Several strong Positions especially on approaching the Lima. This River very broad at the Ferry to Viana. The Road for the most part very bad.

Jan. 20. The Marshal inspected the 10th Regt., Lt. Col. Doyle.

Jan. 21. CAMINHA.—3 Leagues.—The road tolerably good. Here is a Fort originally constructed to defend the Passage of the Minho against the Spaniards. It is at the ' Debouchure ' [*débouchement*] of that River and also at the confluence of the Couva with it, and commands the Ferry over it, and the Road passing there from Valenza to Viana.

The Division of Thomiéres forming the advance of Soult's Army in its march to Oporto attempted to pass here from Galicia in the March of 1809, but the Boats of

his advanced Guard keeping too near the Bar, to avoid
the Guns of the Fort, were carried out and he lost several
hundred Men. Soult then relinquished his project of
crossing here, marched up the River to Orense and there
passed; the French afterwards sent a Detachment from
Oporto, knocked off the Trunnions of some of the Guns
and threw the others into the ditch. The Ferry of the
Coura is fordable except after heavy rains. The Bars
at the mouth of the Minho are difficult of entrance, though
in high tides they have from 14 to 21 feet of water. The
Harbour will contain a considerable number of vessels
not drawing more than 5 or 6 feet of water. The Fort
of Caminha is closely commanded on the Portuguese
side, this, however, if necessary, might be remedied.

Jan. 22. VALENZA on the Minho.—4 Leagues.—Good
Road, passing through the most naturally fertile Country
that can be conceived. Many strong Positions either to
dispute the passage of the River or the Road to Valenza.
Valenza is strong, and when the Breaches made by the
French who blew up a part of the Curtain and Demilune
of one of its fronts are repaired, will be capable of a long
resistance, and is situated certainly in a point of no small
importance. The Brass Guns are perfect still having
only had their Carriages burnt. The Iron Guns have had
their Trunnions broken off.

This Fortress commands Tuy on the one side. Brigadier Azedo of the Engineers is here superintending the
repairs, which he expects to complete in a Month. The
French intentions against the South of Spain develop
themselves more clearly. Joseph Bonaparte left Madrid
on the 8th and moved by Consuegra, with all his Officers
of State to join Victor (Duke de Belluno) in La Mancha;
part of the Garrison of Madrid with 20 pieces of Cannon
and almost all the Troops from Talavera de la Reyna, took
the same direction on the 6th. The Enemy's Force, of
this Army, is reckoned to be from 45 to 50,000 Men. If
they have not already received their expected reinforcements, or a part of them, this statement must, I think, be
exaggerated. At all events it indicates a certainty of
their near approach which may allow of Joseph's collecting
every thing he can lay his hands upon for the South of
Spain, in order to make the attempt on Seville. This
he is reported to have been ordered to do by Napoleon

and that Ney was the bearer. Soult of course is with
Joseph; Victor, Sebastiani and Mortier are with the
Army.

The Advanced Guard being at Canamel on the Road
of Almodovar, has given rise to the idea that the March
will be upon Cordova by the Route of Fuente Caliente.
From Cordova of course they will pursue the High Road
by Ecija. Gerona having fallen and the Army of Aragon
and Valencia being therefore occupied with Augereau
(Duke of Castiglione), the only Spanish Force to oppose
Joseph will be the Duke of Albuquerque, who from Quintana and Zalamla will probably move to his right, and
attempt to dispute the Passes of the Sierras de Fuente
Caliente.

Meanwhile the Enemy are said to have upwards of
11,000 Men [distribution given] upon the line of the Tagus
which are intended to observe the Duke del Parque, whose
crippled Army is at the foot of and in the Perales and the
Gata, and they are fortifying Toledo, thus keeping open
the line of communication with Madrid of the Army of the
South.

Ney is at Salamanca concentrating all that he can,
probably 12,000 Men. This is the natural consequence of
Lord Wellington's movement to the Eastern Frontier.
If His Lordship now moves by the Tormes upon Ney
occupying the Baños while the Duke del Parque remains
upon the Perales and Gata, the French General must be
cut off, or retreat upon the Capital. This would be very
likely to call back Joseph from the South, and at all
events the diversion might be attempted, for the British,
if they don't advance farther than Salamanca, can always
return to their present Cantonments, and that advance
would probably do all one could wish. If, however, the
French Reinforcements have actually passed Burgos this
would be of no use and is better left alone.

Jan. 23. Arcos de Valderez by Monsanto.—This foot
of Monsanto commands the ford of Salvatierra and that
foot also as well as the Road from the Pass of Melgacō
(2 Leagues distant) to Arcos and Braga. From Monsanto
to Arcos 5 Leagues of bad Mountain Road easily destroyed.
Abundance of Corn.

Jan. 24. Braga.—5 Leagues—Mountain Road—easily
rendered impassable—very fertile.

Jan. 25.   GUIMARAES.—3 Leagues—several very strong positions—Road easily broken.

Jan. 26.   SOBRADO.—10 Leagues.—The Roads to the Tamega by Canaveres tolerably good, the Country affording several Positions.   A narrow Bridge over the Tamega, easily destroyed ;   the Roads Entre Ambos os Rios nearly impracticable ;   the descent to the Banks of the Douro very difficult.   The Country between the Rivers strong and mountainous.

1,200 stand of Arms ordered to Almeida, and McMahon at Lamego to be supplied from Peso da Regoa in which there are 2,510 good accoutrements.

Jan. 27.   By ARANCA to PEDRO DE SUL.   All the way a Mountain Road of the very worst description.   The Valley of Aranca fertile beyond measure and capable of furnishing much subsistence.—8 long leagues.

Jan. 28.   VISEU.—3 Leagues.—Country strong and Mountainous and the Banks of the Vouga difficult.   The Road bad, and very difficult in several places for Guns.   Several Positions either way.

Jan. 29.   Santa COMBA DÃO—6 Leagues.

Jan. 30.   COIMBRA.—8 Leagues by the Road of Batao, which though very bad will well admit of Cavalry and Infantry without Guns.

Jan. 31.   LEIRIA.—12 Leagues, the road excellent, and the Country for several leagues well adapted to the movements of Cavalry.

Feb. 1.   ALCOENTRE.—10 Leagues of good road.

Joseph has passed the Sierra Morena, and arrived at Cordova upon the 23rd probably is now at Seville.   The Duke of Albuquerque made no movement to oppose the Enemy in the Passes on the Road to Cordova, but withdrew by that of Llerena to post himself in front of Seville where to disperse his Army will, I fear, be no difficult task for the Usurper.   The Foundry and the fabrics of Leather and Cloth will be the prey of the French ;   and the moral effect which this advance and success may have, there is no calculating ;   perhaps it may do good, it will at least overturn the wretched Junta which has ruined Spain, and if a Revolution follows, tho' late, it may yet perhaps be possible to retrieve their fortunes.   In the mean time Spain has no Army—else—but the Picture is altogether too melancholy to look at.

Feb. 2.　Lisbon.—10 Leagues.

The Works are commenced upon the Position of Castanheira upon the Left, near the heights of Alenquer. Any attempt to make a permanent defence, so as to put any trust in it,—of the Rivulet on the Right, will not fail to be dangerous,—the space is too great to the River,— but the Ground on the Right is a natural Echellon as far as Villa Franca, and properly managed may cost the Enemy, whatever the attempts to push forward there. He must pass along a defile which becomes narrower at every step, and must give his right flank in succession to all that we have there established, and finally his rear to whatever we may choose to attack it with, by means of our lateral communications.

Feb. 3.　Lisbon.

The French entered Seville on the 30th, having detached from Cordova to Jaën and there made themselves Masters of 60 Pieces of Cannon. Joseph, however, has not hazarded his own Person on the other side of the Morena; he remains at Almagro, and Soult near Toledo. Mortier and Victor therefore are the People who have gone forward to play this bold game which, if the arrival of reinforcements from France be impeded, or even delayed, will very possibly end in their destruction.

Feb. 4.　Lisbon.

Feb. 5.　Torres Vedras.—7 Leagues. Marshal Beresford went there to meet Lord Wellington, who has come from Viseu to inspect the Works [1] upon the different defensive Positions determined in October.

Just before leaving Lisbon Lord Burgherst arrived from Mr. Frere at Cadiz. That place is menaced by the French. A sort of Revolution has taken place, the Junta is deposed, and a Regency consisting of Castanos, Saavedra, the Bishop of Orense, etc. established. They anxiously demand a British Garrison for Cadiz. On the Marshal's arriving at Torres Vedras, he urged the great expediency of sending what could be spared, and Lord Wellington upon reading the letters of Mr. Frere, despatched an express to Lisbon, ordering M. Genl. Stewart to embark forthwith, in Command of the 2 Companies of Artillery, lately arrived from England, and the 79th, 87th, and 94th Regts., at least equal to 3,000 Men, and proceed to Cadiz to assist

[1] See memoranda, p 73.

in its defence by every means in his power. This is prompt and as it should be,—and in every respect an important point gained.

Feb. 6. TORRES VEDRAS.—The Works in front in a state of great forwardness, wanting but a few days of their completion, and beautiful specimens of Field Fortification, doing infinite credit to Lt. Col. Fletcher who traced, and Capt. Mulcaster who executed them. The Right hand range of hills, though, covers a Road which turns these works out of shot, and therefore 'tis most likely that an Enemy won't come within their influence, of course not, unless that Road is so effectually obstructed, as to render such a step a *sine qua non* to his advance.

Feb. 7. . . . to Mafra.

Feb. 8. . . . back to Lisbon.

Feb. 9. LISBON.

Feb. 10. . . . to Villa Franca.

Feb. 11. The Marshal General inspected the Works at Sobral; returned by Aranda.

Feb. 12. Position of Castanheira, faulty in many respects, turned by its left—abandoned—Alhandra determined upon. The Marshal General to Santarem on his return to Viseu. Marshal Beresford to Lisbon. Mr. Stewart arrived.

Feb. 13. LISBON.

The Enemy pushed a Detachment from Seville, by the Pass of Sta. Olalla on the High Road to Merida, into the neighbourhood of Zafra,—these are of course advancing upon Badajoz, to try the effect of their appearance. Romana is there, the place can't be taken by a *coup de main*, and I don't think they'll have time for anything more protracted.

Feb. 14. The Enemy advancing to Olivença, probably about 8,000 strong, sent forward 600 Horse and 2,000 Foot to Badajoz to summon it and order rations. Requested the Marshal to allow me (as nothing immediate requires my stay at Lisbon) to go to Elvas for a few days and feel the pulse of things. He did not think it right or necessary at present.

Feb. 15. Straggling French Dragoons crossed the River Guadiana between Badajoz and Talavera Real,— 6 or 7 of them who approached were killed by a Shell.

Feb. 16. General Hill's Division (in addition to his

British he has of Portuguese—Artillery, 2 Brigades,
Major Dickson.—Cavalry, 1 Brigade, M. Genl. Madden.—
Infantry, 4th and 10th Regts., Col. Campbell; 2nd and
14th B. Genl. Luiz) in readiness to move. B. Genl. Madden's
Brigade of Portuguese Cavalry marched to Estremoz.
Sent the Viscount da Lefra to Genl. Hill.

The French are concentrated (from 10 to 15,000 Men)
at Tamames, Fte. de St. Estevan, and Martin del Rio,
apparently intending to attack Ciudad Rodrigo. If they
do this they will commit themselves to Lord Wellington.
Loison Governor of Leon,—6,000 Troops of the last
Conscriptions,—bad Cavalry, excepting 300 Polish Horse.

The movements of the French are so unaccountable
and contradictory, that I've a notion they are only to
hide their weakness and spread terror. It is just possible
that they are disappointed in getting their expected
Reinforcements, and then these Movements are to impose.

Feb. 17. The Enemy under Ney having concentrated
upon Ciudad Rodrigo and summoned it on the same day
(the 12th) on which Mortier summoned Badajoz, Lord
Wellington, who received this intelligence on his way to
Viseu, writes from Espinhal that he intends to concentrate
forward, and that he has therefore moved up the Portu-
guese Brigades of Chasseurs, Infantry and Artillery from
Leiria, Montemor Velha, Condeixa, Isalpensal (?), and
Condeixa and wishes the Marshal to join him. He means
to set out to-morrow. Instructions dispatched to Silveira,
Genl. Miller, and Col. Trant. The Marshal visited Mr.
Forgaz once more upon the subject of Provisions.

Feb. 18. Certain Intelligence of the French Corps
having retired from Badajoz, as well as from Ciudad
Rodrigo, after having fruitlessly summoned both these
places, changes the Marshal's intentions of going to the
Army for these few days to come. He certainly has many
important affairs to transact with the Government, but
I hope he will not let anything keep him more than two
or three days; else 'tis but too likely that he may lose
some forward Command, and be kept in the back ground
during the Campaign.

The French are now more dispersed, or at least as much
so as they were in the middle of 1808. They are scattered
into small Corps of 4, 6, 8, and 10,000 Men each, at Granada,
Cordova, Ecija, Seville (Joseph), Cadiz, Huebla, Banks of

the Albuera, Talavera de la Reyna, between Salamanca and Ciudad Rodrigo, Benavente and the Asturias. What can dictate this policy 'tis difficult to imagine. Either they are sure of reinforcements (which there's great reason to believe is not the case) or they feel confident that England will no longer stir a step to assist the Spaniards, and therefore knowing that Spain has no Armies they take this measure to overrun and terrify and subjugate it, not fearing any opposition. These Detached Corps afford each other no mutual support and may be well enterprised against (those in Castile) by Lord Wellington, almost without hazard.

Feb. 19–21. LISBON.

The forward movement of the Troops is delayed under the present circumstances.

Feb. 22.   Junot who has arrived in Spain is with Loison at Benavente ;   his Corps is stated to be from 15 to 20,000 Men and they appear to indicate an advance to Astorga. This is possible, but I should rather expect an advance upon Braganza (that is if they intend to attack Portugal, as it has been held out at the Tuileries).   It is a better advance for them, by far, than that upon the Minho from Galicia, and answers the same purpose, nor do they risk anything by exposing a flank to that Province as we have nothing there. More Reinforcements than our accounts gave them credit for, have probably arrived, for else their strength, North of the Tagus, could not be what it is, nor could Junot be so strong as he is reported. If Ciudad Rodrigo and Badajoz both fall, then the Enemy will be well posted to attack upon three sides, North, East, and South, but he will find it difficult, if we make the utmost of our means, so to combine his Attack as not to risk the being beaten in detail; meanwhile both these Towns will probably hold out for some time, and unless much larger Reinforcements are following than anything that has yet passed the Pyrenees he cannot venture to strengthen his Army of Portugal at the expense of that of Spain ;   if he do, he will lose the one, in attempting to lay hold of the other.

Feb. 23–25. LISBON.

Reinforcements to the amount of 42,000 Men have entered Spain. The British have arrived at Cadiz, and the Governor has answered the summons of the French General as became him.   This Place may now be considered impregnable. Junot, for some purpose, has gone to Madrid, and Loison commands the Corps at Benavente, which has an advance at Baneza.

Feb. 26. If any dependence can be placed upon some intercepted letters, Bonaparte will (if not prevented) come to Spain himself. Berthier (Prince of Wagram) writes to Soult from Paris (5th Jan.) that the Imperial Guard will march from Bordeaux for Bayonne immediately. The Marquis of Monte Hermoso, writes from Vittoria that the Imperial Guard entered Bordeaux on the 6th Jan. and remained there on the 12th. Berthier also particularises to Soult, that three Divisions of the 8th Corps d'Armée, and 12 Provisional Regiments of Dragoons would enter Spain by the 15th.

Junot's Vanguard marched from Bordeaux on the 3rd. Reynier comes to Spain and remains in Biscay to receive, organise, and discipline the Detachments as they arrive. Lapaye (?) is in Biscay also with the 2nd Division of Ney's Corps. The Brigades of Germin and Corsim are following to join him.

A part of Junot's Corps turned by the Ebro for Arragon; a part, as we know, came with him and Loison to Benavente. Loison is there but Junot gone to Madrid.

Feb. 27–28. 8,000 of the Corps of Soult under a Relation of his [General D. Soult, his brother] have advanced to Merida and Montijo, and have a strong advanced Guard upon the Chebora, and at Villa del Rey. This is of course to co-operate in the investing Badajoz, with the Corps of Mortier, which still continues upon the Albuera, where it retired upon the 14th.

It is not improbable that some of the Regiments of the Duke del Parque's late Army, may be cut off by an advance of this Corps upon the Chebora, especially if their march is loosely conducted, which it most likely is.

Two Spanish Captains of Guerrillas, Lopez and Morales, have deserted to the Enemy at Pedrahieta. This is, I think, the worst symptom that has yet arisen.

March 1–6. The Enemy fell back upon the 27th Feb. from Talavera, Albuera, and Montijo, to Zafra, Los Santos, and Merida. Badajoz is thus left for the present, but (as it is probably only to wait for Artillery, and till the preparations in Castile and Leon are mature, so that the operations upon the South, East, and North may be combined) this falling back is merely to avoid exhausting and eating up the supplies which it will be desirable to find unimpaired when they seriously invest the Place.

Their motive, however, for destroying Provisions before they left Talavera Real is difficult to guess at, probably one of those wanton mischiefs which the great licence prevailing in their Armies has deprived the General of the power to prevent.

March 7–15. During these days the positions of the different Corps of the Enemy have remained nearly the same as they were excepting that Junot has moved nearer to Ney so as to indicate a junction of their respective Corps; these will then be about 35,000 Men of which 5,000 are Cavalry. They give out that they will attack Ciudad Rodrigo, and afterwards Portugal, and they say that the old College of Salamanca, which is fitting up, is preparing for Napoleon; at the same time, however, the French Army don't believe he's coming. I should think not yet, at all events. Joseph has gone back from Seville to Cordova; and the French in Andalusia certainly don't seem much at their ease. The Spaniards are rising in all directions, and are anything but subdued.

Don Gabriel de Mendizabel has conducted 16,000 Men, the remnant of del Parque's Army, to the neighbourhood of Badajoz, and Romana therefore has about 25,000 Men, if he knows but how to make use of them—which I doubt—certainly he is wild and fantastic in all his measures, and as far as one can judge from his previous conduct, by no means an able soldier.

The French with an audacity which they always (and only) evince when they are allowed to do so with impunity, push their Parties beyond the Agueda, and levy contributions in Villa de Ceiros and Villa de la Yegora. Why our Out Posts permit this I can't imagine. While the British Cantonments are where they are, the Agueda is their natural chain of advance, and nothing ought to pass it without being made to smart for it. Just at this moment a little Partisan work would be very judicious to keep the affections and respect of the Natives if for nothing else. The French ramble about more at their ease now in front of the whole British Army, than they either did, or dared to do last year, when nothing overlooked them but Wilson with 600 Men.

The Marshal, to my infinite regret, has withdrawn Colonel Wilson [1] from the Command of the South Eastern Line of Out Posts to the Command of Lecor's Line at Thomar. What has induced him to take this step I cannot think. A British Officer, and a proved one, without doubt almost, if not altogether, the best for the duty he has been filling, that he has under his orders,— thus replaced at a critical moment by a Portuguese, can't fail to be disgusted, and we can't afford to lose men like Wilson, for we have scarcely any like him. We have many *drills*, they are easily replaced if we lose them. Wilson is a Soldier—*they* are not so easily got again. I ventured to remonstrate; without effect I have only to regret it.

March 16–20. By Alcoentre (16th), Batahla (17th), Leiria (18th), Condeixa (19th), to Coimbra (20th) where for the future are the permanent Head Quarters of the Marshal.

The 4 Artillery Brigades at Condeixa under Major von Arentschilde, are in very high order, nothing can be finer, or more to the credit of that Officer who is most excellent.

March 21. The 1st and 2nd Chasseurs marched to join the British Army. Marshal Beresford received a Memorandum (No. 4) from Lord Wellington relative to the defence of the Northern Provinces. In this His Lordship, remarking upon the Instructions (Nos. 1, 2, 3, of 17th and 19th Feb.) sent to the Generals Silveira and Miller, and Col. Trant, for their guidance in the Defence of the Tras os Montes and Minho, wishes their operations to be more connected than by these Instructions is prescribed :—with their means it is difficult to conceive how this can well be. The Marshal wrote Lord Wellington (No. 5) explanatory of his reasons for these Instructions.

The Spaniards are enterprising a little in Estremadura, and the Generals O'Donnel and Contreras have beaten up the French Quarters with success at Valverde and Canres.(?) Mortier's Head Quarters falling back. It is most likely that they will evacuate Estremadura. But Ney and Junot are concentrating upon Ciudad Rodrigo, and

---

[1] To be distinguished from the daring and dashing Sir Robert Wilson, who returned to England at his own request, in October 1809, after the Talavera campaign.

the large depôt of Provisions forming at Salamanca indicates operations in that quarter.

March 22. Colonel Wilson wrote me upon the subject of his recall from the Out Posts, he felt it, of course, as I supposed he would, and I spoke again to the Marshal on the subject ; he proposes to do away (with) the annoyance he has unintentionally given, as well as to make use of Wilson upon a Service, certainly of the greatest importance, to send him as second in Command of the Tras os Montes with positive orders to Silveira to follow his opinion upon all occasions of importance. This is a delicate and arduous Service, but Wilson will do it well, if any Officer can. The Marshal writes for Lord Wellington's acquiescence. I wait the answer to write to Wilson.

March 23–24. Lord Wellington replied to the Marshal's letter (No. 5), still wishing new and more connected Instructions to be given to Trant, Miller and Silveira. The Marshal of course complied, and the Instructions 6, 7 and 8 were sent those Officers with a copy to Lord Wellington on the 25th.

March 26–28. Lord Wellington replied that he fully approved of the New Instructions sent to Trant, Miller, and Silveira (No. 9) ; and acquiesced to Wilson's appointment to the Tras os Montes. Wilson written to.

March 29–30. 9th and 21st Regts. marched to Celorico. The Brigades from Leiria, Figueira, and Oporto to assemble at and near Coimbra.

March 31. In the last fortnight the movements of the French have been incessant throughout Leon, Castile (Old), and Estremadura. In Leon and Castile they have lately constituted two Corps, one under Junot (from 17 to 18,000) at Benavente which has since advanced to the neighbourhood of Astorga, leaving Detachments in the Partido de Sayaya, and another near Salamanca under Ney (22 to 23,000), which latter from its preparations and from the collecting a large quantity of Provisions to form a depôt has indicated an attack upon Ciudad Rodrigo with a view to operations against Portugal.

It has never, I think, been probable that this would seriously take place, nor with the present French force in Spain, do I see how it could, with any prospect of success, considering the unquiet state of that Kingdom and the attitude of Portugal.

Mortier has retired from Badajoz and marched by Sta. Olalla into Andalusia, and Reynier has fallen back from Merida first to Caceres and at length gone also into Andalusia. It is probable that something has gone wrong with the Enemy to the South of the Sierra Morena, for at Salamanca he is very uneasy at the non-arrival of Andalusian Posts, and has even detached a Corps to occupy Baños. A day or two will show, meantime it becomes every day clearer that nothing offensive, to any extent, will be for the present undertaken against Portugal.

This (if Ney has detached considerably towards Estremadura especially) would appear a favourable moment for an attack upon Salamanca and the destruction or seizure of his Magazines, and I hope Lord Wellington meditates some such thing, by his calling up all the remaining Portuguese Brigades to Coimbra.

April 1. Ballasteros and Contreras with Romana's advanced Guard have fallen upon the Rear Guard of Mortier, dislodged it from Sta. Olalla, driven it from Ronquillo, and thus the High Road across the Sierra Morena is again in the hands of the Spaniards.

The Enemy has certainly sustained some disaster in Andalusia. Reynier has advanced from Caceres to Torremocha, thus he is quite in the air, O'Donnel follows him from Albuquerque, and I should think his Division ought to be made an example of. If General Hill be permitted to afford any offensive assistance he may be cut off. In that case the Corps marching by Placencia will retire, or share his fate. The Times require a little enterprise, where it is consistent with the General Safety, and does not involve general measures. Partial Successes, however small, will just now have an excellent moral effect and now perhaps these may be achieved in more quarters than one. Junot is at Astorga. The Tormes very full. Loison in the Sierra de Ledesma may be held in check and prevented from crossing into the Garcey Rey. Ney has detailed to Placencia, and it would appear worth while to attempt the important object of carrying off or destroying the Magazines at Salamanca. This effected,— no matter what reinforcements arrive from France, want of Provisions will secure Portugal for all the Summer, and if it don't fall before the Autumn, I don't think it can fall at all. Even now it will be a hard purchase, and every day of delay on the part of Napoleon strengthens its Position.

April 2–10. During these days the position of the Enemy appeared less favorable in Andalusia as well as in the North. It was learned that Joseph Bonaparte had returned to Madrid ; Sebastiani fell back from Malaga upon Jaca. Ballasteros maintained his post at Ronquilla and Mortier certainly under some inquietude signified to the Magistracy of Seville the probability of his breaking the Bridge over the Guadalquivir. All straggling French were everywhere murdered by the Andalusian Peasants, and the aspect of the Enemy's Affairs to the South of the Sierra Morena is anything but favourable. O'Donnel has fought with success in Catalonia ; and it is very probable that Victor, if he can't immediately succeed at Cadiz will retire. Why there should be any reason to despond as to the fate of that place I can't well imagine, nevertheless General Graham who has lately arrived there from England (where everybody is determined to despond, and from whence perhaps he has come a little infected with the reigning mania) complains of an insufficient Garrison and croaks—therefore I wish he had remained at home—these are not the description of people for the Peninsula. Any General who is not confident is ruin to us. The firmness of mind which Lord Wellington has continued to preserve since the Battle of Talavera, in spite of the despondency of almost every one about him, as well as of all the people at home, and the perseverance with which he has continued in a forward position ready for offensive operations yet fully prepared for defensive ones, has saved Portugal, and may, and probably will, be the Salvation of Spain. This admirable firmness proves him a Hero, if he had done nothing else to deserve the name.

The Junta have foolishly quarrelled with their best soldier the Duke of Albuquerque and he is going Ambassador to England—this is a lamentable step.

Reynier from Torremorcha has marched to Llerena probably on his way to La Mancha. Bonnet has been driven back from Asturia to Santander. Junot with a weak Corps invests Astorga, where he is observed by Generals Garcia and Mahy from Villa Franca, and has given indications of retiring. Loison at Ledesma and Ney at Salamanca. Where these movements are so various and contradictory that for the present it is impossible to decide whether they will go backwards or forwards. Meanwhile they are very sickly; nor can I see what but ruin they can propose by an advance.

April 10. The Brigade of Chasseurs (1st and 2nd) which were sent to General Craufurd, are returned unfit for service; this does not at all astonish me. Why they were sent I wonder—certainly the worst in the Army.

Elder's Corps, and Arentschilde's 6 and 9-pounders ordered to be in readiness to march. Lord Wellington will take from the Marshal all his best Troops piece by piece. 'Tis probable he will soon be without any Division at all—the whole incorporated with the British. I foresaw this long ago. The Marshal might have stopped this once—'tis too late now—the delay in setting out from Lisbon has snatched from him all prospect of the Advanced Command which he had a right to ask, and which *then*, I've no doubt, would have been given.

England always liberal has sent 30,000 Stand of Arms, 2,000 Rifles, 6,000 Swords and Pistols. If we don't fight for this Country hard, we must hide our heads for shame. The period of attack is I think postponed. No further reinforcements have reached the French, and they are too weak for Spain and Portugal too, as they are.

April 11–12. 15,000 Stand of Arms and 1,500,000 Rounds of Ball Cartridge ordered from Lisbon, for the Militia of the Minho, Tras os Montes. Partido d'Oporto, and to the Militia of Abrantes, Obidos and Peniche. Flints also and a proportion of Accoutrements. 2,000 Barrels, 64 lbs. each, ordered to Valença.

Nothing new on the part of the Enemy.

April 13. Elder's Regiment of Chasseurs, and Arentschilde's 6-pounder Brigade marched from Saveira and Condeixa on their way to Pinhel and Celorico respectively.

April 14. The French demonstrations indicate the Siege of Ciudad Rodrigo more perhaps than ever heretofore, for they have collected 40 Guns of different descriptions, some of them heavy ones, at Salamanca where Ney is. Loison at Vitijadas, Kellerman at Alba. 'Tis difficult to bring one'self to believe that Marshal Ney dares undertake this Siege with 22,000 Men, under the very nose of Lord Wellington. It must be actually commenced for me to credit it.

H

April 15. Arentschilde's 9-pounder Brigade which waited the arrival of some newly constructed ammunition Waggons from Lisbon, received them this morning, and followed the 6-pounder Brigade on the Route to Celorico. These Brigades are excellent, and do infinite credit to Arentschilde.

An additional requisition for smaller ammunition ordered to the Tras os Montes for Silveira.

April 15–20. Everything looks adverse to the French in Spain. No additional Reinforcements arrived to them, and therefore, as I predicted, far from attacking Portugal they have enough to do to take care of themselves. The Army that crossed the Sierra Morena is much diminished without having effected any purpose but plunder, and proving the determined hostility of the Southern Spaniards. There is a report from several quarters that the Spaniards are in Madrid, perhaps this is not actually the case, but there is an evident wavering of the French and indecision' in all their movements, and if vigorous steps were now taken many of their Corps would fall in detail. *Offensive* operations to a certain degree now, would avert the necessity of *Defensive* ones for some time to come at least.

1,000,000 Rounds of Musquet Ammunition and 30,000 English Flints ordered from Lisbon to complete the Reserve here. This Division requiring nearly 400,000 Rounds to complete which will require nearly all our available Reserve.

Lord Wellington removed his Head Quarters to Cea, and in two or three days found it inconvenient and ineligible and returned to Viseu.

Upon the 19th the Marshal received letters from Silveira who has moved his Head Quarters to Braganza. This General[1] is the most extraordinary of all the people in this extraordinary Country. Perpetually fluctuating— incapable of standing still—always wishing to move— backwards or forwards, and all his movements to no purpose, but that of harassing the Troops. At one moment he desponds when there is not the shadow of an Enemy, at another talks of moving on when he has no Troops to do it with, and when even if he had, such a step would be foolish and useless. Perpetually boasting or desponding, either attributing the Movements of the French Galician

---

[1] *Cf.* Oman, iii, p. 176, footnote.

Army to the absurd wanderings of his wretched Patroles,
or fancying that half-a-dozen Skirmishes will inevitably
get possession of the Tras os Montes.   This Man is either
a very weak, or a very designing one, or perhaps both,
certainly a dangerous one at any rate, for be he what he
may, he either understands his Country Men well, and
keeps his popularity by acting upon that knowledge, or
is so like the whole Portuguese aggregate of Character,
that they all feel he represents what they would do themselves.   He is a mischievous Charlatan and I wish the
Marshal would not so far yield to the prejudices of this
People and their Government as to employ him as a Military man.   Wilson's appointment will prevent mischief
for the present, as far as a second can prevent it, and the
Marshal has to-day written Silveira, so tying and binding
him down within certain limits, that 'twill require more
than common ingenuity to get out of them without a
direct breach of orders.

April 21–24.   Reynier at Merida.   Mortier again on
the right bank of the Guadalquivir, his advance again at
Sta. Olalla, and also at Aracena, Ballasteros having successively retired from Ronquillo to Vazcera, and from
thence to Aroche.

Mendizabel's advanced Posts at Zalamca(?) attacked by
a party of Reynier's and forced back to La Roca—the Head
Quarters of the 3rd Division.   Much sickness in McMahon's
Brigade at Lamego so as to render the removing it necessary.   Lord Wellington wishes it to go to Celorico; it goes
in consequence, and its Hospital remains behind under
the charge of Dr. Keating who has orders to forward such
Sick and Convalescents as he may think advisable by the
Douro to Oporto.

April 25.   From Coimbra to Viseu.

By intelligence from the Alemtejo it appears that an
advance of Reynier's attacked upon the 21st and drove in
an Advanced Gd. of O'Donnel's at Zalamca(?), that General
fell back upon La Roca.   About the same time the whole
of Mortier's force having come to the right bank of the
Guadalquivir his Advance pushed on by Ronquillo towards Sta. Olalla, and Ballasteros who had for some days
been at Zalamca Real, retired to Aracena from whence he
fell back upon Aroche.   Whether this indicates a real and
combined Attack upon Badajoz, or whether it is to occupy

the attention of Genl. Hill and the Corps of Romana, while the real object is Ciudad Rodrigo remains to be seen. Badajoz would be the most feasible enterprise one would think, for the Guns at Alba and Salamanca might be easily sent by the Road of Baños, and the distance of the main British army does not render Badajoz so formidable an undertaking as Ciudad Rodrigo with Lord Wellington within call.

April 26. The British Army in the highest possible health and order. Lord Wellington orders back the 1st and 2nd Chasseurs to Coimbra. 11 o'clock P.M.—The intelligence of this evening announces the whole Force of the Enemy in the Campo de Salamanca, and Sierra de Ledesma to be in motion. They have moved with their right to Vitigudino and Benavares (?), the front of their Centre to St. Estevan and Martin del Rio, and their Left to Tamames. An Advance has pushed on too, towards Guinaldo upon the Road to Perales. The Guns have not yet, that we know of, been put in motion, *their* bearing will indicate whether the real intention is Ciudad Rodrigo, or Badajoz, or whether, sending a part of their Artillery to Estremadura, they think themselves strong enough for both.

Be the intention what it may, Lord Wellington will watch it well. He has given orders to Col. Murray to move up the British Divisions from the Rear Cantonments towards the Front, to bring up the Cavalry from the neighbourhood of Coimbra and Sta. Comba Dão, and for the British Cavalry of Genl. Hill's Division (Royals and 14th Dragoons) to move across the Tagus by Villa Velha and join him; to-morrow morning he goes himself to Celorico.

By his direction I had received Marshal Beresford's Orders to bring up all the Portuguese Division from Coimbra, and I have despatched an Express to Lt. Col. Hardinge at Coimbra, putting in motion all the undermentioned Corps for Celorico, where the Marshal will go as they get into movement, and for the present he holds his Head Quarters at Viseu.

The Portuguese Division ordered to the front consisted of : 2 Brigades 3-pounder Guns ; 5 Brigades of Infantry composed of the following Regiments ; 4th and 6th Chasseurs ; 1st, 16th, 7th, 9th, 6th, 18th, 11th, 23rd Line.

The Corps [1] all get into March on the 28th and will successively arrive by Brigades at Celorico in 4 days.

The 13th English Light Dragoons just arrived from England and the 4th and 10th Portuguese Dragoons from Salvatierra, reinforce General Hill in lieu of the Royals and 14th Dragoons under Genl. Slade.

April 27. Lord Wellington went to Celorico. He gives us Biscuit from his Depôts, and this makes my mind easy as to Provisions. I have despatched some additional instructions to Hardinge in consequence. The Troops will now march with 6 days' Biscuit.

Went to Celorico by Marshal Beresford's Orders, to arrange with Col. Murray the ultimate routes of the Portuguese Division after arriving at Celorico, and his Head Quarters,—arrived. Nothing new from the Front.

April 29. No decidedly forward movement upon the part of the Enemy, Lord Wellington pauses therefore, and waits further events; the Troops halt, in consequence *pro tempore*, in their respective stages of the march commenced; I have despatched instructions to all the Portuguese Brigades, by Lord Wellington's desire and they are all cantoned provisionally. . . .

. . . Lord Wellington points out Fornos as the Marshal's Head Quarters, it being of easy communication with Celorico, and centrically in front of the Portuguese Brigades on both sides of the Mendego. Having despatched the necessary orders to the Troops I have only time to reach Fornos on my way back to the Marshal. Fixed upon a House for his Head Quarters. The Country from Viseu to Celorico exceedingly strong, especially the Banks of the Mondego, which is about half-way between Fornos and Celorico and although so near its source, a very considerable stream. The Road (for Portugal) good and the Country well cultivated. Carrera and the Guerillas still don't think that a real attack is to be made upon Ciudad Rodrigo; it certainly will be a bold step, for Lord Wellington can assemble 30,000 effective Rank and File, of Infantry (British and Portuguese), and 2,500 British Horse. A Battle near Ciudad Rodrigo, if Ney can be induced to give or receive it, would mean, I should think, a good aspect for us. There must be some risk in all military matters; if we gain it, Salamanca falls and all

[1] See Oman, iii, p. 243, footnote.

the long collecting Magazines, as well as their Battering
Train ; if we lose it, I don't see what's to prevent our
short Retreat upon our strong frontier of the Coa, and
there resuming our defensive attitude. This is supposing
the worst, but it strikes me we have the best possible
chance of success. Physically and morally too our British
force would be a match for Ney's superior numbers,
without reckoning the Portuguese at all ; these last,
however, are now well disciplined and perhaps may fight
better than People expect. I don't at all doubt of their
doing their duty.

Lord Wellington does not wish for Madden's Brigade
of Cavalry. The 9-pounders from Santarem to Condeixa
as soon as they are equipped.

Celorico to Fornos—2 Leagues. To Mangoalde—3
Leagues. Viseu 2 Leagues. Total 7 Leagues.

April 30. Viseu.—Intelligence of a small Battering
Train having passed Baneza on its way to Astorga (Fell
22 April). It is but too probable that its fall cannot long
be delayed, for there is no hurry to relieve it, and even
supposing the attempts to storm it to be ineffectual, after
its walls are breached, yet there can scarcely be any long
supply of Provisions in the Place. Junot has now there
about 16,000 Men for 12,000 having arrived at Valladolid
from Burgos, 4,000 went to him, 4,000 to Ney, and 4,000
to Madrid. Joseph Bonaparte appears to be at Andujar.

The 1st Regiment arrived.

May 1–2. Mangoalde.—1st Regt. marched to Mangoalde. 16th followed to Viseu. Halt there for the present.

Mangoalde.—Astorga surrendered on the 22nd. This
could scarcely be otherwise. Now then will Junot establish himself in Galicia with his whole force ? Or hold
Astorga with a part, and send the remainder to the General
Rendezvous before Ciudad Rodrigo ? As it was on the
26th that Ney advanced, he, of course, knew of the fall of
Astorga when he did so, and therefore probably calculated
upon a consequent Reinforcement ; if Junot spare him
10,000 Men, Lord Wellington is too weak to fight, that is
to advance and fight in the Plain Country before Ciudad
Rodrigo. The odds would be too great, with half our
Infantry Portuguese. If all were British the odds would
be nothing, but as it is they would put so much of risk
into the possible result that I doubt whether the Com-

mander-in-Chief will try it.   At Cadiz the French Batteries
have destroyed Matagorda, and we have abandoned it.
Col. le Ferre (?) the Commanding Engineer of the Allies
has been unfortunately killed.   In the South nothing
material has occurred.   I fear this fall of Astorga will
confine us to defensive measures, unless the Corps of Genl.
Hill could be drawn in, which the vicinity of Reynier and
Mortier forbids.   Meanwhile the Heavy Guns have not
yet been moved from Salamanca.   Probably the rains
have occasioned a little delay.

Wrote to Mr. Stewart at Lisbon.   From the time of
his arrival in Portugal I have been in the habit, by the
Marshal's order, of sending him the substance of all intelligence received from the Enemy.   As my letters, however,
have never contained matter of opinion, but simply a sort
of summing up of the different extracts, when that appeared
to be necessary from their number,   I have hitherto
thought it unnecessary to keep any copies ;   henceforward
perhaps it may be better to do so from the increasing
interest of the scene, and I therefore commence to do it
with this letter of the 2nd May from Mangoalde.

Evening.—Arrived at Fornos where the Marshal has
established his Head Quarters.

May 3.   Fornos de Algodres.—Marshal Beresford
visited Lord Wellington at Celorico.   Every thing remains
as before.   Don Julian in a Sally from Ciudad Rodrigo
has slain a French Officer and some 16 or 20 Men.   This
is good.   Blood spilt under the walls was to be wished—
it will beget inveteracy, and from that the Spaniards both
there and elsewhere must look for their advantage.

The Marshal is arranging with Lord Wellington some
certain means of subsisting the Portuguese Troops, when
their own supplies fail, by the occasional assistance of
the British Commissariat.   This is absolutely requisite
or the Troops will often starve,[1] for such is the poverty,
imbecility, and total want of arrangement of the Portuguese Government, that any regular system of supply is
not to be expected.   In short from one or other or all of
these causes or defects, the whole Civil Branch of the
Army is in such a state of confusion that I hold it utterly
impracticable to carry on operations with it for more
than a week or two together, if even so long.   The many

[1] Quoted Oman, iii, p. 178.

Months of repose since the Spanish Campaign, the evils then experienced, the remonstrances of the Marshal, have produced no effect whatever, and we are about to commence another Campaign destitute of everything that keeps an Army in motion. I have foreseen this, I have represented frequently that it would be so, the Marshal, I fear, hoped otherwise, the promises of this wretched Government have deceived him again for the 100th time.

May 4.   Junot has left 800 Men at Astorga ; from 4 to 5,000 the South of the Benavente Road ; and has marched with his remaining force probably from 8 to 9,000 Men in the direction of Ciudad Rodrigo.

May 5-6.   Nothing new.   The Marshal went (6th) to Guarda to inspect the Brigade of McMahon.   Enquired of Col. Murray the arrangements for sending back the British Sick to the Rear.   Received a Memorandum of it. They are to go once a fortnight and we therefore may send ours by the same Route on the alternate week.

May 7-10.   The Enemy upon the 7th at noon drew in his Parties and Advance near Ciudad Rodrigo, and moved to his right towards St. Felices.   He has also almost entirely evacuated Baños, and has retired from Merida leaving his sick.   These Movements are singular, the two last especially.   A day or two will shew, 'tis quite impossible to form any judgment of what they mean.

May 11-12.   Lord Wellington sent back the 2 three-pounder Brigades to Sampayo near Ponte de Murcella, this principally for want of forage ; both that and provisions are certainly very scarce, to the Portuguese Army, whose wretched system of procuring supplies must of necessity fail.   Nothing is paid for, and even what is not given to the British Commissaries, who pay readily for everything they get, is secreted, which of course the owners would much rather do than give it for the Intendant General's receipt, which he and all the world knows will never be accounted for.

The 25th is the succeeding fortnightly period of sending the Portuguese Sick to the Rear.   Lord Wellington has fixed upon Govea as a temporary Hospital of Rest for the Sick of the Advanced Brigades ; the British allow us the use of their covered Boats from Foz Dão to Coimbra, but cannot spare their covered Carts.   Our Sick will I apprehend suffer greatly, for it rains in torrents every day, and will do all this month, and the casual coverings that can be found for the Country Carts will be but a slender shelter. It strikes me we shall find a difficulty of Transport too, for we do now for the most common and necessary purposes. A new arrangement has been made to prevent a competition of demand for Carriages. The British require the *whole*, and afterwards give us *one third*. The necessary Orders, Routes, and Instructions for the next Convoy of Sick, despatched to the Inspector-General of Hospitals, the Brigades and Regiments, their March arranged, Hospital ordered, etc.

Ferguson rather wishes Figueiras than Coimbra as a General Hospital for the Army of the Beira. His reasons are very convincing; the Marshal acquiesces, and the thing is ordered.

May 13. The Enemy's desertion increases fast.

May 14. Mermet in the name of Ney has again summoned Ciudad Rodrigo. Herrasti adheres to his former answer. A Mr. Jackson has escaped from the French, and has given an account of the state of Preparation and Reinforcements among the French, which must be received, I think, with some caution; a part is improbable, a part impossible, and his own mode of escape suspicious.

Junot went back to Valladolid on the 1st of May, taking with him about 6,000 Infantry. He left 5 or 6,000 in Leon, and can have had few therefore to spare for Ciudad Rodrigo.

To-day and yesterday wrote to Mr. Stewart—gave him the intelligence and my own notions of its substance —represented also the inefficient supplies for the Portuguese Army, the necessity of a regular and increased Meat Ration, and the certainty of its consequences if the Regency did not immediately and effectually apply a remedy.

May 15–17. No Movement. Mr. Jackson has arrived at Head Quarters, and Lord Wellington upon examining him has the same suspicions of his integrity that his written deposition awakened, when we first read it here.

Martiniere's Corps of 10,000 Men (Infantry) which he affirmed to be complete Battalions, and marching upon Ciudad Rodrigo, is probably a Corps of Recruits for the 2nd Corps d'Armée under Soult upon the Guadiana.[1]

---

[1] 'They were complete Battalions,' Sir Charles Oman comments.

The Enemy has again advanced in that direction and reconnoitred both banks almost up to Badajoz. The coming of Masséna to Command in Chief is reported. If it be so, all these movements are but to keep up alarm and expectation, and real measures will be deferred till his arrival. It is not probable, though certainly possible, that Ney will venture a real attack upon Ciudad Rodrigo, risking his Battering Train, and stores, nay Salamanca itself, with Lord Wellington's undivided attention fixed upon him, and the Army close at hand. 'Tis to be supposed that our flanks must be seriously threatened, before anything real is done in our front.

May 18. The Merida Division of the Enemy having advanced to Olivença, General Hill at the desire of the Marquis of Romana, advanced the British and Portuguese Troops comprising his Corps (on the 14th) and the French fell back again on the 15th. On the 16th the Alemtejo Division returned to its former Cantonments. The Division of Reynier which thus advanced towards Badajoz, is about 10,000 Men.

May 19. A French Officer who had killed or wounded (as he said) his Captain in a duel, deserted yesterday. He says that the three French Corps in front of Ciudad Rodrigo consist of two Regts. of Infantry, 1 of Cavalry and a few Light Guns and Howitzers each.

Masséna has been put in orders as Commander-in-Chief of the Army of Portugal, and is said to have arrived at Salamanca. This Army is to consist of the 2nd (Reynier's), 6th (Ney's), 8th (Junot's) Corps d'Armée—stated at 80,000 Men. This number in the outs won't be sufficient. Probably a Reinforcement follows Masséna.

This is the best General France has ; Bonaparte thinks the Defenders of Portugal of some consequence or he would not send him. Though indeed he does not much want him anywhere else at present, and perhaps it is his wish to employ him at a distance, rather than let him be idle near home. In about a Month or at longest 6 weeks, I imagine things will be in motion.

Meanwhile we are like to be starved. The Government, as I feared it would, has again deceived Marshal Beresford as to Provisions. There are not above 5 days' consumption in hand and no hope of more when that's done. If there be no treachery in this, there is the most shameless imbecility, iniquity and sloth that ever disgraced an Executive Government.

May 20–23. During these days there was no movement on the part of the Enemy, nor any change in our own positions. An English Officer named Ryan came over from the Enemy. He was taken in the Adriatic in 1807, and, strange to tell, entered the French Service even by his own account without any coercion. He was a Captain in the Irish Brigade, served at the siege of Astorga and was promised a Cross of the Legion of Honour by Junot.

May 24. The arrangement settled for the English Commissariat supplying the Beef Ration to the Portuguese Troops of the Division of the Beira, 16,540 Men. The Portuguese Commissaries to give receipts for the quantity issued, and the expense to be settled between the two Governments. All the Orders and Instructions for this fortnight's Convoy of Sick are sent off and all the preparations made. Col. Murray is informed that Boats will be required for 90. Ferguson of their arrival at Coimbra on the 30th. The fortnightly Convoy made a Standing Order and the Corps told to continue it on each succeeding fortnight without any new orders.

May 25. Accompanied Lord Wellington and Marshal Beresford to Almeida on their way to visit the Out Posts upon the Line of the Agueda by Celorico, Alversa, Freixedas,—the Country very strong and a very powerful Position near Macal da Chao.

May 26. . . . General Craufurd holds the whole Line of the Agueda from Barca de Puerco to Guinaldo, with the Hussars of the K.G.L. . . . Beacons are well established and the Line of Out Posts under an excellent arrangement, but the Force of Hussars rather too small for the duties.

The French Advanced Corps are where they were excepting that General Ferri who was the other day a little to the Right of St. Espiritus is returned to St. Felices, where he has about 2,500 Men. Desertion increases, but the execution difficult, the Rains having swelled all the Rivers.

The most extraordinary instance of Spanish warped and mistaken judgement has occurred, that imagination can conceive. General Carrera has made overtures to

Marshal Ney, inviting him to come over to the Spanish
Cause and offering him the Rank of Captain-General, he
thinks too he shall succeed. This is too absurd to need
any comment.

Returned to Almeida.

Lord Wellington has determined on occupying Fort
Conception upon the right Bank of the Tormes and
left of Duas Casas. This it would appear is a very
good measure. If the Enemy got possession of it they
might range all over the Country to the Banks of the Coa
and the Gates of Almeida, and it would render the relief
of Ciudad Rodrigo very difficult. We holding it, can at
any time advance upon the Agueda, to all the approaches
of which it is the Key, and it is at the same time a strong
support to our Out Posts. Cox provides 6 Guns from
Almeida, and the 6-pounder Brigade, 9th Portuguese
Infantry, and 4 Companies of the 45th Regt. from General
Picton's Division at Pinhel occupy the Fort, that is they
are cantoned in Valde la Marta and Vald'Obispo, and held
in readiness to go into it upon the first alarm. Joseph
has returned to Madrid, and the intelligence from the
Enemy would lead one to suppose that Masséna meditates
an Attack upon Portugal before an attack upon Ciudad
Rodrigo. Ney moving upon Alcanides and La Puebla
de Senabria and himself upon the Agueda and Coa. In
this case he knows that if he beats the British Army,
Ciudad Rodrigo and Almeida together with Portugal fall
of course, and perhaps thinks it better therefore to attack
Lord Wellington, trying at the same time to distract his
attention by Ney's flank demonstration, than to be
attacked by him while he is besieging Ciudad Rodrigo.
The French Troops are very sickly, the natural consequence
of being constantly exposed to the inclemency of the
weather.

May 27. Lord Wellington returned to Celorico,
Marshal Beresford to Fornos.

May 28–30. The issue of Meat arranged from the
British Supplies at 1 lb. a day to the Portuguese Troops.—
Orders given.

May 31. The Enemy's Battering Train, and Heavy
Guns have at length been actually put in motion from
Salamanca for Ciudad Rodrigo. They moved on the 28th,
and are now of course near the Town, but the Reports

did not come in till this day at 2 o'clock. The C. in C.
holds himself in readiness for an immediate March, and
the Troops have been advised to be in readiness to move.
There is no reason to suppose that anything more than
the Corps of Ney has yet advanced, whatever may be
following. What if Lord Wellington, should this be the
case, determines upon falling rapidly upon him ? I don't
see why he should not be beaten, and his Guns taken
before he can be supported ; the moral effect of such a
thing, to say nothing of its real and Physical one, would
be infinite.

A Courier despatched to Foz d'Alva to expedite the
30,000 Flints to the Brigades and the Ammunition which
the carelessness of the 6th Regt. has made it deficient in.

June 1.   The Enemy are without doubt concentrating
everything they can collect in the Campo de Salamanca.
All the Troops from Leon are moving upon Zamora and
Reynier is said to be in March for Alva with the 2nd Corps.
Whether Mortier again crosses the Sierra with the 4th
Corps is not yet certain, 'tis reported and will most likely
be so. Silveira reports that 26 Battalions have followed
Masséna and that they are beginning to arrive between
Valladolid. There is also a corroborating report of the
same thing from another quarter. If this be the case,
and the Corps of Reynier arrive from the Tagus, while
Mortier, crossing the Sierra Masques General Hill (for I
don't hold Romana for much), then the French General
may perhaps have force sufficient to besiege Ciudad
Rodrigo and cross the Coa also. All this depends upon
this 9th Corps, these 26 Battalions. If they be full and
strong it throws much into the scale, but still, considering
ground and circumstances, I think we may fight him with
advantage, and a Battle gained would be everything for
our affairs now. It would act in a double ratio, and its
consequences to us both physically and morally would be
incalculable. Lord Wellington has moved up the Germans
from Trancoso to Alversa, put the Cavalry in motion from
Mello and Margoraldes to the front. B. Genl. Craufurd's
Portuguese Brigade to Mello, Blunt's to Goveã, Chasseurs
to Torrecillo, 1st to Algodres and Figueira, 16th to Mar-
goralde.

Wrote to Mr. Stewart Intelligence.

June 2.   Fort Conception was occupied fully yesterday

by 5 Companies 45th Regt. The 9th Portuguese and 14 Guns, 12- and 6-pounders from Almeida with a Company of Artillery. Sir Brent Spencer arrived from England—second in Command.

June 3. Lord Wellington wishes to get up something more on his present Left. The 1st Regt. is ordered to move from Figueira and Algodres to Trancoso ; the 16th to Maclira and Sobral.

The Enemy on the 31st began to throw a Bridge over the Agueda upon Trellises (Chevalets) at the Convent of Caridad.

June 4. God bless the King ! [George III.]

June 5. The Enemy have completed their Bridge over the Agueda near La Caridad, this was finished on the 3rd and they have begun one near Carboniso, that is they have thrown it over the smaller branch of the stream to a little Island ; the return of Rain has delayed his effecting the Bridge of the larger Stream for perhaps two or three days till it sinks again. He pushes Parties over, however, every day, and of course will occupy the heights above La Caridad. When the Bridges are complete he will effect the Investment of the Place, and communication will cease.

General Craufurd's Head Quarters of the Out Posts still continues at Gallegos, but he can't well prevent the occupying the heights opposite La Caridad, because to do so he must go with all his force, and then if the Enemy crossed at Carbonero he could not retire upon Fort Conception and Almeida.

June 6. The French Sergeants of Dragoons and a Trumpeter came in. Masséna reviewed the Investing Army before Ciudad Rodrigo and went away again. The Heavy Guns have stuck fast in the mud near Matilla. The state of the Roads must prevent their arrival for a few days. At all events I imagine the Enemy would rather wish to complete his Investment, establish his Position, and have his Batteries ready before he brings his Guns. This will risk them less, they will come into the Batteries as soon as they arrive, and the fire will open at once.

Ney's Corps is before the Town,—Loison, Marchard, Mermet.

June 7. 1st and 16th both at Trancoso. 4th and 6th

Caçadores march to-morrow from Torrecillo to Figueiro and Algodres,—arrive 9th.

June 8. The Enemy has completed his Bridge at Carbonero; the Town is therefore upon the point of being closely invested, and a Letter of the Governor's is in a still more desponding vein than might be wished, in short, there is a tone in it that augurs but a weak resistance,—I shall be happy to be mistaken.

June 9. 4th and 6th Chasseurs arrived in the Cantonments at Figueiro and Algodres. Instructions to Trant and Miller to be ready to co-operate with Silveira and Mahy in a forward movement of demonstration by Torre de Moncorvo and so looking at Zamora. This is well enough imagined, but Bonnet has moved down out of the Asturias and will probably watch that quarter while everything else is in the Campo de Salamanca and before Ciudad Rodrigo; he is weak, however, about 4,000 Infantry, and perhaps may commit himself to the attack of our People though their Troops are very irregular.

June 10. The Enemy has completed the investing of Ciudad Rodrigo, has pushed 2 or 3,000 Infantry over the Agueda and has his Pickets on the Roads of Guinaldo and Gallegos. General Craufurd has succeeded in throwing in 300,000 Balls. The Cavalry has gone out to join Carrera, excepting Don Julian Sanchez. The retaining this celebrated Partizan in the Place may give confidence to its other defenders and so far be right, otherwise 'tis pity to shut up him; for he is worth all their other People of the same description.

General Craufurd rates the disposable Enemy in Castile at 50,000. Rumar at 30,000. The truth probably lies between.

Some Trees have been sent down the stream by the Spaniards, but without effect. It winds so much and the banks are so rocky that 'tis difficult to send them down any distance and the Enemy would prevent its being done near the Bridge.

June 11. The Enemy are constructing a Tête du Pont to the Carboneros Bridge. A little skirmishing between the Carpio and Marialva Pickets.

General Craufurd writes Lord Wellington that he did not choose to attack the Carboneros Infantry, because his right and rear would have been exposed to La Caridad, without His Lordship's express orders. Perhaps he's right, and indeed the attack, excepting to destroy the Bridge would not have been for much use, nor even then, for the dry weather has now, I fancy, commenced in earnest. The Enemy too would have been supported more readily and expeditiously than it was possible for the General to be, and perhaps it would have ended in his Corps being driven back, whereas 'tis decidedly an advantage for it to remain where it is, as long as it can, and supposing that Lord Wellington intends to attack the Besieging Army 'tis not yet time to do so, for their Guns are not arrived,—it will be well to wait till they are in the Batteries and then the Battering Train will be the fruit of Victory. When this arrives a well concealed and bold movement with 8 or 10,000 Men by the Ford of Valdespiro, Serravilla, and Mastilla, so across to the rear of the Sierra de Ciudad Rodrigo on the St. Espiritus.

June 11.   Road while 20,000 advance in front will do the business past all doubt. Herrasti talks very firmly in a letter to Carrera.

June 12–16.   During these days little occurred in front. The Enemy has occupied a wooded hill in front of Carboneros, which commanding Palacios prevents Genl. Craufurd from keeping his Cavalry Picket here any longer. The best accounts make the 6th and 8th Corps only amount from 33 to 35,000 Men. No Reinforcements have passed into the Peninsula since April 16th, but 13,000 Infantry and 1,800 Cavalry, Germans, Italians, etc. With Masséna have come a Conde de Recede, the Marquis of Tancos and the Marquis d'Albuera; these are Portuguese Traitors, and the last of them a very able man, eccentric, devoted to the French, and likely to render them good service.

June 17.   The Enemy opened the Trenches before Ciudad Rodrigo on the night of the 15th on the hill of St. Francisco, and appeared in the morning of yesterday to have traced the greater part of his first Parallel, with two approaches; one on the Left, the other on the Right leading to some houses by the River side covering the Right. On the reverse of the hill, towards the tail of the Trenches, there are two or three small works, probably for Mortar Batteries. General Craufurd seems to think what I have all along supposed, that they won't bring up

the Guns till the Attack is pretty well prepared. Marshal
Beresford has to-day talked with me as to the feasibility
of doing something when the Guns arrive and the idea of
a flank movement by Valdespiro has struck him also.
This confirms me in my own previous notion of its expediency, and I hope Lord W. may see fit to attack so.
The National Honor requires us to do something for 'twill
be bearing an absolute insult to have the Town taken
under our Noses without an attempt to save it. We had
better have remained out of sight altogether. Marshal
Beresford does not seem to carry his idea further than the
Flank Demonstration, and build upon the Enemy's extreme
jealousy, that even that might make him retire. The
Flanking Corps always preserving the power of retiring.
This may be more prudent, but I should incline to make
the thing real. No Country can be more advantageous
for Battle. You turn the Enemy without the possibility
of prevention, attack his rear while you attack his front,
and you fight under the Guns of the Town.

Note.—Upon this day a Spy of Don Julian corroborates all
the estimates of Rumar, making out the whole force between
Salamanca and Ciudad Rodrigo to amount to no more than
from 33 to 35,000; of these 23,000 with Ney at Ciudad Rodrigo,
the others with Junot.

The Enemy will not be weaker, we shall not be stronger,
but the very reverse of each, by waiting. Our Troops
both physically and morally are superior to theirs, and I
am clear that a forward movement upon the general idea
in my Memorandum of the 11th would be crowned with
success. 'Tis needless to waste a moment in commenting
upon the infinite value of such a success to us now in every
possible point of view.

The Returns of Elvas prove it to be by no means
sufficiently supplied with provisions. These were Returns
casually called for. The Governor would never have
reported it, though 'twas impossible to divine it, because
two months ago his returns accounted for a complete
1,500,000 (equal to 187 days supply for 8,000 Men) Rations
of every description, and he has made no representation
since, either of having expended any provisions, or of
having found a difficulty of supply. This man too, Genl.
Leite, is one of the best of our Portuguese Chiefs. Who

can deal with such people, or make a good work with such instruments ? The Devil—nobody else.

June 18. Orders to all the Corps who have changed their quarters within this fortnight, with instructions for the ensuing convoy of Sick. (4th and 6th Chasseurs ; 1st and 16th Line.)

The Marshal met Lord Wellington at Trancoso to inspect the 1st and 16th Regts. Reflecting upon his conversation of yesterday and looking back to what I have myself thought, and considering what 1 do think upon the subject. I conceive it a duty (though it is an unpleasant one to venture a suggestion to those superior to ourselves in judgement and experience) to give him a hasty abstract of my opinion, and as hasty an outline of what I think may be successful. I have accordingly left upon his table the Paper ' A.' There are many things that the present knowledge of the People at the Out Posts must furnish, many that must depend upon the Commander-in-Chief, many that an acquaintance with the actual resources of ourselves must afford before this outline can be filled up. I have given a *mere outline*, resulting from some little practical knowledge of the Ground, acquired while I had the good fortune to be with Sir Robert Wilson in the beginning of 1809, and from my ideas of what we can do, and may do.

June 19. The Curate of Garci-Rey received letters some days ago from People at Ledesma and St. Felices which said that with Junot 9,000 Men marched from Salamanca towards Zamora ; Don Julian's Spy from Salamanca corroborated this, and a letter from Wilson at Braganza, just received, speaks of a strong and circumstantial Report of a Corps being at Zamora which has come from Salamanca, and of Bessières and Kellerman having passed through Benavente for Astorga. If these reports have any foundation, and coming from so many quarters one can't refuse credit to their general import, we shortly have a demonstration at least upon our Northern flank. It accords too with an indication upon the Southern one, for Reynier has suddenly assembled everything he has at Merida. All this renders the present moment precious, 'tis the one on which it rests to disconcert all their plans, not yet quite ripe, and by fighting the Enemy before Ciudad Rodrigo—the success of which I cannot but feel very confident of—to strike at their centre, and leave their Wings in the air, Ney's Corps destroyed, their destruction or flight follows of course. There's no time to be lost though, for if their preparations are suffered to proceed to maturity, their combined movement will *walk* us back. They must take the law from us now, 'twould be better to give it, than to wait and take it from them.

Intercepted returns of the 2nd May make the strength of Ney's Division *then* 31,000 effectives; they can scarcely be so strong now at all events, for their losses between that time and the present have been great by sickness.

The Marshal approves my project but rather inclines to make the Body of Army advance by the Fords and the Town attack a feint.

JOURNAL IV

1810, *June–September*

PORTUGUESE CAMPAIGN (*continued*)
THE FALL OF CIUDAD RODRIGO AND ALMEIDA
THE BATTLE OF BUSSACO

June 20. Fornos de Algodres.

A part of the Corps of Junot are coming to Ciudad Rodrigo. Small Divisions of from 2 to 3,000 men have passed through St. Felices, Banavares, and St. Felices el Chico, from Ledesma. Most probably this indicates that the Batteries are almost ready for the Guns. Of course they'll collect everything they intend for the Siege at the time they propose them to arrive.

The fire of the Town is very trifling and gives the approaches little interruption.

Sent Mr. Stuart all the intelligence worth his having.

June 21. An intercepted letter of the 10th May from Marshal Ney (Duc de Elchingen) to Marshal Soult (Duc de Dalmatie) pretty strongly shows how seasonable the arrival of Masséna (Prince of Essling) was for the French interests. There appears to have been such a misunderstanding between Ney and Junot (Duc d'Abrantes) that the Corps of the latter would afford him no support, nor co-operate with him in any way., It is to be lamented that with the great means of Money, in our power, we don't contrive to unlock some of the Enemy's secrets. When Ney wrote the letter in question he owns that in case of Attack his force does not exceed 12,000 fighting men.— What infinite benefit if we had fought him in the end of May !—All this time Lord Wellington was rating him at 30,000 men and General Craufurd supposed the disposable force at Campo de Salamanca to be 50,000. To be sure this included Junot, but his force is not more than 16,000.

(6th, or Corps of Ney, 12th May.—Infantry 23,105; Cavalry 4,056; Foot Artillery 1,259; Heavy Do. 1,893: —Total Force 31,307. This includes everything; therefore, deducting for Officers, etc., 1/6th, his Fighting Force is 26,000 at the utmost.)

My conjecture as to the Battery Guns is fulfilled. Ney says they remain at Salamanca guarded by the 2nd Battalion of the Hanoverian Legion, till the Trenches are quite ready for them.

Yesterday the Enemy began to advance from his Parallel. Between 12 and 2 o'clock, there was the appearance of some Guns being brought into the Trenches.

Strong Infantry Pickets of the Enemy are now posted at the Valdespiro and Copene Fords of the Agueda. Of course he begins to be jealous of his Right and Rear, and he committed a most egregious blunder in not taking care of it before. An operation somewhat like that I proposed would any time before yesterday have actually taken him by surprise. It would lose that advantage now indeed, for these Pickets would give the alarm—but it is still, I think, a feasible measure and of good prospect—and if executed within eight and forty hours, we shall beat the Besieging Army. This, however, is mere matter of opinion, and to be considered as thought, not spoken,—the first I've a right to do, and can't help, the last would be presumptuous.

The Place fires very little. This is unaccountable. General Craufurd does not think it will bear 48 hours fire. Their present slackness almost makes me agree with him. 'Tis of infinite importance to us to save it. 'Tis well worth a Battle. We shall know its infinite importance to Portugal when 'tis ours no longer. Carrera has joined Genl. Craufurd. Conception is ordered to be effectually mined. I'm afraid things look like retiring. 'Tis impossible to fathom my Lord W. or otherwise I should think that by advancing so far, and yet not fighting, even where the ground was favourable, and powerful motives must have urged him to fight—he means to let the Enemy pass him, and then follow him. This is no doubt an excellent mode of Mountain War—and if the Harvest were gathered would be good—but now—*Nous verrons*.

The 2nd Chasseurs are thought unfit for service and are coming back from the front.

June 22. To-day the Sick Convoy assembles at Guarda. Fewer than last fortnight. The Army very healthy.

June 23. The Marshal determined upon removing his Head Quarters from Fornos to Trancoso. Sent Harvey with the Captain of Guides to arrange the new Head Quarters which he means to occupy on the 25th. The 2nd Bat. of Chasseurs arrive on the 24th at Reteiro on the Mondego. They halt there till the Marshal shall have inspected them, which he proposes to do on the 25th and then they will proceed to Coimbra. This Corps has been sent back in consequence of General Craufurd's Report of their being unfit for service, and he has also reported the 1st Chasseurs to be so, because of the bad and weak physical qualities of the Men ;—as (whatever their discipline may be, which certainly might have been improved by this time, as they have been at the Out Posts with Genl. Craufurd for those three months) they have never appeared to the Marshal inefficient for want of strength, or deficient in point of stature, considering the Standard height of the Country ; indeed he has long used every exertion to get rid of every old, feeble, and infirm Soldier from this as well as the other Corps ;—as Men therefore he has always judged them fit for Service, and his Returns have so stated them to Lord Wellington and to the Government. The decisive way in which General Craufurd has stated this Corps to be unserviceable, must of course wear an odd aspect, and it is necessary that it should be inspected, and reported upon in its present state ;—in sending me to the Out Posts therefore (which several circumstances have induced the Marshal to direct me to visit) he has ordered me (see ' Y ') to inspect the 1st Chasseurs most minutely and carefully, and to make a Report upon them as to the points of inefficiency above mentioned.

Evening at Alverça. At Alverça I expected to have met the 2nd Chasseurs according to the route sent by Col. Delancy. They are not here, however. I have dispatched therefore to Reteiro an Order for them to be in readiness for the Marshal's Inspection at 12 o'clock on the 25th.

June 24. Almeida—Cox—had the conversation with him that the Marshal directed. That Officer in himself will do his duty zealously and well, whenever the day of trial comes, but it is very possible that having fallen, without perhaps knowing it himself, into a habit of seeing

the black side of things, he may have injured unwittingly
the instruments with which he will have to work. Despondency will beget despondency, although we endeavour
to conceal it most carefully, and confidence engenders
confidence though not a word be spoken. The Countenance is sufficient to indicate either one or the other, and
Soldiers read countenances accurately. Cox is a most
active, zealous, excellent Officer but the Correspondence,
and other sedentary duties of his present post, have almost
imperiously detained him from the more active and more
important ones of being constantly amongst his Garrison
and not only watching over their discipline, but training
and fashioning their minds to the confidence necessary
for what may perhaps be required of them.

Every thing is going on well and rapidly at the Fort
(Fort of Conception) and the zeal, attention, and ability
of Sutton have contrived to work wonders, for it will in a
few days be completed as far as is requisite.

General Craufurd's whole Division concentrated here
(Gallegos). The Enemy has this day had a Field Day of
his Cavalry which lasted from 10 in the morning till 5 in
the evening. The Batteries of the Trenches have not
opened. The Town has been firing the whole evening.
Don Julian cut his way through the French Posts the night
before last with 200 Men, coming out by the Bridge Gate.
He is with Carrera. Carrera and Mera with General
Craufurd. Mentioned to that General the Marshal's Order
that I should Inspect the 1st Chasseurs; this I shall do
while I stay here.

The evening too far clouded in to observe the French
Position clearly; to-morrow I shall be able to see it.

This unfortunate Ciudad Rodrigo! 'Tis lamentable
that it should fall before our very eyes without an effort.
We had better have kept at a distance. I'm afraid it
won't tell in favour of our National Honor.

June 25. At day-break the Enemy's Batteries opened
upon the Town. It was very promptly answered and
perseveringly continued.

At 5 o'clock General Craufurd arrived at the hill above
Minaloa, across which from that place to Carpio were his
chain of advanced Videttes, supplied by two small Cavalry
Pickets, one at each of these Villages.

At 8 o'clock the Enemy brought from his Camp near

La Caridad 3 Battalions, 2 Regiments of Cavalry, and 6 Guns to drive in our Pickets from the Right Bank of the Azava. They advanced very prettily (as people do very easily against less than a twentieth Part of their strength), in two Columns, and when they reached the Palanios Ridge, they formed their Cavalry in line between the Carpio and Marialva Roads, and advanced throwing out a long line of Skirmishers. General Craufurd withdrew his handful of Pickets (about 60 men) in excellent order. The Right Bank of the Azava was thus yielded to the Enemy, who have rather surprised one in so long abstaining from taking what they have always, since the investment of the Town, had the means to take, and which was important for them to have. A little skirmishing without loss, was all that occurred. The Enemy took up one chain and we that on the Left bank of the Azava.

At half past 8 o'clock the fire of the Garrison blew up a large Magazine in the Trenches, and from the size of the column of smoke and the explosion, I trust the French have suffered considerable mischief. This is confirmed by a long silence at the points of Explosion,— that Battery did not recover itself all day, and the Deserters say the loss in the Trenches has been very great. The firing continued all day and with slight intervals all night.

The General's change in his Out Post disposition, in consequence of the Ground gained by the Enemy, very judicious. He remains with 3,000 Infantry and 350 Horse in the face of the Enemy,—6 leagues in front of our Army, yet the French respect his Corps too much to meddle with it seriously.

(This Corps consisted of 1 Troop Horse Artillery; 43rd, 52nd, 95th, English Infantry, 1st, 3rd, Portuguese Caçadores; 2 Squadrons German Hussars; 2 Squadrons 16th Light Dragoons—the latter arrived at 12 o'clock A.M.)

Deserters say that Masséna has arrived and that it was he who reviewed the Cavalry the day before the Batteries opened. Wrote the Marshal the occurrences of the day, and mentioned the probability of my being detained a few days.

June 26. Firing all night. Town discovered to have a house on fire at day-break. Firing continued briskly. The Garrison are doing themselves infinite credit—'tis a thousand pities they are not to be relieved. They have passed the Rubicon—they have committed themselves deeply in being our friends—and in firing with such determination and effect, and I fancy despair may now make them continue obstinately to fight. Masséna I suppose will soon shew his sense of their conduct by punishing them with their gentle Military chastisement.

Lord Wellington arrived at Gallegos from Almeida,—rode to the Rio Molino Picket,—looked at the Town and some of the French Posts,—and then immediately got on horseback and went back to Almeida. I'm afraid he does not mean to move forwards and relieve the Place. Firing all day, but the French Guns have not discovered any heavy calibre since the Explosion of yesterday morning.

June 27. This morning the French have reestablished their heavy Battery, and the firing upon the Town is heavier than at any time since the Batteries opened. The Place fires more briskly in proportion as the Trenches fire more heavily. No appearance of the fires that were visible yesterday. The Posts all quiet this morning, but the Infantry Pickets on their Right are strengthened, and they have moved some Infantry more to the Left by Carpio. Their appearance indicates much jealousy, more than usual, as they would naturally have observed the Head Quarter Staff at Molino das Flores yesterday, and that accounts for it.

About noon a Peasant came out of the Town from the Governor. The walls are not yet materially injured, but they have lost 7 or 800 men, and of these about 100 Artillery men. Herrasti urges to Lord W. the necessity of coming soon if he comes at all. Lord W. returned an answer to the Governor and the Peasant set off on his way back; he seemed confident of entering, and perhaps will. The purport of Lord W.'s answer I am as yet ignorant of.

June 28. The firing which had continued at intervals through the night recommenced both from the Town and Trenches at 4 o'clock, and was supported on both sides with as much vigour as yesterday. It ceased a little towards the middle of the day, and in the evening commenced again with more fury than ever. This poor Town deserved a better fate than it will find. I fear it is not to expect any help from us. General Stewart (the Adjutant General) came to the Outposts to-day. The Alarm Posts are to be in Rear instead of in Front. This, one would think, looks backwards. What an infinite delight it would be to have this conjecture proved wrong. Independent of all one has hitherto felt for this unfortunate Town, its gallant defence has thrown a dignity around it that mixes respect with our pity, and certainly there is not a Man or Officer of this Advanced Guard that would not be rejoiced and gratified in getting the order to move to the attack of the Trenches. The relief of this Town would be most glorious, as well as most politic, and the brightest Laurel that has yet adorned the brow of Lord Wellington.

Inspected three Companies of the 1st Chasseurs.

Junot has arrived ; he visited the Outposts this morning ; he was at Marialva to-day and sent his compliments to General Craufurd by the Flag of Truce which has been sent in about their flags approaching the Bridge.

June 29. The firing from the Town and Trenches continued all night, with occasional musketry, and for three hours after day-break was heavier than it has yet been. The Posts all quiet, nothing to be seen but the Cavalry Pickets upon the hill of Marialva. A General Officer of the Enemy reconnoitred the Passage of the Azava at and below the Bridge of Marialva at 8 o'clock.

Finished the Inspection of the 1st Chasseurs.

At about one o'clock Lord Wellington ordered to retire tonight to Almeida. The Pickets ordered to be withdrawn at 10. The Division under arms at 11.

The unfortunate Town that we thus leave to its fate still continues to fire resolutely. It has two breaches— one in the Inner, the other in the outer wall.

June 30. The Infantry marched to Almeida, bivouacked in the wood. Cavalry remained. A Peasant came out of the Town last night to Carrera with a letter from Herrasti. This excellent and gallant Spaniard says that the Breach is practicable, and the Garrison fatigued, and in some measure dispirited at their being totally abandoned. Upon the whole he says that if Lord Wellington does not soon advance the Town, he fears, will be lost.

Evening to Pinhel.

July 1. Returned to Trancoso. Found that the Marshal had ordered the 3rd and 15th to Thomar and the 8th to Coimbra.

Intercepted Letters from France, say as follows :—

1st from Berthier to Soult dated Dieppe 27th May.

Informs him that the Emperor commands (now that Lerida and Hostalrich are taken) Suchet to march against Tortosa, and MacDonald against Tarragona, these taken, Suchet with 30,000 men and the necessary Battering Train, is to besiege Valençia.

As the Siege of Ciudad Rodrigo may probably bring on a Battle, Reynier with the 2nd Corps is to be near Abrantes, and hold himself under the orders of Masséna, to manœuvre up on the Right Bank of the Tagus. The 1st, 4th and 5th Corps and the Division of Dissolle are more than sufficient for the South ; the 5th Corps therefore are to hold the Portuguese in check on the side of Badajoz.

The Emperor [1] is much astonished that Arms should have been given to the Spaniards. Experience has shown the bad policy of this, and the pernicious use they make of them. He is astonished also that the Country is not made to pay, and feed the Troops.

2nd from Berthier to Reynier, Dieppe, 27th May, Orders the plan of Operations of which Soult is apprised in the letter No. 1.

3rd to Joseph, Havre 28th May.

Deprecates the Arming the Spaniards. Informs him of the destination of Masséna and Reynier. Of the Siege of Ciudad Rodrigo and of the disposition of the 1st, 4th and 5th Corps and the Division of Dissolle. Directs the King to give no orders to Suchet, all the necessary ones shall be sent direct to that General from the Emperor.

4th Berthier to Masséna, Havre, 28th May.

Commands him to lose no time in reducing Ciudad Rodrigo, and orders him to *beat* the English if they advance to relieve it. Tells him that he has about 50,000 men, that by the English Papers their Army in the Beira does not amount to above 23,000 men, and that of Portugal about the same, making a less force than that of Masséna. He says nothing of subsequent operations against Portugal.

5th. Berthier to Kellerman, same date :—

Tells him that he shall have a Corps of 12,000 men and he is to keep open the Communications with the Army of Masséna.

Sent these to Mr. Stuart.

July 2. Brigadier Genl. Madden and Col. Trant

---

[1] See Oman, iii, p. 246, footnote.

ordered to proceed in the execution of the Instructions of the 8th June for a Diversion upon Zamora, which from circumstances had been suspended. Hardinge went to the Outposts. Lord Wellington has ordered the six-pounder Brigade of Arentschilde to remain in Almeida. Surely this is not the best possible disposition of an excellent Brigade of Field Artillery, probably as good a one as can be found, even in the British Army. Received the Marshal's directions to march the L.L. Legion from Thomar to Torres Novas, the 9-pounder Brigade from Condeixa to Golegão, and the Cavalry Brigade of Madden from Salva-tierra de Mayor to Santarem, and its adjacents, if requisite. This Corps behind the Zezere to be under General Leith, some English Regiments to be with it. Expedited the two first Orders to Miranda and the last to the Count of St. Payo.

Wrote Mr. Stuart, enclosed him copies of the inter-cepted letters received yesterday, and told him the heads of the Siege of Ciudad Rodrigo. Colonel Pack arrived and is to have the Brigade 1st and 16th. This is a great acquisition,—an Officer of tried service, sound judgement, and proved intrepidity.

All the Northern Forces united under Baccelar, and Wilson his *Chef de l'Etat Major* with very full powers,— instructions sent.

July 3. The Marquis of Romana, and the Marquis of Coupigni at Lord Wellington's Head Quarters. Accom-panied Marshal Beresford there. Ciudad Rodrigo still holds out.

July 4. Ciudad Rodrigo still defends itself. We do nothing for it, but it does a great deal for us, for a Siege of this sort not only detains the Army of Portugal, but it exhausts its provisions.

Hardinge writes from the Outposts.

July 5. . . . At day-break on the morning of the 4th the Enemy moved forward 10 Squadrons of Cavalry, 2 Brigades of Infantry and some guns, and drove in the Cavalry Pickets from Gallegos, upon the Post taken up on the 30th June in front of Almeida. A good deal of Skirmishing and Capt. Krauchenberg of the German Hussars had an occasion to behave very brilliantly charging a superior number of the French Dragoons, and cutting down the Squadron Officer with his own hand. My friend

Elder brought his Portuguese Chasseurs into fire for the first time with excellent effect. The Advanced Division is now according to its previous orders, when it should be attacked, fallen back upon Fort Conception.

July 6. The Enemy's Outposts in front of Gallegos; ours in front of Val de la Mula. All quiet. Wilson written to as to the new arrangement for him with Baccelar.

July 7. Hardinge returned from the Outposts. Nothing new and the Town still holds out. Wrote Mr. Stuart.

July 8. Town still defends itself.

July 9. The Town still holds out. Letter from Mr. Stuart adverting to Militia desertion. Answered. No want of precaution or exertion on the part of the Marshal, but the wretched want of vigor in the Magistracy, from the imbecility of the Government.

July 10. Ciudad Rodrigo [1] still holds out.

July 11. Town still defends itself, much Musquetry all yesterday and this morning. The Marshal proposes to McMahon to be Governor of Valença de Minho; for this he is well calculated. 'Tis a very important Fortress, and no man will hold it better, but the principle of removing him from his Brigade, because Senior British Officers now choose to vote it a fashionable Service to belong to this Army, now that the fag and uphill work is over, and therefore, that those who have worked at the Regiments through the burden and heat of the day, are to get out of the way for them, is hard and difficult to reconcile with common justice. One Squadron of Madden's Brigade at Santarem ordered to March to Castel Branco, and then that of the 11th Dragoons, now there, to hold itself in readiness to march at the order of the British Quarter Master General. The Squadron of the 11th Dragoons at Golegão to march to Lamego, and there to be with Baccelar, and the 1½ Squadrons at Lisbon to go there also by Troops as soon as they are successively complete and fit to march. Requisite orders sent to Miranda, Baccelar, Madden and St. Payo.

Surrender of Ciudad Rodrigo

July 12. The Report yesterday from the Outposts was unfounded; there might have been firing in the

---

[1] Surrendered on this same night.

evening of the 10th, but there could be none on the morning
of yesterday.   The Town surrendered in the night of the
10th, when every thing was prepared for a General Assault,
and the Breach more than sufficiently wide to admit of a
Column of Companies.   Ney offered to. accept a Capitula-
tion—the Governor (Don Antonio Herrasti) acquiesced.
What terms he has got we don't yet know, but I trust good
ones.   His defence has been excellent and he was perfectly
right in surrendering when he did, his provisions were
nearly exhausted—he was quite abandoned to his fate—
he could no longer hope for relief from the British Army
which had made no effort to save or to succour him, and
he would have been at once an unfeeling man and a Mad-
man, if so circumstanced he had exposed the numerous
population of the Town to all the horrors of a Storm.   I
think the time may soon come when our eyes will be
opened to the policy of having done something for Ciudad
Rodrigo.   I shall be right glad to be mistaken. . . .

   . . . An Outpost Skirmish[1] yesterday morning cost
us Lt. Col. Talbot of the 14th Dragoons.   Leading his
Squadron to charge a small body of French Infantry at
Barquilla, he was shot through the body and fell dead
at the points of their Bayonets.   This is a heavy loss,
for I don't think we shine as formerly, in good Light
Dragoon Officers, and he was one of the very best class.

   July 13.   Nothing new.   Out Posts where they were.
Hardinge is gone to the Out Posts.

   July 14.   The duplicates of the intercepted Orders
have by this time reached Spain.   Reynier has received
his instructions and is marched for the Tagus.   A Corps
has advanced from Seville and driven in Ballasteros a little
to the rear of his position at Castellijo de las Guardias.
This Corps is perhaps intended to occupy the attention
of our Alemtejo Division.   I suppose Lord Wellington
watches well the Road between the Navar and Zezere that
turns the latter and leads upon Thomar ?

   Douglas writes from Coimbra that he wishes to move
to Condeixa to be out of the influence of a Fever which
prevails amongst the Peasantry and which he fears may
reach his people.

   July 15.   Wilson accepts the situation of *Chef de
l'État Major*, to the Army of the North, and I hope it

[1] See Oman, iii, p. 255, and *Sir Harry Smith's Autobiography*, i, p. 22.

gives him pleasure. McMahon declines being Governor of Valença. I am sorry for this, for I think he was well calculated for it, he says he is unequal to the task, and evidently does not like it. Douglas ordered to Pombal—better ground for drill than Condeixa.

July 16. The Army of Ballasteros dispersed. This gives the Liren (?) to Mortier, and as General Hill must attend the motions of Reynier, leaves Romana to himself.

July 17. Hardinge returned from the Out Posts. The Infantry Posts fallen back to Junca . . . [page cut] upon the Coa. Cavalry Pickets up the Las Casas Hill.

July 18. Duplicate of the Order of the 12th with regard to Ammunition for Abrantes sent to Rosa.

July 19. Reynier has crossed the Tagus, his Advanced Guard is at Coria. General Hill crosses also and comes to Castel Branco. . . .

July 20. All the Troops in the Rear closed up, and Lord Wellington seems to intend taking a Position from Guarda on his Right to near Freixadas on the Left.

Telegraphic Signals arranged with the Governor of Almeida. Mortier's Head Quarters at Castillijo de las Guardias. His Advance at St. Olalla.

July 21. . This morning the Enemy crossed the Dos Casas River in some force of Cavalry, and Infantry. General Craufurd therefore blew up Fort Conception. His Position—Right upon Junca,—Left upon the Wind-mill Hill.

July 22. Enemy advanced to General Craufurd, skirmished and retired. General Hill at Castel Branco . . .

July 23. Enemy ordered Rations at Sepera, Zibreira and Castel Rodrigo.

July 24. General Craufurd attacked and driven over the Coa. (This intelligence received at 12 P.M.)

4th and 6th Chasseurs ordered to remain at Povoa de Conselho instead of proceeding to Aldea Nova and Valverde.

ALMEIDA INVESTED

July 25. General Craufurd's loss yesterday was greater than would be pleasant to hear of, especially as the Action was incurred without necessity. 26 Officers killed and wounded, 300 men. The French there in force. Masséna present in person, and as they had 10,000 Infantry, 23

Squadrons of Cavalry and 15 Guns, they were of course enabled to turn General Craufurd's Right and obliged him to gain the Bridge expeditiously. Elder's Chasseurs behaved perfectly well. . . . The 1st . . . [obliterated]. General Craufurd is withdrawing to the heights of Carvalhos. All the Troops in readiness and well concentrated. This morning at Day-break :—General Picton as usual at Pinhel; General Cole at Guarda—Guards—G. Legion. General Cameron's English and the Portuguese Brigades of Campbell and Coleman between Celorico and Alversa; General Pack's at Trancoso and the 4th and 6th Caçadores at Povoa de Conselho.

July 26. The French in Force between the Coa and the Pinhel. At 12 o'clock Lord Wellington informed Marshal Beresford that he wished him to remove his Head Quarters to Avelar de Ribeira. General Picton withdrawn from Pinhel, at Carejo; Genl. Anson's—Povoa del Rey, observing the road to Trancozo—reporting to Marshal Beresford. Genl. Craufurd's advance Freixedas and Vendado. Campbell's Portuguese Rotoeiro. Colman's Ditto. Pack's Trancoso,—4th and 6th Caçadores Minacal, and 27th, Pine Wood by Celorico.

July 27. Rode by the Out Post of Povoa del Rey to Pinhel,—found a Peasant who left Almeida at 4 A.M. Letters from Cox. Loison's summons in the name of the Duke of Elchingen—takes Cox for a Portuguese. Offers most honorable terms—continue Governor—and concludes by saying that the Marques d'Alava, and the other Portuguese with the French, can assure him that all promises will be. fulfilled. The Garrison in good spirits. Cox was in the Covered Way by the Barrier Gate when the French Summons arrived,—the Officer did not enter therefore. He gave him a verbal answer of refusal.

Returned by Souse Pires. Not finding General Cotton there, opened the Packet, and returned by Alverça. Shewed the letter to Lord Wellington. He charged me with a Message for the Marshal.

He wishes Infantry in Rear of Celorico, Cavalry only in Front. Guns withdrawn from the Division at Guarda, and then it can retire upon Linhares. Left upon the Mondego—Advance in Celorico—Genl. Hill to look well to his Line and the Left. Reynier is passing the Perales. Rode to Trancoso—met the Marshal on his way to Lord

Wellington—gave him his Lordship's Message, and Cox's Packet. Night—Avellas de Ribeira.

July 28. Marshal's Head Quarters, Largiosa. Lord Wellington's Celorico. Movements of the Troops according to Lord Wellington's message of yesterday.

Arrangement :—Head Quarters Alverça to observe the Roads leading from Pinhel to Trancoso and Alverça, the direct road from Almeida, and the Roads coming from the side of Jerumelia.

Troops stationed. . . .

July 29. Movements. . . .

July 30. 1st and 3rd Caçadores moved into rear of Celorico, and halted with the rest of the Light Division.

Lt. Col. Windham of the Royals patroled into a French Picket in front of Freixedas, and was taken Prisoner. No Movements.

July 31. The Enemy hides (as might be supposed he would) his real Attack 'till the last moment, and this is very easy for him to do, for, as by holding the whole line from Alfayates to Almeida, he has the entrances of all the Roads leading into the Beira. The tidings of his real march must be brought in the blow, and 'till that falls 'twill be very difficult to distinguish his true Columns of Attack from his feigned ones. Meanwhile the Army would appear to be very well posted for any event. General Hill's main body at Sarzadas, Genl. Leith supporting him upon the Zezere in Second Line, and Lord Wellington at Celorico, with his People so laid along the Base of the Estrella, in the direction of Pte. de Murcella, that they can be easily rendered to the Front, if the Advance be there, to the Left if any thing of consequence be pushed along the Right bank of the Mondego, and can take General Hill by the hand if that be requisite. These movements are all to be executed partially or generally, and the Position therefore seems according to circumstances the best possible. Trancoso is a Post of Observation. Guarda, while occupied, is a Watch Tower of the Retreat upon Linhares easy enough, or upon Celorico.

Aug. 1. Lord Wellington as before. No movement on the part of the Enemy—if there be any appearance 'tis rather a looking backwards on his part,—this however is nothing and only a change in the disposition of his Posts. General Hill in consequence of a forward appearance

of Reynier on the 29th and 30th July—was yesterday
at Tenillas ready to move upon Zarzedas. Le Cor taking
care of the Estrada Nova, and Campbell at Sarnadas
defending the space between the Ocreza and the Tagus.

The atrocities of the Enemy's advance upon the
Frontier Line have exasperated the Peasantry. The
Towns therefore are deserted at his approach and every-
thing retires into the Strongholds, each man getting a
Gun or some weapon for defence and revenge.

Orders for Convoy of Sick to set out on the 4th from
Guarda given to all concerned.

Aug. 2. To Guarda and returned. Sent by the Marshal's
orders two Officers (Major Harvey and Capt. Chapuset) to
encourage the Magistrates and Inhabitants who are taking
Arms, at Villa Mayor and upon both banks of the Coa
between Almeida and Alfayates. The atrocious cruelties
every day committed by the French very much tend to
create the spirit of revenge in the People. 'Tis strange
and certainly impolitic that they should have given in to
this. A Peasantry may be quieted by the influence of terror
where they have no Army to rally to ; where they have,
as now, 'twill be quite otherwise. These Officers are to
bring off the ——— ? of the Mda. Sourda who has assisted
the Enemy, to communicate with Don Julian and return.
Pinhel quitted by the French, the Out Posts patrolled
into it at 12 o'clock.

Aug. 3–5. At the Out Posts. Sir Stapleton Cotton's
Head Quarters at Alverça. The Chain of Posts. . . .
French came into Pinhel night of the 3rd at 8 o'clock.
Their Front Line on the Right Bank of the Pinhel ; their
Left pretty strongly encamped in front of CastelMendo,—
a Battalion at Misquitella and the Peninsula between the
Coa and Noherina occupied, Centre at Valverde and so on
to Pinhel. Their advances on the other bank of the
Pinhel at Carvallal and to the Right and Left. They
conduct themselves with great caution, never sending even
a Patrol without Infantry. Communicated by Telegraph
with Cox at Almeida. The Enemy has not opened the
Trenches. He surrounds the Town out of Gun-shot.
The immediate Corps in sight is about 5,000 Men. All
well, but run out of Firewood, Signified the Marshal's
orders to him that if Firewood failed he must use the
Roofs of Houses. The Marshal's satisfaction at the

accounts in his Letters of the 25th, and 26th July, and our good wishes. Upon the whole it appears at present more like a Blockade than a Siege. Many deserters—scarcity of Provisions in the Enemy's Army. Returned to Lagiosa evening of the 5th.

Aug. 6–7. Harvey and Chapuset returned from the Coa. Very active; the People most willing to rise, and as a first fruit Jose Ribeira, Curate of Villa Mayor, killed yesterday an Officer and five and twenty French Dragoons. 3rd Dragoons at Lagiosa. The Marshal gives them Rifles to complete. The other Chasseurs are attached to Brigades under British Officers . . . and will therefore improve rapidly. 200 Rifles ordered also for each of the Chasseurs 1st, 4th, 6th.

Aug. 8–9. Nothing new. Insurrection going well. Don Julian Sanchez invited to Celorico and employed by Lord Wellington. This is an excellent measure and will ensure the best intelligence. The Enemy is very tardy. He waits for the arrival of Bonaparte, or perhaps waits for his Birthday (15th August); more probably than either, he has no provisions.

Hatchets enough found at Coimbra to complete the deficiencies in the Beira Army,—ordered up.

Shoes to the 1st and 3rd Chasseurs.

Aug. 10–11. The Portuguese Cavalry in the Out Post Skirmishes are behaving well . . . officers in the Tras os Montes, . . . and near Atalaya have distinguished themselves and their Regiments by great coolness and good conduct, and in both instances succeeded against the Enemy completely. Silveira blockades a Battalion in the Castle of Puebla da Senabria. These will fall in a day or two if not relieved.

Aug. 12. The Insurrections going on very well. Harvey very active. Silveira a little too much inclined to commit himself with Serras the French General. Marshal wrote to him express to be cautious. Promotions from the Brazils,—the Marshal's resistance!

Aug. 13. Desertions from the Enemy everywhere gaining ground. Loison and Mortier very ill. The Battalion in the Castle of Puebla de Senabria surrendered on the 10th to Silveira. The Enemy has made no movement.

Aug. 14. Silveira writes that he has taken up his

position of Bragança. Serras faintly pursued about 1¼ leagues and then retired.

Aug. 15. An almost incredible report brought to the British Head Quarters at Celorico, by a Commissary, that the French have pushed a Corps of 4,000 Men over the Coa to Villa Nova de Foscoa. Sent out Flagini for the Marshal's satisfaction, but there can be no good foundation for this Report, or if there be our Out Posts at Carejo are asleep.

Letter to Dubrawa ordering him from d'Essada Cista into the angle of the Druro and Coa, by the Marshal's Order. One would have rather wished him to remain, for he gets excellent and early Intelligence where he is, and where he is going he'll get none.

Aug. 16. There is an appearance of an Assembly upon the side of Puebla de Senabria. Thomier has marched from the Lower Tormes upon Ledesma, as a part of this. They feel the loss of their Squadron and Battalion, and mean to attempt a Revenge upon Silveira. The utmost they can intend, and I should think the very utmost they can effect, is to get him out of Bragança; this they may do, and send him for a time to the Right bank of the Tua.

Aug. 17. Accompanied the Marshal General and the Marshal to the advanced Posts. Pack's Brigade at Trancoso. Almeida was firing fast upon the Enemy's approaches. Telegraphed that the Enemy had not as yet opened any fire but occasional Musquetry, but that his works were nearly complete and that his fire would probably open tonight or tomorrow morning.

The Enemy seems to be collecting every possible means for the attack of Almeida and to be proceeding in Form. He is making great preparations in provisions and ammunition, and according to all accounts of Deserters, the daily Working Party for the Parallels is 6,000 Men. This for the first time looks like the coming of Napoleon in person ; why do they wait else to besiege a Place at a great expense of time, now becoming very precious, when the possession of it, though without doubt desirable, is certainly not essential to their attack upon Portugal. If he comes he has ensured the power of bringing Reinforcements, for he will not risk either his Fame or his Safety in an attack, personally conducted, upon Portugal unless he is at the head of greater means than those now wielded by Masséna.

As Almeida is made so serious an object, and as there will be an enormous collection of Artillery and Stores before it, it is very probable that Lord Wellington, who now having Genl. Hill within reach, is strong, will make a movement to relieve the Place, and get possession of or destroy them.   I should be tempted to think that a movement, turning the difficult part of the Coa, with our Right and Centre, consisting of the principal part of our force (including Genl. Hill) then marching down the River along the Right Bank and driving in the Post upon the Pinhel River with our Left, which must afterwards advance to the Coa, watch it, so as to secure our Left and then act according to circumstances, I should think, I say, that such a Movement well combined and rapidly executed, would make us Masters of their Siege Stores and Artillery, and beat their Besieging Army   A very few Marches would strike this blow and the Army can well fall back again upon the Line of Sabugal, Guarda and Celorico, if upon a very near approach appearances should ultimately bespeak the actual attempt too full of risk   Nor will the Retreat upon the same line be a bad one, if any unfortunate event should make it fail in the execution.

The Desertion of the Enemy increases and the Disgust of all Ranks of his Army at the War and its fatigues and privations is at a height that cannot fail of being very embarrassing to him.

Returned to Lagiosa.   A Mail going to France intercepted by a Spanish Guerilla, and sent in to the Marshal. The Letters from the Ministers and Principal Officers of the Army give such a description of the wants and miseries of the Government and the Armies.   Of the determined and inveterate resistance of the Spaniards, of recent losses in consequence in the South, and of a strong sensation lately felt at Madrid connected with a design upon the person of Joseph, that all we have believed and collected for some time past of the melancholy aspect of French Affairs in the Peninsula is fully confirmed, and the total want of Provisions, Money, and resources of every kind are likely to fulfil all that we have looked forward to of the Enemy's ultimate failure.

Flagini reported the French Party only one of plunder, 600 Men returned across the Coa.

Aug. 18.   Forward   movement   ordered.   Necessary

Directions given for what concerned the Portuguese Troops.

Aug. 19.   Movements made. . . .

. . . Eagle of the Swiss Battalion arrived.

Aug. 20.   Sent Dr. M. Forjaz the state of things by the Marshal's orders. Serras retired from the Tras os Montes Frontier. Ballasteros defeated in the Sierra Morena. Division dispersed. Romana obliged to retire. Ballasteros advanced contrary to the order of Romana and the misfortune seems to have been the consequence.

Deserters increasing—54 to Silveira in one day. Movement continued. . . .

Head Quarters British, Alverça. The Head Quarters don't move till tomorrow—sent to take up the Marshal's. Marshal Beresford—Avellar de Ribeira.

This day a continuation of the movement was ordered for tomorrow but late in the evening countermanded, and the Army remain as by this day's distribution.

Aug. 21.   Lord Wellington's Head Quarters to Alverça, Marshal Beresford to Avellar de Ribeira. Sent orders to Baccelar to Occupy Torre de Moncorvo and João de Pesquera with the Oporto Division under Col. Trant. A Battalion in Freixo de Namão and Villa Nova de Porocoa. A Company of Cavalry at Meda or in the neighbourhood communicating with Trant, and watching the Front and Right. The Minho division under B. Genl. Miller to Villa Real and Lamego. Orders to the Intendent of Provisions accordingly. Dubrawa ordered back again to Freixo d'Espada Cista. I hope he will not have moved.

Aug. 22.   Marshal at Trancoso and Meda. Almeida firing fast. Batteries not opened. Cox telegraphs that some embrasures are opened. The Deserters give out that the Batteries will open the 25th and that the Fire of the Garrison has already killed and wounded 800 Men.

Aug. 23.   Following Movement and Distribution :—
Almeida firing very heavily.

Aug. 24.   Batteries not yet opened upon Almeida. The 3rd Division near Villa Franca and the Troops more closed up than herebefore. Additional orders and instructions to Baccelar for his Guidance in defending the Ground from the angle of the Coa and Douro to Lamego. Romana's Head Quarters at Salvatierra—Advance at Zafra—

Guerillas at Bicnorda—Ballasteros assembling his scattered Division at Xeres de los Caballeros.

Head Quarters of the French Division at Leiria—Cantonments Berlaya, Valverde, Villa Garcia, etc.

Aug. 25. Heavy fire from Almeida in the morning and some shells thrown in by the Enemy. The Governor telegraphed that the Batteries would open to-day certainly.

Aug. 26. Almeida fired rapidly all the middle of the night and again for half-an-hour before day-break. At twenty minutes past five in the morning the Enemy opened his Batteries upon the Place. His Firing heavy and quick, but the fog so thick that it was not possible to distinguish how much of it belonged to the Town.

The Consul at Corunna writes of a Diversion in the Northern Provinces and Silveira sends some intercepted Correspondence which looks like a March by Serras upon the Tras os Montes. Dubrawa writes some accounts that look like this.

Arrangements made for the next Convoy of Sick to the Rear,—to reach Coimbra September 5th.

Aug. 27. This morning the firing from and upon Almeida ceased at 8 o'clock and the silence has continued through the day; a heavy explosion took place in the Town last night (7 P.M.).[1] The Church has been knocked down, and the place on fire. The appearance is suspicious, and although it is difficult to conceive a possibility of the Town having fallen after thirty hours of open Batteries, yet the general notion is that it has already surrendered. Lord Wellington inclines to this opinion, and determines to place the Infantry again along the Pta. de Murcella Road, so that there may be no jostling or obstruction in their breaking up for the defensive positions heretofore fixed upon. The Cavalry to keep the advance as before the last forward movement.

The following Movements ordered. . . .

Many things short of a surrender may have occasioned the silence which appears to all so conclusive. I must suspend my belief for the present. This night and the morning will show.

12 o'clock P.M. The Town and Batteries commenced firing again at 9 o'clock and have continued till just now. Lord Wellington has suspended the backward movement.

---

[1] Fall took place eleven o'clock in the evening.

Aug. 28. The Town and Batteries ceased firing between 12 [1] and 1 o'clock Lord Wellington and Marshal Beresford at the advanced Posts. The silence continuing till half past 5 o'clock His Lordship considered it certain that the Town was gone and ordered the Movement directed last night to be carried into effect. The Fog so thick that the Town can't be seen.

Between 5 and 6 the Enemy began skirmishing with the Vendada Pickets in the Centre, and soon after on the Right and Left. They pushed in the Videttes with a Reconnaisance of intermingled Infantry and Cavalry, and then retired, not having put back the Pickets. Lord Wellington to Celorico, and the Marshal to Lagiosa, and the following Movement ordered for 24th August.

Movement to take place August 29th. . . .

Aug. 29. Lagiosa.—Deserters who have come in, and a French Colonel of Gendarmerie, who has been taken, make the fall of Almeida certain. It surrendered finally about 11 o'clock yesterday morning the 28th. On the evening of the 27th the principal, and indeed almost only, Magazine having been blown up and the Town in ruins, the Governor finding his Powder almost exhausted proposed Terms to Masséna. The terms he proposed appear to have been rejected and the firing commenced again ; at 5 o'clock in the morning of the 28th it finally ceased, and at 11 the Place capitulated. 'Till one has other accounts than those of French Prisoners and Deserters 'tis impossible to comment upon what we so uncertainly know.

The Enemy's Advance drove in the Videttes at Freixedas yesterday evening, and were for a short time in possession of that Place where they cut down the Telegraph, but were shortly driven out by the supporting Pickets under General Keith, some of them cut up and some Prisoners made ; the remainder fell back and the Chain is as before. Movement for 30th August. . . .

Aug. 30. To the Out Posts. Sir S. Cotton's Day Post Baça Cova ; Night Post Alversa. Picket Freixedas ; Advanced Vidette no further than the Telegraph :—this has been the arrangement since the French advanced the other day to Freixedas. All quiet in Front. Major Gordon went in to the French Posts with a Flag of Truce—Money

[1] See Oman, iii, p. 275, who says Cox was forced to surrender at 11 P.M.

for the Prisoners at Almeida, and a proposal to exchange the French Colonel of Gendarmerie for Cox. The Colonel, Officers, and 400 Men of the Regiment of Arganil Militia came into the Posts this evening from Aldea d'Obispo. The Guarda and Trancoso Regiments (Militia) also taken at Almeida will follow tomorrow. These People with the exception of a working party of 600 Men (200 from each Regiment) have been released and sent back under a condition of not serving again. This is a politic measure on the part of the Enemy,—they get rid of an incumbrance, —send us back people of no use to us and above all introduce hundreds of emissaries of the Marquis d'Alorna into the Country. To make this mischief[1] more effectual this Traitor has spoken separately and individually to each Man and Officer, and preparing them by saying that this grace was accorded to them at his instance, exhorted them to inform their Countrymen of the lenient treatment they received, of his influence with the French Commander in Chief as exemplified in their being sent back at his desire, and putting it to their judgments thereupon whether it is not better to assist as far as they can the French, who only make war against their Tyrants the English and who of themselves are inclined to behave with the utmost mildness to the Portuguese and will certainly do so under his protection and suggestion. This is calculated to do much mischief as the Marquis d'Alorna is popular in the Beira. The unfortunate Peasantry are naturally tired of the miseries they endure and will be easily led to look for an end of them to the French having quiet possession. The Contest should be settled therefore as soon as possible, and the more speedily the Enemy can be induced to advance to the spot where he is to be encountered and made to fight his first General Battle the better. These Officers report that the 24th Regt. and the Troop of the Almeida Dragoons have taken service under the French, with the exception of the English Officers and the Portuguese Major of the 24th. The Enemy appears to exult in this, and plumes himself greatly upon the speedy fall of Almeida. Gordon returned. The Enemy appear to be preparing for the attack of Guarda.

Aug. 31. All quiet in Front. Along the road from Almeida to Guarda, and at Guarda itself, the Enemy has

[1] Quoted Oman, iii, p. 276.

not advanced beyond Pinzio. At 4 o'clock afternoon an order received from Head Quarters to move back the Cavalry at Alverça to the front of Baça Cova. This done at 6 o'clock, and the Pickets left posted till daybreak. . .

Returned at night to Galerda. Beresford at Lagiosa. Movement made 31st. . . .

Sept. 1. He has this day sent to the Marshal some letters going to France, taken near Madrid by a Spanish Guerilla Troop. A letter from Mortier (Duc de Treviso) to Bonaparte asks for leave to return to France on account of ill health, and also on account of a disgust which he freely expresses and accounts for, at the manner in which the Troops of his Corps have been frittered without utility or a prospect of advantage ; he laments the fate of these Troops, left destitute of every thing, scattered all over Andalusia and every day falling victims to the People without ; he speaks with great discontent of Soult, dates the misfortunes of his Corps from the period of his becoming Major General of the Army of Spain, and consequently attributes them to measures suggested by him.

These letters contain also the . . . returns of French losses. . . .

SUMMARY

Thus the Army of Masséna exclusive of the Corps of Reynier amounted in the beginning of July to no more than 37,322 Infantry fit for Duty ; from here must now be deducted all the losses by sickness, desertion, and the Siege of Almeida, for two months up to this 1st September.

Austin writes that a Corps under Genl. Lasci landed at Moguer, near Ayamonte, on the 24th August, beat the Division of the Prince of Arenberg and, seconded by Ballasteros, pursued him closely. This will be an excellent Diversion, and embarras Mortier beyond measure, nor can he now have the Corps at Llerena for operations upon Badajoz. (This turned out afterwards to be a very partial and uncertain success. Lasci re-embarked the day after and returned to Cadiz.)

The 22nd Regt. and the most effective Regiment of Militia at Abrantes ordered to be in readiness for the Field, and the Regiments of Setubal and Alcacer ordered from Setubal to Torres Vedras and Sobral. These replaced at Setubal and Palmela by the Eastern Regiment

of Lisbon.   Thus two Regiments will be gained for the
Zezere, two for the home defences. . . .

Sept. 2.   The Enemy were reported to have driven
back our Cavalry upon Baça Cova, and to be following
it up.   The Marshal communicated this to me at 3 P.M.
in a note from Celorico whither he had gone to see Lord
Wellington, and directed me to move the Head Quarters
to Cortica.   Moved the Head Quarters accordingly.
Night at the Out Posts (Macal de Chão)—all quiet.   The
Enemy came forward at about 11 this morning with 3,000
Infantry and strong in Cavalry.   Our Pickets of course
were forced to retire but they skirmished in the coolest
and most excellent manner, notwithstanding the Enemy's
advantage in having Infantry while we had none.   The
Prince of Salm came in with a Flag of Truce and brought
letters from Cox and the English Officers taken at Almeida.
Masséna has given them their Parole to go to England but
they go by the way of France.

Sept. 3.   Morning.—All quiet in Front.   Enemy retired even from Freixedas.   Returned towards Cortica
by way of Celorico at half past eight.   Marshal Beresford
there.   Head Quarters moved again to Moinerta de Sierra.
Lord Wellington's to Gouveã.

Following Movements take place to-day. . . .

. . . A report of an Enemy's Corps advancing toward
Convilharos.   Harvey and Chapuset sent to watch and
report.

Every thing withdrawn from Guarda but Capt. Cock's
16th Dragoons, with a small *Corps d'avertissement.*   This
movement savours altogether too much of precipitation
and will occasion an alarm, perhaps unnecessary because
the Enemy did not press.   To Moinearta.   Wrote Wilson
by the Marshal's Order to come to Baccelar.   If the
Army of the North is pressed to get into the strongholds
of the Northern Provinces ; if this should by any unforeseen movement of the Enemy be rendered impracticable,
then it must cross the Douro and come to us by Coimbra.

The 140,000 Cartridges intended for the Beira, and on
their way to Baccelar, to be distributed by the Governor
of Vizeu to the Ordenanza of the Estrella and to the Right
and Left of the Mondego opposite Pta. de Murcella.   But
above all to those of the Estrella.   Ordered.

Sept. 4–5.   The Enemy have retired from Sabugal

upon Penamacor, Peragorcia, and Monsanto. Upon the Almeida side they show no indication of advancing, they have not approached Guarda, although there's nothing left there. 'Tis much to be wished there had not been so great a degree of precipitation. This begging the question, this yielding country before it is demanded, can never have a good effect. The Enemy are certainly not so strong as Lord Wellington has thought them, nor have they ever been.

Sept. 6. [1]Upon the 2nd and from that day to the evening of the 4th, 450 Men and 18 Officers of the 24th Regt. came in, having escaped from the French, and arrived at Torre de Moncorvo. Orders to Silveira to unite them at Chaves. Dubrawa facilitated their passage of the Douro at Freixo d'Estada Cinta with his usual activity.

A war between Russia and Austria confidently talked of in the French Army.

Sept. 7–8. No appearance of any advance on the part of the Enemy. Rather an inclination towards the Tagus. It is very probable he will besiege Badajoz, and perhaps Elvas. For these purposes he is strong enough, especially as he knows, from the experience of Ciudad Rodrigo and Almeida, that it is not our system to fight for the preservation of Fortresses, no matter how important. For the attack of Portugal he is not strong enough at present— this he knows well,—better than we do, or choose to do. These Frontier places taken and held, will give Masséna the power of commencing the Invasion with infinite advantages next year,—Supposing him to be reinforced, as he probably will be. There is besides much to do in Spain, which can be attended to during the winter and spring, and in which a part of the Army of Portugal may well be employed. This is the Sure Game and I have inclined to fancy it the probable one from the instant he formed regularly the Siege of Almeida, and he threw away 5 or 6 weeks of most precious time, upon a place by no means essential to him in an immediate Attack upon Portugal. Certainly he is not strong enough now, and it is much to be wished that he may advance with his present force. His destruction ought to be the certain consequence.

The Enemy has formally shot some Guerilla Prisoners.

[1] Quoted Oman, iii, p. 276, footnote.

The Marshal represents it to Lord Wellington.[1] If remonstrating don't succeed certainly we should resort to retaliation. With the French 'tis the only check ; they acknowledge no other barrier to atrocities but the dread of being judged by the *Lex Talionis*.

Sept. 9. Reille's Corps (9 to 10,000 Men) which has been stated to be at Valladolid, and afterwards at Toro, appears never to have been at either, but to have been countermanded and sent to Navarre and Biscay. It appears that Joseph's authority is, or is about to be superseded by his Brother. He dethrones his own family with as little remorse and hesitation as others when they don't answer his purposes.

Lord Wellington replies to the Marshal's communication with respect to the Murder of the Ordenanaes, that he will write to Masséna.

Sept. 10–12. Strong Detachments of Infantry and Cavalry, with some Guns, Ammunition Carts, and Provision Waggons, moved to Idanha Velha and afterwards by Aldea de João Pyrez to Escalajos, then turned towards Sabugal, and finally as far as Roto, 2 Leagues from Guarda. All these successive Movements reported by Harvey and the appearance at Roto by Capt. Cocks who stated them to be in *force*, this I doubt.

Sept. 13. The Enemy who came into Guarda yesterday left it this morning and retired towards the Coa. Several considerable Detachments have been for some days marching to and fro upon all the line between Rosmaninhal and Guarda. This perhaps may be to conceal and feel the way for something serious collecting behind ; a report of Reynier having moved to his Right would appear to countenance this notion, but I should rather think that 'tis only to clear their front from the Guerillas, walk over the line we have left, by way of taking possession, and pick up all the subsistence and plunder that's to be got there.

A Portuguese Captain and Lieutenant of the Almeida [garrison] came in. Their examination annexed—nothing in it.

Sept. 14. Lord Wellington reviewed General Cole's Division near Rosmaninhal. A report from Silveira of Junot and Solignac bending towards Zamora. This may be, but I can't credit it's being in force, or with any serious

[1] See Oman, iii, pp. 34, *et seq.*

intention, Masséna can't spare enough to do any thing
effectual there, unless he weakens himself not only so
much as to give away all power of the offensive, but so as
to throw that power into the hands of Lord Wellington.
However, the giving out such an idea is politic on his part,
for he may calculate upon keeping in check our Northern
Army if he march by the Beira and distracting our attention here if he intend to move upon Badajoz.

Sept. 15.   Three separate Detachments or Corps have
moved from the side of the Parales and closed in between
Alfayates and Guarda.   (Letter of 10th from Mr. Stuart.)
In the evening it was reported to Lord Wellington that the
Enemy had passed through Guarda, and his advance
came to Lagiosa, while at the same time he advanced in
some strength from Freixedas upon Barracal and drove
in General Cotton to Celorico.

This may be the forerunner of a real Advance, and the
closing in of the Corps from the left looks like it.   After
all it may be only a determination to have all the front
of Celorico clear and this would be ensured by the movement upon Lagiosa, as nothing could stay at Barracal
then.   Tomorrow will probably shew.   Meanwhile Lord
Wellington ordered for tomorrow morning the following
movements.

Movements ordered 15th Sept. 1810. . . .

. . . A Lady, not a little suspicious, came in from
the Enemy yesterday, and says, amongst other things,
that Masséna will be at Pinhel today, and tomorrow at
Trancoso.

Afternoon at St. Romão.—Wrote Wilson, Baccelar
and Trant to mention the Advance, the probabilities, to
beg them to look out sharp, and not move till the Enemy
be well drawn on the road to Porta de Murcella.

Sept. 16.   The heads of the Enemy's Columns, or
perhaps more properly to speak, the Enemy's Detachments, in the Val de Mondego, and in front of Celorico,
being reported strong, the Peasants agreeing in their
accounts that many Troops were following, and other
circumstances concurring to make Lord Wellington believe
the Enemy's advance real, at about 10 in the morning His
Lordship withdrew the Cavalry and moved back the Troops
according to the following. . . . Movements for the
16th September (1810). . . .

Sept. 17. The Reports of last night and this morning make out that a Corps is passing by the Right Bank of the Mondego, and were last night at Mangualde. This is said to be Junot with the 8th Corps. The 2nd and 6th are in the Val de Mondego. The Enemy's Advance at Villa Cortez. The annexed Notes give the principal news of this morning.

. . . Wellington to . . . Beresford.

Coa, half past 5 P.M. Sept. 17th, 1810.

. . . I enclose a report received in the night. The Column mentioned as marching upon our left went off by Jasooa yesterday morning, and was at Fornos at about three P.M. It can scarcely have got as far as Margualde last night. It can have no Guns with it, and the Prisoner says that Junot has marched upon Oporto, which I conclude means upon Moinerta from the lower part of the Coa ; and this column is intended to keep up the communication with him.

You should order all your Sick away from Coimbra at all events ; and send people down to be in readiness to remove or destroy your Ammunition, and other Stores there without loss of time. I am going to give similar orders.

Ever Yours, etc.

(P.S.)—I have ordered every thing to be prepared for a short move in the afternoon if the Enemy then should move. The whole of the 2nd and 6th Corps are in the Valley of the Mondego.

I write another Report from Walters.

Received 8 o'clock morning of the 17th Sept. at St. Romão.

Copied by Order of M.G. Anson.

8½ P.M. 16th Sept.

' A French Column has marched on our left consisting of Cavalry and Infantry, seen marching by my Patroles, and are actually in Camp near Mangoalde.'

T. S. ARENTSCHILDE, Lt. Col. 1st Hussars.

Forwarded by Genl. Cotton to Lord Wellington at 1 o'clock.

Sept. 17. The Stores and Sick ordered from Coimbra to Figueira,—the Biscuit there to Miranda de Corvo. Flangini sent to Raina and Foz d'Alva to turn back the Rifles and Stores and if practicable send the former to Thomar. Heavy Bureau to Thomar,—Civil Departments beyond Puerta de Murcella. Nixon take care of himself and retire upon Thomar.

Movements to take place 17th Sept. . . .

Sept. 18. By Report of last night it appears that the 2 Corps in the Valley of the Mondego have followed the Advance, and that the whole, therefore, now moves by the Right of the Mondego,—if this be the case it makes Lord Wellington's game a much simpler one than he expected. Instead of being distracted by the uncertainty of the Line of the Enemy's approach, who had his choice of Three or Four Routes, he will now only have to look to one and fight upon whatever part of that he likes best.

Movements ordered last Night. . . .

Head Quarters of the Army Cortica ; Marshal Beresford's Carapida. Evening at Carapida.

Leith's Division moving up to the Puerta de Murcella and that of Hill, with the exception of Lecor, to come down also by the Pampilhosa Route,—this he may safely do for all Reynier has joined Masséna by the Road of Guarda. This Corps is that which moved by Detachments along the line between Rosmaninhal and Guarda.

If the Enemy thinks to be before hand at Coimbra he will be disappointed, for today there will be two Regiments there, and tomorrow 6 Brigades. If he actually moves altogether by the Right Bank, *à la bonheur* we can meet him in the strong position about Mortagua (Busaco). The Troops are well laid to cross the Mondego. The Coimbra Division will become the Reserve. A part of Leith or Hill will take care of the Puerta de Murcella and all is in the natural order of march. . . .

Sept. 19. Head Quarters ordered to move from Cortica to the Convent of Lorvao and from Carapida to Botão. Lord Wellington did not move, however, and the Marshal remained for the night at Murcella.

The passing of the whole force of the Enemy to the Left Bank of the Mondego is ascertained. The following Movements. . . .

Sept. 20. The Marshal to Botão. Baccelar ordered to form an Advanced Guard for Wilson, of two Battalions of Grenadiers and two Battalions of Chasseurs of the Divisions of Miller and Silveira, and three Squadrons of Cavalry. Wilson written to to act immediately with his advance upon Vizeu and Tordella. Following Movements ordered for tomorrow :—

Movements . . . 21st September. . . .

Sept. 21. The Bridge over the Criz leading from Sta.

Comba Dão was blown up yesterday and General Pack's Brigade remained watching the Criz; this morning the Enemy were observed forming in two Columns, altogether about 20,000 Men, on the opposite side of the River. When the Columns were closed our General according to Orders withdrew his people, and the Enemy retired. Cavalry Pickets in front of Barril. 4th Regt. of Caçadores in Barril, Videttes of the Cavalry observing the River, and the Brigade of Pack and Division of Craufurd in the Town of Mortagua. Cavalry behind Mortagua. Head Quarters :—Lord Wellington—Convent of Bussaco :—the Marshal—Sta. Eufemia.

Sept. 22. Lord Wellington at the Out Posts and the Marshal. About 11 o'clock, about 1,500 French Infantry came over the Criz and began to take post on the heights between one and two. Loison crossed the River and reconnoitred from a Height in front of the Bridge for some time. He sent in a Flag of Truce, and the Enemy kept the heights on this side the River at Nightfall.

Sept. 23. Mr. Thomas ordered to bake biscuit instead of Bread, and to get 20,000 Rations of Biscuit for immediate use. It is impracticable to introduce regularity into the issues and arrangements of a Portuguese Commissariat, and altogether a hopeless case.

Sept. 24. In the morning at half past 8 the Enemy shewed a few Squadrons and a Battalion or two of Infantry about Barril and began skirmishing with our Pickets of Cavalry on the Right at ¼ before 9—these retired to the skirts of the plain of Mortagua and the skirmishing ceased.

About 2 o'clock two Columns of Infantry and one of Cavalry appeared from the Groves behind Barril, and at 3 o'clock came down into the Plain in front of Mortagua. They were deployed and appeared to be 6 Battalions of Infantry and three Squadrons of Cavalry. Some detachments of Infantry were sent out to our Right *en Tirailleur*, and then at a little before 4 their Cavalry advanced. Pack's Brigade attended to it with the Mountain Guns. Our Pickets retired upon the Light Division formed in Echellon of Brigades upon the Heights of Mellejozo; our Skirmishers[1] were pushed back upon their Picket by the Enemy's Cavalry, and when they had reached it, it charged

[1] See Oman, iii, p. 356, footnote.

and dispersed his advance though superior in number, sabred 8 or 10 and took about the same number of Prisoners. The Enemy's Cavalry retired at half past 5, but threw some Infantry into the woods on the Right of the Mortagua Road. The Light Division Bivouacked upon the Heights of Mellejozo.

Sept. 25. At about half past 10 in the morning when the fog cleared the Enemy appeared in force having a Column upon each of the Roads leading from the Criz to Mortagua,—at 12 the Heads of his Columns of Infantry having reached the lower falls leading from the Mortagua Valley, he pushed forward his Cavalry,[1] and began to skirmish with our Pickets. It not being the intention of Lord Wellington to dispute this Ground but rather to do everything that might entice Masséna to follow and attack him in his Position of Boçaco, the advanced Division was gradually withdrawn, the 95th and 43rd covering its retreat and Capt. Ross's Horse Artillery acting upon the Enemy's Advance from hill to hill; at 5 the Enemy was halted by the fire of the 43rd Regt. above the Village of Sulla, and at about 6 o'clock the firing ceased and the whole advanced Division, as well as General Cole's had taken up their Ground upon the heights of Boçaco. (Heretofore at Moura and Sulla.)

Sept. 26. The Enemy shewed some force in front above the village of Sulla, and on his left above and below St. Antonio de Cantaro. He appeared about 15,000— but the gorges and broken ground might well conceal troops and therefore 'tis most likely we don't see all he has up. Towards the middle of the day a few shots from the Position Guns on either side, and in the evening a sharp Skirmish with our Pickets on the Right in front of Sto. Antonio de Cantaro. The Pickets of the 88th Regt. and three Companies of the 4th Portuguese Caçadores behaved very well, and repulsed and drove back the Enemy.

BATTLE OF BUSSACO[2] (BOÇACO)

Sept. 27. The Sierra de Boçaco, a ridge extending from the Mondego to a little beyond the High Road from

---

[1] Quoted Oman, iii, p. 357, footnote.
[2] An excellent map, drawn by a Portuguese officer, is enclosed but not reproduced here.

Coimbra to Vizeu, is as strong as any ground can well be, and affords a most excellent defensive Position for checking an advance from Vizeu upon Coimbra by the Right Bank of the Mondego ;—all the Roads from the Criz and the Dão cross it, excepting two which crossing the Sierra de Caramula, turn its left and enter the high Oporto Road at Avelans and Sardão. It is evident, however, that the three Corps d'Armée of the Army of Portugal are now in the Valley before us, and too far advanced to have any other intention than that of forcing their way by the Roads crossing the Sierra de Boçaco. Lord Wellington last night put the Divisions of Hill and Leith at Pena Cova and St. Miguel de Payeres, and that of Sir Brent Spencer at Mealheada in march, and they have this morning arrived. These Corps were left within one march of Boçaco, but yet sufficiently near to the Mondego to have been rapidly thrown back to the Puerta de Murcella in case of Masséna's again taking that direction, or upon Coimbra in case of his passing by the Caramula to Sardão and Avellans.

The General Order of Battle now stands thus :—

1. Lt. General Hill's Corps on the Right near the Road which proceeds from Foz d'Alva through Gondelim and Vozeiras and crosses the Sierra de Boçaco to Allagoa and Botão.
2. M. General Leith's Corps on the left of General Hill and reaching nearly to the Road which proceeds by St. Antonio de Cantaro, crossing the Boçaco to Palheiros and so to Botão.
3. M. General Picton on the left of M. Genl. Leith across that Road, and his left extending nearly to the foot of the steep fall from knoll of the Convent Garden of Boçaco.
4. Upon this knoll, on the left of Genl. Picton, the Reserve or 1st Division of the Army under Sir Brent Spencer, 2nd in Command.
5. On his left the Brigade of Genl. Pack, its left upon the Convent Garden Wall, in the prolongation of the Eastern Front of which and extending beyond the high road of Vit to the front of the Chapel of Santa Anna dos Alvas.
6. The Portuguese Brigade of B. Genl. Colman. The

wall opposite the only assailable gorge is lowered to fire over, pierced with loop-holes, and forms an excellent Breast-work for the Troops behind it.

7. On the left of Genl. Colman the Light Division under B. Genl. Craufurd, extending a little beyond the hill above Moura.

8. On the left of the Light Division the Portuguese Brigade of Brig. Genl. Campbell and on his left and closing the

9. Line the Division of M. Genl. Cole (4th Division).

From the nature of the Ground on the left the Light Division forms a Reserve and Second Line to the Brigade of Campbell and the Division of Cole and even should the enemy succeed in forcing the extreme left, these Troops have an excellent Retreat, under the protection of Genl. Craufurd, and in their turn become a reserve and second line to him upon the heights of the Chapel of Sta. Anna dos Alvas.

The Division of Sir Brent Spencer can equally render support to Right or Left, for either of which purposes its situation is admirably calculated, and a Regiment of Heavy Cavalry (3rd Dragoon Guards) is under the Southern wall of the Convent Garden and in case of anything forcing its way through the Brigade of Pack, will fall upon it in flank,—for the Ground is so favourable that a charge executed here will probably destroy whatever is in its way. All was ready before day-break, and at the dawn, some Batteries were observed that the Enemy had established in the Night, during which also he had brought down his Columns of Attack into the Valleys.

At about ¼ past 6 he attacked at once the Left of the Centre under General Craufurd, and the Right of the Centre under the Generals Picton and Leith. These were both heavy Columns, and came up the hill very gallantly, but their fate was the same and speedily determined. The Light Division upon their Right Column approaching the crest of the hill, advanced—gave them one volley and then charging, drove them to the bottom in the utmost confusion, wounding and taking Prisoner General Simon who led the Attack and almost annihilating the Column. This Column consisted of two Divisions and was composed of the best Troops of the 6th Corps which formed their

Right Wing. The Enemy's Left Column was composed
of three Divisions principally of the Corps of Reynier,—
it attacked by the Gorge opposite St. Antonio de Cantaro,
and was like the other driven down again and almost
entirely destroyed or dispersed by the Division of Genl.
Picton, and a part of that of Genl. Leith. This Attack
as the ground was weaker was pushed further by the
Enemy and longer contested than that on the Left; a
portion of the Column, in consequence of having advanced
along a Channel of the Gorge where they had not been
observed on their ascent, gained the summit of the hill and
consequently the advantage of the Ground, but notwithstanding this the 88th British and 8th Portuguese Regiments under the Lt. Colonels Wallace and Douglas advanced
against them firing up the hill, took them at length in
flank and then charging, drove them to the Bottom,
bayonneting great numbers. The repulse upon both
flanks was complete and decisive, and was completed by
$\frac{1}{2}$ past 7 o'clock. Two Guns (9-pounders) which were
placed by Lord Wellington himself, and which flanked this
attacking Column, were of infinite use, crossing their fire
with that of Major Arentschilde's Guns attached to Genl.
Picton's Division, and making great havoc. All the Regiments engaged behaved most excellently, and the Portuguese in this their *Coup d'essai* have proved themselves
very gallant Troops. The Regiments that had particular
occasions to distinguish themselves were the 9th British
and 8th Portuguese of the Division of Leith; the 45th
and 88th British of that of Picton; and the 43rd, 52nd,
95th and 3rd Caçadores of the Division of Craufurd.
Also a wing of the 19th Regt. of Colman's Brigade under
Lt. Col. McBean.

The Artillery of Arentschilde was excellently served,
they dismounted 3 of the Enemy's Guns and blew up two
of his Tumbrils.

There was some reason to expect that about the middle
of the day when the Enemy had cooked and dined, he
would attack again, but this did not take place. A good
deal of Skirmishing and sharp firing *en tirailleur* took place
with the Enemy in the Fir Groves to the Right of Moura,
and the 4th Caçadores, and Light Companies of the 1st and
16th Regts. behaved well.

The Enemy's killed and wounded probably amount to

8,000 Men.[1]—ours to 1,000. Lord Wellington's arrangements, presence of mind, and coolness in the Field are
admirable.

Sept. 28.   There was every reason to expect a general
and persevering attack this morning, for it has not been
the habit of Masséna to give up his point. Towards day-
break appearances were suspicious for instead of becoming
fainter the Enemy's fires became brighter. At 8 o'clock
he was discovered in March and by 11 o'clock was evidently
retiring. This is probably either to go to his left, recross
the Mondego and recommence his operations on the Left
Bank, or to his Right by the Caramula into the high
Oporto Road and after turning this Position either march
upon Oporto, refit, refresh, and content himself with the
North for the Winter, or come down upon Coimbra, and
try to force his way to Lisbon. In either case Lord Wellington is prepared. General Fane will report from the Right,
and Sir Stapleton Cotton is gone to the Left with the
Cavalry. The Commander-in-Chief therefore waits intelligence and will act accordingly.

Sept. 29.   Reports from Sir S. Cotton arriving at 10
o'clock appear to ascertain the Enemy's decided march
upon Sardão and Avelans. The following Destinations
therefore assigned for the Troops, and Halting and Re-
freshing discretionary, they will tomorrow be as follows.

Distribution of the Army . . . 30th September . . .
Head Quarters, Coimbra.

Thus we are again prepared for him and his wiles won't
gain him a single march. Should he turn upon Oporto
with his Army weakened as it is and no doubt proportion-
ately disheartened, Trant, in retiring will destroy the Bridge,
and if Lord Wellington choose to follow, with the British
Regiments (94th, 71st, 76th) now on the march, which will
trebly supply his late loss, Wilson and Baccelar at the
same time closing in by the Mountains of St. Pedro de Sul,
what may be the fate of the ' Spoiled Child of Victory ' ?

The Light Division and the Hussars remained at
Bussaco, to watch the Enemy's Rear Guard of 4 or 5
Battalions and 3 Squadrons, which remained; at 8 o'clock
these got into march. Hardinge and myself followed
them with a Patrole of Hussars, they halted on the heights
above Mellejozo. Returned by the front of General

---

[1] See Oman, iii, app. xiii. and xiv.

Picton's Position. The Enemy's loss had everywhere been greater than we imagined. He left many Wounded behind who all agreed in calling his loss 10,000 Men killed and wounded. Two Generals wounded, and one killed, besides Genl. Simon.

Returned to Coimbra. Ordered all stores to Peniche, Sick to Lisbon, Boats to be collected, and Rifles at Miranda de Corvo to the Tagus and Lisbon, by the Marshal's directions.

Sept. 30.   Everything from Thomar and Santarem to Lisbon by the Marshal's order. Wrote Mirada. . . .

JOURNAL V

September 1810–March 1811

WELLESLEY'S RETREAT TO THE FAMOUS 'LINES,' OF
TORRES VEDRAS, FOLLOWED BY MASSÉNA, WHO SOON
DISCOVERED THAT IT WAS IMPOSSIBLE TO ATTACK HIM,
AND ' SO BEGAN THAT GRADUAL RETREAT WHICH WAS
TO END AT TOULOUSE.'

Sept. 30. Coimbra.—Everything ordered to Peniche
near Lisbon with the utmost expedition. The whole of
the Enemy's Force decidedly in march, having entered
the high Oporto Road by Avelans and Sardão.

Movements. . . .

Oct. 1. The Enemy pushed forward an Advanced
Guard of Infantry and Cavalry, drove in our Cavalry from
Fornos and approached Coimbra about 10 in the Morning ;
this was rather sudden and not reported by Sir Stapleton
Cotton, till they were within about two miles of the Town.
The Head Quarters moved in some haste, for Condeixa,
but circumstances rendered it necessary to change that
place for Redinha. Infinite confusion was occasioned on
this day's march from the quantity and irregularity of the
Baggage. Fortunately the Enemy is extremely cautious
in advancing for if he had been otherwise, there is no calculating how far the confusion might have spread. He con-
tented himself with putting two Battalions over the River,
and the March was unmolested. The Baggage continued
moving all night, and by the morning of the 2nd was
tolerably clear of the Troops, though mixed and in great
disorder.

Movements. . . .

Oct. 2. March continued according to yesterday's
arrangement. Less confusion in the Baggage, and things
getting into order. Fortunately the Enemy having

marched over the Caramula without his Guns, and having hastened the movements of his advanced Guard, waits for the arrival of his Artillery and stores, and to concentrate and bring up his Rear, our having marched a day too late therefore will be recovered and our confusion and disorder lead to no bad consequences excepting that the Portuguese Regiments have lost more discipline in three days than they'll recover in three weeks. This has been a striking lesson.

Movements. . . .

Oct. 3. The Enemy's Outposts are still but little advanced, and we shall get into our proposed Positions in good time and without hurry. If he do not unfortunately content himself with the North, but follow us up, a short time will probably conclude the career of the Army of Masséna.—We become stronger every day,—British Regiments meet us,—our Positions are prepared, our Resources near. The very reverse of all this is the case of the Enemy. The decisive Battle will probably be an obstinate one, but everything warrants the sanguine hope of its being in favour of England and of Justice. For Masséna there is no mean between Success and Destruction. For him if he be defeated there is no Escape. Severe punishments inflicted upon all stragglers and Marauders and every means taken to collect and concentrate the Troops and to push the Baggage forwards.

Oct. 4. The Enemy not having advanced the Army halts to-day, and order is restoring. The Portuguese Commissariat infamous beyond all description.

Movements . . .

Oct. 5. In the middle of last night Major Gordon, who had gone in from Lord Wellington with a Flag of Truce, returned. The Enemy's advance was at Redinha, his Vedettes near Pombal, and the thing altogether so far indicated an advance that Lord Wellington ordered the following Movements. . . .

Head Quarters—Alcobaça.

Leiria 5th Oct. These Movements took place accordingly and the confusion which the March had hitherto worn is got rid of. Movements. . . .

Head Quarters.—Rio Mayor.

Oct. 6. Some Charges of the Cavalry Pickets. Capt. Cocks of the 16th Dragoons distinguished himself. The

Enemy got within Case-shot range of Capt. Ball's Guns, and
suffered considerably.—Yesterday the 5th near Leyria.
Movements as ordered yesterday made.   Movements. . . .
    Head Quarters.—Alemquera.
    The Corps of Genl. Hill was yesterday at Santarem.
    Foolish conduct of a Pt. of the Regency.   Pc. de S. and
the P.   These wretches are beyond belief.

Lord Wellington now organized the Anglo-Portuguese
Army after a manner peculiarly his own, different from the
formation of any other modern army, and closely resembling
the Roman Legion.   He distributed it into divisions of about
6,000 men respectively, each having all the component parts
of an Army, and thus becoming independent and capable of
taking care of itself.   One of these Divisions, usually commanded
by a Lt.-General, consisted of Artillery (Cavalry where the
country admitted of its use), Riflemen, Light and Heavy Infantry and an Engineers' Commissariat, Medical, Quarter
Master-General's and Adjutant-General's staff, and was thus
an Army in miniature, which could be adventured to make a
separate movement by itself :   a most judicious formation
indeed, which manifested the Simplicity and Genius of a master
of his art.   It afforded great facility of action, and may be
considered the mainspring of the admirable movements which
distinguished the Campaign of this Great Captain.

The Commander-in-Chief this day ordered the following
new arrangements for the Divisioning [1] and Brigading of
the Army.
    Rio Mayor, October 6th, 1810.
No. 1. The Regiments are to be arranged in Brigades and
        Divisions as follows until further Orders :—

    2. The 50th 71st, and 92nd are to form a Brigade
        under the Command of M. Genl. Sir William
        Erskine, and to be in the First Division.
    3. The 94th are to be in a Brigade with the 2nd
        Battalion 5th and 2nd Battalion 83rd under the
        Command of the Senior Officer till further
        Orders.   This Brigade is to continue in the 3rd
        Division.
    4. The 79th are to be in General Cameron's Brigade
        and in the First Division.
    5. The First Battalion Fusiliers, and the 61st, and

―――――――
[1] See D'Urban's annotation to Jones's *Account*.

the Brunswick Infantry are to be in a Brigade together under the Command of the Hon. Col. Packenham, and to be in the 4th Division.

No. 6. The 5th Division of Infantry is to consist of B. Genl. Hay's Brigade, and of a Brigade of British Infantry composed of the 1st Batt. 4th, 2nd Batt. 30th, 2nd Batt. 44th under the Command of the Senior Officer till further Orders, and of Brigadier General Spry's Brigade of Portuguese Infantry.

7. The 6th Division of Infantry is to be Commanded by Major General A. Campbell and is to consist of M. Gl. A. Campbell's Brigade of British Infantry, and Baron Eben's Brigade of Portuguese Infantry (8th Regt. L.L. Legion).

8. Col. Packenham's Brigade, M. Gl. Campbell's Brigade, and Baron Eben's Bde. are to be continued with the several Divisions with which they are now marching till opportunities offer of forming the Divisions, in the meantime the Commissary General will make arrangements for placing a Commissariat Staff with Sir William Erskine's Brigade to be added to the 1st Division.

Army

1st Division.—Lt. Genl. Sir B. Spencer.
2nd   ,,   Lt. Genl. Hill.
3rd   ,,   M. Genl. Picton.
4th   ,,   M. Genl. Cole.
5th   ,,   M. Genl. Leith.
6th   ,,   M. Genl. A. Campbell.
Cavalry.—Lt. Genl. Sir S. Cotton.
Artillery.—B. Genl. Howorth.
Light Division.—B. Genl. Craufurd.
Chief Engineer.—Lt. Col. Fletcher.
Quarter Master Genl. Col. Murray.
Adjutant Genl. M. Genl. C. Stuart.
Commissary Genl. Mr. Kennedy.

Oct. 7. . . . Rains commenced to-night. La Romana in march for the Tagus. Enemy's advance this morning at Cavalhos.

Oct. 8. Movements for to-day. Head Quarters.—Aranda. . . . All Sick and Wounded safely arrived at Lisbon—911.

Oct. 9.   Lord Wellington inspected the Line of Defence from Alhandra to Ereceyra.

The Enemy pushed his Advance to Alcoentre.   There his Advanced Squadron of the 14th Chasseurs à Cheval was charged by the 16th and its Colonel Le Febre (son of the Marshal) killed.   Some Prisoners.   No loss on our part.   Rains continue.   Mr. Stuart arrived.   500,000 Rd. Am. 60,000 Fts. to Sacaren.

Oct. 10.   Enemy's advance at Quinta de Torre.

20,000 pairs of Shoes to Alveres.   60 Camp Kettles and 40 B Hooks ordered to the Regiments of Douglas to replace those lost on the 27th at Bussaco.

Mr. Stuart returned to Lisbon.   There the people appear quiet and well-disposed to await and abide by the result of the British efforts.   The Troops were under cover last night.

Distribution. . . . 10th October. . . .

Head Quarters Sta. Quintina close to Sobral.

Enemy's Advance in Alemquer.

The Reserve ordered from Sacaren to [MS. illegible].

Oct. 11.   At about 4 o'clock in the afternoon the Enemy reconnoitred in some force in front of Sobral, and by some mistake were unmolested, our Light Dragoons fell back upon the Infantry of the 1st Division with a rapidity which one would have wished let alone, and afterwards a Company of the 95th who were in the Town and the Vineyards about it abandoned it without a shot ; [1] 'tis difficult to account for all this which must be vexatious enough to the Commander-in-Chief, who aware of the importance of the heights in front of Sobral, must have wished them kept for the present.   Forty-second Regiment the advance for the night.   All the 1st Division alert.

Oct. 12.   In the morning the Enemy were no more to be seen, and what we should never have given up, we were fortunately permitted to reoccupy.   The heights above Sobral were taken up by the 71st and 95th ; and a Company of the 50th in the Town.   A Hussar who escaped from him (the enemy) last night states the Corps to have been 4 Regts. of Cavalry and 8 Regts. of Infantry.   In the night the Enemy with about 6 Battalions retook the heights and the Town of Sobral.

Oct. 13.   In the morning the Enemy made some barri-

[1] Quoted Oman, iii, p. 439, footnote ; likewise entry for October 12.

cades and breastworks of casks and other things. At about 3 in the afternoon there was an Affair of Pickets near Dos Portas in front of Genl. Cole's position.—The Portuguese behaved perfectly well but having charged the Enemy back on his support, and their support being rather at a distance, were obliged to retire,—Col. Harvey commanding the Brigade (11th and 23rd) of Portuguese Infantry wounded,—the loss of his services is a heavy one,—a very excellent Officer.

Oct. 14. The Enemy was discovered to have some Guns behind his Barricades of Casks at Sobral,[1]—between 12 and 1 o'clock, he endeavoured with these and a swarm of Tirailleurs to dislodge Sir Brent Spencer's advance from the lower slopes of the Sobral Hill. He was repulsed in about half-an-hour by the 71st and 95th Regts. and retired up the hill.

A considerable Column marched into Sobral by the Alemquer Road, and a General Officer reconnoitred. They also reconnoitred at Alhandra in the afternoon of yesterday.

Oct. 15. At 4 o'clock this morning Sir Brent Spencer's advance was withdrawn in silence, and the most perfect good order from the foot of the hill of Sobral, and the Villages of Sta. Quintina and its adjuncts, and the Divisions of the Centre and Right occupied a Position determined upon by the Commander-in-Chief yesterday. The Right is formed by Sir Brent Spencer's Division upon the Hill of Zibreira stretching towards the Great Redoubt No. 14. This Division occupies about 1,000 yds. The 3rd Division on the left of the 1st 800 yds. The 4th on the left of the 3rd 1,500 yds., and the 6th on the left of the 4th, closes the left of the Position in the Mountains of Ribaldeira. The two Portuguese Brigades of Campbell and Colman form a Reserve in the Rear of the left, and the 5th Division in like manner in Rear of the Right.[2] Each individual Division has besides more than sufficient Troops to occupy the space allotted to it, and the overplus will form a Reserve to each respectively. If this Force thus posted beats the attacking Enemy, of which there is little doubt, a Telegraphic com-

---

[1] *Cf.* ' The high water-mark of French conquest in Europe was reached on the Knoll of Sobral on the wet and gusty 14th of October, 1810 '—Oman, iii, p. 436.

[2] Quoted Oman, iii, p. 446.

munication will bring down Hill and Craufurd from Alhandra and Arruda and the affair will be complete. There is much appearance that the Enemy will attack this Position with his whole force. Alhandra is too strong for him to attempt, and Torres Vedras under his present circumstances and the state of the roads, too long a detour for him to make. He cannot well retire, and his distress for provision will it is to be hoped, compel him to bring the thing to a speedy decision. A part of the Northern Army with Miller, Wilson and Trant moved upon Coimbra on the 8th and the whole of the Enemy's Depôt there fell into their hands. All the Wounded of Bussaco,—and a small Garrison amounting to about 4,000 Men. This event, which is already known to the French Army, has occasioned much consternation and dismay. The General of Cavalry St Croix [1] was killed by a Cannon Shot from one of the batteries at Alhandra, in the Reconnaissance of the 13th. This Officer was very highly Prized. (Note made at a subsequent date.—It was from one of our Gun-boats on the Tagus off Alhandra.)

Oct. 16. All quiet on the part of the Enemy; upon ours active preparation. Romana arrived at Aldea Gallega.

Oct. 17. The Enemy throwing up some works; otherwise all still. . . .

Oct. 18. All quiet.—Our preparations completing.— The Deserters give out that the Enemy is waiting for his Guns, and for Bread to be made from the Corn taken in the Corn-country about Golegão. The Regency visited Lord Wellington.

Oct. 19. Still all quiet. Fewer of the Enemy are visible than yesterday, and this morning he withdrew his Guns from the Barricade of Casks near Sobral. It would appear that he is executing some movement, all this however may be feint. Cantonment Distribution. . . .

These Troops though close to their Ground are kept under cover.

Oct. 20. Frequent desertion from the Enemy. Some movements apparent on the part of the Enemy, probably not of much moment notwithstanding they are preparatory to something decided, backwards or forwards, one would think the latter. The former without a Battle would be

[1] *Cf.* Oman, iii, p. 441.

so great a loss of reputation to the French Army, that it is not to be supposed Masséna will incur it.

Trant's details of the affair at Coimbra received;—conducted with much spirit and ability.—5,000 sick and wounded,—80 Officers and M. Flaudin the *Commissaire Ordinateur en Chef* of the French Army fell into his hands.

Oct. 21. Desertion continuing.[1]—No apparent change on the part of the Enemy. Wilson at Leyria on the 19th. 3,000 Spaniards under O'Donnel arrived at Cavalleros.

Oct. 22. Nothing new.—Desertion as usual.—Orders to Baccelar to give Trant's Squadron to Wilson's advance.

Oct. 23. No apparent change in the Enemy, but Deserters and Prisoners all concur in their accounts as to something like a Bridge over the Tagus being worked at, in parts, and the completion pressed. A communication with the Alemtejo cannot be desirable to Masséna whether he retreats without fighting or intends to secure that communication before he fights. In either case a Bridge at Santarem would be a great point gained, for the Ground on the Right Bank here affords Positions to cover the Passage.

Oct. 24–26. Upon these days everything remained perfectly tranquil, the Deserters and Prisoners continued to report a Bridge in preparation, and the Tagus, though not fordable, will be in a few days.

If it were not presumptuous, one would be inclined to think these people are left too quiet, they may detach or do as they please, certainly their posts might be driven in, and their Right made very anxious without compromising our defensive attitude.

Loison is reported to have gone to Thomar with his Division,—this may be either to collect Provisions or provide for a Retreat. Meanwhile Lord Wellington has ordered Wilson to stretch down in that direction to circumscribe and confine the Enemy's parties. If Loison be there, Wilson is too weak to be of use. Masséna had agreed upon an exchange of Prisoners and all the British and Portuguese in his Possession amounting to 30 Officers and 421 men were to have been given to us today for an equal number of his people in our hands,—they were

[1] See Oman, iii, p. 451.

accordingly brought to the Outposts ;—the Enemy made some excuse for defering the exchange and it is of course postponed to another occasion. He is probably about something that he does not wish us to hear about.

Oct. 28–29. All quiet.—The Enemy's detachment at Thomar examining the Pte de Codes and inquiring about the Roads crossing the Zezere and Alva. This looks backwards but unless some corroborating movement takes place 'tis impossible to judge.

Oct. 30. All tranquil. We have been overreached in our exchange of Prisoners. The Officer charged with that duty appears to have given the Enemy our Prisoners back, before he received his in return,—and as might be expected this rascally foe gave back Portuguese stragglers and Captain Mors instead of British Soldiers and the British Officers.

Some fresh Ammunition issued to the French Infantry, 45 rounds a man, probably in lieu of that spoiled in the rain.

Oct. 31. Lord Wellington having received intelligence of Bonnet's having quitted the Asturias altogether, and thinking it possible, though not probable, that he may make some attempt upon the Northern Provinces, has directed new Instructions to be sent to the Army of the North. These were accordingly sent by a Courier of the Adjutant General's to Genl. Baccelar through Genl. Blunt at Peniche, and their purport is to lay Trant's people along from Coimbra to the Vouga, Miller's from Mortagua to Vizen, Silveira where he is holding himself prepared to cross the Douro, and Wilson as near as practicable to Thomar, throwing his Infantry along the road to Foz d'Arone. These Divisions all communicate with each other easily, and are thus so disposed that they can either concentrate Northwards for Bonnet or Southwards should Masséna retreat.

Nov. 1. All quiet. French Cavalry ordered to hold itself in readiness for a march of 8 days.

Nov. 2. The 15 Battalions under Claparede at Vittoria confirmed. Surely they will not be permitted to join Masséna unmolested, he waits perhaps for these to attack, or for their near approach, to open and prepare his road of retreat.

Don Carlos D'Espagne at C. Branco. Carrera arrived

with the rest of the Spaniards, in all 7 or 8,000, altogether undisciplined.

Nov. 3–6.   Upon these days the Enemy continued to send detachments across the Zezere to Villa del Rey, etc. and to examine the different roads in that direction.   All quiet in his lines and no movement reported or seen. Silveira at Pinhel has surrounded Almeida, driven in their Foragers and Outposts, compelled the Garrison to shut its Gates and in fact placed it in a state of Siege.   Of course no supplies can enter the Town.   Genl. Fane's Cavalry and a Brigade of Guns sent over the Tagus.

Nov. 7.   Marshal Beresford invested with the Order of the Bath by Lord Wellington in the Palace of Mafra.

Nov. 8.   Despatches intercepted at Linhares upon Mascarenhas, a Portuguese Aide-de-Camp of Junot. Account of Bussaco,—tolerably correct,—a little French lying of course.   Silveira reports the march of 2,000 men from Salamanca to Ciudad Rodrigo, the following of 6,000 more, and the arrival at Valladolid of the Advance Guard of reinforcements.

Nov. 9–13.   During these days there was no movement. Letters from the South mention various movements in Andalusia of which the object can't yet be seen;—and letters from the North and East confirm the march and arrival of some reinforcements, at Valladolid, Salamanca, etc.

Nov 14.   Wilson writes from Cabacos on the Zezere that his Quarters were beat up there on the 9th by a superior Force of the Enemy from Thomar.   After some skirmishing and a Manœuvre of Wilson's which imposed on him in some measure he retired.

Nov. 15.   At day-break the Enemy were discovered to have retreated altogether.   In the evening their Rear Guard was at Villa Nova.   Little of their actual intention can yet be seen.   Tomorrow may tell us more.

Nov. 16.   The Enemy is continuing his retreat today, left his rear guard for the night a little in front of Cartaxo,— he left some troops at or near Azambaga, but as he has had some days to complete his arrangements of course there is as yet no disorder in his march.   The Light Division with Genl. Craufurd at Azambaga, its advance between that place and Cartaxo.

By absence of (orders (?)) the Division did not move

M

till 3 o'clock yesterday,—should have moved at 9 in the morning.

Nov. 17. The Enemy were discovered early in the morning, to have withdrawn everything but his Cavalry from Cartaxo ; these were put back, soon after daybreak by Genl. Craufurd, and each post retired, with very little skirmishing, upon a support of three or four Squadrons, near the centre of the plain between Cartaxo and the Ponte d'Ancea.—Sir Stapleton Cotton, Commanding the Cavalry, arrived about 1 o'clock, but the Cavalry not being up no attack was judged advisable. Genl. C., however, determined to make it, but the arrival of Lord Wellington put a stop to what would have had no great result in success, and probably would not have succeeded.

Distribution. . . .[1]

. . . Head Quarters tomorrow at Cartaxo or Santarem.

Nov. 18. The Enemy retired this morning to the left bank of the Rio Mayor and his Rear Guard occupied the lower falls of the heights of Santarem, his Pickets and Posts extended beyond the Causeway Ford ¾ of a League higher up the River,—the Bridge and Causeway on the road *abbatued*. Major Genl. Anson arrived upon our left from the Rio Mayor approach,—General Craufurd early in the morning sent Colonel Elder's Chasseurs to the upper Causeway with a view to co-operating in an attack upon the Enemy's Rear Guard. This, however, appeared so strong by its position that the Commander-in-Chief did not conceive it expedient to attack it with the Light Division only. Lt. Col. Harvey of the 14th Lt. Dragoons patrolled past the Enemy's left nearly to Santarem. The Enemy's force uncertain. The Position, if he be in force, a most admirable one.

Distribution. . . .

Nov. 19. Lord Wellington intended this morning to attack the Enemy's Rear Guard on the left of the Rio Mayor, with the Light Division turning his Right,—Genl. Pack (posted there in the night) turning his left by the Causeway Ford, and Sir B. Spencer to sustain by the high road and advance according to the progress of the flank attacks. The late arrival of the Artillery ordered to Genl. Pack as well as that of the Cavalry, prevented the attack taking place. This may be considered fortunate, for his

[1] See Oman, iii, p. 475.

way over the inundation and swamp was so impracticable,
that his being able to get over at all was very doubtful.
The Enemy appears in greater force than Lord Wellington
at first imagined and therefore defers the attack till
tomorrow, ordering the Distribution 4.

Sir William Erskine's Brigade to Almosteira. B. Genl.
Pack Azambuja. Elder remains at the Ford.

Nov. 20. This morning it is evident that the Enemy is
in force in Santarem,—he has completed an Abbatis along
the whole face of the Upper Heights ; he has reinforced
his Right with a considerable body of Infantry, and it is
now clear that if the attack yesterday had not fortunately
been prevented by the late arrival of the Guns to Genl.
Pack, we should have fallen into the Trap which had been
set for us and sacrificed the two attacking Divisions
probably, certainly that of Pack, not only by *determining*
to believe that a Rear Guard, which was in fact two Corps
d'Armée, and perhaps half of another, but by blindly
making a straggling and unsupported attempt in defiance
of local difficulties and with the Body of the Army at a
distance. Good fortune has supplied what was deficient
on the score of Prudence, and the late arrival of means for
attack has averted the evils that would have followed.

Masséna came to Santarem last night. Genl. Leith's
Division arrived this morning. One Brigade is thrown to
the left opposite the Ford. We must now do, if we attack
at all, what we ought to have done three days ago ;—
strengthen the Pte de Affera and turn the Enemy by the
Rio Mayor and Torres Novas.

Genl. Hill halted at Almeira and he can therefore be
easily got back. Genl. Fane is up to Abrantes. The
heavy rains of last night and this morning have inundated
the whole plain of the Rio Mayor. Flangini gone to
Wilson.

Nov. 21. This morning the Enemy has continued his
Abbatis along the whole face of the Hill of Santarem round
his left flank ; probably Major Stuart's Reconnaissance
into the rear of his left last evening has induced him to do
this. For the rest all is as it was. He skirmishes pretty
sharply with Genl. Anson's picquets in front of Caljeria
towards evening, and shewed some Infantry to Genl. Pack,
who is rather awkwardly posted if he be thought worth
serious attention by the Enemy, having two branches of

the Rio Mayor to cross in his retreat over inundated Causeways.

Nov. 22. Again some skirmishing on the left. Pack withdrawn to Almosteria, upon Sir Wm. Erskine's Brigade, the water having unexpectedly fallen made this movement feasible, and fortunately so, for the Enemy shewed about 6,000 men in his front.

Gazan returned to Seville ; Mortier in movement upon Estremadura with 8,000 men.

Rizonvales who had sailed for the coast of Biscay has returned to Corunna. The object of his expedition having been frustrated by a Storm in which a Spanish Frigate and Brigantine perished, and two English Frigates were left in great danger in a Bay in the Northern Coast.

Nov. 23. This morning the Enemy has withdrawn all that he had in front of Genl. Pack's Post at Azambuja leaving a Picket of Cavalry and Infantry in front of Pero Filho.

Nov. 24. . . . ' Resolved to take no further offensive action and to let famine do its work, Wellington gave orders for the Army to draw back and go into winter quarters.' . . . [1]

Distribution. . . .[2]

The Army thus placed at once takes care of Abrantes, observes the Enemy at Santarem, defends the Passes of the Rio Mayor, has a Division upon the High Rio Mayor Road to commence the March upon the Enemy's Right, should that become expedient, and still appuis itself upon its intrenched Position, Its retreat into which its Echelon Posture secures, should that measure be adopted. Means are ready to pass over Genl. Hill to the Right Bank of the Tagus with such celerity, that his Division can be calculated upon for its order of March or Battle on that side as certainly as if it were already there.

Col. Otway of Genl. Fane's Division reconnoitred the Left Bank of the Zezere yesterday and found a Detachment of the Enemy of about 5,000 men, at and near to Punhete, Villa de Rey, etc. General Baccelar reports from Coimbra that on the 18th a Corps of from 5 to 6,000 men were at Leiria, and that on the same day about 5,000 passed Pintado on their way from Thomar towards Cabacos.

[1] See Oman, iii, p. 478.
[2] ' The allied army is now disposed as follows,' see *ibid.*, p. 478.

These last will thus drive back and perhaps follow Wilson, but their venturing thus to detach will probably expose them with diminished numbers to Lord Wellington's attack should he determine to make it by Rio Mayor and thus turn the Right of their Santarem Position and separate the Army there from its branches at Leiria, etc., etc. Instructions sent to Wilson that if the sudden appearance of the Reinforcements should cut him off from the Mondego, he will throw himself into the Estrella or use his own discretion.

Nov. 25–27. Flangini reports the Enemy at Leiria and many of the adjacent Villages on the 22nd. The Detachment therefore permanently remains there. Silveira has had some success upon the Advanced Guard of the Reinforcements under Claparede in the neighbourhood of Valvada. 300 men, 10 Officers of the Enemy killed. No movement on the part of the Enemy: his expected reinforcements have probably arrived, as certain intelligence makes them to have been at Sabugal on the 19th. They don't probably consist of more than 10,000 men and the greatest part of these are Convalescents who were left sick, belonging to the Army of Portugal when it advanced, and the Garrisons of Salamanca, Ciudad Rodrigo, and Almeida. The whole of these are under Genl. Claparéde and their Advance Guard under Genl. Gardanne were defeated by Silveira on the 15th with the loss of 17 Officers and 400 men left dead on the field. This was a very brilliant exploit; it was done almost entirely with the Bayonet and principally by the 24th Regt. which was taken at Almeida and afterwards escaped from the Enemy. Genl. Drouet (Count of Erlon) commanding the 9th Corps d'Armée had arrived at Almeida before the Reinforcements marched. His Troops relieved the different Garrisons from which those were taken who marched to Portugal, and he himself furnished an additional number from his own Corps which is not under the orders of Masséna. Upon the whole these Reinforcements can be of little weight in the scale, and both in point of Numbers and description would not appear to be much worth the having.

Nov. 29. Movements. . . .

Nov. 29–30. No Change.

Dec. 1–2. No Change in the position of the Enemy between the Rio Mayor and the Zezere, excepting some

appearance of a partial movement on his Right. The
Detachment of Genl. Gardanne, whatever was its view in
coming so far has again gone back and on the 28th was at
Atalaya near Castel Branco,—this Corps perhaps is merely
a sort of Escort to stand mid-way between Drouet and
Masséna and to forward securely whatever Despatches may
have to pass between them.

Dec. 3. ¶Yesterday, although the Coronation of Napoleon and the Anniversary of Austerlitz, passed quietly.

Dec. 4. Upon these days nothing new occurred.
Major Fenwick was unfortunately wounded mortally in a
Skirmish [1] on the side of Alcobaça. Gardanne's Corps
arrived near Ciudad Rodrigo.

Dec. 10. Lord Wellington, thinking it possible that the
Corps of Drouet may intend to menace or perhaps move
upon the Northern Provinces, has directed Provisional
Instructions for the Army of the North. These have
accordingly been prepared, and sent off to General Baccelar
by Express. The General is also directed to drive the
Country between the Mondego and the Vouga without
delay, removing everything to the Right Bank of the latter
River, and this because it would appear from Col. Wilson's
Reports that the Enemy has approached the Mondego and
given indications of a design to pass it.—This is not
unlikely ; Masséna has now pretty well eaten up the plains
of the Tagus, and while he suspends offensive operations,
awaiting the orders of his Court, he will be better off
between the Mondego and the Douro where there is yet
plenty of subsistence ;—he can advance again from there
just as well as from where he is, he can retire better, and
he will be able to make, *en attendant*, an attempt upon
Oporto.

Dec. 11–14. No change.—General Walker writes from
Corunna that all is inactive in Galicia, that it is quite
impossible to stimulate Mahy to exertion and that lately
when he urged the making some attempt upon Drouet's
Military Chest, left at Valladolid under a weak Guard
when that General marched upon Ciudad Rodrigo, the
Spanish Commander answered that his Army had no great-
coats and could not move. During the whole Campaign
from the 25th July when Masséna invested Almeida to the
present day, the Galician Army though furnished by

[1] See Oman, iv, p. 7, footnote.

England with clothing, Money, Arms, and Provisions, has
not made one effort either of demonstration or reality to
create a diversion or in any way give uneasiness to the
Enemy. One might reasonably have expected some effort
however faint, and there have been times when much
might have been done. This Spanish General would
appear to have flagrantly neglected his duty to his Country
and the Common Cause of the Peninsula.

Mem.—No Forage for Arentschilde's Mules at St.
Astoneira. They are sent for the present therefore to
St. Astorio de Tejal.

Dec. 15. Towards evening Sir William Erksine reported from the left that he had seen 6 Squadrons and
three Battalions in movement upon the side of Rio Mayor,
and there was some slight skirmishing with the advance of
his Cavalry. The Troops were held in readiness to move,
but the demonstration or reconnaissance of the Enemy
led to nothing. Very possibly it is a part of some bending
towards Coimbra and the Mondego. He has strengthened
his left, having thrown up a work upon the hill above the
Causeway, and may under cover of his left prepare and
commence any measure of movement upon his Right.
Want of provisions may induce Masséna to go on the other
side of the Mondego. He will sacrifice perhaps only one
advantage of any consequence by this step, that of resting
his Left upon the Tagus, and thus being able to hold out
his hand to anything that may be ordered to come from
the South to co-operate on the side of Alemtejo. In every
other respect he will be just as well between the Mondego
and Douro. Although it is to be considered that in the
event of his advancing again, his Line of Operations will
be rather longer from Coimbra than from Santarem, which
will be material in as much as he must bring all his subsistence with him, for he can't as before feed in the Country
through which he passes, that Country exhausted by two
Armies is quite eaten up and little better than a desert.
These considerations however must give way to the paramount one of placing himself where there is Food and
Forage, and if he seriously wants these before he receives
his orders he will cross the Mondego.

Dec. 16. Blunt reports that the Enemy have shown
from 5 to 6,000 near Pombal, and that some Cannon have
been seen on the Coimbra road.

Dec. 17. A variety of reports corroborating each other, indicate an intention of the Enemy upon the Line of the Mondego. Wilson moved on the 7th and 8th to intercept the Advanced Party at Condeixa; he was too late by a few hours, it had retired upon its support near Pombal.

A letter from Col. Trant reports his having discovered that the Portuguese Government have formed a Depôt at Coimbra of above 600,000 Rations. This is the most unheard of infatuation if it be nothing worse. Two vessels also laden with Rice have arrived in the Prondago and are at Figueira. Yet with all this General Baccelar has never been apprised of it, so that the Divisions of his Army have been starving with plenty near them. Nor has any intimation of such a Depôt been made to the Commander in Chief. One doesn't know what to think of all this, but it is lamentable to have to do with people who either from folly or treachery have taken almost sure means to throw into the Enemy's hands subsistence for his whole Army for 10, or 12 days, while the supplies of our own are irregular and precarious, and inability is alleged by the Government as the cause. Orders despatched by Express to General Baccelar to take immediate measures for the safety of all these Provisions, the means being pointed out, and instructions given for the future.

Dec. 18. Copons has contrived to be again defeated upon the frontier of Algarve and his Division dispersed ;— this is the third time within these few months that he has done the same thing.

The Enemy is at present necessarily rather loosely Cantoned, and our long adherence to a quiet defensive, may be supposed to have lulled him into security and a firm belief that any enterprise against him is out of the question. If the Divisions were speedily closed up to our left, he might probably be attacked by his Right with success. It is not too much to suppose that a part of his Army would be destroyed before the arrival of the other to support it. If beaten he can't get away. He is in a sort of cul-de-sac and his Army is lost. This blow therefore if successful would brilliantly terminate the Campaign and the French cause would have little further to hope in the Peninsula. If we fail the Retreat might be well effected to the Lines, which the Enemy would be too much crippled to attempt. There would be as little risk as any measure of such importance can ever have about it, and there are the most urgent reasons for attempting it. It becomes very necessary that this state of things should have an end, for the complete destruction of the Peasantry by Famine will be the consequence of its continuance as well as the ruin of the better orders. These considerations should have some weight for we are here in the Character of Defenders and Protectors. While the present warfare goes on we can scarcely be justly called either one or the other. Meanwhile the French if they are to remain will certainly be reinforced. Shall we be as certainly ? If not our present relative force points out this as the time for active measures. It would well justify some adventure to destroy the Army of Masséna. The effect upon all Europe, upon France herself even, would be electric. 'Tis difficult to conceive any future occasion so fair as the present. If he stays he will be reinforced. If he is to retire he will take cautious measures and have all prepared before he begins his Retreat, will arrange his previous steps—and his loss, except perhaps some of his Artillery, will very likely be trifling. Upon the whole, while it is his interest and his wish to remain quiet and undisturbed, it must be ours to deny him both one and the other.

Dec. 19. A considerable degree of sickness has appeared in the 4th Regt. and in other parts of Genl. Leith's Division, principally among the Regiments that were at Walcheren, the 3rd Division therefore from Torres Vedras will replace the 5th which will take up the Cantonments of the former.

Movements. . . .

Dec. 20–22. No change. Vague reports of the Enemy having pushed something over the Coa.

Dec. 23. The Marshal went to Lisbon. His presence necessary enough there for the Government with its usual infatuation and folly (if nothing worse) has stopped the payment of subsistence to the Army, and this without a communication of any kind either to Mr. Stuart, Lord Wellington or the Marshal, the latter having only become acquainted with it by the representations of several Brigadiers to whose Corps the issue of pay has been refused. Yet has the Money for the Army Expenditure been received by the Regency, but of course, in its way through the corrupt channels of the Government, has been appropriated to other purposes and hence the deficit. This might be and no great harm done,—'tis only the loss, and a proof afforded that the British subsidy must be applied by British hands,—but the criminal secrecy, the concealment of a want of such importance, situated as the Country is—is not to be endured.

Dec. 24. The Division of Gardanne reinforced, has again entered Portugal to effect its junction with Masséna. On the 14th and 16th it crossed the Coa, and on the 18th and 19th was at Trancoso and Celorico. The Pte Novo near Celorico did not blow up, that of Alamandra did. Baccelar has directed Silveira to follow this Corps. Miller to remain watching events at Vizeu. Trant to take care of Coimbra, and Wilson to march upon Bocase.

Towards evening [1] the Marshal wrote that he must necessarily remain some time at Lisbon, and that his Head-quarters therefore would be provisionally transported there.

If Gardanne's Corps be as reported 9,000 Infantry and 2,000 Horse he may take the Right Bank of the Mondego and the Enemy is immediately in possession of it and all its advantages.

Dec. 25. The Departments moved to Lisbon. Transmitted the Intelligence of the Enemy's Corps. In the possibility of the Marshal's return being influenced by it, retain my Department at Cartaxo. I remain here till I hear from him.

Dec. 26–29. The Corps which has entered is not the Division of Gardanne but the Corps of Drouet, it passed the Pte de Murcella on the 24th and of course has formed its junction. Will its arrival be followed by a Retreat, an Advance, or a movement between the Mondego and the Douro?

Dec. 29, 1811–March 1812.

BERESFORD IN CHARGE OF THE ESTREMADURAN ARMY
WITH D'URBAN AS CHIEF OF THE STAFF.

On the 29th the Marshal received Lord Wellington's orders to repair to Chamusca on the Right Bank of the Tagus, and take the Command of the Right Division of the British and Portuguese Army. General Hill indisposed.

---

[1] See Oman, iv, p. 20.

Dec. 30. Marshal Beresford crossed the River and established his Head Quarters at Chamusca and assumed the Command of the Right Div.

Dec. 31. The Marshal received the Reports, Details, etc., etc. from Genl. Wm. Stewart.

Mendizabal has defeated Mortier's Advance at Larese and Soult has marched from Cadiz with 4,000 men.

1811, *Jan.* 1. Visited the Corps of Don Carlos d'Espagne at Magarida, Baños, etc. and reconnoitred the Enemy's entrenched position at Punhete, and his works of Boats and Bridges in the Zezere. A large collection of Planks, Boats, and Materials, and a good deal of activity in the Yards upon the Left Bank of the River. A large Park of Carriages on the Right Bank, but no Guns to be distinguished. Two only further back than the Park. There is however a Howitzer and a Gun near the Church from which the Enemy fired 4 or 5 times this morning into Arriprada where the Grenadiers of the Regiment of Zamora of Don Carlos's Corps are quartered. No injury was sustained. The preparations in the Zezere may be only to ensure the passage of that River under any circumstances, and relays of Boats and Bridges if those now existing are carried away by sudden rains. They may however have a view to passing the Tagus, at present 'tis difficult to decide what is their drift. Positions fixed on for three Batteries to command the entrance of the Zezere. The Marshal reported to Lord Wellington.

Jan. 2. The Marshal determined upon throwing up works at the three points fixed upon yesterday, and putting two Six Pounders into each. Capt. Wilson, Asst. Q.M.Gl., went over to arrange Commissariat for the Artillery. Capt. Squires, Chief Engineer of the Division, to arrange the Works. Raposo ordered to give Ordnance to him.

Wilson attacked the Rear Guard of the 1st Division of Drouet's (9th) Corps on the 27th [1] near Miranda de Corvo. Took 26 Prisoners. This Division 9,000 men,—reports 2 others following. Silveira reports one of 4,000 men at Pinhel.

The position at Punhete becoming respectable, knolls on the left fortified.

Jan. 3. Capt. Squires having reported the range of 6 Pounders insufficient for the purpose of reaching the

[1] *Cf.* Oman, v, p. 21.

Mouth of the Zezere from the opposite bank,—the German 6 Pounders ordered to Barca and Magarida have been countermanded, and the Portuguese 9 Pounders ordered there in lieu of them, the two German 6 Pounders however already with Don Carlos will remain and be posted opposite Praya.

Jan. 4.   On the Marshal's arrival the following . . . Distribution. . . .

Jan. 5.   Heavy rains commenced,—Tagus rose 7 to 8 feet.

The Sor (or Benavente River) has become impassable, in consequence of which Colonel Campbell's Brigade has not been able to pass to Benavente.   It appears that everyone has been in complete ignorance as to the passages of the Sor as influenced by change of weather.   Lord Wellington had instructed Marshal Beresford upon assuming the Command of the Division, that if the River became impracticable between Salvatierra and Benavente he must cross it, if such a measure should become necessary, at Cornate.   Thence the Marshal conceived that the passage there was a certain one, whereas upon wishing in consequence of the Benavente passage failing to send the Brigade of Campbell by Cornate, he finds most unexpectedly that not only there is no Bridge but that if there were, the plain of the River would be impassable as it is inundated for the breadth of a quarter of a league. There is no bridge at Ponte de Sor, and even if there were, the detour is a very long one.   As it is, Lieut. Forster of the Engineers is ordered to go up the River and search for a practicable place for establishing a Bridge.   At present if it were necessary for the Division to march to the Westward it must turn the sources of the Sor and by consequence march very nearly by Abrantes.   The Enemy is not likely to make any movement across the Tagus, at all events till the arrival of the Army from the South.   If he does this Division cannot retire whatever may be Lord Wellington's wish.   That this inconvenience should not have been previously attended to is the more extraordinary because in the end of November when the Division first came over the Tagus the Rains were heavier than they have now been and of course the evil must have been visible enough.

Jan. 6.   The Enemy continues at work at his Boats, and is probably preparing them for communication with

the Southern Army. I don't think he has any intention
of passing till that is at hand. However he may attempt
it and I think may succeed in carrying Don Carlos's post
and establishing himself on the heights of Barca, unless he
comes in great force, however, we shall drive him into the
River so soon as the Division can be assembled. During
these days the Marshal repeatedly visited the advanced
posts. Lord Wellington sent over Col. Fletcher, the Chief
Engineer, who approved of the sites of the Batteries fixed
upon by the Marshal. The Marshal reported the circumstances of his situation every day to Lord Wellington.
The Government is at length almost without resources in
point of supplies. This is all imbecility or treachery. It
has long been foreseen—long represented—they have been
long and strongly exhorted to no effect. This weak or
criminal negligence will conquer Portugal. Without it,
twice the present French forces would fail in doing it.

Mortier is certainly in motion now. He can't be very
strong though, even with the addition of Soult. If he
advance, this Division, leaving the passage at Punhete
strongly guarded, must of course advance to meet him and
it will beat him if he be not much stronger than I imagine.
Supposing him 15,000—ourselves 11,000. One thing
appears certain, that if we suffer the Enemy to possess the
Alemtejo—*la chose est finie*—we may embark and go
home—or this, or advance and fight Masséna—certainly
the only other alternative is to stand.

Jan. 10. Col. Campbell and Genl. Lumley will be able
to pass at Benavente and the Distribution will stand
tomorrow thus :—No. 3.

The Marshal this day orders Don Carlos to charge himself with the defence of the River, in case of the Enemy's
attempting the passage. The 5th Caçadores at Tramagal
to march to his assistance upon the first alarm and to be
under his orders. The Brigade of Col. Colborne at Arripiada, Carregeira and Pinheiro to do the same. He
commands till a superior British Officer arrives. If
Enemy approaches from the Southward, Bridge of Alvantes
removed to the North Bank.

Jan. 11. Mortier has moved upon Merida which he has
taken possession of. The Spaniards having retired without resistance and the orders given by Lord Wellington
through the Marquis of Romana to destroy the Bridges of

Merida and Medellin, and render the passage of the Guadiana as difficult as possible, having been disobeyed.   This
conduct of Mendizabal is extraordinary enough.   If the
Spaniards don't commence to make severe examples of
their Generals in cases of actual disobedience their Military
measures must all miscarry.

Jan. 12.   There is now no obstacle to the progress of
this Corps of Mortier's and it is to be supposed that it will
do all that it can to effect its junction, or at least communication with Masséna.   His preparations at Punhete still
continue active, and his passing the River is feasible
enough.   When Mortier is within reach, he will probably
attempt it.   As this Division is posted, it can neither move
with advantage to attack him after he shall have done so,
advance to oppose Mortier, nor provide for its own security.

The Benavente River is at length proved to be impassable after Rains, even at Benavente, and the space between
it and the Tagus is therefore a Cul-de-sac, in which we are
so posted as to be of no proportional service to the risk
incurred.

To unite the objects of watching the passage of the
Tagus with that of the approach of Mortier, and to ensure
at the same time the power of retiring upon Aldea Gallega
at any time, and in any weather, our proper Post would be
between Abrantes and Gavião, with a strong Rear Guard
opposite to Punhete, and a good Advance towards Gavião,
or Advance according to Circumstances.   Thus with a good
look out each way, one might rapidly advance a March to
fight Mortier, retire a March to attack whatever crossed
from the Zezere, or retire by the high Alemtejo Road if that
became expedient, while the destruction of the Benavente
and Mugem Bridges would secure against the possibility of
the Corps from the Zezere getting over the Sor.

Having ventured to point this out to the Marshal he
appeared to approve it, perhaps it had already struck him,
but this evening a letter from Lord Wellington by Major
Gordon, of which the substance is in ' Y,' put it out of the
question.   It would be presumptuous to suppose that his
Lordship does not advert to the peculiarity of the Ground,
which nevertheless is such that the disjointed sort of
distribution his directions lead to, will put it out of the
power of the Marshal to oppose any effectual resistance to
anything crossing from the Zezere.   While it will in case

of heavy Rain, which may be expected, give him sufficient
occupation to save his Rear Guard, and pretty well tie up
his hands from doing anything effectual against Mortier.

The Marshal is well aware of all this. However he has
but one course to pursue and this he takes by ordering the
Movement No. 4 for tomorrow the 13th, writing however
to the Commander-in-Chief the disjointed state in which
the Division will be placed and the sort of half measure
that will be the result.

Jan. 13. The Conde de Lumières returned from Lord
Wellington who repeats his wish to have the Division
lightened, that is, a part thrown over the Benavente River,
and the Movement No. 4 therefore takes place, with the
exception of the 13th Dragoons who not having moved
are provisionally halted in their old quarters, the tenor of
a part of his Lordship's letter rather looking like a
possibility of change.

Meanwhile [1] the concurring testimonies of Deserters,
of Observation and of Intercepted letter ' X ' from Drouet
to Claparéde announce some general Movement on the
part of the Enemy to be near. Lord Wellington inclines
rather to imagine that this Movement will be a Retreat,
and that the Retreat will be by the Mondego, to this he is
inclined by Claparéde's being ordered to take post at
Guarda. Supposing the Retreat, the route his Lordship
imagines is certainly very likely and the taking post at
Guarda by Claparéde's Division would well warrant the
idea. But I have my doubts if anything like Retreat has
entered the head of Masséna. Much indeed must depend
upon Mortier's communication, not as to the additional
force he will bring, but in consideration that there will be
thereby established with the Alemtejo an intercourse
which will give to Masséna abundant supplies and enable
him to turn the Siege of the Lines into such a Blockade
that the alternative is upon the cards of coming out of
them to attack him, starving or embarking. Be this as it
may, whether Retreat or Staying be his intention, I am
quite certain the most prudent as well as the most military
step is that this Division should fight Mortier as he advances
and put his co-operation, and Alemtejo supplies out of the
question. The French Retreat will then indeed be made
under a complication of disadvantages beyond all idea,—

[1] Quoted Oman, v, p. 64, footnote.

with nothing to cover his Right Flank,—no supply previous to marching,—no diversion against the efforts of this Corps to turn him. Claparéde at Guarda is nothing. If he intends to stay there, when all hope of Mortier's co-operation ceases,—so must his of success, and his ruin is not far behind.

Jan. 14. Lord Clinton arrived from Lord Wellington in the middle of last night. His Lordship is very strongly impressed with the idea that the Enemy must retreat immediately if he can't communicate with Mortier, and wishes the throwing this Division on the other side the Benavente in order that every measure may be taken to prevent this communication. Col. Colborne's Brigade (Buffs, 2 Companies 5th Batt. 60th, 2nd Batt. 45th, 66th, 31st,) therefore resume after nightfall the Posts they occupied according to No. 3 before the movements ordered yesterday with the exception of the left Batt. of the Brigade (31st) which remains at Chamusca for the moment. The Regiments (2nd, 14th, 5th, Portuguese Infantry ; 4th, 10th, 1st, 7th Portuguese Cavalry ; 6-Pounder Brigade Portuguese Artillery) pushed on to Mugem, Almeiria, Corrucha, Salvatierra, etc. will remain a day for rest and then return. The 9-Pounder Portuguese Brigade which has lost its way and been moving all night, only arriving at 9 this morning from Sta. Margarita, will also remain to rest before it returns.

In the evening the Marshal received letters from Lord Wellington in which his Lordship directs the whole Division to be brought to this bank of the Benavente River, laying aside all idea of lightening, or placing any part of it on the Left Bank, and pointing out to the Marshal's attention the objects of observing closely the Zezere Corps, and intercepting their communication with Mortier, or their establishing themselves on the left bank of the Tagus.

His Lordship at the same time *attributes* this change to Intelligence received from Mendizabal of Mortier being occupied for the present with Olivenza under which plea Romana has required Don Carlos d'Espagna to march to the Guadiana.

Be this as it may, the reuniting the Division is a measure to rejoice in, both partially and generally, and if it be well thrown up to the Head of the Sor, it will answer all the purposes expected of it especially if it be allowed to meet Mortier should occasion serve.

Received the Marshal's orders to have the Division back according to Lord Wellington's desire, and the Distribution No. 5 is therefore ordered. The Orders all setting out for their respective points before 12 P.M. Nothing known, nor any movement on the part of the Enemy, but preparation of Boats continuing in the Zezere.

Jan. 15. A part of the Enemy's Force is certainly occupied about Olivenza. His views for the conduct of this Andalusian delusion are not yet sufficiently developed to allow of a judgment that would have a chance of being correct.

Jan. 17. All the Troops at their Posts according to No. 5.

Jan. 18. No Movement. Part of the Southern Corps forming the Siege of Olivenza, the other at Merida. Reports of this latter marching by Truxillo with a large Convoy of Clothing etc.

Jan. 19. Letters intercepted ' R,' ' S.' They mark very strongly the antipathy, abhorrence, and horror entertained by the French towards the War in Spain. Women are the very Mirrors of Men. (Note:—These letters[1] were from the Duchesse D'Abrantes and Madame Thomières to their Husbands and were taken from a Spanish Peasant endeavouring to reach the French Head Quarters upon the Tagus, 15th Jan. 1811. Originals sent to Lord Wellington.)

Jan. 20. Lord Wellington writes that about noon yesterday 3 Battalions and 6 Squadrons moved upon Rio

---

[1] STATE OF CIUDAD RODRIGO.

One from Duchesse d'Abrantes, 13th Dec., a pathetic letter of domestic news . ∴ ' all my attempts to send you a letter have been ineffectual . . .'

She goes on to describe her position . . . ' inhabiting a tomb surrounded by the dead and dying, deprived of news. . . . I cannot go to my window without seeing cartfuls of dead bodies which they throw outside the town without taking the trouble to bury them, the number of the dead (without counting the inhabitants) is nine a day in a hospital as small as this one is. At Salamanca where it is much larger the smallest number during the past days was forty-two a day. . . .'

A similar letter from Madame Thomières; she had written fifteen letters . . . ' I doubt much if you have received one of them ' (a pathetic tribute to the vigilance of the Ordenanza). . . . ' I could not stay here. They will no longer sell food for the horses or servants. The continual passage of the Troops has emptied the stores.'

Cf. Oman, iii, p. 447.

Mayor. Our post there retired. His Lordship attributes this to an idea upon the part of the Enemy from the movements of the other day that he had reinforced this Division, and that this demonstration is the commencement of a movement of Diversion. The Enemy is still busy about his Boats in the Zezere and has perhaps about 80 completed. I can't imagine his attempting the River till the Southern Army can come near.

Jan. 21. Nothing new.—Beacons established so that the alarm may be very quickly conveyed from Barcas to Mugem.

Jan. 22. To Abrantes.—In going to Abrantes along the bank of the Tagus, it becomes apparent that the difficulty of passing that River must be very great and indeed so much so that [1] it is altogether improbable he will commit himself for the consequences unless in combination with the Army arriving from the South. The stream is very rapid. The Boats cannot return to the original place of embarkation for a second load, nor to the second for a third, but must cross at each time to a point lower down. This must and will occasion great disunion and scattering amongst the several parts of the Division or Corps who will have to pass in the first instance, and vigorously opposed as they will be. It appears to me that no attempt of the kind will succeed. It has long been considered a very practicable thing for an Army to pass a River in the face of an Enemy, and so it undoubtedly is, where circumstances afford many points of collecting means of crossing, and this gives the power of concealing the real point of attempt by several feints. Here this is not the case, the Zezere alone is the *place d'armes*, and leaves little else to watch, hence arises a difficulty of accomplishing this enterprise that would appear almost insurmountable.

Abrantes is in a very forward state of defence, is quite out of danger from a *coup de main*, and even very respectably provided against a formal attack. (Memoranda ' Y,' ' Z,' [2] for the Marshal.)

Boats diminished near the mouth of the Zezere between

---

[1] Quoted Oman, iv, p. 74.

[2] Memoranda of information about the enemy's numbers obtained from peasants. These figures tally substantially with those given by Sir Charles Oman of the French Army of Portugal, see iii, app. viii, and iv, app. i.

the 21st and 22nd Rockets and Blue-lights along the
Enemy's line.

This morning the 22nd the number of Boats in the
mouth of the Zezere was considerably diminished, probably
wanted higher up the River, either for the passage of
Troops or to be put in security.

Jan. 24. The Marquis of Romana died suddenly
yesterday at Cartaxo, and his loss is a severe one to the
cause of the Peninsula. The Marquis was a true Patriot,
and devoted himself to the interests of his Country with
an enthusiasm and a perseverance of which it is impossible
to speak too highly.

It appears that General Junot was dangerously wounded
upon the 20th at the Rio Mayor, and that he is at Santarem
with little hopes of recovery.

Silveira has been driven across the Douro and the
Division of Claparéde entered Lanego on the 14th.
Brigadier Genl. Miller and Col. Wilson held the Line of the
Pavia, and the latter is with the Advance at Castro Dairo.

The French seem to be in some agitation, and a movement will in all probability take place almost immediately ;
what that will be it is altogether impossible to predict.
Mortier's delay upon the Guadiana will very likely send
them between the Mondego and the Douro.

Jan. 25. Memoranda ' Y,' ' Z,' of Abrantes sub-
mitted to the Marshal. A change of system ordered in
Abrantes. 22nd Regt. into Billets instead of the Convent
of St. Antonio. The other things attended to as far as
possibility goes.

Jan. 26. Olivenza surrendered at 9 in the morning of
the 23rd reduced by blockade and for want of provisions.
The Spaniards lost there four Battalions. The South of
the Alemtejo will now be open to ravage. Mortier and
Soult will next turn their attention to Badajoz; if they can
reduce it speedily, well and good, if not they'll proceed.
The infamous neglect of this Government in furnishing
supplies for the Portuguese Troops is every day more fully
apparent as well as the villainy of the Commissaries they
employ. They make 9 Rations of Bread out of the same
quantity of Flour that provides 15½ to the British Bakers.[1]

No effort made to collect the resources of Algarve, the
Alemtejo, and the Minho. Everything left for the Enemy

[1] Quoted Oman, iv, p. 70.

if he chose to come and take it. Nothing drawn in for ourselves. We shall never succeed in this war of supplies. There have been two or three moments since the affair of Bussaco when 'tis to be wished the thing had been put to the arbitration of the Sword. However, 'tis better late than never, and to do it now would be better than to delay it any longer.

Jan. 27. Lord Wellington met the Marshal at Almeiria. Masséna met the principal Generals at Loisson's House at Golegão a day or two ago.

Jan. 28. Masséna has moved his head quarters to a quinta near Golegão from Torres Novas.

Jan. 29. The Marshal visited the line of posts and remained the night at Abrantes.

Jan. 30. Inspected the works and Hospitals. Ordered several essential changes, left Dr. Halliday there and returned to Chamusca.

Jan. 31. The Andalusian Army has approached Badajoz and cut off communication with Elvas. Ballasteros has been defeated in supporting Campos near Aracena. French Cavalry reconnoitred Elvas on the 29th—retired before the Spanish Cavalry and Portuguese Brigade of Madden. Tortosa has surrendered in the South. Grant has destroyed a few of the Rear of the Escort that marched for Spain by Somiera Formosa and Pasamedor, and prevented their plundering the Villages. The advance of Claparéde has appeared near Celorico. The Enemy have six Boats, mounted upon two Cars each, on the left bank of the Zezere near the Bridge-foot.

Feb. 1. The Brigade of Campbell's Infantry moved from Mugem to Salvatierra and the 5th Caçadores from Quinta da Braga to Ulme for the advantage of more healthy and commodious quarters.

A small Division moving from Madrid down the Tagus to join the Army of Estramadura. The Enemy evidently endeavouring to bring as much as he can to bear on Portugal. He might be attacked by his Right now with great advantage—he does not expect it. If the pure defensive be adhered to much longer we shall wish, when it is too late, we had laid it aside sooner.

Feb. 2. Appearances of Movement increasing on the part of the Enemy.

Feb. 3. Heavy Rains, Tagus much swelled. Many

concurring accounts of the Enemy's distress. There is now some probability of this being true. Badajoz invested. Lagos Regiment ordered to Elvas.

Distribution as ' B.'

Feb. 4–5. Much despondency and discontent in Badajoz—dislike of Mendizabal. If the Enemy persist and the place be not speedily relieved, there is too much reason to apprehend its loss.

Meanwhile every delay of this Southern Army becomes every day more and more distressing to Masséna. 'Tis to be doubted whether it would not have been better policy in Soult to have risked much and leaving places behind him, advanced to the Tagus without waiting for Badajoz, or Olivenza. He however is not aware of Masséna's immediate wants. His orders have in all probability come direct from Paris, and when that General made his Report to his Court, very possibly he overestimated his resources.

Feb. 6–8. Foy has returned from France ; he left Ciudad Rodrigo with an Escort of 3,000 Men. Grant attacked him on the 1st with about 100 Ordenanças near Alfridanha and slew about 230 of his people, amongst them Colonel Besson of the 70th Regt. of the Line. Great part of his Baggage, and a herd of Cattle fell into the hands of Grant.

The principal part of Claparéde's Division has moved upon Guarda and on the 2nd its advance was in Belmonte and Coria. This movement accords with Drouet's letter to that General. What further march he is to make or what he has come there for *nous verrons.*

Badajoz has sustained a slight Bombardment and Mendizabal having come out of the Town and repaired to Elvas, has concocted an enterprise with Butson, Leith, and Madden. The Spanish Division of O'Donnel and the Portuguese Brigade of Cavalry of Madden, are to cross the Guadiana in the night by the Bridge of Badajoz, and with the Garrison attack the French Lines. Surprise may do much, and if the execution be as prompt and secret as the project is spirited and plausible the best effects may be augured. But . . . we shall see.

The Rains for the last few days have ceased. The Tagus still however continues very full. Passing appears to be out of the question. If Badajoz does not fall, the

Army of Masséna ought to be a devoted one, and God
forbid that one man of it should escape us.   If that place
does not fall, it is still a devoted Army if this Division
may advance two or three marches to meet Soult.

The reinforcements arriving will probably put Lord
Wellington upon active measures, perhaps not though—
as a general measure he may be right, inasmuch as a
partial one against Soult and Mortier are concerned
perhaps, but he is a Judge that one has no right to dispute
the opinion of, and we may safely trust in him.

Feb. 9.   The enterprise at Badajoz has been badly
managed.   Mendizabal got into the Town at 3 o'clock
in the morning, but instead of attacking immediately, or
after a short rest, and so taking advantage of the surprise,
he waited the whole day, all the next night, and attacked
at 2 o'clock in the afternoon.   The Spaniards behaved
very gallantly, but the Enemy were prepared and of course
superior discipline prevailed; the Spaniards retired into
the Town.   Madden's Brigade which remained upon the
Gebora, charged a Detachment of 300 French Cavalry
and routed them, but in the pursuit fell into a sort of
ambuscade, and was obliged to retire with some loss to his
rear guard.

The Marshal determines to move up the 1st and 7th
Cavalry to Apalhão, Gafeita, etc.   Col. Otway goes with
this Brigade leaving his own at Almeiria, etc. to re-establish
the Horses.

Feb. 10–12.   The Cavalry Brigade marched and will
arrive at Alpalhão and Gaifeita the 14th.   Two Guns of
the Portuguese 6-Pounders were brought from Quinta de
Santa Martha to Chamusca on the 12th.

The Spanish Army, with the exception of the Garrison,
has come out of Badajoz and also the Portuguese Brigade.
It would seem that the Enemy has become acquainted with
the circumstances of Badajoz being invested by Soult and
Mortier, and indeed it might well be conceived that he
would.   Of course he will hold his ground as long as he
can.

On the 11th the Marshal visited the posts.

Feb. 13.   The Enemy concentrated about 2,000 Men
between 6 and 8 o'clock P.M. yesterday at Montalvão.
This led to nothing; this morning all was as usual.

Badajoz is now pretty closely invested upon the left

bank of the River. It is well worth an effort to save it.
Whether Lord Wellington will make it I doubt. If the
Siege be raised, and this Division, well managed, can
raise it, the intelligence will be the signal of Masséna's
retreat.

Tavira Militia will reach Elvas on the 19th.

Feb. 14–16. No change. Enemy completing his third
Parallel at Badajoz. Distribution ' C.'

Feb. 17–18. Increasing indications of a movement on
the part of the Enemy and the reports of the Spies accord
with these appearances.

The attack on Badajoz does not proceed with much
activity. General Leith ordered to send the Militia of
Lagos back to Mortinor Novo, so soon as that of Tavira
shall have arrived at Elvas.

Feb. 19. No change.

Feb. 20. Last night the Enemy brought 9 Boats out
of the Zezere, they were perceived and fired upon by the
Post at Foz, when 5 returned, and 4 continued to fall
down the Tagus, passing all the Posts and not being seen
after falling below Arripiada and Tarcos.

Feb. 21.—The Enemy at break of day passed over a
detachment in five Boats from the right Bank of the Tagus
to the Isla dos Inglese opposite Alpiaça, surprised and
carried off the Guard of Ordananza, and endeavoured to
collect and drive the Cattle to their own side. He only
succeeded however in getting off a few—nine or ten.

It was not easy in the first instance to determine
whether this was a forage, or a serious intention to hold
the island, nor was it possible to ascertain the number he
had sent into it. Before commencing to drive him out
therefore the Marshal intended to be sufficiently strong to
do it effectually and therefore ordered up the Brigade of
General Lumley from Almeiria and the Portuguese Brigade
of Genl. Augustin Lumley (2nd, 14th, 5th) from Chamusca
with 2 6-pounders. The Cavalry Brigade 4 and 10
(Viscount de Barbacena) were upon the spot, it being upon
the centre of his Cantonments. Lord Wellington who had
met the Marshal at Almeiria upon other business, accompanied him to the ford between the left bank of the River
and the Island and having arrived the Cavalry Brigade,
and the Light Infantry of the 39th Regt. upon horses of
dismounted Dragoons, crossed the Ford with some

difficulty. The Enemy abandoned the Island, took to his Boats and escaped, and this he had full time to do, because his high ground on the right Bank enabled him to see the approach of the Columns and apprize the detachments in the Island accordingly.

A strong piquet of Cavalry and Infantry occupied the Island for the night. The Cattle were driven to the left Bank and the Forage is ordered to be brought off without delay. Genl. Lumley has received orders to practise small to command the Roads. This Island would be of importance for the Enemy to hold, and would afford him an excellent *Tête du Pont* for the passing his Army if such were his intention, his position on the right bank commands it altogether. On the left bank the ground is flat and does not discover the reverse surface of the Island. There are two fords out of it on the Alemtejo side, and moreover by towing round the Boats from the North channel, Troops might be very rapidly passed over. I have yet seen no part of the Tagus so well calculated for a passage. The Troops returned to their Cantonments except that a Brigade of Genl. Lumley remained at Alpiaça. Campbell's Brigade closed up from Salvatierra to Mugem. Lord Wellington returned to Cartaxo.

Upon the 18th the besieging Army of Badajoz crossed the Guadiana in force, and passing the Xibosa attacked, (indeed surprised) the Army of Mendizabal, and totally routed it. Another, and indeed the last, Spanish Army thrown away by the ignorance, stupidity, and inability of their Generals. They have even abandoned Campo Mayor, and are flying over the country in utter dispersion to Estremoz.

The Portuguese Brigade of Madden has suffered considerably and what is worse, has behaved very ill, notwithstanding every effort of its General and some of its Officers. This however I have foreseen. It conducted itself most heroically when it was first brought against the Enemy in September last, but after having been several times left unsupported by the Spaniards to whom it has been attached, after having daily witnessed their panics, and confusions, and flights, it was to be expected that it should lose confidence in them and itself, and catch the contagion of their pernicious example.

Feb. 22.   Nothing new.

Feb. 23–26. Within ' X,' ' Y,' ' Z ' :—but on the 24th. Distribution ' L.'

Feb. 23. The Marshal told me Lord Wellington [1] means to attack and his own share to turn and force the left when the reinforcements should arrive. It had been brought upon the *tapis* in the short interview opposite the Isla dos Inglese.

Reinforcements having arrived in the Tagus and some of them being on their march from Lisbon, on their arrival Lord Wellington would attack the French right by the side of the Rio Mayor.

Marshal Beresford to cross the Tagus at Abrantes and attack his Left on the Zezere at the same time.

Feb. 24. The Marshal visited the Posts and I proceeded to Abrantes, having orders to inquire and discover, how far in attacking the Corps at Punhete, Amoreira could be turned, the Heights of Montalvão gained, and afterwards the consequent advantage of ground to come at the Enemy upon the Zezere. Arrived in the evening.

Feb. 25. The Governor produced the most intelligent people of the country between Abrantes and the Zezere. The result of their examination is in ' Y.'

Rode out as far as the Enemy's Posts would permit, the result of this reconnaissance in ' Z.'

Feb. 26. Inspected the Hospitals and returned to Chamusca. The Sickness is decreasing and Doctor Halliday's diligence and ability has put things in good order. The Garrison however is very weak.

Carefully compared the Country as seen from the left bank of the Tagus with my reconnaissance of yesterday and the accounts I have collected. In consequence ' X.' A few general ideas and the detail very sparingly entered into.

Feb. 27. The Marshal visited the Isla dos Inglese and the left bank of the river beyond Santarem.

Feb. 28. Gave in to the Marshal a corrected copy of ' X ' and a Memorandum of Roads, Local, and Boats arranged from the substance of ' Y,' ' X.'

The Enemy opened at 7 A.M. of the 26th upon Badajoz, from 4 Guns and 2 Mortar Batteries, and continued till past 3 P.M. The Town answered briskly.

Col. Colborne reports that on the 26th the Enemy

---

[1] Quoted Oman, iv, p. 83, footnote.

constructed something like a frame-work on the right bank
of the Zezere below the Bridge, as if for the purpose of
drawing up Boats upon it, and that on the 27th they were
occupied all day in carrying things from the Left to the
Right Bank.   Reported to the Marshal upon the Abrantes
Hospitals.

March 1.   Enemy continues to press the Siege of
Badajoz.   Letters from Wilson of the 24th at Villa Caja
upon the Aloa (where he has moved to save the right
bank of that River, and if possible, a part of the Estrella
from Ravage) give a most horrible picture of the Atrocities
of the French in their late march of plunder from Pedrogao
and Figueira dos Vinhos to Goes and Arganil.   Upon the
first two days of their excursion they murdered more than
100 persons and after making a desert of the Country,
carried off many families and every female above 12 years
old for the use of the Soldiery.   This they do all round us,
this they do everywhere, and excepting by a few Guerillas
we disturb them nowhere.   I trust the hour of retribution
is yet to come.   Meanwhile our pure defensive system has
rendered the French General so presumptuous that he
detaches for days together, as in this last instance, more
than 5,000 Men to many leagues distance, to forage and to
plunder, in one point only, boldly weakening his Army
upon the conviction of our tameness.

For the first time that I have known, or heard, or read
of in the Annals of our English Military History an English
Officer (4th or 5th Lieut. 45 Regt.) has deserted to the
Enemy.

JOURNAL 6

1811, *March–May*

GENERAL RETREAT OF THE FRENCH UNDER MASSÉNA.[1]
BERESFORD'S CAMPAIGN IN ESTREMADURA. PART II.
1ST SIEGE OF BADAJOZ

INTRODUCTION

IN connexion with these events D'Urban conducted a lengthy
correspondence (preserved in his papers) with various highly
placed officials in England, including Sir Herbert Taylor,
secretary to the King. At the conclusion of the war he wrote
up the whole Albuera campaign, which he read over and
discussed with Beresford, and then had it privately printed on
his return to England in 1817 under the title *Report of the Operations of the Right Wing of the Allied Army under Field-Marshal
Sir. Wm. Carr Beresford in the Alemtejo and Spanish Estremadura
during the Campaign of 1811* (not in 1811, as Sir Charles Oman has
it, vol. iv, p. 267, footnote). Years after, as a result of the
appearance of Napier's third volume in 1830, a good deal of
controversy was aroused, and the writer of 'Strictures' and
'Further Strictures,' championing Beresford, communicated
with D'Urban for a copy of his publication. It is interesting
to find that there is among the enclosed papers a letter from
Colonel J. Freeth of the Horse Guards, saying that Beresford
had expressed great anxiety for a copy of the pamphlet, and that
he had tried everywhere to obtain one, but in vain. There is a
further private letter on the same subject, but it is difficult to
decipher the signature. Beresford intended replying himself and
so commenced a lengthy correspondence with D'Urban. As

---

[1] Sir Charles Oman remarks (vol. iv, p. 174) that the maps used by
Masséna 'were very bad'—the actual set used by his headquarters
staff is in existence. See also vol. iii, p. 347, where he refers to the capture
of these maps, their subsequent presentation to Queen's College Library,
Belfast, and their description in an article by Mr. T. J. Andrews in the
English Historical Review, xvi (1901), p. 472. It is further interesting that
the two maps of Salamanca ('second part comprising the battlefield and
the country around the city and of Cuenca'), missing from the Irish
collection, are to be found enclosed with these papers.

the life of Beresford remains among the *desiderata* in the annals of British military history, and as his papers, so far, have not been traced, his letters, including several from Wellington, and memoranda, should prove of great value to a future biographer.

March 1-3. The Enemy's transport of Stores to the rear continues with great activity. He has apparently weakened himself more upon the Zezere.

March 4. A reconnaissance was ordered from Abrantes towards Montalvão and Amoreira to make the Enemy show his force. It was rather too late the evening closing in.

March 5. The party of Reconnaissance again moved upon Amoreira at daylight from Abrantes ; the Enemy's Advance retired upon Montalvão, and here the whole appeared about 900 Infantry.

He passed over 8 or 10 Boats upon Carriages from the left to the right bank of the Zezere in the course of the morning, and certainly gave indications of an intention to abandon the former bank.

The Reinforcements *are* arrived in the Tagus. Lord Wellington writes the Marshal, dated in the evening of yesterday, that from all the observations he can make in his front and indeed from his information generally, there can be no doubt of the Enemy's preparing to move to his rear, but that at present he does not conceive anything has actually moved except Baggage and Artillery and Stores. He directs the Marshal ' *when the movement in his front shall be decided,*' to send a British Brigade by Abrantes to occupy the Country to the right from the Tagus to the Zezere and then to bring down the Bridge of Boats from Abrantes to form a short communication between this Division and the Army.

The Marshal in consequence directs the 5th Caçadores to march immediately to Abrantes. One Regiment of Col. Otway's Cavalry to move back to the Roscia quarters to be in readiness at Abrantes for a British Brigade. General Hoghton's Brigade to hold itself in readiness, and the Sailors and the Boats at Abrantes to be assembled and ready. Capt. Patton is directed also to have all belonging to the Bridge in readiness to move. This according to his Lordship's letter is all that can at present be done for the movement in front is not quite ' decided.'

The Divisions on the right bank of the river closed up as in ' D.'

In the middle of the night, a letter from the Correspondent in Santarem, as well as many concurring reports and accounts make the movement opposite apparently ' decided,' and the Marshal orders Genl. Hoghton's Brigade to march for Abrantes, as well as the 4 six-pounders of the German Brigade from Margarida. The Squadrons at Crucifixe also will march and be replaced by that at Carregueira.

The Marshal despatches an express to Lord Wellington with the letter from Santarem, some other accounts, and a report of what he has ordered, and how he stands. Badajoz holds out well. It would be well to give it spirits, and send express to fix a day for its relief.

March 6. The Enemy quitted Santarem at 1 o'clock morning. At day-light it became known, and every preparation was made by the Marshal to follow up the instructions given in Lord Wellington's letter of yesterday. Major General Stewart went to Abrantes to take the command of the Corps which to-morrow is to proceed to the Zezere. (' B ' copy of his orders). Portuguese Regiments of Cavalry of Otway's Brigade, 1 Squadron 13th Light Dragoons, Major General Hoghton's British Brigade of Infantry (29th, 48th, 57th), the 5th Caçadores, the 2nd Portuguese Regt. and to have at his disposal also, the 13th and 22nd Portuguese Regiments from the Garrison of Abrantes. The Major General will proceed by two roads from Abrantes, one across the plain by the road of Rio de Moinhos, the other by the heights of Pai Gallege as recommended in ' X ' page 63. One Squadron of the 13th from Chamusca replaces that which has moved from thence to Crucifixe. The 2nd Portuguese Regt. marches direct to Abrantes from Chamusca, the 14th and 5th to Pineiros and Carregueira, the British Brigade of Lumley (28th, 34th, 39th), and the Portuguese Brigade (4th and 10th) of Campbell, together with the 4 Portuguese six-pounders from Almeiria and adjacents to Chamusca. The heads of the Columns advanced beyond Santarem. The French Cavalry broke down the Porto de Aloiela and kept the Golegão plain during the day. Orders despatched and the necessary arrangements made.

March 7. The Enemy evacuated Punhete in the night

burning his Boats and destroying his Bridge. Major General Stewart received this intelligence on his march, (Order of March ' E ') to execute the Orders contained in ' B.' The Marshal arrived at Punhete at day-break. The Boats fell down from Abrantes, and by 12 o'clock at noon all the Corps of Major Genl. Stewart (as in the Margin of ' B ') were passed to the right bank of the Zezere (excepting the 5th Caçadores, the 2nd Portuguese Regt. and the 62nd Colborne's Brigade (one Company 5th Batt. 60th, Buffs, 31st, 48th, 66th, see ' E ') also crossed from Foz to Praya ; the 31st crossed at Tancos and joined its Brigade by its right at Praya. The advance of Genl. Stewart's Corps on the right was pushed on a little on the road to Santa Cinta, that of Col. Colborne's on that of Moita—then one Squadron of the 13th Light Dragoons was attached to each of these, and the roads both lead upon Thomar. Everything halted thus for Lord Wellington's orders.

The Marshal despatched two Staff Officers to his Lordship at Golegão, and proceeded to Tancos, crossed the River, and returned in the evening to Chamusca, where the Count Alva brought him ' F,' and orders were despatched by Capt. Chapuzet to march Genl. Stewart accordingly, and to bring down the Boats from Punhete to Tancos.

March 8. Capt. Chapuzet reached Punhete at 3 o'clock A.M., the Division of Genl. Stewart was in march upon Thomar before 4 A.M. and Capt. Chapuzet sent the Boats down to Tancos and returned to Chamusca.

At 3 o'clock A.M. also, the Marshal[1] crossed the River to Torres Novas and had an interview with Lord Wellington. The immediate relief of Badajoz whose danger becomes imminent has been judged desirable (this to be done with the 2nd and 4th Divisions, the latter under Genl. Cole). The Marshal returned at 8. Orders were immediately sent to Capt. Squire at Punhete to throw the Bridge of Boats over the Tagus near Tancos for the re-passage of Genl. Stewart, and the passage of Genl. Cole, and the Troops which have remained on the left bank of the Tagus were immediately marched as from ' a ' to ' b ' in the Distribution ' W ' by which arrangement they are well thrown up in their March upon Portalegre. Communicated to Mr. Ogilvie the Commissary Genl. of the Division the

---

[1] See Oman, iv, p. 60, footnote.

probable bent of this movement, and he proceeded to take measures for the Supplies Southward. In the evening the further movement ' XL ' ordered for to-morrow by which Carregueira and Pinhero are left free for the Head of Genl. Stewart's Column when it shall re-cross the River.

An Officer arrived from Badajoz. The Governor has made a most gallant sortie,—destroyed several of the Enemy's Works, and the Battery upon the covered way that was to breach. He (Don Raphael de Menacho) is unfortunately killed. This exploit gains time, and the gallantry of the Spaniard and his Garrison have probably saved the place by this very gaining of time even but for a few additional days. The relief may now arrive before it is too late.

March 9. Lord Wellington following the Army of Masséna has his headquarters to-day in Peruche beyond Thomar. Distribution and movement ' SB.' Col. De Grey's Brigade of Heavy Cavalry and the 4th Division under General Cole are attached to the Marshal's Division, and the March for the Relief of Badajoz commences with the Movements in ' TC.' All the orders given in consequence. The Bridge of Boats will be ready at Arripiada at 12 o'clock to-night.

Mem.—In the evening Lord Wellington ordered the Marshal to join him, for Masséna shows fight at Peruche (near Thomar).

March 10.[1] Peruche—Enemy between Touraso and Pombal.

March 11. Enemy marched all night.—Rear Guard seen at 7—followed—drove his Rear out of Pombal—he occupied the heights beyond and extended in echelons along the Pombal River right bank. His Lordship would have attacked but the 3rd, 1st, and 5th Divisions arrived so late that it would have been dark.—Divisions took their places to attack his right and front in the morning. Army bivouacqued. Casalinho de Mulge.

March 12. Redinha.—The Enemy continued to retreat all night and in the morning about 7 the Rear Guard was found in position upon the heights in front of Redinha.

[1] *Endorsement on a small packet:*
' 10th to the 17th March inclusive.
' During these days—having left everything at Chamusca but my two Horses—riding one and leading the other alternately—I could get no paper but these scraps for my Journal.—B. D '.

He occupied the Fir-woods on his right looking down upon
the valley of the Pombal—very strongly. He had six
guns and a howitzer on the heights commanding the Fir-
woods, the high road leading through his centre, and
approaches to his left. The Fir-woods were carried very
dashingly by the 95th and 3rd Caçadores of the Light
Division, supported by the Division, between 9 and 10 and
the Enemy then retired his right and stood across the high
road leading to Redinha.   At 12 the heads of the Columns
were all up, they moved forward, ascended the heights,
deployed, advanced in two lines as at a Field Day, and by
1 o'clock the Enemy was driven from his position across
the plain and through the Town of Redinha to the heights
beyond it.

1.

Left.   Light Division—4th Div.—G. Pack—G. Picton.
Right.

2.

5th.   1st.   6th.

Cavalry in front of the first line.
The position was turned by the right and left by the
movement of Lord Wellington, masterly and well executed.
This was the Corps of Marshal Ney.   Masséna commanded.
3 or 4 Officers taken.   He retired behind Porto Calheiro
which with the heights beyond were occupied by our
advance.
Orders to Genl. Stewart to fix his head quarters at
Tramagal to move the 13th to Crato or Carragueira for the
convenience of forage, and to let the Troops remain as at
present, unless it should become necessary to concentrate
for the protection of the Bridge of Tancos.[1]
Chapuzet ordered to go to Pernes and Santarem to
make enquiries as to Guns and Ammunition supposed to
be left by the French. Lobes ordered to march the
9th Dragoons to Elvas.
March 13.   The Enemy held Condeixa and the heights
and woods and began to put his Rear Guard in motion from
his left upon the road to Miranda de Corve.   The 5th and
3rd Divisions marched by the right upon Abriganza across
the Mountains to cut his line of march and the remaining

[1] Quoted Oman, iv, p. 248.

Divisions were intended to advance upon Condeixa. A
Corps, however, that had marched by one of the intermediate routes formed its junction with the line of march
upon the Miranda de Corve road and put on an appearance
that caused Lord Wellington to suspend the movements on
the right, more especially as the appearance of the Division
crossing the hills hastened the Enemy's march, who
evacuated Condeixa, having first set fire to it, about
2 P.M. The Advance followed about a league, and the
Army bivouacqued in its order of march.

Hardinge was sent into Coimbra with a patrol to
Communicate with Trant. That Officer, however, had
quitted the place in the morning, leaving a Rear Guard
and fallen back upon the Vanya. Hardinge wrote him his
instructions and returned, then went to prepare Hospitals
and use every effort to draw in supplies. Hardinge took
a picket of the Enemy which had been left behind to keep
fires and burn straw.

March 14. Thick fog. The heads of the Columns were
halted. Between 7 and 8 Sir W. Erskine's Light Troops
were warmly engaged with those of the Enemy's Rear
Guards and Lord Wellington found them as soon as the
fog cleared. John Stewart wounded !!! The Columns
were put in motion, the 3rd and 5th Division forced the
Enemy's left. Sir W. Erskine with the Light Division on
his right. Lord Wellington with the 1st and 6th
Divisions and the Horse Artillery of Ball & Ross advanced
upon his front. He disputed every inch and retired very
handsomely to the heights beyond Chão de Lamas burning
the place. He suffered severely by being closed with by
the flanking Corps of the Right and Left, and from the
Guns of the Centre Column which reached his Columns in
the Valley of Chão de Lamas. His gaining the heights was
rather precipitate but his formation was prompt and good.
The Troops had made a long march. Lord Wellington
made his dispositions for the morning's attack and the
Army bivouacqued in its position of march and Battle—
its left towards Villa Sella where headquarters were for
the night.

March 15. In the morning the fog was impenetrably
thick till towards 10 o'clock. Lord Wellington would not
suffer the Troops to move till he could see, for the great
height of Miranda de Corve might have enabled the Enemy

to mask himself with advantage. As soon as the fog cleared
the Columns moved in the same order. General Pack's
Brigade was sent off by the left to turn the Enemy's right,
further than the extension of Sir W. Erskine's Division.
The Troops in movement. Lord Wellington rode forward.
The Enemy had marched all night burning many of his
wheeled Carriages and leaving several hundreds of Baggage
Asses [1] maimed upon the road. Lord Wellington at length
discovered their Rear Guard upon the western heights of
the Ceira about a league and half in front of Miranda de
Corve :—he determined to dislodge them and the heads of
the Columns arriving in the Plain of Louzão were put in
motion for the attack. Genl. Picton turned the Enemy's
left ; the 95th and Horse Artillery of Sir W. Erskine
forced his Light Troops from the heights of the Centre.
Both attacks succeeded, the Enemy was driven over the
Ceira just as day closed. The Army bivouacqued. Genl.
Picton had a strong opposition for nearly an hour. He
took the Colonel of the 39th Regt. John Stewart died ! ! !
Head Quarters at Louzão. The French Rear Guard on
the other (Eastern) bank of the Ceira. No Movement.—
The Army rested and (waited) for the arrival of Biscuit
which from the nature of things had been a little behind.

Yesterday Genl. Houghton, his heavy Brigade of
Cavalry and the 4th Division began to march back to
the Tagus, it being clear that the Enemy don't intend to
give Battle. Besides Badajoz has surrendered [2] and the
Alemtejo is laid open. The Marshal rode to Thomar on his
return to his Division.

  March 17. Thomar.—Troops put in motion. Orders
expedited for tomorrow according to ' NV ' Chamusca.

  March 18. Rode to Portalegre. Marshal at Pte. de Sor.

  March 19. Arrived in the morning. Arrangements
for the arrival of the Army. Campo Mayor invested.
Soult marched for Andalusia with 5,000 men, Mortier
remaining. Enemy's detachments to Albufueza and
Valesa d'Alentan. Wrote the Marshal the state of things.
Sent a man to the Governor of Campo Mayor to say that
the Marshal is in march to his relief and to exhort him to
hold out. Marshal at Crato.

---

[1] See Oman, iv, p. 154.
[2] In D'Urban's ' Report ' (1817) he mentions that ' on the 13th his
Lordship apprised of the Fall of Badajoz.'

March **20.** Looked at the country by Assumar, Monforte, and Arronches. The Marshal arrived at Portalegre.

March **21.** The Army continued to arrive according to ' NP.' Colonel Campbell to Allegretto to take care of the Passes in the Mountains of Ougalla. The Marshal not having got any instructions from Lord Wellington, which were to have been sent after him—is anxious in the meantime to relieve Campo Mayor—and proposes to move so soon as the Troops of the 4th Division are up,—laid before him ' SS '—approved. The Town becoming very crowded and it being now evident (as I have supposed it would) that it can't hold what will arrive tomorrow—Col. Colborne's advanced Guard, to which is attached the six-pounder Brigade German Artillery, and three Squadrons of Cavalry (1–13th, 2—Portuguese), Genl. Lumley's Brigade, march tomorrow for Arronches. Genl. Houghton will rest tomorrow and then follow. Informed Ogilvie of Movement.

March **22.** General Stewart with the Brigade of Colborne and Lumley marched for Arronches. B. Genl. Long with the 13th Dragoons and Portuguese Cavalry of his Division to Assumar. The Heavy Brigade of Cavalry and Hamilton's Division of Portuguese Infantry (excepting the Brigade of Campbell already at Allegretto) ordered to march tomorrow to Arronches. Road excellent. Reported to the Marshal Campo Mayor surrendered at 2 P.M. after a very gallant defence.

March **23.** Patrolled to Campo Mayor, all still—one vedette only to be seen. Marshal arrived at Arronches, determined to move on and get between Campo Mayor and the Guadiana. A letter from Lord Wellington at Arganil confirmed him. 4th Division which arrived yesterday at Portalegre ordered up to Arronches. The other two Divisions and the Cavalry to move tomorrow according to ground to be taken up.

March **24.** Reconnoitred by the right bank of the Caya, crossed by the Ford of Santa Olaya, fixed upon a position at Monte Regongo, the right resting on the Caya fronting Campo Mayor. Returned at 11. Army marched at 12. Army bivouacqued. Genl. Cole arrived at Arronches. Head Quarters Monte Regongo.

March **25.** Reconnoitred at day break to the Atalaya

da Loupa da Moita within half-a-league of Campo Mayor.
2 or 3 French Pickets shewed. This ridge of the Atalaya
after passing the Corteada is well calculated for a Cavalry
advance forming the right attack upon the Enemy at
Campo Mayor.

Returned at 8. General Cole arrived at 9. Army
marched in one Column at 10 upon the direct road to
Campo Mayor by the Atalaya da Loupa da Moita. General
Long ordered with the 13th Dragoons and Portuguese
Brigade of Cavalry to march by the right approach reconnoitred this morning and turn the left of the Enemy's
posts in front of Campo Mayor. At about ½ past 10 it
rained hard and the thickness of the weather induced the
Marshal to change his intention with respect to the Cavalry
and to recall it to the Principal Column. This it joined
at the Corteada. At 11 the Army advanced upon the
Atalaya da Loupa Road. General Long with the Light
Cavalry by the left Ridge followed by the Division of
General Hamilton. General Stewart's Division and Col.
de Grey's Cavalry by the high road. Colonel Colborne
and the Cavalry of the advanced guard by the right hand
ridge, Genl. Cole following by the centre and supporting.
The Enemy had nothing but Cavalry at the Post of the
Atalaya. He retired skirmishing, evacuated the Town
before 12, and marched rapidly upon Badajoz. In this
march the Enemy had so much the start that only the
Cavalry and two six-pounders could overtake him at about
1½ leagues from Campo Mayor. He retired in good order,
and his Infantry beat off the Portuguese Cavalry but the
two Squadrons of the 13th Light Dragoons led by Col.
Head charged his 26th Regt. of Dragoons, to which were
attached some Hussars, routed them and pursued them
to the Gates of Badajoz, cutting down and taking great
numbers. In this pursuit the Regt. took 15 pieces of
Cannon, cutting the traces, and abundance of Horses,
killed the Colonel and Lt. Col. of the 26th and many
Officers and brought back a Lieutenant. They continued
the pursuit, however, too far,[1] and as no report was made
from them to the Marshal (and indeed could not because
they had passed the Enemy's Corps and could not communicate with him) he supposed them cut off, Genl. Long
having stated his apprehensions on that head. And as

[1] See Oman, iv, p. 261, also p. 263, footnote.

his Infantry could not arrive in time, and he considered the 13th Dragoons lost, he would not allow the Heavy Cavalry to charge at the risk of losing or weakening his only British Cavalry remaining. He discontinued the pursuit therefore and the arriving Columns of Infantry were halted and laid down.

It is difficult to conceive how the apprehension for the safety of the 13th Dragoons could have been so strongly entertained by Genl. Long; Light Cavalry in an open country can scarcely be cut off and the event proved it,— the Regiment and two Squadrons of the 7th Portuguese Cavalry that under Col. Otway had followed it after the charge to support, returned in good order having gone to within a short Grapeshot range of the Guns of Badajoz. The 13th cut down about 700. The Enemy lost something by the fire of two of the German six-pounders. The Enemy's force was about 3,500 men.

The Army returned to Campo Mayor. The Cavalry and 2nd Division bivouacqued. The 4th and Genl. Hamilton's in the Town.

HEAD QUARTERS CAMPO MAYOR

March 26. Army cantoned to rest in and between Campo Mayor and Elvas. Cavalry in Santa Olaya and St. Viseta. 4th Division, Campo Mayor. 2nd and Portuguese Division, Elvas.

March 27. Lagos Militia halted at Utrenol. Faro Militia sent to Campo Mayor in order to hold it, in case Genl. Cole should be obliged to leave it for a time to join the other Divisions.

March 28. Capt. Squire reported upon the passage of the River at Jerumenha, and every exertion is making to prepare a Bridge according to what he recommends— this must be principally on Chevalets for want of Boats or sufficiently strong Pontoons.

The great evil is the want of shoes which, however, it strikes me has been in some measure exaggerated, and if it be of importance to march the Portuguese Brigade, by equalizing what they have might certainly get on for some days very well.

March 29. The Enemy's loss was considerable on the 25th. He has carried into Badajoz above 400 Wounded.

All his Artillery Men who had been employed in the Siege of Campo Mayor were sabred and of 16 Officers who were in the field of the 26th Dragoons 8 were killed or wounded. The 10th Regt. of Hussars and the 2nd Hussars suffered severely.

What he has in Badajoz is stated to be as in ' YY.'

Mortier, Commanding in Chief, Girald.   Cavalry Latour Maubourg, Bris ; Infantry Regiments—21st, 34th, 40th, 88th, 100th—4,000.   Cavalry Regiments—4th, 26th, 14th, Hussars and Dragoons two strong Regiments—850.

March 30.   Jerumenha reconnoitred,—the point for the Bridge fixed upon—the work commenced.   Castaños arrived.

March 31.   Laid the sketch ' RD ' before the Marshal at 7 o'clock A.M.   At one the Marshal ordered for to-morrow morning :—Cavalry and 2nd Division, Villa Viciosa and Borba ; 4th Division, Elvas.   Madden from Jerumenha to Campo Mayor.   Militia of Lagos to Jeru-menha.   Lord Wellington at Santa Mancha on the 25th. The Enemy passing the Coa at Aveida, Castel Bom, and Sabugal, not pressed very hard by us for the last few days from want of provisions on our part.

April 1.   Preparations for the Bridge continued.   An express sent off to hasten the shoes.

April 2.   At Jerumenha.—Preparations for the Bridge complete.—Fit for passing in 12 hours from the time it commences to be laid down.   Reconnoitred.   Deter-mined a Bivouac for the Army to assemble, 1½ English Miles behind Jerumenha.   Returned, reported to the Marshal.

April 3.   In the morning laid before the Marshal ' CS.' Orders of march given to assemble and Bivouac to-morrow morning in the wood near Condeira.—the place determined on the 2nd.   Cavalry and 2nd Division from Villa Viciosa and Barba ; 4th and Hamilton's from Elvas.

April 4.   Troops in their Bivouac at 10 o'clock and 11. But the Guadiana which has hitherto been perfectly quiet and still, has risen since nightfall of yesterday three feet.[1] In consequence the Chevalets have been overturned,—the Ford rendered impassable for Cavalry, and the means of passage very insecure and unsubstantial,—depending entirely on some floating Bridges of no great size.   Sent

[1] See Oman, iv, p. 268.

back a report to the Marshal who arrived at Jerumenha soon after. Every exertion made through the day to increase and strengthen the means of passage. Pickets and patrols over to the left bank occupying Villa Real.

April 5. Establishing a Bridge is out of question, the River continues to rise and increase in rapidity. The means are anything but secure either for passing the Army, (tedious beyond measure too no doubt) or establish a communication either for supplies or other purposes after-wards.—Nevertheless the state of things and above all Lord Wellington's reiterated orders received this morning render it necessary to pass.[1] Position of Assembly deter-mined. General Stewart 2nd Division, and three Squadrons of Cavalry get orders to cross to-night. Then General Hamilton—then Genl. Long's Cavalry, and then the 4th Division. Passage going on all night.

April 6. General Stewart and Genl. Hamilton in their position ; the first at 6 A.M. ; the last at 4 P.M. A proof of the wretched slowness of the passage. General Long and Genl. Cole passing all night.

April 7. A little before day-break Major Morris's Picket surprised. Two Squadrons taken ; fault of the Staff Officer placing the Picket. 4th Division all over by 2 P.M. Cavalry in the middle of the night.

April 8. Biscuit, Ammunition and Division Baggage passing till 8 o'clock, when the 9-pounder Brigade began to pass and finished at 3 afternoon. Two Spanish Flying Guns joined, ordered to pass the River and be attached to Genl. Long. Two Squadrons 5th Dragoons relieved at the Advance Pickets. After collecting all the information possible as to the Roads, etc., gave the Marshal the sketch 'D.T.'—Approved. The march of the Army unavoidably postponed till to-morrow on account of closing the supplies. Orders given for the execution of ' D.T.'

See Gordon's Letter of 31st for Lord Wellington's movements.

April 9. The Army (which was bivouacqued, by Brigades in succession as it had crossed, in a position of Assembly, of which the Right was upon and beyond Villa Real, on a boggy rivulet, and the Left upon the Guadiana and which formed an angle at about 1½ English Miles on the road from Villa Real to Badajoz and thus fronted both

[1] Quoted Oman, iv, pp. 268-69.

Badajoz and Olivenza), assembled at an hour after day-
break, at the respective Bivouacs of Divisions, and at a
¼ before 7 the whole moved upon Olivenza according to
'D.T.' and arrived there at 9.   The Enemy, however, had
retired during the preceding days to Valverde and Albuera,
and not even a Vedette was seen upon the march to
Olivenza. The order of march was dictated by the ground.
The 2nd Division marched by its Right, the 4th by its
Left so that the Line could be formed at any moment
readily, while the Division of Genl. Hamilton followed the
2nd and by turning to the right would be easily thrown
into second line.   Meanwhile as the Country was favourable for the movements of Cavalry, especially in the space
between the Columns, the Cavalry moved along that space
between the heads of them, protecting the Centre of the
Movement, and to act according to circumstances; the
Pickets of two Squadrons B, and two other Squadrons C
flanked the Left of the 2nd, and Right of the 4th Divisions.
Capt. Burroughs sent out by Alconchel and Barcanote to
make certain of Mortier's route.

Upon reaching Olivenza the Army halted so as to secure
the objects recommended in the 6th Paragraph of 'D.T.'—
The Town summonsed.—It was soon found that the Enemy
had retired altogether from Badajoz as well as from
Olivenza leaving a Garrison of 1200 men in the former
and of 300 in the latter. The Town returned an answer of
refusal. The Army bivouacqued in the Woods close to
the place, with a Brigade upon the hill of Atalaya de Donna
Anna. Major Dickson and Mr. Ogilvie dispatched to
Elvas, the one to assort and expedite the Transport of the
requisites for breaching the Town, the other to hasten the
arrival of supplies, which have almost failed.   This failure
is as unfortunate as unlooked for, the Commissary charged
by Lord Wellington with the collection of subsistence for
this Army, having reported their readiness to the Marshal
on the 7th. Patrolled into Valverde which the Enemy
had left.

April 10. The Reports of the morning giving certain
hopes of the arrival of some supplies, the 2nd Division and
British Cavalry marched at 2 o'clock beyond Valverde and
bivouacqued about 1½ English Miles in front of it.

Captain Squire of the Engineers arrived at Olivenza,
reconnoitred it, and agreed with Major Dickson as to its

weak points. So soon as the Guns arrive a Breaching
Battery will be established,—Genl. Hamilton's Division
will follow the 2nd tomorrow and the 4th remain to shut
up the place till its surrender.

See Gordon's account of Lord Wellington's movements
6th April.

April 11. Genl. Hamilton's Division and the Portuguese Cavalry marched at Day-break for the Bivouac at
Valverde ; on reaching it, the Cavalry passed to the front
of the 2nd Division, the Portuguese Div. closed to its rear,
and then the whole moved in one Column to Albuera.
The Cavalry headed the Column because the Country is
all open. Bivouacqued on the wooded heights upon the
right bank of the Albuera. The Army thus stands upon
and between the Albuera and Olivenza as recommended in
' R.B.' and ' C.S.,' and cuts the communication between
Badajoz and Seville. Crossed by two good Bridges, and
a shallow ford between. A small detachment of the
Enemy's Rear Guard at Santa Martha. The remainder
of his Army at and beyond Fuente del Maestre. Castaños
has engaged to get possession of Merida. Ballasteros at
Fregenal. Mortier at Llerena.

April 12. Patrolled into Santa Martha.—Enemy gone.
—Gone also from Talavera Real and from Lobon. There
will be no opposition therefore to the executing Lord
Wellington's Orders and Investing Badajoz. To clear the
Rear of the Enemy from Fuente del Maestre and hasten his
retiring from Zafra, Col. de Grey's Brigade of Cavalry will
march tomorrow to Santa Martha, to patrol to Fuente del
Maestre and to ascertain and feel him. One Brigade of
the 2nd Division with two Guns and two Squadrons of
Portuguese Cavalry tomorrow to Talavera Real to occupy
the Cantonments, and give a little confidence, which will
bring supplies.

The old out-work at Olivenza was taken possession of
last night with the loss of one man, and the Battery will
be ready to receive the six 24-pounders tonight ; they will
arrive from Jerumenha in the course of the day.

Count Penne Villemur in possession of Merida, his
advance at Almendralejo.

April 13. The troops marched from Talavera and
Santa Martha, as ordered yesterday. The rest remain in
the Bivouac near Albuera.

April 14.   A Division under Prince D'Arenberg coming
up from Niobla is pushing back Ballasteros, who was last
night at Xerez de los Caballeros.   The accounts, however,
of the exact position of this French Division, or its strength,
or probable intentions, were very vague ; as well as the
certainty of Zafra being clear and the whole of Mortier in
march for Cordoba.   Rode in the afternoon to Martha.
From thence to La Favre.   Zafra evacuated and even
many of Mortier's people beyond Llerena.   Learned that
Ballasteros was at Salvatierra de los Barros, and that the
Enemy were in Xerez.   Went to Salvatierra de los Barros.
Proposed to Ballasteros to do his utmost to draw
D'Arenberg after him that the Marshal may cut off his
Retreat.   He agrees and will fall back if attacked upon
Nogales—making a good show of resistance not to excite
suspicion.   If D'Arenberg takes the bait he must be lost
altogether ; if he halts at Xerez to consider for only two
days we ought to also get hold of him.[1]   Ballasteros 2,000
Infantry, 250 Horse.   D'Arenberg 4,000 Infantry, 500
Horse, 2 Light Guns.

April 15.   Early in the morning went back to Albuera.
On my way threw together ' P.Z.' gave it to the Marshal
on my arrival at 10 o'clock.   Breaching Battery at
Olivenza opened at day-break.

Troops put in motion for the neighbourhood of Zafra.
Detached Brigade of the 2nd Division recalled from Tala-
vera-Real to accompany the Division.—Cavalry and 2
Guns there also recalled.   Genl. Cole remains at Olivenza.
Cavalry, 2nd and Portuguese Divisions Bivouacqued by
Santa Martha.   Olivenza surrendered at Discretion at
11 o'clock, after the Breaching Battery had continued its
fire from day-break, in which time each of the 5 24-pounders
fired 72 Rounds.   400 Infantry taken there.

The intelligence of the Enemy gave the Marshal reason
to think that the Enemy were assembling something at
Llerena.—Genl. Cole's Division and the 9-pounder Brigade
of Reserve ordered to march as in ' P.Z.'

April 16.   Troops arrived near Zafra.—500 Cavalry of
the Enemy came to Los Santos—charged and pursued by
our Cavalry—Enemy's loss 3 Officers, 200 men, killed,
wounded and prisoners.   Our loss none.   Troops quartered
to Zafra—Los Santos—Puebla—as in ' P.Z.'

[1] Quoted Oman, iv, p. 278, note.

April 17. Troops resting—provisional orders given to the Generals of Division for their guidance in case of an alarm—position determined. Letter in Cypher to the Commandant of the Division that followed Ballasteros, intercepted from Latour Maubourg—waits to see our intentions—confesses a great loss of his Cavalry—says he apprehends being turned by Hornaches. Cole halted at Santa Martha.

April 18. Penne Villemur in Asagre last night. The Enemy still remains in Llerena, from whence it is necessary he should be sent before the operations are confined to the Siege of Badajoz. The Cavalry and the two Divisions will assemble therefore tomorrow morning soon after daybreak and march upon Fuente de Castos. If then Latour Maubourg still stays at Llerena one more march will enable the Marshal to cut him off at once from Seville and from Guadalcanal. Orders given—Roads pointed out—Points of Assembly marked.

April 19. Torrents of rain—so heavy that for the sake of the Troops the March was suspended at ½ past 4 A.M.

At 9 received a letter from Count Penne Villemur. He got into Llerena at 3 P.M. yesterday, the Enemy having marched at 10 A.M. ' Y.A.' Latour Maubourg's order of march for Guadalcanal. Maransin's Division has moved in the same direction from Aracena by Zafra. The Marshal's movement upon Zafra and Los Santos has thus cleared Estremadura without fatiguing the Troops, without the loss of a man, and saved the Magazines preparing upon the Guadiana, by living altogether in the Country he has occupied. Meanwhile no time has been lost as to Badajoz, for this position shuts it up as well and better than any other, while at the same time it has opened us channels of supply to the foot of the Sierra Morena. Major Dickson and Capt. Squire are pressing the arrangements and requisites *for the Siege of Badajoz*, at Elvas. Lord Wellington arrives at Elvas tomorrow, and the Marshal can now, notwithstanding all the want of means with which he started, put into his Lordship's hands, Olivenza and Estremadura, which have been acquired without loss and without any expense of Store supplies.

April 20. Letter from Lord Wellington announcing his arrival at Elvas on the 21st induce the Marshal to put the Troops in movement for Badajoz. This one rather

regrets.—Cole's Division with Alten—the Loyal Lusitanian Legion at Olivenza, and the Militia would be
sufficient for the Siege,—and with the Cavalry and other
two Divisions then occupying Llerena, we keep all Estramadura, and maintain a most imposing attitude towards
Andalusia. Supplies too are every day pouring in. The
confidence of our forward position has procured them, and
the opposite feeling that will arise from our going back,
will perhaps stop them again.

Marshal to Almendral. Cavalry Zafra, Los Santos,
Villa Franca ; 2nd Division Almendralejo ; Hamilton
Santa Martha ; Cole Almendral and Torre.

April 21. Almendral. — Distribution — Instructions
sent to Genl. Long at Los Santos, and Genl. Stewart at
Almendralejo.—Points of Retiring—Intelligence—Self at
Olivenza. Marshal to Elvas.

April 22. Lord Wellington reconnoitred Badajoz.
The Enemy not expecting this reconnaissance had out
in a wood a party of 200 men. This returned while the
Escort (Baron Alten's Brigade and two Squadrons of
Portuguese Cavalry) were under the place, and three
Battalions came out to protect its retiring, shewed them-
selves upon a point, where two companies only had been
left and effected his purpose.

Lord Wellington returned to Elvas. Marshal Beresford
to Olivenza. The Brigade of Cole's at Valverde ordered
to Elvas, replaced by one of those from Almendral.

April 23. Marshal Beresford went to Elvas. Kemmis's
Brigade of the 4th Division passed in part but the 40th
Regt. could not and remained at Villa Real.

April 24.—River rose in the night. Carried away the
Bridges and all the materials and cut off the communica-
tion. At $\frac{1}{2}$ past 2 A.M. received ' Z.L.' from the Marshal.
All ordered.

The 40th Regt. unable to pass. This Jerumenha communication therefore, as I have always supposed, is insecure and subject to be cut in 24 hours. This Bivouac
in the woods is for no other use than to destroy the Troops,
for the Engineers are not ready.

The Marshal returned at 4 P.M. He wishes to have his
rear upon Merida and to be *appuis* to the line from thence
to Los Santos.—' P.C.' ordered.—One would have wished
to have let Hamilton alone for the present who is well off,

and quite near enough to the line proposed. The Marshal however did not think fit to adopt the Paragraph ' T.' The whole of ' P.C.' therefore ordered.   We were sure to do wrong when we left Zafra, it has led to nothing but fatigue, and we were better there than where we are returning.   If we had remained for a short time at Zafra and the neighbourhood as I proposed and begged to do, occupying Llerena,—we should have possessed all Estremadura with its resources and confidence of the people, watched Andalusia, forced Soult to declare himself, for he could not have waited, and must either have assembled everything, and advanced to drive us back,—or gone to Cordoba or Cadiz. If he advanced we were excellently posted and the result could not have been doubtful for a moment. Meanwhile no time would have been lost, for preparations for the Siege of Badajoz would have been going on, and after resting and feeding the Army in good Cantonments, and developing the intentions of Soult, the rainy season would have passed and when all was ready we should have returned direct upon the Town and commenced the Siege in fine weather, in high health, in full possession of Estremadura, its opinions and supplies. This was urged beforehand, but it could not be !

April 25. Troops marched as ordered. Head Quarters at Santa Martha. Blake landed in the Nieble.

Enemy pillaging the foot of the Sierra between Guadalcanal and Llerena, but not advancing. The removing of Artillery from the former place to Cazalla—the road to Cordoba, indicates rather a retiring altogether.

Genl. Stewart's Brigade in Merida. D'Armagnal retired to Medellin. Head Quarters Almendralejo.

Genl. Cole having arrived at Merida with two Brigades of the 4th Division, the 9-pounder Brigade of Reserve, and a Squadron of Portuguese Cavalry according to ' P.C.', the Brigade of the 2nd Division, and Genl. Lumley with the two 6-pounders and the half Squadron of Heavy Cavalry from Villa Franca are ordered back and will return tomorrow to their respective quarters.

The 40th Regt. which has marched with Baron Alten to Talavera Real will march to Lobor on the 27th and remain in communication with the Brigade of Kemmis at Montijo. This Brigade (two Regts. of it) which had crossed the Guadiana at Jerumenha, has gone by Campo Mayor.

April 27. Troops arrived as mentioned yesterday. Count Penne Villemur left Llerena last night in consequence of exaggerated reports of an Enemy's advance upon him and returned again when he found his mistake. Meanwhile B. Genl. Long moved forward some Squadrons to Usagre to support him.

April 28. A French Officer, Le Baron Le Jeune, Colonel and A.D.C. to Berthier (Prince of Wagram) going with dispatches from Soult to Madrid and Paris taken near Madrid by Guerillas. ' V.B.' and ' V.C.' found upon him. The central Army of La Houssaye has retired from Truxillo and fallen back upon the Tagus and Toledo. If this Army advances now upon Andalusia—co-operated with by Blake from the Niedla and Genl. Graham from Cadiz— Victor is cut off and Andalusia recovered. Badajoz will fall of course afterwards—but it is lost time, precious time lost—to wait about it now.

April 29.—Ordered to prepare instructions for Genl. Colborne upon the basis of ' W.T.' giving, however, only 2 Squadrons. Did so ' Z.Z.' Colborne marched accordingly.

April 80. Castaños had a conference with the Marshal. Colborne being to reach Llera tonight, rode forward by Villa Franca and Los Santos to Usagre. On arriving wrote Colborne that the Cavalry here should move upon Higueira in the Morning—to continue his march upon Maguilla—begged him to say when he would march, that the Squadrons might accordingly—and also to say at what hour he could meet me at Higueira—to talk fully upon some points connected with his further progress. Wrote Count Penne Villemur that the Cavalry would be in Llerena tomorrow—the movement of Colborne upon Maguilla and La Graja, and begged him to look out well to Reyna and Fuente del Arco. Also begged him to order for the quartering of the Squadrons.

May 1. At 4 A.M. Orderly returned from Llera. Colborne it appears has marched on—could not be found. At 5 an Officer of the 7th confirmed this. Wrote Colborne and sent by an Officer of the 7th to say that we would march upon the Berlanga Loão where I hoped to get his answer, and thence to Llerena—begged to hear where he was, and would be tonight. Wrote the Marshal. Cavalry without corn—recommended that Castaños should be called upon to make an example of the Alcaldes.

Marched at 7 upon the road of Berlanga, passed Llerena and halted and dismounted for two or three hours at about 2 leagues from Berlanga—waiting the return of the Officer sent to Col. Colborne. As he did not return, and as of course it was uncertain whether the moving upon Berlanga would be of any service commensurate with the fatigue of the Troops, marched into Llerena. Troops quartered. Officer returned from Col. Colborne at ½ past 4. He will be at La Graja at 11 tonight. Visited the Count de Penne —the purpose of the 4 Squadrons being here fully explained and understood. He proposed a Reconnaissance for the morning upon Pte. del Arco. This I should have been obliged to decline joining in, because it would have taken me out of the way of Colborne; he probably saw my backwardness and proposed another movement—upon Valverde and Azuaga. This excellently answers my purpose of standing near Colborne for tomorrow's march and gives me the Spanish Cavalry too. 'Tis probable that Colborne's appearance combined with ours will clear Azuaga and Valverde. At all events we countenance his march to Berlanga. Wrote Colborne by a confidential man. Cavalry ordered at 4 A.M. tomorrow. Wrote the Marshal and Long.

May 2. Marched with Count Penne Villemur upon Ayllones and Berlanga at 4 in the morning. His Picadores under Colonel Loto cleared Valverde on our right flank. The 70 Enemy there saved themselves at full speed and gained the Pass of Puerto de Guadalcanal. Arrived near Azuaga after some delay from the blunders of the Spaniards, opened a communication with Colborne who had received my letter and kept his appointment. The Enemy (500 Infantry and 300 Horse) retired rapidly down the hill on the Guadalcanal road, and gained the Sierra by which they retreated on Guadalcanal. This Demonstration will perhaps clear Guadalcanal. The Enemy believes Colborne much stronger than he is and this Cavalry hovering about and then moving to meet him at Azuaga will puzzle him a little. Wrote the Marshal.

May 3. Colborne to Berlanga to rest for a day, then by Carpillo and Hornaches to Almendralejo. Marched with the Count Penne Villemur by Valverde upon Llerena.

The movement of yesterday has succeeded fully, the fugitives from Azuaga reached Guadalcanal at 9 last night and Latour Maubourg's whole force were in march for the Rear by 11. He has fallen back upon Cazalla towards Seville. Fuente Ovejuna is also evacuated and the whole Province ours. The Movement of the *Colomne mobile* therefore has had its full effect, even more perhaps than what we expected and Colonel Colborne's judgement and ability in the conduct of the Duty he has been charged with have been most conspicuous. Wrote the Marshal from Valverde. Returned with the 4 Squadrons to Llerena. Estremadura is thus decidedly cleared, without the loss of a man, Latour Maubourg's force thus deceived and manœuvred into a retreat was 3 times more in Infantry and 3 times in Cavalry. At Guadalcanal—Cavalry 1500, Infantry 5500, Artillery 11 pieces; at Alanis 4 Squadrons; at Valverde Cavalry 70; at Azuaga Infantry 500, Cavalry 250; Puerte de Ovejuna Infantry 500, Cavalry 150. Total:—Cavalry 2200, Infantry 6300, Artillery 11 pieces. Colborne's force was:—Infantry 2200, Cavalry 150, Guns 2; 2 Squadrons with me 300; Spaniards 350; Total, Infantry 2200; Cavalry 800, Guns 2.

May 4. Colborne marched this morning at 2 A.M., he will pass through or near La Granja, shew towards Pte. d'Ovejuna, and bivouac on the road to Campille, shew towards the Sierra and thus be heard of in La Mancha, march upon Hornaches and Ribeira towards Almendral and arrive by the 8th having thus completed his Tour, with great ability and effect in 10 days. This is the same time he would have taken to return by Llerena and Fuente de Cantos, and circumstances have now. rendered his returning by that route unnecessary. Colborne proposed this change to me at Azuaga when I met him there, after the Enemy had retreated, and I of course agreed to it, as well because I respect his judgement, as that the Marshal had a view to this return, should the other become unnecessary, and gave me, before I left him, discretionary power to adopt it if I should think proper.

Dispatched a letter to the Marshal which I wrote last night and left open for the news of the morning. Detailed to him Colborne's route and explained the reasons. Told him my intention of returning to Head Quarters tomorrow if nothing should occur here to prevent it. Called his attention to the foregoing, and provisioning the Troops, and reminded him of calling in the aid of Castaños to effect this purpose at Usagre and elsewhere, wherever good will failed and coercion became necessary. There are abundant means everywhere. In all these marches both this Cavalry and Colborne's Corps have had the most ample supplies. In our Commissary there's neither the conciliation to persuade, nor energy to enforce.

The Count communicates to me that Ballasteros refuses to send one of his Battalions to Guadalcanal from Monte-molin, unless he gets orders from the Marshal or Castaños. This childish stickling for forms at a distance from Head Quarters, and when occasion presses, is very mischievous. Reported it to the Marshal before I closed my letter and begged his interference.

Suggested to him also to urge Castaños to cause the important post of Fuente de Ovejuna, the key to the road to Cordova, to be immediately occupied by a Battalion, a Squadron and Gun or two, under an Officer of trust. It can scarcely be conceived the Enemy have gone to any great distance, and it is not at all impossible that they may return when the coast is clear of the British Troops, and hold their former posts. This however will not be very easy if the Spaniards occupy them in the manner their local importance demands, and their local advantages admit of ; they are very strong by nature.

The Intelligence of the Count Penne Villemur, who certainly ought to have good, if it be in the power of any one to get it, is upon all occasions very vague, uncertain, and indefinite. He has no positive intelligence yet where the main body of the Enemy has halted, he knows from the reports of Peasants that a part of him is in Cazalla, but where the others are he has no idea. At all events the rapid way in which the Enemy's Division retired from the important pass of the Puenta de Guadalcanal, is a clear proof that he has no intention to stand and that he would instantly fall back before a real advance, who has given up a post of such consequence to a demonstration. The French Officers were at Supper when the detachment from Azuaga arrived, and they mounted and marched in the greatest hurry and precipitation.

5 P.M. It would appear that the French or their Rear Guard still occupy the heights of Alaris upon the high

road to Seville by the Barcas de Torina, but not so far advanced as Cazella.

Colonel Nivis of the Catalonian Brigade of Light Infantry sent to Guadalcanal by the Count reports that they are encamped there but does not state their numbers. This is the true style of a Spanish report; but that they are there, few or many, I don't doubt, for by enquiring carefully since the report came in of some Peasants who are acquainted with the country, I find that Alaris is a very excellent and important Post, and if the whole Division has halted there it would be no matter of surprise to me —for it now appears that this Alaris that Count Penne Villemur and his Officers scarcely knew by name, has a road leading directly to Azuega, better than that of Guadalcanal and as near,—and these good Spaniards were quite ignorant that by one short march upon this road from Azuega whatever was posted at Guadalcanal might be cut off entirely from the roads from Cordova and Seville. The knowledge of this road in his rear accounts for the Enemy's alarm and precipitation, when he supposed us in force at Azuega and standing upon it. This makes it very likely that he has stopped at Alaris, to see what is to be undertaken against him. Where he is he can see well about him and his retreat is open, and secure from this side. It is very clear, however, that retreat is his object,—and Blake who is arrived at Zeres de los Caballos, may effect it if he will by two or three marches of himself and Ballasteros upon Mortenolin and Cazella,—this would place him in the rear of Latour Maubourg who with the fear of the British before him would want to cross the Guadalquivir.

May 5.[1] Marched off the 4 Squadrons at 5 A.M. for Usagre. The Count's Reports of this morning make the Enemy certainly to have sent off his baggage and Guns to Constantina. Some of them affirm him to have marched from Alaris in that direction altogether. The first of these reports is probably authentic, and the latter probably

---

[1] On May 5 Wellington also fought the Battle of Fuentes de Oñoro, about which there are several interesting letters from Colonel Alexander Gordon. ' I must now with regret inform you,' he adds, ' that the fruits of this brilliant victory have been most unfortunately lost to us, that the laurels most deservedly gained by Lord Wellington and the Army on the 5th have been snatched from us most unaccountably. The Garrison of Almeida, after having blown up the works, succeeded in making their escape on the night of the 10th.' See Oman, iv, pp. 349 *et seq.*

premature, although every appearance indicates his immediate march. The fact is his Camp was at St. Nicholas, near Constantina, and his Rear Guard only at Alaris.

Hellier sets out immediately for Guadalcanal to ascertain the true state of this, for no report procured by the Count can in any way be depended upon. Returned by Usagre and Villa Franca to Almendralejo. The preparations for the Siege being at length reported complete by Colonel Fletcher the Commanding Engineer, and the Bridge over the Guadiana near the confluence of the Caya in readiness, the Marshal has ordered the investment and the Troops have begun to move according to ' L.P.' which I met on my return. It appears that Bessières (Duke of Istria) has assembled all that he can at Valladolid to join Masséna, near Ciudad Rodrigo, and that this latter General has received orders from Bonaparte to wipe off the blot from the French Military reputation sustained in the Campaign in Portugal by bringing Lord Wellington immediately to action. If this be so a General Action will shortly, in all probability, take place—perhaps nothing is more to be wished for, a complete defeat, which there can scarcely exist a doubt of, to the Enemy, will settle affairs in that quarter, and by allowing Lord Wellington, if he thinks fit, to send two additional Divisions to this Army, enable him, so soon as Badajoz shall be ours, rapidly to clear Andalusia and most likely even Murcia.

May 6. Head Quarters—Talavera Real.

BADAJOZ INVESTED. Major General Stewart reports that he completed the investment of Badajoz, by 9 o'clock in the morning of yesterday the 5th without loss, with the Brigades of Lumley, Alten, and the Portuguese Brigade of Algarve.

Colonel Kemmis's Brigade from Montijo to Bivouac to-morrow between El Tesorio on the Left bank of the Gebora and Pte. de Gebora. The rest of the Army to Bivouac in the nearest part of the Oak-wood on the Valverde side of Badajoz, and the duty be taken by Brigades.

The Fords of the Guadiana everywhere practicable. To Badajoz/

May 7. Fixed the Bivouac for the Besieging Army, about three miles from the place, in the Oak-wood, the Left upon the Olvenza Road. The place has been very ably invested by General Stewart. Dickson destines 14 24-pounders and two 8-inch Howitzers for the principal attack on the left bank, and five 24-Pounders and two 8-inch Howitzers for that of St. Cristobal, on the right. General Lumley sent to Elvas, from thence taking with him 4 6-Pounders, 2 Squadrons Portuguese Cavalry and the 17th Portuguese Regt. of Infantry, he will proceed to Santa Espacia, behind St. Cristobal, and be met there before day-light by Colonel Kemmis from El Tesorio, the attack of St. Cristobal then to proceed under General Lumley and Capt. Squire.

Colborne remains at Almendralejo till further orders.

Returned to Talavera. Ordered Kemmis's march to rejoin his Division. The Marshal arrived from Olivenza.

May 8.   Talavera Real and Camp before Badajoz.

The Corps under Major General Lumley.—Brigade of Genl. Kemmis :—27th, 40th, 97th Regiments ; 17th Portuguese Infantry. 2 Squadrons 3rd Portuguese Cavalry ; 4 four-pounders, assembled in the morning near Santa Espacia and took possession of the heights behind St. Cristobal. The Enemy opposed this, but was driven back ; our loss was from 20 to 30 wounded, a few badly ; the 17th Portuguese Regt. (their first time under fire) behaved remarkably well. At 8 P.M. the Trenches were opened near the River on (Pardelliras) the Left, and upon the side of Picurina on the Right, upon the left Bank, and about 400 yards from the Fort of St. Cristobal on the Right Bank of the Guadiana. The loss was very trifling. The work went on all night, and the progress made was good. The Enemy's shot and shell badly thrown, most of the latter failed in exploding.

May 9.   In the morning returned to Talavera.

Letter from Col. Colborne. He has a little extended his Tour and very judiciously by Belalcazar, Valsez, and Campanacio, and is returning by Alanje to Almendralejo ; he'll arrive there on the 11th. The French had a Subaltern and 60 men in the Castle of Belalcazar, and Colborne could not get into it. He has skirted upon La Mancha, and passed through part of the Serera, shewing in all those parts where his appearance could be of effect, and has performed the service given him admirably. Wrote him by the Officer's return. Sent a distribution to Col. Murray.

Two Captains of Engineers and one (English) of the 17th Portuguese Regiment were wounded in the approaches of St. Cristobal. The Enemy has turned his principal attention towards it, and has given so much obstruction that it will not be practicable to get in the Guns to the Battery there before tomorrow night. Blake has arrived at Frejenal. Count Lumières sent to Blake.

May 10. Working parties going on. Enemy made a Sortie into work behind St. Cristobal. Driven out immediately with great spirit, but the Covering Party suffered severely both in advancing and returning by the shot and shell from the Fort and Town. Loss being today on the side of Lumley; on the side of Pardelliras and Picurina nothing.

May 11. Battery opened upon St. Cristobal before it was intended. The Fire therefore very inferior to the Enemy. Our loss there today very considerable. Yesterday and today, 6 Engineers out of 9, killed or wounded at St. Cristobal. Soult reported to be advancing to attempt Raising the Siege. Works going on. Battery opened upon Picurina.

May 12. March of Soult confirmed. 20,000 Infantry; 2 to 3,000 Cavalry last night at Santa Olalla. Lumières returned. Blake falling back upon Barcarotta. Move up to meet Soult and fight him some where near Albuera according to Lord Wellington's instructions. We can return to the Siege afterwards, meanwhile the operations must be to a certain degree suspended, and the Stores as far as is practicable put in safety during the Contest.

May 13. Head Quarters removed to Valverde. 2nd and Portuguese Divisions and 9-pounder Brigade also ordered to March in the morning, in consequence of Intelligence received by the Marshal after his arrival, of the actual Advance of Soult from the Mountains.

May 14. General Long at Santa Martha. Madden at Solana. Rode over the ground to the Albuera and to the Left.

May 15. Head Quarters Albuera. Marched the Divisions of Hamilton and Stewart and the Brigade of Alten to Albuera. Took up with Hamilton and Stewart a Line following the contour of the Ground parallel to the Albuera, about ¾ of an English Mile from the River, the

Right upon the High Road from Valverde. Orders sent
to Long to fall back upon Albuera from Santa Martha ; to
Madden to march from Solana upon Talavera, and to
Genl. Blake to march his Spanish Division from Almendral
to Albuera ;—the prolongation of the English Line was
destined for the Spanish Troops of Blake, his Left upon the
Valverde Road, his Front along the contour of the ground
parallel to the Albuera. This is not a good position, but
it is the only one. Blake and his Division did not arrive
till past midnight and then in spite of all instruction took
up wrong ground in the dark. Alten held the Village of
Albuera and Campbell's Portuguese Brigade was attached
to him. Cole ordered to march at 2 o'clock tomorrow
from the Bivouac, and Kemmis's Brigade by Jerumenha
after the Stores should be all sent off to Elvas.

Long [1] was driven rather faster than one could have
wished from Santa Martha and retiring precipitately,
crossed the Albuera, and gave up the whole Right bank to
the Enemy. This haste is a bad thing, because the woods
masque all the Enemy's movements.[1] Madden ordered to
Albuera.[2]

May 16. At day-break the Spaniards commenced to
get into their General alignment, which their total want of
all system of movement, and consequent unwieldiness,
took up such a length of time that they were not in till
7 A.M. The Cavalry which had covered the ground
destined for the Spaniards, were now moved to a Bivouac
in the rear of the right of the British, for rest and forage.
Cole arrived at 8 o'clock. The Officer sent to Madden
returned from Talavera without finding him—it appears
he has retired from thence without orders, where no one
knows.

At 8 o'clock the Enemy were seen beginning to pass the
River. He menaced our centre and left pretty strongly
and directed his real Attack upon our Right. (The
Spaniards 2nd Line thrown *en potence* upon the heights of
the Right.) For this he had good reason, it was the key
of the Position and was also the direct road to cut off our

---

[1] Quoted Oman, iv, p. 372.
[2] See Oman, iv, p. 374, footnote.

Communications. The Firing began at half past 8. The Enemy advanced upon the Right and drove the Spaniards from the Heights. It was necessary to retake them promptly. The Enemy had rapidly established himself upon them and got up a powerful Artillery. The Spaniards to save time as being the nearest Troops were to attack and General Stewart's Division to support. General Hamilton remaining in Reserve to move to either point and sustain if required, either the Centre or Right. Meanwhile the Division of Cole was placed obliquely, behind the Right of the British Line, to cover its Flank or support its Rear. General Lumley with the Cavalry, British and Spanish, was in front of Cole upon the plain, and Col. Otway with the Portuguese Cavalry covered and watched the Left of the whole, beyond the Town of Albuera. The French occupied the heights they had gained with 18,000 Infantry and some Cavalry,—of the latter they had an overwhelming superiority, and with 26 Squadrons to Lumley's 12, manœuvred on our Right.

The contest was bloody and obstinate, it lasted from 10 A.M. *till* 2 P.M. An uninterrupted fire of Artillery and Musketry, the latter frequently at 20 paces asunder, varied at short intervals by partial charges of the Bayonet, continued for the four hours. From 12 till 2 it was the hottest action of the Peninsular War and unequalled in the memory of the oldest soldier. The Enemy brought up reserve upon reserve, but at 2 he could make no further efforts, he was turned by both flanks. The heights were carried and the battle gained by the invincible valour of the British and Portuguese Troops. The Spaniards behaved gallantly but were so devoid of discipline that they stood in the way and did more harm than good. The Enemy retired to his Camp, a Fusillade and Cannonade lasted till night-fall, and each Army occupied itself in repairing its disasters as far as practicable, in sending off its wounded, and in making arrangements for a renewal of the Action tomorrow. Soult will probably attack again. An Officer despatched to hasten Kemmis's Brigade. Even that small reinforcement is necessary to us, for the loss has fallen heavily upon our most precious people, our British. Out of about 6,000 of them engaged, I'm afraid we shall find nearly 3,000 *hors de combat*. They have nobly upheld the honour of their name, and whatever may be the fruits of the Victory of Albuera, it has been desperately fought for and brilliantly achieved.

May 17.   The Enemy quiet.   His loss has been severe. Three Generals of Division killed, three dangerously wounded, with a host of Officers Supérieurs, 2,000 dead upon the field and more than 4,000 wounded.   This he has paid for his attempt.   I doubt his renewing it.[1]   Kemmis arrived.   This makes us better and if he saw the Brigade arrive he'll give up the task.

May 18.   At day-break the Enemy had abandoned the Bridge, and there was reason to suppose he was moving to his right or rear.   Early in the morning this became manifest and by 11 o'clock he was in full march covering his rear with all his Cavalry; he took the road of Solana and Almendralejo.   The Cavalry followed.   The Infantry remained.   Hamilton ordered to reinvest Badajoz at day-break.

REINVESTMENT OF BADAJOZ

May 19.   Badajoz reinvested at Day-break.   Not a supply of any kind received by the Town.   Not even a French advanced post got in sight of it.   Not a *fascine* of the Siege stores lost.

The Enemy still remained at Solana, or at least a very strong Rear Guard ; the Cavalry continued watching, but the Marshal very judiciously determines not to pursue, as he is not strong enough to complete their destruction. Badajoz reinvested on the South bank by General Hamilton's Division and Brigadier Genl. Madden's Cavalry Brigade.   Otway to Talavera.   2nd and 4th Divisions removed to the wood on the Right bank of the Albuera. Baron Alten placed there yesterday.

Every effort to get all the Wounded moved.   The 4th Division employed all day with 1,500 Spaniards in this work.   The French Wounded brought to Albuera ; English Surgeons attend them.   English Commissary to provision them.   Spanish Troops to Cantonments road Almendral, for they have nothing to eat.

May 20.   The Enemy's Rear Guard, 18 Squadrons and 4,000 Infantry, broke up at 5 A.M. and marched from Solana upon Fuente del Maestre.   Cavalry followed. Marshal despatched Arbuthnot with the Official Detail of the Battle to Lord Wellington who arrived at Elvas yester-

[1] See Oman, iv, p. 396, footnote.

day. Near 1,000 Killed. Killed and Wounded 4.500
British and Portuguese; 3,600 of the whole British.
Soult is wounded in the shoulder, three Generals dead,
Four Generals grievously wounded, a crowd of Officers
Supérieurs, and from 7 to 8,000 Killed and Wounded.

May 21. Lord Wellington arrived, and rode over the
Field of Battle. He is perfectly satisfied and well-pleased.
The Marshal gave out his orders of thanks to the Troops.[1]

Intercepted letter of Gazan to Soult proves their Army
to be in the greatest confusion and disorder, and that they
carry with them near 5,000 Wounded with only 5 Surgeons
to attend them. This with above 2,000 Dead, and 1,000
Prisoners left in our hands, brings their loss to 8,000 at
once, and it will probably be found to reach 9,000.

Second Division, 4th Division, Baron Alten and the
British 9-pounders ordered to march at day-break in the
morning upon Solana. Cavalry near Almendralejo and
Azeuchal. The Marshal sent a Flag of Truce to Badajoz,
demanding Medical Assistance, clothing, &c. for the French
Wounded. We have none for them. We have fed and
dressed and attended them, but we can't cover, or remove
them. He answered 'We can't,' and thus they must perish.

May 22. Column of Infantry and Artillery marched
as ordered last night.

Enemy withdrew from Azeuchal and Almendralejo.
Saw his Rear Guard entering Villa Franca. His Infantry
at Fuente del Maestre. Cavalry at Almendralejo. Posts
upon the Road in part. Infantry for the night at Solana.
Blake required to push a Division to Feria and to march to
Zafra. 320 Wounded French found here. Most of them
never dressed.

May 23. The Enemy pretty strong in Cavalry at
Villa Franca at day-break. His Post of Infantry, 5,000
Men and 4 Guns, marched yesterday to Ribera from
Fuente del Maestre and this morning at day-break to
Usagre. The Cavalry remained till ½ past 8 A.M. and then
broke up from Villa Franca and marched upon Usagre.
The Enemy has sent his great Column of Wounded &c. by
Hornaches and Fuente Ovejuna to Cordova.[2]

The Cavalry to follow up the Enemy past Llerena and
then to take up their former Cantonments, Los Santos,

---

[1] See D'Urban's *Report* . . . app. iii.
[2] 'As a matter of fact, they moved by Constantina to Seville,' Sir
Charles Oman notes.

Zafra, Villa Franca, Ribera, etc.   2nd Division from Solana to Almendralejo.   4th and Alten to Azeuchal.

The total loss of the French more than 10,000 Men, admitted by Latour Maubourg's Chief of the Staff.

Head Quarters as yesterday Almendralejo.

May 24.   French still in full retreat.   Cavalry near Villa-Garcia.   Alten to Villa Alba.   Troops resting.

May 25.   This morning at ½ past 5 A.M. the Enemy's Cavalry in force, about 2,000 with 4 Light Guns, pressed back the Spanish advance from Villa-Garcia and pushed it upon Usagre; so soon as they crossed the Rivulet of Usagre in pursuit, they were charged by M. Genl. Lumley with the 3rd Dragoon Guards and 4th Dragoons flanked by a charge of Madden's Portuguese Cavalry, and driven back in confusion with the loss of 350 Dragoons killed, a Colonel, two Officers Supérieurs, several other Officers, and 72 Men Prisoners.

The Marshal goes to Elvas tomorrow to see Lord Wellington.   Orders to that effect.

May 26.   The Marshal went by Santa Martha, Valverde, and Olivenza to Elvas.   He had an interview with General Blake at the former place, and pressed upon him the pushing forward to Monasterio and the occupying permanently, as soon as the retiring of the Enemy should have rendered it possible, the Posts of Guadalcanal, Heights of Alaris, Fuente Ovejuna, and ultimately Belalcazar.   All this had been before recommended in writing both to Genl. Blake, Castaños, and Lord Wellington.   Its execution is of the utmost consequence.

At Valverde and Olivenza the Marshal visited all the Wounded.

May 27.   The Marshal continued his route to Elvas. He there found Lord Wellington occupied with the recommenced Siege of Badajoz, which the Marshal had reinvested on the Left Bank of the River on the 19th with one Division and a Brigade of Cavalry sent back from Albuera, and which his Lordship invested on the 26th with the 3rd Division on the Right Bank.

Marshal Beresford here relinquished the Command of the separate Army of Estremadura, Lord Wellington having permanently assumed the conduct of the Operations in the South.[1]

[1] There follows a summary of these events.

JOURNAL VII

Second Siege of Badajoz

1811, *May* 28. No. 1 is a Memorandum for the Siege
of Badajoz and operations connected with it. The Enemy
still remained yesterday at Llerena, and held Usagre with
his Rear Guard,—of course as long as it continues to be a
matter of convenience to him, from whatever reason, to
do so, he will, as not pressed, and sees no Infantry following.
It is difficult, however, to conceive his views in staying or
how he can be spared so long from Andalusia.

May 29. Preparations for the Siege going on. Memorandum No. 2, a very excellent and able distribution.
The Marshal moved to the Bishop's Quinta.

May 30. The Marshal's strong recommendations of
Officers under the Rank of Lt. Colonel, who distinguished
themselves on the 16th for Promotion, favourably received
by Lord Wellington, who promises to support and forward
them. Plan of Albuera sent to Genl. Browning.

May 31. The Trenches opened night of 30th and
morning of 31st, with very little loss on both sides the
Guadiana. The Engineers made great progress all night,
and all the forenoon. The Fire will be ready to open everywhere upon the 2nd June. Letter intercepted from
Philippon, dated 29th to Soult,—by this it appears that
the Town did not communicate with him during his
advance, for this Letter is a Journal of proceedings, since
the Investment on the 4th May. At the end of this Letter
he says in Cypher ' with strict economy, I have bread for
3 weeks.'

June 1. The Approaches going on rapidly on both
sides of the River. No considerable loss today. The
Engineers reckoned upon opening their Fire on the morning of the 2nd; they can't however be ready till that of
the 3rd.

June 2. The Approaches carried on actively, and little loss sustained. The Garrison firing sparingly.

June 3. This morning all the Batteries opened upon the Right Bank—one of 4 Sixteen-Pounders and two Ten-inch Howitzers to enfilade the Bridge and shell the Castle : one of 4 Twenty-four Pounders and a Ten-inch Howitzer to fire upon the defences of St. Christopher : one of 5 Twenty-four Pounders and a Howitzer to breach St. Christopher ; one of 4 Twenty-four Pounders and a Howitzer, to flank St. Christopher, and batter the Castle and take the Eastern Batteries of the Place in reverse ; one on the Left Bank, a Breaching Battery for the Eastern Face, Twenty twenty-four Pounders, at 600 yards.

The Fire admirably supported through the day. No answer, excepting a few shells ; loss trifling.

June 4. Birthday of the King, whom God bless. Batteries continue. Enemy fires rather more ; trifling loss. St. Christopher's Breach in great forwardness. Breach in the Eastern Face on the Left Bank forward. All the wall down by 9 A.M. this day, but the natural slope of the hill's side forms an embankment behind it.   A New Battery of 4 Twenty-four Pounders and a Howitzer begun in the night, 400 yards to the right, and 200 yards in front of the Twenty-Gun Battery, this to Breach a Salient Angle on the right of the Breach, where they have made 4 New Embrasures, and fire well from them. Loss hitherto trifling. Two Deserters,—Garrison at ¾ Rations.

June 5. The New Battery began to play this morning and with good effect, but not with all that had been expected. The Battery continued all day very briskly. The Enemy got a Howitzer to work from St. Christopher, and another from the Ravelin near the Gate.

June 6. The Enemy opened another Battery further to his own right of the Breach, near the Turret and white House, which fired with great effect into our Breaching Battery while they were flanked, and a good deal annoyed by the Howitzers from the Ravelin and St. Christopher's. Several people killed in the approach of the New Battery. Another Battery 200 yards more in advance begun upon. The Brass Guns bad and above a third of them are become unserviceable. Some Iron ones expected tomorrow. Lt. Hawker of the Artillery killed by a shell in the enfilading Battery on the Right Bank, No. 1—a great loss—a most excellent Officer. An attempt to storm St. Christopher at 12 o'clock tonight failed, with 12 men killed and 80 wounded. The Breach was scarcely practicable, in addition to which a mistake was made. Lt. Forster, Engineers, mortally wounded—very great loss.

June 7. Drouet has passed Toledo, he has not more than 5,000 Men and this reinforcement is little or nothing for Soult. Marmont has moved his Head Quarters to Ciudad Rodrigo, and an Assembly of Troops is going on there, to what extent, or with what view, is not yet developed. I adhere to my original opinion that Soult should have been *ruined* before we thought of Badajoz. It must have fallen to the Conqueror. We were the Conqueror if we willed it. Had Marshal Beresford been permitted to do as he wished, he had been at Seville now, and the Siege of Cadiz raised. Sir Brent Spencer would have taken care of Marmont, the South would have been conquered, Marmont if he had chosen to come to Estremadura, would have come too late to save, too feeble to retake it. He would have shared the ruin of Soult, and Badajoz would have fallen of course.

The New Battery with 7 Guns got to play this evening with good effect.

June 8. The New battery continued an excellent fire through the night and all day. The truth is that a Battery at 400 is sure to aim better than one at 800 or 600 yards. Hence the superiority of the New Battery in Breach to the two others which had preceded it. Towards morning the Enemy attempted a Working party upon the Breach, seen immediately and driven back by our Case-shot. The Breach continued to improve all day, and so did that in St. Christopher.

There was much mismanagement in the Storm of the night before last, and it failed, which is most lamentable, because nothing that English Troops attempt ought to fail, but the Attempt certainly ought not to have been made, and the Breach was by no means practicable. It was in effect the escalade of a wall, not the storm of a Breach. The Iron Guns were got into the New Battery, but the platforms were too high and there was a consequent delay in their beginning to fire.

The Enemy found means to get out a Working Party during the night upon the Breach, and clearing away the

Earth and rubbish, left at day-break about 10 feet of perpendicular ascent. Captain Patton of the Engineers badly wounded in reconnoitring the Breach.

June 9. Everything continued as usual through the day, the firing on both parts pretty much as before. At 9 o'clock in the evening another attempt was made to carry St. Christopher. It failed with the loss of some valuable Officers and Men. In fact the Breach was not, nor has it ever been, practicable.

June 10. In the morning a Sergeant of Sappers deserted from the Place. He affirms that we shall never breach where we are attempting it, that it is a solid Rock behind, and that to make all sure, the Enemy has cut a ditch behind of 10 yards wide, throwing the Earth inwards *en Banquette* to give an Infantry upon the Crest of the Breach; be this as it may, the Battery has had very little Additional effect, and our Guns become rapidly unserviceable; the fact is the Engineers have begun on the wrong side.[1] Towards the middle of the day Lord Wellington became certain of the march of the whole Army under Marmont for the Tagus by Puerto de Baños; this gives a new face to things; the whole War will be transferred to Estremadura or Andalusia, a few movements will shew which, meanwhile His Lordship raises the Siege of Badajoz tonight, removes the Stores again to Elvas, and gets ready to take the field with clear hands; now it is most clear that had this infernal Siege been deferred, there has been full time since the Battle of Albuera, and arrival of the 3rd and 7th Divisions to have ruined Soult, raised the Siege of Cadiz, and returned to take Sir Brent Spencer by the hand on his arrival, and fight the Battle with Marmont, under very auspicious circumstances. Soult must have been destroyed or fled before us with a disheartened and broken Army, Drouet could have arrived at Cordova without anything to join when he got there and must have remained useless upon the Skirts of Andalusia till it was our pleasure to destroy him, or retread his steps to the Tagus with a Division fatigued and jaded out of the Field.

Drouet was at Cordova on the 8th, he has collected detachments in his way till he is now said to amount to between 8 and 10,000 Men.

June 11. Removal of Siege Stores carried on with the

[1] Quoted Oman, iv, p. 418.

greatest activity. The Siege therefore may be said to have been raised last night, but the close blockade will of course continue till the last moment. Lord Wellington, very justly perhaps, conceives that if the whole Army of Marmont moves down to form a junction with Soult, there is something more in the wind than the driving us out of Estremadura. How far he is equally correct as to what that something may be, remains to be proved ; His Lordship thinks that a serious and rapid attempt will be made upon Portugal, indeed an attempt to get possession of the works at Almada before he can occupy them ; or that the Enemy will form the Siege of Elvas. He probably is right for his conception of things is almost always just, to a degree of intuition, but in the present instance,—a supply to Badajoz in the first place, and then the whole French Force proceeding into Andalusia to press the Siege of Cadiz, and secure their interests, now tottering in that Province, appears most likely.

June 12. Every Siege Store, Guns, Ammunition, etc., etc., brought off and the Siege turned into a Blockade.

Siege Raised.

B. D.

ANNEX No. 1
(Circular)

Siege of Badajoz. Memorandum by Lord Wellington. May 24th, 1811 (see ' Dispatches,' vol. vii, pp. 601–2).

ANNEX No. 2

Covering the Siege of Badajoz. Memorandum by Lord Wellington, May 29th, 1811 (see ' Dispatches,' vol. vii, pp. 618–20).

JOURNAL VIII

1811. *June* 13. The Reports from the front announced
to Lord Wellington that The Enemy were in movement on
the side of Llerena, and Hellier reported that Drouet had
reached Cordova on the 8th, was at Azuaga and Berlanga
on the 12th, and so may be said to have formed his junction
with Soult upon that day. Hamilton's Division ordered
to march to Albuera ; 7th and 3rd remain for the moment
to continue the Investment and Blockade of Badajoz.
One can never enough lament the having preferred this
Siege to effecting the total ruin of Soult, should have
allowed him time to take breath, and to receive reinforcements. He now again becomes a formidable separate
Army to act in co-operation with Marmont, and a very
great reinforcement if the Armies join ; and this neglect
alone will very likely change the War on our part from the
Offensive to the Defensive.

June 14. Albuera.—Lord Wellington rode in the night
to Albuera. Soult's Head Quarters at Los Santos, his
Advances at Villa Franca and Fuente del Maestre. Our
Cavalry at Almendralejo and Azenshal. Our Infantry
fallen back to the woods of Albuera there joined by
Hamilton from Badajoz and all bivouacked in the wood.
It is an object to Soult to get the Cantonments we have
been occupying upon every account, and we have given
them up upon his demonstration without waiting to see
his Troops in motion. Our Out Posts now and then make
their reports from the histories of Peasants, and this leads
to a precipitation and uncertainty that is much to be
regretted. Soult has opened his right and front towards
Merida, and easily takes Marmont by the hand upon his

arrival, which will now, in all probability be speedy, for it appears that his People have been passing at Almaraz upon flying Bridges and that the Advanced Guard was at Jaruicejo on the 12th. If his Rear be decently well closed up, he can, according to this report, be at Merida upon the 16th or 17th. Blake came from Almendral and a conference with Lord Wellington.

June 15. ALBUERA.—Marmont's Advanced Guard having reached Truxillo on the 12th may be at Merida the 16th, and the Corps of Soult is evidently making a corresponding movement so that they are in all probability in communication today, and may begin their junction to-morrow. The appearances at Sta. Marta have been merely show, and the slightest expectation that Soult will fight us again upon this ground is at an end. Lord Wellington of course intends to concentrate without loss of time. This afternoon General Hamilton marches back to his old ground before Badajoz. General Hill with the 2nd and 3rd Divisions and Baron Alten, General Howard's Brigade, and that of Colonel Ashworth, fall back at day close from the Bivouac in the wood to the heights behind Albuera, and at Moon Rising continue their march to the Bivouac in the wood upon the road from Valverde to Badajoz, where they were during the short Siege of Badajoz, previous to the Battle of Albuera. The Cavalry at Moon Rising will fall back upon Albuera communicating with Madden at Talavera Real on its left, and having its advances towards Solana and Sta. Marta. Blake informed of the intended retiring movement, which has now become absolutely necessary. He too retires to the other side of the Guadiana, and will probably afterwards move into the Condado de Niebla, where he can enterprise upon Seville, should it be practicable. This pointed out to him by Lord Wellington, and he agrees with an appearance of cordiality.

June 16. Last night and this morning the arrangement of Movements determined yesterday carried into execution. Our march now puts us into the Frontiers of Alemtejo and unites us with Brent Spencer whose advance is tomorrow at Portalegre.

Lord Wellington returned at night to the Quinta de Granispi on the right bank of the Guadiana.

June 17. All the Army crossed the Guadiana. Lord Wellington's Head Quarters removed to Elvas.

Q

June 18.   Army covered in Elvas and Camp Mayor. Soult at Almendralejo.   Reynier between Truxillo and Merida, Marmont on his march to Truxillo.

June 19.   The Army between Elvas and Campo Mayor. Part in the latter ;   part bivouacked on the Caya.   Head Quarters Sta. Olala.

Lord Wellington at Quinta de St. João, near Vicente.

June 20.   French advance of 1,500 Horse entered Badajoz.   Castaños fixed his Head Quarters at Sta. Olala.

June 21.   His Lordship's proposed Position will probably be from Ouguella on the Left, to the Rear of Campo Mayor and to the Caya on the Right, that is to the Atalaya de Loupo de Maita ;   having a Redoubt there to close the Flank.   This will be an excellent Position if the Enemy will come there, and he will move with much risk if he ventures to pass it.

June 22.   The Enemy reconnoitred this morning with 14 Squadrons upon Campo Mayor, and with something stronger upon Elvas ;   in the former direction he was checked before he could see our Infantry.   In the latter he gave us the misfortune (by the blunder of a Brigadier Genl.) to cut off a Captain's Picket of the 11th Dragoons.

June 23.   Army assembled.   All the Divisions arrived from the Beira.

June 24–25.   The Enemy made some movements that indicated nothing decisive.   His Columns moved backwards and forwards on the Left Bank of the River between Olivenza and Badajoz, and Badajoz to Montijo and Corte de Peleas and Talavera Real ;   no judging what he means yet ;   meanwhile everything is ready for him.[2]

June 26–28.   No movements of consequence.   Reconnaissances, Foraging Parties and Appearances to occupy our attention.

June 29–*July* 1–2.   Appearances of separating movement upon the part of the Enemy.   Soult gone to Seville. Marmont reported to be in march for Truxillo.   The Marshal set out for Lisbon.

July 3–11.   No change.

---

[1] Wellington's letter, June 18, 1811, to Beresford on the defence of Elvas is enclosed—*Despatches* . . . viii, pp. 33–35.

[2] Memorandum enclosed . . . 'in the event of the enemy making a movement in such force as to render expedient a greater concentration of troops.'

Blake has never got to Seville, and has, after having, with his characteristic stupidity, lost some days at Catelligos, been shamefully foiled by 300 French at Niebla. Marmont has suspended, if he ever intended, the prosecution of his march towards the Tagus. The Cavalry of his Rear Guard are yet no further than Montijo.

July 12–14. Lord Wellington reviewing the Divisions in succession. Reinforcements arriving at Lisbon, where General Graham landed from Cadiz on the evening of the 9th.

July 15. An intercepted letter of the 4th July from Belliard, Governor of Madrid, to Marmont, begs for reinforcements at Madrid, because Bassecourt with 12,000 Men had arrived from Cuenca, within 3 or 4 marches.

July 16–17.[1] The Enemy are certainly falling back and so much so as to allow of his Lordship's taking up Summer Cantonments, which he has determined upon doing forthwith. (See A.P.)

Present Strength of Lord Wellington :—

	Rank and File
Artillery	2,200
Cavalry	4,200
Infantry	44,600
	51,000 Total Rank and File [2]

July 18. 3rd and 6th Divisions marched for Castello Branco.

July 19. 7th Division marched for Niza.

Lord Wellington proposes to open with Ciudad Rodrigo. Dickson gone by Abrantes to Oporto. (Battering Train there :—32 Twenty-four Pounders ; 8 Ten-inch Mortars ; 2 Eight-inch Howitzers.) 'Tis the only way, he was not strong enough to make Marmont sure, less for Cadiz, independent of the unhealthy season, but in 6 weeks or

[1] Two letters from Beresford to D'Urban, the second from Lisbon, July 11.

'. . . I write to say . . . that I hope you understand your stay with the army is quite in your own option [D'Urban was probably offered leave for a period of rest] and that I shall be glad when you can get down to me, though I do not press it if you wish to stay some time longer, or if you think it necessary so to do, tho' I should think Harvey [assistant to Wellington's Q.M.G., George Murray] now quite *au fait* to execute any instructions you may leave with him . . .'

[2] Quoted Oman, iv, p. 450.

2 Months he will be 60,000 effectives,—probably the Enemy not much stronger than at present. They must give him Ciudad Rodrigo, or fight to save it. The first a most important acquisition. The last sure for him for he will be stronger. Meanwhile when he moves, he'll leave 2 Divisions to watch the 5th Corps—if it closes upon Marmont, the 2 Divisions will close upon Lord Wellington.

July 20. Tarragona has fallen. [28th June.]

July 21. Remaining Divisions break up and march to their Quarters of Summer. All will have arrived on the 24th.

July 22. Rode to Aldea Gallega to rejoin the Marshal.

July 23. To Lisbon.

July 24.[1] Lord Wellington removed his Quarters to Portalegre and the last of the Troops entered into their Summer Quarters.

There follows a summary of events since May 1810 that is so excellently written that it must be given. Its perusal heightens one's regrets that D'Urban never wrote a history himself. He led, perhaps, too active a life for such an undertaking, but that he seems to be ever thinking of it is shown by the profuse annotations he made in Jones's ' Journal of the Siege ' and the eagerness with which he joined in refuting the charges of Napier against his chief, Beresford, and other officers.

SUMMARY

1811. *July* 24. Thus at length has closed for the moment this long and important Campaign of 15 Months' duration, which began in the May of 1810 by the Assembly of the 'Army of Portugal ' before Ciudad Rodrigo. Its operations have been marked by Four Pitched Battles, Bussaco, Barrosa, Fuentes de Oñoro and Albuera, and many Affairs that in common periods would have received the Name of Battles. It has presented to the World what have been seen with astonishment, because in prospect it could scarcely have been looked for. An Army of 100,000 French Men, Warriors accustomed to Conquest, who had beaten and bullied all Continental Europe, magnificently appointed, and led by the most eminent of the Peers of the

---

[1] In another letter of July 24 from Cintra, Beresford says that he is glad to hear of D'Urban's arrival at Lisbon, ' as we shall soon see you here, where your rooms are ready and tho' my house is pretty full, unoccupied. . . . I am getting here much better,' he concludes, ' and indeed to see me I do not suppose one would think much ailed me and I hope they would not be far wrong. . . '

Modern Charlemagne, 'the Spoiled Child of Fortune,' was collected and prepared for the avowed and sole object of Conquering Portugal and driving the English into the Sea. This was its object—nothing short of this—this Bonaparte held out to France, to the Peninsula, and to the World,—this Masséna proclaimed to his Army,—of this they wrote, and talked and dreamed, and of effecting it they were assured and confident. Mark the Sequel! Against this Army Lord Wellington defended the Country, and with what?—25,000 British Troops, 30,000 Portuguese. This was their very utmost amount. The Former indeed, though few in number, were of tried valour and transcendant discipline. Europe had witnessed, and the Enemy had felt their Prowess at Roliça, Vimiero, and Talavera. But the Latter were New Levies, and of an Infant Army. They had never been in Fire, were of a Nation that had sunk in Military Renown, and what their bearing would be when tried, the Trial was yet to prove. Our able and dexterous Chief conducted Masséna almost in the outset to a spot of all others in Portugal (and which the latter might have avoided), best calculated to make this Trial with the least risk of ruinous consequences from its failure. Bussaco proved that the painful labours of Marshal Beresford had not been thrown away, that the Troops he had formed were steady, and could be relied on, and from that instant Lord Wellington was confident of his ultimate success, and firmly and tranquilly adhered to the Plan his own superior Genius had formed,—the only measure that could have saved Portugal. It did save it, and in the March of 1811, the French Army, diminished by one half, again reached Ciudad Rodrigo, from whence it had marched in September, after a Retreat of unparalleled hardships and privations, and a succession of bloody partial Actions, every one of which they lost, and if this Campaign had produced no greater Battles,—if Bussaco, Barrosa, Fuentes de Oñoro, and Albuera, had never been fought,—Redhina, Chao de Lammas, the Ceira, and Sabugal would have well attested the Enemy's inferiority.

With fresh Troops, and as a last desperate effort, Masséna tried his Fortune once again at Fuentes de Oñoro,—and for the last time foiled and baffled, beaten and out-generalled, returned to the Emperor to lay before his Throne, the Trophies, the Triumphs (?) and the Spoils of his Army of Portugal.

These Operations North of the Tagus cost the French Army from 50, to 60,000 Men; and the Allies 5, to 6,000.

While this great game was playing in the North, subordinate, and co-operating ones were upon the Cards in the South; Cadiz was besieged without effect by Victor, who in the end of March again proved the edge of the weapon he had felt before, and beaten at Barrosa by half his numbers, read General Graham's [1] commentary upon the Text of Talavera.

Meanwhile Soult from Seville, with the Andalusian and part of the Murcian Armies, advanced to the Guadiana, and with much ability, aided by the treachery of Imas, and the imbecility of Mendizabal, defeated and dispersed the Spanish Army and took Badajoz.

One small allied Army could not be infinitely multiplied. To root out Masséna was the great and paramount object, and till that was effected Lord Wellington's Force would not admit of his detaching for any other purpose ; upon the instant, however, that he was decidedly in retreat, upon the third day of it even, he did not hesitate to detach three Divisions under Marshal Beresford to the South. This Force succeeded in all its preliminary measures, cleared Alemtejo, which Mortier had just begun to tread upon, purged Estremadura of the French from the Guadiana to the Sierra Morena, and formed the Siege of Badajoz. To save the Town which he had taken, and justly held as a very precious possession, Soult moved Heaven and Earth in Andalusia, collected a most splendid Army, the best at that time which remained to the Enemy in Spain, and advanced by rapid marches to raise the Siege ; for a moment he did so, Marshal Beresford had not a sufficient Force to Besiege and fight at once. He raised the Siege therefore, advanced one March to meet the Enemy, and fought the Battle of Albuera. Here as in all former Battles of the Peninsular War the French were defeated, with immense comparative loss, and would have been destroyed Root and Branch but for their doubly superior Cavalry.

The march of all the French Armies collected from the North and South were just sufficient at the close of the Campaign to save Badajoz for the present, and Lord Wellington raised the Second Siege of the Place, when the Junction of Marmont with the whole collected Army of the South rendered it imprudent any longer to carry on that operation against a superior Force.

Thus closed the Campaign ; the Enemy failed in every great Object for which he had begun it, was beaten out of Portugal, lost 4 Pitched Battles, and 80,000 Men, Masséna, Ney, Junot, Reynier, Victor, Soult, Marmont, and Bessières, and Loison, the Conquerors of Austria, Prussia, Poland, Italy, and Egypt, all had a part, all were in succession foiled, and beaten, and the Peninsula has at once become the Grave of Hosts of the French Warriors and of the Military Supremacy of France.   B. D.

[1] Founder of ' the United Service Club as a place of rendezvous for his old Peninsular comrades, who looked upon him as a kind of father.' (Oman, iv, p. 97, footnote.)

JOURNAL IX

1811, *July–December*

INTRODUCTION

THESE months while D'Urban is in Lisbon (making ' arrange-ments in his office ') are comparatively uneventful.

Wellington, having re-organized the Anglo-Portuguese Army and placed his troops in cantonments, is now ' in such a strong position, being at last in possession of an adequate proportion of mounted men,' that he can confidently await the French offensive that comes in September, when they make an attempt to relieve Ciudad Rodrigo. But though the blockade is raised, they are not in strong enough numbers to attack Wellington—in short from July to December there is much manœuvring but little change comes from it.

The Journal is therefore sketchy but attached are full details of the Army's cantonment.

1811, *July* 22.   Arrived in Lisbon from the Alemtejo. The Marshal at Cintra.

July 23.   Arrangements of my Office in Lisbon.

July 30.   Army taking up Cantonments ; all arriving on the 25th.

July 31.   Joined the Marshal at Cintra.

Aug. 1–25.   CINTRA.—Upon the 28th July Lord Wellington received intelligence of Ciudad Rodrigo being in great want of Provisions and thought it a sufficient object to induce him to break up immediately from his Cantonments, contrary to his original intentions and march to beat up the Town, he did so accordingly (see Distri-bution X).—And for his views, objects, and opinions of probable events, see A.B. (the substance of his Letter to the Marshal of the 7th August.

Aug. 26–*Sept.* 18.   The Marshal remained at Cintra. Lord Wellington in his Cantonments on the Beira.

Sept. 19.   Marshal at Prayas.

Sept. 30. Marmont collected his whole Force, called in Dorsenne, that is all that had been Bessières's, and threw in a Convoy into Ciudad Rodrigo.   Lord Wellington, after one or two smart Affairs of Posts, fell back two marches into the Position of Soito.   Dorsenne who had driven back Abadia to Villa Franca obliged to quit Galicia for the moment.   Marmont retired to Placencia—first—then Cantoned his Army along the Tagus to Talavera de la Reyna, and took up his Head Quarters there.   Lord Wellington moved up again.   But did not return to Fuente Quinaldo, his Head Quarters remained at Fresneda.

Oct. 1–30.   The Governor of Ciudad Rodrigo, General Regnaud, taken and Cattle carried off under the Guns of the Place by Don Julian Sanchez.   A new Governor, Genl. Barcois, and a supply of Cattle, thrown into the Town. Lord Wellington moved some Divisions to prevent it, but the coup failed.   General Hill in the Alemtejo marched upon Giraud's Division at Caceres,—this affair was admirably conducted and succeeded accordingly.   Giraud was surprised at Arroyo de Moliños, his Division dispersed. General Bron and Prince D'Arenberg taken, 37 Officers and 1,400 Men also, 500 killed.   Giraud escaped, wounded, with about 300 Men but he would not have done so but for some mismanagement and want of promptness on the part of —— (?).

Middle of October Marshal Beresford returned to Lisbon.

Nov. 1–30.   All quiet in the Quarters of Portugal. Lord Wellington had intelligence of a Convoy to be sent into Ciudad Rodrigo.   He moved some Divisions up and went himself to Fuente Guinaldo.   The Enemy was alarmed and desisted from his intention.

Lord Wellington moved back the Troops and returned to Fresneda.

Bonnet entered Asturias and advanced to Oviedo.   This was only a predatory movement; but it spread great consternation.   He pillaged all the Spanish Magazines, dispersed what Troops were in his way and retired again. The Guerilla warfare is active and more efficient than ever, but the Spaniards have no longer any Army, General or Provincial—that of Murcia has been lost by the folly and inability of Blake,—that of Valencia defeated, and its remnants shut up in Valencia, where it will fall a prey to

Suchet, by the treachery of Mahy, and that of Galicia disorganized and good for nothing, no longer deserves the Name. This latter Province is as disorganized as the Army; this has also been the work of the treachery of Mahy who was for a long time intrusted with the Province, and who when he could no longer do any mischief here was very wisely removed to ruin the affairs of his Country in Valencia.

For the last two months perpetual relapses of a lingering Feverish affection and great debility have detained the Marshal from his Army. He is better now in the end of November, and his Head Quarters will be immediately at Villa Formosa, near Lord Wellington.

Dec. 1. During the last three months the Enemy has been making great progress in the North of Spain and all the strong places there have been falling in succession, and he has received generally about 40,000 Reinforcements by driblets.

Dec. 31. To the end of the Year nothing.

The Marshal by repeated relapses has been prevented from leaving Lisbon.

B. D'URBAN.

JOURNAL X

1812, *January–March*

SIEGE AND FALL OF CIUDAD RODRIGO

INTRODUCTION

THESE months cover the first part of Wellington's campaign.
' The true backbone of the war,' says Sir Charles Oman, ' and
the central fact which governed all the rest. Here we follow
the working out of a definite plan conceived by a master mind
. . . for the initiative had at last passed into Wellington's
hands. . . .'

Beresford with his chief-of-staff, D'Urban, returns to the
' front,' and both are present at the siege and fall of Ciudad
Rodrigo.

1812, *Jan.* 1–16. The Marshal left Lisbon, inspected
Abrantes and its Garrison, and then proceeded by Thomar,
and Coimbra to Lord Wellington's Head Quarters. These
when he left Lisbon had been at Fresneda, but the Siege of
Ciudad Rodrigo had moved them upon the 6th of January
to Gallegos.

MEMORANDUM.

Lord Wellington had long been meditating the Siege of
Ciudad Rodrigo, and even before he quitted the Alemtejo
in the July of 1811, had ordered round his English Battering
Train from the Tagus to Oporto, and dispatched Major
Dickson of the Royal Artillery to the latter place to receive
and arrange it. Meanwhile from the instant that he
arrived upon the frontiers of the Beira, he never ceased to
prosecute the Repairs of Almeida so that the Train might
be received into that Fortress, and placed out of the risk
of insult. Towards the end of December Almeida was
already in a state to answer this end, and the Train and
Siege Stores were brought up the Douro and deposited
there, while a certain number of the Divisions of the Army,

whose Cantonments were nearest to Ciudad Rodrigo were ordered to make Fascines and Gabions and to hold them in readiness.

In the close of December and beginning of January, Marmont had withdrawn his Army to such a distance (as far as and beyond Madrid), that Lord Wellington saw within his reach the occasion he had looked and prepared for, and upon the 2nd January resolved upon commencing the Siege immediately. Upon a consultation with the Chief Engineer, it appeared to be the opinion of the latter, that, considering the necessities and the means, it would be impossible to be perfectly prepared to break ground before the 20th of the Month. His Lordship in reply went through every computation and every detail of preparation with the readiness of a Professed Engineer of the first order, and insisted upon what resulted from these computations, that the operations of the Siege could commence upon the 6th, but that to be sure of the whole Machine working together, he would postpone them to the 8th.

He was right,—all was ready,—and on the

Jan. 6.   Head Quarters were at Gallegos.

Jan. 7.   The Place was invested.

Jan. 8.   The Redoubt upon the Hill of St. Francisco was stormed by Col. Colborne and the Engineers broke ground there.

Jan. 9.   The Suburbs and Convent of St. Francisco were taken.

Jan. 10–12.   The work of the Trenches and Batteries were unintermitted.

Jan. 13.   Fire opened up on the Place.

Jan. 15.   The Marshal joined Lord Wellington.

Jan. 16–17.   Fire continued. New 7-Gun Battery to make a new Breach on the left of the principal one.

Jan. 18.   Seven-Gun Battery opened at Sun-rise. In the evening two Breaches were considered as practicable by some, as nearly so by all. Firing continued all night.

Jan. 19.   Breaches practicable.—Lord Wellington made his Disposition for Assaulting the Place in the evening :—

The Troops destined for this enterprise were the
  Light Division, General Craufurd,
  3rd Division, General Picton,
  Portuguese Brigade of Genl. Pack,

and the Disposition was as follows :—

1. The 2nd Portuguese Caçadores, Light Company of the 83rd and 5th Regt., all of the 3rd Division, to enter the Fausse Braye Wickets near the Almeida Gate, sweep the Fausse Braye to the Right or Greater Breach, and scale the Rampart where ever most practicable along that extent.
2. General McKinnon's Brigade and the remainder of the 3rd Division, forming in the Trenches of the Breaching Batteries, to Storm the Right Breach.
3. Light Division to Storm the Left or Lesser Breach, forming for that purpose behind the St. Francisco Convent.
4. B. Genl. Pack's Brigade to make a feint attack on the left, by the St. Jago Gate and to be guided by circumstances.

As the Sap had not been carried to the Crest of the Glacis, so that the Counterscarp retained its original height, and the Ditch its original depth, it became necessary to provide for the descent into the Ditch ; and the Advance of each Column therefore carried Wool and Hay-Bags to drop into the Ditch, and thus prepare a slope and a break for their leap down. These were succeeded by the Parties of Ladders to scale the unbreached part of the Fausse Braye, and of the Rampart.

These preparations made, the Assaults commenced at the same time, at 25 Minutes past 7 in the evening,[1] and the Town was carried by a Quarter before 8. Every Attack succeeded. The Great and original Breach had been cut off by the Enemy, but the smaller Breach having been only begun upon on the 18th could not be cut off— the People in the defence of the Great Breach, therefore, found themselves turned by the assailants of the Smaller one and abandoned it. General Pack finding little opposition on the side of St. Jago Gate changed his feint attack into a real one, and entered the Town upon that side at the same time as the other Columns.

Part of the Troops on entering lined the Ramparts, the others penetrated to the Great Square where they formed, sending out Pickets and Patroles ; resistance ceased. The Governor was taken in the Castle by Lt. Gurwood, the

[1] Cf. Oman, v, p. 177.

leader of the Forlorn Hope of the Light Division, where he had fled for safety.

His Conduct can scarcely admit of defence—to save himself with his Master, he continued to defend what was no longer defensible and exposed his Garrison to all the consequences of an assault, while he spared his own person and withdrew from the extremity which his own obstinacy had brought upon those under his command. (*Note.* I heard Lord Wellington use these words to him, a day or two after the affair, upon his making frivolous complaints of the loss of some of his Baggage. B. D.)

Thus fell Ciudad Rodrigo and this Enterprise whether viewed in its conduct or its consequences, is equally brilliant and satisfactory. Lord Wellington has baffled Marmont, as he has before done every other French General opposed to him, and has possessed himself of this most important Fortress after a Siege of eleven days, and before it was possible for Marmont to assemble and come to interrupt him.

This French General who is making every effort to unite his Corps at Salamanca, will now in all probability retire again, for he has no inducement equivalent to the risk of Fighting.

Jan. 20. The Storming Divisions moved out of the Town to their Cantonments. The 5th Division moved into it, and every exertion commenced for the putting all things in order, and into a state of defence.

Jan. 21. Marshal's Head Quarters to Villa Formosa.

Jan. 22–24. Bridge at Rio de Molina (on the Agueda, constructed for the Siege) taken up. Works repairing. Marmont and Dorsenne assembling.

Jan. 25. An Advance of 3,000 French pushed to Fuente St. Estevan. General Robert Craufurd who died last night of his wounds received in advancing to storm the Left Breach, and the bones of M. General McKinnon killed in the Right Breach, buried in the ditch at the foot of the Breach. All the Staff and the greater part of the Division Generals with the Commander-in-Chief attended the Funeral.—This latter Officer is a very great loss to the Service. Able, active, and intelligent. All the Corps held in readiness to move [1] at a short notice.

Jan. 26–31. The Repairing Ciudad Rodrigo going on

[1] See Oman, v, p. 212, footnote, for movements.

with all possible activity. Major Dickson dispatched to Setubal and Elvas to prepare for the Siege Stores of Badajoz which will be the next operation undertaken. The Troops will fall back (when the French decidedly separate) for Quarters of Rest and Re-equipment, on the Tagus and Mondego.

Feb. 1–6. At Villa Formosa. Lord Wellington having determined upon the Siege of Badajoz, and proposing to move the Troops and himself into the Alemtejo towards the beginning of March, everything also being quiet upon the Frontier of Castile, Marshal Beresford set out for Lisbon, where his presence was indispensably necessary, for many arrangements with the Government, and to ascertain the actual proportion of our Means to our Expenditure ; an investigation, which strange to say, has never been fully entered into hitherto, and which now becomes imperiously necessary, for the Machine, after many expedients to keep it going, at length defies them altogether, as might well be foreseen, and threatening to stop altogether. Pay, Provisions, Transport, all wanting—all in ruins.

A Radical Reform, grounded upon a bold and fearless Enquiry into every branch of the Revenue, Expenditure, and Subsidy, and an addition to the latter from England, can alone put a period to these evils, alone continue the efforts of this Country as a Nation allied to us. To this, Lord Wellington, though late, is now I trust, opening his eyes. And when the Marshal in conjunction with the Ambassador shall have made his Report, it must be immediately acted upon, for there is no time to lose.[1]

Feb. 6–16. On Route to Lisbon, by Coimbra and Leiria. The loss of Population in the Beira by the enormities of the French, and the consequent miseries of the People, has been enormous. The Comuesca of Leiria alone is reduced from 42,000 to 18,000 souls. The aggregate loss upon this ratio will have been from 80,000 to 100,000 Souls.

General Lenos, the Marshal's Military Secretary, has returned from the Brazils. The Marshal's powers are much increased—(by orders from the Prince Regent at Rio Janeiro [2]) President of the Council of War, etc.

Feb. 16–29. The Marshal at Lisbon. After a perfect

[1] See Oman, v, p. 228.
[2] See Oman, v, p. 149.

investigation it appears that the Expenditure must be nearly £6,000,000. The Means at present £3,500,000. *Nous verrons.*

March 1. The Troops in March from the Beira to the Alemtejo.

March 2. The Marshal left Lisbon for Elvas, to meet Lord Wellington there on the 5th.

JOURNAL XI

1812, *March–April*

IN ESTREMADURA—SIEGE AND FALL OF BADAJOZ—PRE-PARATIONS TO RECEIVE SOULT—HIS RETIREMENT—MARMONT'S DEVASTATION OF THE BEIRA — THE BLOCKADE OF ALMEIDA AND CIUDAD RODRIGO.

1812, *March* **2–6.** LISBON. Lord Wellington having signified his intention of setting out from Fresneda on the 1st for Elvas, the Marshal left Lisbon and proceeded by Salvatierra, Cornesa, Estremoz, Boita, and Villa Vicosa to Elvas. Arrived on the 6th.

March **7.** ELVAS. Lord Wellington has not left Fresneda 'til the 3rd. He visits Abrantes and therefore will not arrive till the 9th or 10th probably. 'Tis likely he wishes all to be in readiness to begin the Siege of Badajoz, so that his arrival may be the signal for breaking ground. The Enemy has been working hard for some months at Badajoz, particularly since the Fall of Ciudad Rodrigo. He has moved Heaven and Earth to provision it, and has replaced the weak Battalions of the Garrison by strong ones. It is now completed at 5,000 Men ; this is probably a little overrated, certainly, however, he calculates upon a defence of considerable length, which indeed, it must make, if he hopes to assemble Suchet, Soult, and Marmont to fight for its ultimate relief. Mr. Stuart arrived yesterday in the expectation of finding Lord Wellington.

March **8.** The 5th Corps is at Villa Franca, but Soult has moved upon Corunna.—Divisions arriving—*vide* ' A.'

March **9–10.** Nothing.

March **11.** Lord Wellington arrived. Battering Train and some Tin Pontoons.

March **12–13.** Distribution ' B.' Bridge ready to be laid down.

March **14.** Project ' C.'—Distribution ' D.'

March 15.   Arrangement ' E.'   Called upon to accompany Sir Thomas Graham with the Covering Corps d'Armée, which is to clear Estremadura of the 5th Corps.   This during the early part of the Siege and then return to it.

This, and from my having in the operations of last year necessarily become acquainted with the Roads and Country in which Sir Thomas Graham was going to act.

Badajoz Invested

March 16.   Lord Wellington directed Marshal Beresford to invest Badajoz.   (Divisions :—Light, 3rd, 4th, 1 Troop 3rd Regt.   Portuguese Cavalry,—Left Bank of the River ; Algarve Brigade, 1 Troop Light Cavalry, Right Bank.)

The 3rd and 4th Divisions which had been ordered to cross the River at the Bridge of Pontoons, were so late, that the Head of the Leading Division did not arrive at the River till 1 P.M. so that they were not upon their Ground till nearly 6 in the evening.

When the Marshal had posted the Divisions, I rode to Valverde and joined Sir Thomas Graham, who had crossed the River before the Investing Divisions in the morning, and who is charged with the driving out of Estremadura and clearing the Province to the Sierra Morena.   Meanwhile General Hill will be at Merida tomorrow.

Sir Thomas Graham's Corps . . . bivouacqued at Valverde.

March 17.   The General marched upon Santa Marta in Two Columns :—1 of one Division by Albuera ; 1 of Two by Almendral.

A French Battalion retired out of the Town, by Azenchal upon Villa Franca, at the approach of the Cavalry one Brigade of which overtook the Columns here having come from Olivenza.   They marched in good order, however, and no occasion offered of making an impression upon them, so that they got clean off.   General Graham rode over the Field of the Battle of Albuera.   Drouet is reported to be in Villa Franca with some Cavalry and Infantry. The probability is that he will call in immediately all his Posts and retire.

Corps Bivouacqued round Sta. Marta ; Cavalry and Head Quarters in the Town.   General Hill at Merida.

March 18.   The General is well aware that it will be

R

next to impracticable to cut off Drouet, who has so many
Roads of retreat, but there are reports that lead him to
suppose there is at least a possibility of laying hold of a
Depot, and some Magazincs, at Llerena. He therefore
proposed to give the Corps a short March today, to give
them cover for the Night, and then by a Forced March to
reach Llerena on the following night. Two Divisions
therefore to La Parca ; one and Head Quarters to Feria.
The Cavalry to Azenchal and Fuente del Maestre.

General Hill at Almendralejo.

March 19. Drouet having retired his Posts the night
before last, went himself to Ribera at 9 o'clock yesterday
morning. Villa Franca was evacuated in the night. The
General entered it at 9 this morning. The Enemy appears
to have retreated upon Hornaches, so probably to join the
Army assembling near Medellin. Everything is gone from
Llerena. No Depot. The Magazines removed to Belars
hal. The General therefore Halts the Troops at Zafra 2
Divisions ; Sancho Puez one Division. Cavalry and
Artillery Los Santos, Villa Franca, Adeira. Chain Ribera
by Usagre and Bienvenide to Fuente Cantos. Head
Quarters Zafra.

March 20. The Advanced Guard of Marmont is
advancing upon Truxillo, then to the General Rendezvous
near Medellin. All gone from Llerena. General Hill
therefore goes back to Merida. Sir Thomas Graham
occupies with the Three Divisions of Infantry, Almendralejo, Villa Franca, Azenchal, Fuente de Maestre. The
Cavalry Zafra, in addition to the places of yesterday.
Chain the same ; but a Brigade and Squadron sent to
Llerena—*pour l'eclairer*—and return by Villa Franca.
Head Quarters Villa Franca.

March 21. VILLA FRANCA.—The Enemy still held
Hornaches ; and as a part of his Infantry had been seen
at Maguilla and some had also appeared in March upon
Llerena from the side of Fregenal, the General withdrew
the small Detachment under Colonel Mitchell from Llerena
to Usagre in the evening and strengthened it by one
Squadron of the 3rd Dragoon Guards in addition. A
letter intercepted from Drouet to Genl. Rignoux at
Freyza ordering him to march upon Llerena, and if gone
from thence to cover Fuente Ovejaiz and Guadalcanal.

March 22. Enemy retired from Hornaches, from which

the General had ordered him to be dislodged at daybreak tomorrow morning. Reports agree that he is collecting everything in the Serena at Zalamea, probably 8,000. This may form the Advanced Guard of the Army of the South and Cover its debouche.

March 23. Drouet's Head Quarters reported to be at Zalamea.

Suggested something like ' Z.' The Dispersion of the 5th Corps putting the reconstruction of any part of it out of the question, must greatly embarrass the enemy and retard his assembly. The General had the goodness to think it worth while to attend to it, and charged me with a dispatch to Lord Wellington upon the subject.

Rode from Almendralejo to the Camp before Badajoz.

March 24. Reached Lord Wellington at 2 in the morning. He approved of the General's suggestion, and directed him to move accordingly. [See Dispatches of the Duke of Wellington, Vol. 9, pages 12, 13, 14.] General Hill also. Returned to Sir Thomas Graham, reached him at Villa Franca at 9 in the evening. Meanwhile corroborating reports received by —— made Drouet in movement upon Llerena. Others announced arrival of one half of the 5th Corps there, and the following of the other half. Upon receiving Lord Wellington's sanction to move, the General ordered the assembly of his Corps d'Armée at Usagre upon tomorrow morning the 25th, and so early as to enable, after resting there, to reach Llerena at daybreak on the 25th. This movement may not surprise, but at all events will dislodge and disperse Drouet, and if the report of his being at Llerena, however apparently well founded, should not be so, then very little time will have been lost, the first movement of ' Z ' will have been made, and the others can follow.

March 25–26. Assembly at Usagre. Everything up by 4 in the afternoon. Reports still make a Division of the 5th Corps (3,500) at Llerena,—not Drouet, but the General of Division Quiot. Assembly ordered at midnight at Villa Garcia. Took place accordingly. The General made his dispositions for a silent advance and attack at daybreak. The whole to move in 4 parallel Columns close to the Town. Then :—

1. Two-thirds of the Cavalry, a Battalion, and a Brigade of the Artillery, to branch off to the Left and

moving rapidly by 'a.a.a.' to get upon the Road of Guadalcanal and Valverde and cut off that escape.

2. The 7th Division to rush into the town at 'W' and 'Y' by 'b.b.b.' and 'c.c.c.'

3. The 1st Division (Guards) to support and follow.

4. Lord Blantyre's Highland Brigade and one third of the Cavalry by 'd.d.d.' to pass the Town by the front of the Mountain, and cut off that escape, ultimately meeting the Cavalry at 'x.'

5. The 6th Division in Reserve to support the whole.

The March was made in the best possible order—the arrival exactly timed,—when just at the moment of branching off, and as the morning broke—something too like a Panic was occasioned at the Head of the 7th and 1st Divisions by the appearance of a few French Dragoons, and by the galloping back of some of the Staff and Orderlies. A confused firing took place in Column! without object. General disorder ensued, and half-an-hour's delay was occasioned. This aided the escape of the Enemy about 1,300 Men, without Artillery, who took to a Mountain path 'e.e.e.' and got off.

Their escape, however, but not with such *complete impunity* would in all probability have been effected, for in spite of all precautions, their Intelligence was so perfect, that notwithstanding the Troops had made a Forced March of 10 Leagues in one day, to reach them unexpectedly, they were aware of what we were about before 12 o'clock at night, and were under arms accordingly, and we should therefore, notwithstanding the excellent dispositions of the General, not have succeeded in getting anything more than a few stragglers.

A proportion of the People of this Province have become so entirely French that the Enemy would not have more willing or more efficient Spies in France itself ! ! !

Memorandum.—Even British Troops must never be permitted to Load for a Night Attack.[1]

Troops put in Llerena and Villa Garcia. Movement ordered for tomorrow upon Maguilla.

March 27.[2] 2nd of 'Z.'

The Corps d'Armée moved to Maguilla, Llerena, Valencia

---

[1] Quoted Oman, v, p. 231, footnote.
[2] See Oman, v, p. 232, footnote.

de las Torres and Higuera.   [See Duke of Wellington's
Despatches, Vol. 9, p. 17.] Some Intelligence of an
appearance of an Assembly upon Cordova.

At the Siege of Badajoz—the Picarina taken by Storm
with considerable loss in the night of the 25th between
9 and 10.   Malcaster killed by a Cannon-shot—Established
in the Work, a Communication made.   Foot of the Scarp
seen at 300 yards.   See ' Y,' a most clear and excellent
account by Colonel Hardinge who was with Sir James
Kempt and who distinguished himself (according to his
custom) in the Storm, having been the first Man of the
Centre Attack who got into the Work.

Marmont remains in Castile.

March 28.   MAGUILLA.—Intercepted letters from Quiot
and Remord to Drouet announcing their junction at and
Occupation of Azuaga;   the General therefore ordered
Genl. Le Marchant's Brigade of Cavalry and Genl. Clinton's
Division (6th) of Infantry to Bulaya, proposing that the
1st Division marching this Evening after Nightfall, should
Halt and rest in the Wood of La Graja, and that then it
should co-operate with the 6th Division and the Cavalry
in attempting to cut off the Enemy in Azuaga . . .
Somewhat thus :—[Sketch map is enclosed]

The Cavalry found that of the Enemy on the heights
of Berlarga, drove it into Azuaga, and effectually concealed
the approach of the Infantry, which bivouacqued in the
Wood.   Towards the close of the evening the General
received intelligence which induced him to conceive that
the Enemy had left nothing more than a Post in Azuaga.
To save the Troops therefore unnecessary fatigue, he only
ordered the 6th Division with 3 Squadrons of Cavalry to
move into and Occupy Azuaga.

March 29.   The 6th Division and Cavalry ordered for
the Duty marched upon Azuaga, and the Enemy left it
without resistance.   It was now found that he had Quiot
and Remord there with 4 or 5 Battalions of Infantry and
3 to 400 Horse.   The movement originally intended by the
General might have caught a few of the Enemy, because
the approach of the 1st Division from La Graja could
perhaps have gained the Fuente de Ovejuna Road before
him, or at all events before his Rear Guard.   'Tis doubtful
however, whether his numerous informers would not have
advertised him of the movement upon La Graja and would

have retired in the night. Be that as it may he got off by the Fuente de Ovejuna Road and marched upon that Place. The total want of Bread and Forage Corn delays our movement upon Drouet at Zalamea and Castuera.

March 30. Drouet has gone to Fuente de Ovejuna taking with him everything from the Serena but a few Posts. Has met there the two Detachments of Quiot and Remord, and as it appears, has already received a few Troops from Cordova. Soult has broken up from before Cadiz, and is doing all he can to assemble something at Cordova of which Drouet is the Advanced Guard. Sir Thomas Graham having got rid of him from Zalamea and Castuera and occupied La Graja and Azuaga, stands upon his Communications in such a way that his Assembling in the Plains can't be effected but with much delay (which is everything for the Siege of Badajoz), and even after Assembling in the Mountains 'twill be difficult for him to get into the Plains without committing the Head of his Columns and perhaps afterwards the following Divisions in succession. [Duke of Wellington's Despatches, Vol. 9, page 24.]

An Aide-de-Camp arrived from Lord Wellington with orders to fall back to the Villa Franca Cantonments. Genl. Hill back to Merida. *Il faut.*

March 31. Drouet is decidedly very apprehensive of being attacked, has moved his Head Quarters to Valasquillo one March in rear of Pte. Ovejuna on the road to Cordova and has been drawing in his Troops from the side of the Serena by Montrubio.

The apprehension, however, which was about to have had all the effect that could be wished and to have promised a delay in the Enemy's assembling very much to be desired, will subside fast enough, for Lord Wellington's orders are so positive that there is no alternative but to obey them, although the doing so will throw away some of the fruits of the late movements of General Graham which had already almost done everything proposed, and which in two or three days would have succeeded to the fullest extent and left the Siege unmolested.

All encumbrances are already gone to the rear, and the Troops commence moving tomorrow morning back to their old Cantonments.

April 1-2. Maguilla and Valencia de la Torres—

The General obeyed Lord Wellington's orders and gradually, and with as little shew as possible, withdrew the Troops into their old Cantonments. Advances from Llera on the Left to Fuente Catos on the right Ribera and Hornaches occupied by Infantry, Zafra and Feria all General Anson's Brigade of Light Cavalry to the Front for Out Post duty. Heavy Cavalry to rest in the Valley of Almendral. Divisions of Infantry :—

> 1st. Fuente del Maestre.
> 6th. Almendralejo.
> 7th. Azenchal.
> &c. &c. &c.

April 2. The General arrived at Villa Franca.—Operations therefore concluded.

Soult is collecting and moving towards Estremadura. This effectual dislodging and scattering of Drouet, who has fallen back to within two Marches of Cordova, will have made 5 or 6 days delay at least in the assembling of the Army of the South ; had the recall been delayed two or three days, that Assembly must have taken place at Cordova, and this would have occasioned a delay of 10 or 12 days.

Rode to the Camp before Badajoz from Valencia de las Torres.

April 3. Arrived in the Camp before Badajoz. Two Breaches (one ' a ' in the inner face of La Trinidad, the other ' b ' in the shoulder of that of Sta. Maria) fast advancing.

Marmont is moving towards the Frontier of the Beira. He has 15 days Provisions. Whether he means to attack Ciudad Rodrigo or to make an inroad into Portugal cannot yet be determined. At all events the Breaches will probably be practicable tomorrow night. If so, Lord Wellington will immediately assault the Place and then put as many Troops as may be requisite in march for the Beira and Frontier of Castile.

April 4. Breaches fast advancing. Excellent practice of the Artillery in the Breaching Batteries. Enemy working at Daybreak behind the main Breach. Driven off by Spherical Case-shot. Enemy fires very little. Losses in the Batteries and Trenches few.

Assault postponed till tomorrow, the Breaches not

being considered quite practicable. Commenced to batter
the Curtain ' c.'

Soult at Guadalcanal with about 8,000—Drouet proceeding to join him by Azuaga with about 8,000—equal to
16,000. Then Lord Wellington computes Troops from
Grenada equal to 16,000, in all he imagines that Soult will
be 32 to 35,000 strong. That he will be assembled at
Llerena on the 4th and reach Albuera on the 7th. All the
Troops on the Right Bank of the Guadiana over the river
at night. Bivouac in the Wood. The Place to be carried
tomorrow night. The instant that it is so, the Investing
Brigade from the Right Bank to be brought over. The
Troops put in movement for Albuera. Lord Wellington
will meet Soult there, if he will come, on the 7th. General
Hill makes one move to his Right to take hands with
General Graham. He will be at Villa Alba as long as he
can.

April 5. The Breaches seem very good. But Lord
Wellington does not appear to think the Defences sufficiently destroyed. A little demur takes place in consideration of the undamaged Counterscarp and depth of
the Ditch, so that in case of failure nothing could well
get back again. However this be, the attack is again
postponed.

April 6. The Breach in the Curtain between the
Bastions of La Trinidad and Sta. Maria, being considered
practicable, as well as the Breaches in the shoulder of Sta.
Maria, and in the face of the Trinidad Lord Wellington
has ordered the Assault for tonight at 10 o'clock according to the Disposition ' R,' with the difference that the
5th Division is to make a Real Attack, and get into
the Works by Escalade on the Left near the River.
Thus :—[Sketch plan enclosed.]

The 3rd Division scales the Castle ' a.'

The 4th and Light Divisions assault the three Breaches,
' d, c, d.'

The 5th Division scales the Works on the Left near the
River at ' e.'

B. Genl. Power's Portuguese Brigade watches the Right
Bank ' f, f, f.'

April 7. BADAJOZ HAS FALLEN !

The 4 Columns moved to the Assault at 10 o'clock last
night, and the Town was carried at 3 This morning, after a

most obstinate resistance, and as tough a struggle as
British Troops were ever turned to.[1]

The obstacles to the approaches to the Breaches were
found so numerous, and the retrenchments and Stockades
of Sword-blades within them so insuperable, that notwithstanding the most persevering efforts of a Valour that was
never surpassed, the 4th and Light Divisions could not get
into them, until the 3rd Division scaled and carried the
Castle, and the 5th the Works on the Left and entered the
Town near the River.

The loss has been very great, probably 3,500 Killed and
Wounded, and with a great proportion of valuable Officers,
in this hard fought night. The Garrison was numerous
and well composed and defended itself everywhere
excellently.

Badajoz cost Marshal Soult 79 days of open Trenches,
it has fallen to Lord Wellington upon the 20th day, but
it has been dearly bought, and all the loss of the 20 days
of Siege thrown away, because the Breaches were of no
assistance, the Defences were all left perfect, and the Place
might as well have been carried by escalade altogether upon
one of the dark rainy Nights after it was first invested
between the 16th and 20th March.

Phillipon taken in Fort San Cristobal, with the second
in Command, Chief Engineer, and about 3,000 of the
Garrison.

April 8–9. Resting the Troops. Soult not advancing.

April 10–11. Soult retiring. Ballesteros reported at
Seville. Marmont's advance near Frendão.

Army in movement upon Castello Branco, leaving
Hill's Corps.

Lord Wellington's Head Quarters Badajoz.

Camp before Badajoz 11th April, 1812.

---

[1] There is no mention of the frightful atrocities committed (see
Oman, v, pp. 256 *et seq.*), also Sir Harry Smith's *Autobiography*, i, pp. 63
et seq., where his romantic marriage is described—the only bright spot in
this otherwise terrible picture.

JOURNAL XII

April–June

WELLINGTON'S CAMPAIGN (*contd.*) EXCEPT FOR A BRIEF REST (APRIL TO MAY) IN CANTONMENT—RETREAT OF MARMONT—RELIEF OF ALMEIDA AND CIUDAD ROD-RIGO—PREPARATIONS FOR ADVANCE INTO SPAIN—ATTACK AND CAPTURE AND DESTRUCTION OF ALMA-RAZ

1812, *April* 7–10. Badajoz having fallen on the Morning of the 7th, and Soult continuing to advance, the Corps d'Armée of General Graham fell back from its Cantonments as taken up on the 2nd, and Bivouacqued in the Wood of Albuera. The General having his Head Quarters at Torre de Almendral. General Hill extended his Right to Loboz to communicate with General Graham's Left upon the Albuera and Guadajoz and finally bivouacqued the greater part of his Corps upon the Arroyo de Lesten near Talavera Real. Meanwhile Lord Wellington held everything in readiness to move up also to Albuera, and was fully occupied in preparing his Dispatches, getting the Town in order, and reorganizing the Divisions that assaulted, and whose loss (*hors de Combat*) has not fallen short of 3,700 Men and 250 Officers, by the Storm alone.

Ballasteros has arrived at Seville according to a Plan concerted by Lord Wellington where he will attempt to destroy the Enemy's Establishments of Magazines, Foundry, &c., &c. Soult has in consequence, and also hearing of the fall of Badajoz, commenced his return to Andalusia on the 9th and 10th.

The Corps d'Armée generally reoccupied the Cantonments as in 'A.'

April 11. Marmont has blockaded Ciudad Rodrigo, reconnoitred Almeira, and made an inroad into Portugal as far as to the neighbourhood of Fundão.

All this obliges a movement towards him ; [1] and the intention appears to be to leave General Hill's Corps d'Armée in Estremadura, and to move Northward with all the rest. This commences today with the Movement ' B.'

Lord Wellington moved his Head Quarters from Camp to Badajoz.

April 12. General Hill takes up the Cantonments from Almendralejo to Feria, with his Cavalry at Zafra and Los Santos. His Posts at Ribera, Usagre and Fuente Cantos. The Movement ' C,' and the 1st Division follows the 6th General Power's Portuguese Brigade, and the 22nd Portuguese Regt. remain at Badajoz with Col. Fletcher the Chief Engineer, who is charged with the repairing and restoring it.

April 12. Marshal Beresford removed from the Camp to Badajoz.

April 13. Head Quarters Elvas.

April 14. Head Quarters Portalegre.

April 15. 3rd Division Niza. Light pushed on to Castello Branco which the French quitted yesterday. 'Twas a Party of Pillage, and discovery,—2,000 Foot, 6 Squadrons Horse. Back to Penamacor last night. Head Quarters Niza. Villa Velha Bridge saved.

April 16. NIZA.—Lord Wellington would appear inclined to Halt the Body of the Troops with the Head of the Column at Castello Branco, and so to Niza, and Portalegre, getting on himself with some cavalry and spreading the Report of the Army's Advance. Thus if possible to raise the Blockade of Ciudad Rodrigo, without the necessity of taking up the Army.

April 17. CASTELLO BRANCO.—Marmont is at Sabugal. He has with him the 2nd, 3rd, 4th, 5th, and 6th Divisions of his Army, and has called in the Division of detachments under General Souham which remained at Benevente, Salamanca, etc., and in short has commenced to strengthen himself by all the means in his power. He occupies from Ciudad Rodrigo to Penamacor, and has an advance at Pedrogão. This apparent decision to stand as long as he can makes a real Movement upon the part of Lord Wellington absolutely necessary and His Lordship inclines to think he is,—if he pleases, to us 35,000—and that he

[1] Quoted Oman, v, p. 290.

will be obstinate upon standing as long as he can. The Troops to be brought up as fast as they can and the 3rd and Light Divisions with the Cavalry pushed on one March in Front of Castello Branco.

April 18.[1]   CASTELLO BRANCO.—Enemy's Advance withdrawn from Pedrogão. Light Division to Escalhão de Cima. Hussars to Pedrogão and St. Miguel d'Alba. It is evident that the French General besides the chance of creating a diversion in favour of Badajoz has reckoned on getting Ciudad Rodrigo either by hunger or assault and it would appear that he has received very positive orders from his Court to get it *coûte qu'il coûte*. He has supposed no doubt that Badajoz would have defended itself longer, and that no interruption, in force, would be given to the execution of his design ;—he expected perhaps that one or two Divisions would be detached against him ; hence his forward Position at Sabugal, that he might be prepared to stand in their way, and hence his calling in Souham and indeed everything but Foy's Division (1st) which standing upon the Tagus and Tietar maintained his communication with La Mancha and Estremadura, that he might be strong enough to carry on his operations against Ciudad Rodrigo, and cover them at the same time. By his anxious desire to get the Place, and his probable ignorance of the real force in movement against him, he has perhaps been led into a measure which may end in a misfortune to him, if not in destruction, for he has put the Agueda in his rear, which the late rains have rendered impassable, and his situation is thus very critical. If he has discovered his error he may go off his left, down the Perales road, and so to Placencia, but if he have not, and if he wait to be *driven* out of the ground he holds, I don't see how he is to get away. Lord Wellington will be all closed up by the 21st. Meanwhile he shows little in his Front, and if the giving any serious alarm can be avoided till the General Movement commences, the fairest hopes may be entertained of his striking a successful and decisive blow. It is possible that Marmont may be somewhat stronger than he is generally made out to be (and Lord Wellington seems to hold that opinion) in which case he may be aware, pretty nearly, of the force opposed to him, and yet (considering the feeling

---

[1] The letter of the date to Charles Stewart is quoted in part in Oman, v, p. 292.

that exists at, and the Orders he is supposed to have received from, his Court about Ciudad Rodrigo) may have made up his mind to fight a Battle to prevent its relief. It is difficult to imagine this, but it is possible, and then the proceedings on both sides will be simple enough, and the remains of the ' Army of Portugal ' will soon be done away. It is perhaps upon the Cards to relieve the Place without a Battle, if Lord Wellington should incline to do so, for the Convoy destined for it is actually in Almeida, and Trant and Wilson with the Militia Divisions of the North, are at and in the neighbourhood of Guarda, so that if His Lordship manœuvre in Front of the Enemy and fixes his attention to Sabugal, it is far from impossible for those Officers to introduce the Provisions into the Town. This done all is safe, and want of subsistence from which the Enemy has already suffered much, must compel him to retreat, if he can, should it be thought desirable on our part to spare the expenditure of a Battle. In any event the Town will be provisioned and out of the reach of contingencies.

Trant and Wilson at Guarda, and Silveira at Villa Nova de Pascoa. Lord Wellington has a letter from the Governor of Ciudad Rodrigo in good spirits.

April 19. Enemy withdrawn from Penamacor. Reports of some disaster to Wilson and Trant at Guarda, no making anything clear of it, but something has occurred. 3rd Division to Alcains.

April 20–21. Marmont going back with as much expedition as possible. Lord Wellington follows with as little delay as may be. Movements ' D, E, F.'

There was some truth in the report of the misfortune to the Militia at Guarda. They were driven back by Marmont who massed against them in person on the 14th with 2 Divisions of his Army and his Cavalry. It was something too like a Dispersion, but unfortunately the Enemy did not pursue far. *No trusting to Militia ! ! !*

Head Quarters :—20th.—Escalhão de Cima, de Baiso. 21st.—Pedrogão, Branca. 22nd.—Penamacor.

April 23. Head Quarters at Sabugal, Malsata.

Marmont retreating, and he has probably re-established his Bridge above La Caridado upon the Agueda. The Rain has ceased some days, and the River has fallen. Movements ' G.'

April 24.   Marmont clear off.   Movements 'H.' Head Quarters Alfayates Nave.   Thus has ended this Expedition of the French General which he seems to have conducted with as little ability as determination.   He made no effort to possess himself of the Villa Velha Bridge, or to occupy a Post on the right Bank of the Tagus, which he might have done, and by which he would have forced Lord Wellington to such a distance, that Ciudad Rodrigo would have been starved by the delay.   He has not taken Ciudad Rodrigo, the avowed object of his enterprise—he has not occasioned any Diversion in favour of Badajoz— he has not fought for the preservation of his Blockade, though the Place had not above 5 days Provisions.   In fact he has effected no one object but the driving off some Cattle, the burning some Cottages, and the ruin of a few wretched Peasants.[1]   He fled out of Portugal at Lord Wellington's approach, so rapidly that the Hussars of our advance scarcely got sight of those of his Rear Guard.

Bridge of Almaraz

April 25.   Head Quarters Fuente Guinaldo.
Marmont being decidedly in Retreat the Troops Halted, as in ' I,' and afterwards the Distribution ' J.'
April 26–May 5.   Lord Wellington thus throws back the Cavalry, and the 1st, 6th, and 7th Divisions, and the rest to the Douro near the Depots for subsistence.   While Marmont remains in Old Castile, he must keep a certain force near the Frontier of the Beira.   But leaving the 3rd, 4th, 5th, Divisions, and the Brigades of Pack and Bradford (perhaps 13,000 Men) for that purpose, he can move upon Andalusia if he wishes with the 1st, 6th, 7th, and Light Divs., and afterwards the Brigade of Power and General Hill's Corps d'Armée (perhaps 36,000 Infantry).   This will do.[2]—Lt. Colonel Sturgeon dispatched on the 2nd May, to prepare the broken Arch of the Bridge of Alcantara for the passage of the Troops.   This is a very important object. A glance at the Map will shew its advantages, and that without we can't reap half the benefit of possessing the two fortresses.   Before those were ours the Bridge was better impassable.   Now its assistance is a *sine qua non*.
May 6–17.   The retiring of Marmont within a given

[1] Quoted Oman, v, p. 283.   [2] Quoted Oman, v, p. 317.

distance, the slow progress made by the Spaniards at
Rodrigo, which rendered it unsafe to leave the Place or the
Frontier, the retiring altogether of Soult, and the state of
his Army not making him dangerous now ; these and many
other combining reasons determine Lord Wellington to
make his Offensive Operations North of the Tagus, and
to move upon Marmont. All the necessary preparations
making but secretly, and from circumstances it will be very
feasible to keep his Movements unforeseen and unknown till
they begin.

Meanwhile he diverts General Hill with a part of his
Force to move upon and destroy everything at Almaraz.[1]
During which Genl. Graham makes a March or two to-
wards Elvas. Thus securing all possibility of any danger to
Badajoz during the absence of Genl. Hill, and blinding the
Enemy, who will never imagine that a movement upon
Castile will be begun by the return of two Divisions towards
the Guadiana. ' Z ' are the heads of an intercepted
Letter from an A.D.C. of Marmont who had been to Paris
to represent Difficulties, to remonstrate, to solicit Supplies,
to beg to be relieved from his Irksome and Disgusting
Command. This Officer's conversation with Berthier, and
Marshal Soult's Letter also, pretty well shew how Spanish
Affairs are now regarded, or rather forgotten and given up.
Bonaparte would wish to forget, and to make France
forget, Spain and the Armies ruined there, and amid the
blaze of a successful Russian War to throw the Peninsula
and his Defeats and Disasters there into the shade. Perhaps to gain some occasion for withdrawing the Remnant
of his Forces altogether, at least beyond the Ebro.

Shoes, Ammunition, etc., for the Portuguese Troops
brought forward to the Frontier.

May 18–21. GUINALDO. No change. A certain
appearance of two Divisions of Marmont taken at Tordesillas, by the treachery of an Apothecary. This was a
remarkable Man.

May 22. GUINALDO. In the Evening arrived Major
Currie an Aide-de-Camp of Sir Rowland Hill ; that General
succeeded upon the 18th and 19th in getting possession of
everything at Almaraz, after storming two or three very
respectable redoubts, with little comparative loss. About
700 of the Enemy had been killed, drowned, and taken

[1] Quoted Oman, v, p. 820.

(Lt. Col. of the 59th Commandant taken wounded), when Major Currie left Sir Rowland, and he was proceeding to destroy everything and then to return. (See letter from Capt. Thorn.)

The French had collected here very considerable Magazines of Provisions and Ammunition, a Dock Yard for Boat Building, and an Arsenal of Cable, Timber, and River Stores; and had in fact formed an extensive Permanent Establishment. This therefore had become an Entrepôt for the Supply of anything moving upon, or acting in Estremadura with which it was the point of Communication, and to which it was the Key. Its Capture and Destruction is of infinite importance both real and moral, and is indeed the most advantageous Coup of the Second Class during the War.

May 23–27. No change.

May 28. The Commissary General being in readiness, Lord Wellington ordered the Movement ' W.' This closes up the Troops by the 7th or 8th, and by the 10th of June 'tis likely all will be ready to move.

May 29–31. No Change.

June 1–3. ' T.T.' ordered. The Army assembles therefore in the Wood of Espieje and prepares to advance.

I have received the orders of the Marshal to take Charge of Three Regiments of Portuguese Cavalry to be assembled for a Detached Service at Braganza. Sent the orders for their Assembly and March.

June 4–7. Preparations continuing. No other change.

June 8. Received my final Orders.

June 9. Set out from Fuente Guinaldo for Braganza.

JOURNAL XIII [1]

1812, *June–August*

INTRODUCTION

WELLINGTON'S Salamanca campaign, 'the first great offensive movement . . . since Talavera in 1809,' gave D'Urban his first independent command. This detached service was not very much to his liking, for it seemed as if he were going to lose 'the best lesson and perhaps the most brilliant battle of the war,' just as he had missed active service when sent on reconnaissance immediately after his arrival in the Peninsula.

But he need not have been so despondent, for, as Sir Charles Oman points out (vol. v, p. 358) the 'operations of his small [Portuguese] brigade were of far more service to the main army than that of the whole of the Galicians.'

It may also be noted this is an extremely critical period of the European war. In June the United States of America declared war on Great Britain, but too late to serve the purpose of Napoleon, who had by this time embarked upon the Russian campaign.

1812, *June* 2. Received the Marshal's orders to hold myself in readiness to repair to the Tras os Montes and take the Command of a Corps of Portuguese Cavalry, intended to act from that side against the Rear and Communications of the Enemy as occasion may serve.—This Corps to consist of the 1st, 11th, and 12th Regiments. Their Horses are at Grass.—Sent Orders for them to assemble and prepare to march.

June 3. Sent Orders through the Visconde de Monte-Alegre at Lamego for the three Regiments to march to Braganza, and to prepare for their Forage, and Reception, on the Road and at Braganza.

The 11th being near Lamego, and the 12th near Chaves, will (allowing time for the Orders to reach them and for the

---

[1] This Journal is particularly rich in letters, including nine from Wellington to D'Urban. These have been published in the *Cambridge Historical Journal*, iii, No. 1, October 1929.

collecting the Horses), arrive at Braganza about the 13th, and the 1st which is near Oporto can scarcely do so before the 21st.

June 5–6. Gave up the concerns of the Bureau to Hardinge [his assistant].

June 7–8. Received Lord Wellington's Memorandum ; the Marshal's Instructions to Silveira (Conde de Amaranthe), and his Orders about the matter verbally.

June 9. Set out for Braganza.—Rode to Torre de Moncorvo.—Found here that Silveira (Conde de Amaranthe) was at Villa Real, not at Braganza.—Sent his Instructions which I was charged with for him, by Express to Villa Real, reporting myself to him of my being on the way to Braganza.—Reported myself also to Baccelar (Visconde de Monte-Alegre) at Lamego.

June 10–11. Torre de Moncorvo and Macedo.

June 12. BRAGANZA.—On arriving I found Letters from the Conde de Amaranthe and Visconde de Monte-Alegre. The former wrote upon the 10th from Villa Real before my Letter from Torre de Moncorvo had reached him ; the latter sent me the Routes of the 1st and 11th Regts.—By the first it appears that Silveira has only two Regiments of Militia embodied.—This is not of much consequence but the lateness of sending him his Instructions will be severely felt in the delay of getting Transport Cattle for the Cavalry.—In fact the lateness will prevent the measure, in all probability (if there ever was a chance of advantage from it) from doing any good,—for not to say that Silveira's Orders were sent to him much later than was necessary because they might have been sent on the 2nd and were not till the 8th—the thing itself should have been thought of before, and indeed as soon as the North Eastern Advance was determined.—Now it was not proposed till the Troops were almost assembled about Espeja, and by consequence two of the three Regiments of Cavalry which were at Grass—one near Oporto and the other two marches to the South of Lamego—will arrive too late (if Lord Wellington moves as soon as he is assembled) to have any thing to do.—This appears by the Routes sent in Baccelar's Despatch.—The 12th Regt. which happened to be at Grass near Braganza is assembled, and with that and the Company of the 11th from Almeida, all must be done that can be done. Little enough—but 'tis a farce to wait till the 21st and 22nd. Wrote the Marshal 1W. Told him the tardy state of things and my intentions. Wrote Silveira.—Told him I was here and hoped to see him.—I must communicate with him from the nature of things.

June 13. Having taken the precaution on the 3rd at Guinaldo, to write to Rumar for information of Country, &c., he writes me in reply and I got his Letters today. Little information of Country,—but Letters of Introduction to two Spanish Gentlemen which may be of use.—Received a Letter from Silveira.

June 14. Inspected the 12th Regiment of Cavalry.— In good order enough considering 'tis just from Grass, but it wants two or three essential arrangements before it can possibly move. Gave Orders and Memoranda. Wrote to Silveira.—Wrote Sir W. Beresford, 2W. Having given the most pressing orders to the Commissary for the hastening up the Corn and Provisions, the 12th Regt. being in the midst of its arrangements, the others not having arrived, and no time lost by my absence for a day, set out for the neighbourhood of the Esla,—as well to see the lay and line of the Country as to talk with the Persons to whom I have Letters of Introduction from Rumar,—by Quintalilla and Travancos.

June 15. ALCANIZAS.—Don Manuel du Puelles, Regidor Perpetuo ; and Carvajales,—Don Santiago Uiver-Valle, Commissionado. Both intelligent Men, and with the most perfect wish to be civil and useful. The latter has the best means of intelligence in Castile, and I have arranged that he is to send me all he gets.

The 7th Division (formerly that of Souham) is at Zamora and in the neighbourhood, extending its Posts of Communication to Benavente where there are 600 Infantry and 200 Horse under Carrié. Posts of Battalions in San Cebrian, Villafafilla, and Argurilleros.—Small ones at Corbillas and Monta Marta. The Bridge of Zamora is entrenched and mined. General Seveure is at Toro with the 4th Division. All have orders to march at an hour's notice, and are in considerable anxiety. Whether Marmont meditates a defensive Position on the Right Bank of the Douro, or a Retreat upon Burgos, or first one and then the other, 'tis not clear. I think mining the Bridges and the other movements made, and orders given will answer either or both.

The getting over the Esla to act in the Enemy's Rear, or to cut Communications between Zamora and Benavente, according to the Instructions of Lord Wellington, will be no easy matter, for this River has no Ford nor Bridge but near Benavente.—During its course from thence to the Douro below Zamora there are two Ferry Boats, but these won't do much, for they forbid retreat, even if they allow of passing a small Corps in one night without observation.

However as soon as I have effected the arrangement for, and been able to commence the movement of, the Brigade from Braganza, or rather of the 12th Regt.   I shall carefully reconnoitre the whole line of the Esla and shall very likely find some place that the Country People have not.—Returned to Braganza.—Not a word yet from Head Quarters.—If I am expected to do anything, this keeping me in the dark is to double my difficulties and take away half of my chance of success.

June 16.   Established a Post at Alcanizas to pass on Don Santiago's Letters and mine to him.   Wrote him in compliance with the 5th Paragraph of Lord Wellington's Memorandum.   Put by a portion of Biscuit that arrived yesterday for a three or four days reserve for the Cavalry to march with.   Some Corn arrived.   Repeated my Instructions to the Commissary (made him send Expresses to the Commissary-in-Chief at Chaves,—to the Commissary of Cavalry,—and to the Cattle Contractors)—upon all the subjects of Supply, Money, Bread, Corn, Slaughter Cattle, and Transport Cattle.   The 12th getting on slowly enough with its arrangements.   It can't be ready before the 19th at soonest.   However its Transport Cattle are not arrived.   By the time they do it will be ready.

April 17.   Ordered 38 badly Glandered Horses to be shot.—No arrival of Money, Transport, Cattle, or Provisions to any extent.   ' A ' is the State of Supplies for the four Regiments of Militia, and three Regiments of Cavalry, 1,200 Horse (it ought to be) and 4,500 Infantry, with all that is hoped for to the 21st inclusive.   Received a Letter from the Conde de Amaranthe and wrote to him.   Wrote the Marshall 3W.—enclosed him copies of the foregoing letters.   Not a word from Head Quarters so that I don't know where the Army is, but of course it must be in movement, and I am sure I shall be too late to be of any

use. However vexation is useless, I can't overcome
impossibilities or control events. The very late period
at which the idea of this Partizan Corps was first taken up,
—the distance of the Regiments to form it, from their point
of assembly and their dispersion at Grass,—will have been
one great cause that the Corps won't be ready to march
'till the time to do good is gone by. But this is not by
any means all ; for when they do come 'tis impossible to
say when they can move. I have not been able to complete
the little Regiment here with the absolutely necessary
equipment. Not a single Transport Animal.—Some Corn
Biscuit there is since yesterday, but even this can't be
carried, and how to feed either Man or Horse when the
three days of each, even supposing them to be able to carry
so much, is consumed ?

With a little Money one might live with a small Corps
anywhere in Spain but not without, except by pillage,
and how far it is intended that I should pillage our Allies
I doubt, probably I should do more harm to the cause
than my utmost services with such a Corps would do good.
Of one thing however I'm certain, that a small Partizan
Corps can't act with effect upon an Enemy's Rear, Flanks,
and Communication without the good will of the Peasantry,
—without that there can be no secrecy,—without secrecy
there can be no success.

June 18. A Packet from Head Quarters, of the 11th,
only two days after I left them at Fuente Guinaldo.
Hardinge encloses me the Ordered Movements and Formation ' R.'—I must be too late, and Marmont if he has stood,
is beaten by this time, and this cursed detached Corps has
lost me the best lesson and perhaps the most brilliant
Battle of the War. I have the consolation that although
I did not venture to object to take charge of it,—for a
Soldier has no right to choose Service,—yet I received it
with as much reluctance as was consistent without starting
objections. I foresaw that there were a thousand obstacles
to my rendering any service. I recorded my opinion to
Hardinge. I have lost no time. I have been here many
days before any Corps, I have done my utmost to equip
and arrange the one Regiment already here, that I might
move with it alone. Even today there is nothing arrived.
—No Transport,—No Money,—Nothing has arrived, and
whether anything will tomorrow is doubtful. There is no

Money, even the sum the Commissary expects is but 2,000 Dollars. The arrival of this is rather a hope than an expectation. He is already in debt to one Gentleman of this Place 10,000 Dollars upon the Commissiary Account; the Government can't or won't pay it, and of consequence his Credit is gone, for if these people advance more they are aware 'tis a gift, they have no hope of repayment.

The Cattle Contractors, not having been paid for what they have long ago provided will furnish no more. Indeed, by their Contract they are authorised to refuse, but to cut the matter short, and for fear of force, they have absconded upon being told a second time yesterday that my necessity for some Slaughter Cattle was urgent, and must be supplied. *Voilà tout. Que faut on faire ?*

Evening.—Received a letter from Silveira. By the assistance of the people one has collected a few Transport Mules for the 12th, and five head of Slaughter Cattle. They will be ready tomorrow, and that Regiment at least shall move, on the 20th. It won't give me 250 Sabres, but I know it to be a trustworthy and good Corps. I have some hope that the 11th may bring some Transport Cattle with them, and the 1st ought to do so from Oporto. I shall make sure of the 12th, however. How to feed them must be the work of Providence I suppose—that feeds the young Ravens—for hang me if I see any Human means, ordinary or extraordinary—to do it, without we turn Banditti,—*nous verrons.*

Sent the Commissary a Schedule and returned his answer upon its practicability.

June 19. Having got the small equipment I expected for the 12th Regiment ordered it to march tomorrow morning. Wrote a Letter for Silveira with the date of tomorrow morning to be sent upon my going if nothing makes a change in it requisite. Received 4W. from the Marshal at noon. At 10 at night received 5W. from the Marshal and the Disposition ' R.R.' Wrote to the Marshal all that part of 6W. of the 19th date.

June 20. Wrote the Marshal the remainder of 6W. Sent my letter to the Conde de Amaranthe, adding a note to give him the news from Salamanca.

Evening.—Had proposed to set out at day-break, and going by Puebla de Senabria get to Alcanizas in the evening, but having just got a letter from Silveira 'tis necessary that I should wait to see him. I shall, therefore, go straight to Alcanizas without going to La Puebla. Directed Lieut. Paulino however to go to Alcanizas in the morning and to be there as soon as the Regt. Wrote to Hardinge, —No hope of Money,—made an effort with three or four Money-Lenders to make a Loan of 5,000 Dollars, but the Government Credit is so bad that they denied having any to give.

June 21. Received a Letter from Silveira. He arrived in the evening. Had a conversation with him in which I represented all I had done in writing previously, and begged him to make efforts,—this he promised,—approved of what I had proposed,—said he intended to advance some Infantry according to his Letter,—*Voilà tout*.

June 22. Left Braganza.—At Alcanizas.—Began to learn that everything was gone from Zamora and supposed to be so from Toro.—Ordered the 12th to be in readiness to march, and proceed to Carvajales.

Evening.—Here by Don Santiago de Uiver-Valle and his Intelligence it is clearly confirmed that the Enemy has assembled everything, drawn in all from every quarter, and marched from Toro upon Fuente Sauco and Medina del Campo. This must be to cover Madrid and give Lord Wellington Battle.

All the original objects of my Corps are now out of the question. Everything is retired from those points I was instructed to operate against, there are now no longer any communications where I was told to cut them off, and the Position supposed by Lord Wellington to be occupied by the Enemy is changed altogether;—He is on the other side of the Douro,—and all the data upon which my Instructions were founded are done away. It strikes me therefore to adhere to the general object although the details no longer apply,—and to get up the Douro beyond Toro,—perhaps cross it between Zamora and Toro, —and according to Circumstances execute all the Partisan annoyances I can. Perhaps bear in towards Valladolid. In short to seek my fortune. Perhaps I may be able so to manage as to get near the Army for the great Day.—They'll scarcely send me back again with my 800 sabres when I come, though they would not think me enough worth having to order me there. I'll go and look as close as I can, to do whatever little good I may, and be in the way of occasion.—To this end and to lose as little time as possible, despatched the orders of March.—Thus I'll have all closed up by the 25th and on the 26th I'll be on the left bank of the Esla and assemble in the Woods of Palomares.

June 23.   Examined the Ford of Almendra over the Esla,—quite practicable. Despatched from Almendra a Spaniard of trust to examine the Fords of Carrascal and Villaralbo over the Douro.—12th Regt. arrived.—Wrote Orders for the Brigade.—Wrote 7W. to Sir William Beresford.

June 24.   Rode over the country between Zamora and Toro and by Cubillos &c.—By a Man from near Fuente Sauco it appears there was an Action on the 22nd, and he says the Enemy afterwards marched upon Peñaranda.— Everything gone but the Garrisons.—Proposed therefore to make a stretch up the Douro without loss of time and either to cross at the Villaralbo Ford if anything presented there, or go on in the direction of Valladolid, watching occasions. —Returned.—Gave the Order of March.

Resolved moving with two Regiments and trusting to the 1st which arrives tomorrow to follow.—Received two Letters from Silveira.—Wrote to him.—The Marquis of Angeja arrived with Letters 9W. from Sir Wm. Beresford. There has been a partial affair, and the French indicate moving again upon the Douro.   This is rather corroborated by other accounts,—one inclines to doubt that they will do so however.—the Marshal's caution will tend to make me wary.—I shall let the 1st arrive at all events and take the news of tomorrow.

June 25.   Wrote the Marshal 10W.—Gave the Order for the 1st Regt.   Received Letter[1] from Hardinge, and the Key of his Cypher.   Wrote him my intention to pass

---

[1]   'Salamanca, *June* 23rd, 1 P.M.

'The last three days have been full of expectation of great events, and this morning at day-light we found the Enemy had occupied, and taken up a position about two leagues from ours on the Valladolid road. . . .

' . . . Lord W. will never have so advantageous an opportunity of defeating him, but under all views of the Campaign, I am not sure whether he will not derive more essential benefits by his temperance in keeping his Army uncrippled, than to have gained a great Victory before the Spanish combination was sufficiently in forwardness to ensure the total destruction of his antagonist, Pyrrhus-like his victories would ruin him.   The Fort possibly may be stormed tonight.'

See *Cambridge Historical Journal*, ' Unpublished Letters of Wellington,' iii, No. 1, pp. 96–97.

the River tomorrow with all the Regiments if nothing should occur to render it improper.

Sent out an Officer to the Banks of the Esla.—Rode to Cubillos.—Nothing certain.—The Enemy and everything appear to be in the same position. But there is also an appearance of an immediate return of Marmont to the Douro,—it would rather seem that there is a slight move of his to the Left. Returned to Carvajales.

June 26. Crossed the River Esla with the three Regiments. Halted and assembled at Andarias.—Moved and Bivouacqued behind Cubillos.—Rode to Coreses and Fresno. —Inspected the Fords of Villaralbo and Villalazan. Both good—Villalazan (of Fresno) best.—Wrote to open a communication with Don Julian Sanchez on the other side of the River.—Despatched a confidential Man to the French Army to bring me its position.

June 27. Gave orders for the regulation of Out Post and Bivouac Duties. Wait the return from Don Julian and the Enemy.—Think to march tonight.—Either for the neighbourhood of Toro, or over the River in a direct line upon the Enemy's communication. The return of the Men will determine the which.—Meanwhile this day's repose is most necessary. It is the first assembly of the Brigade and a day's Halt is most important. Received two Letters from Silveira.—Wrote to him.

June 28. Marched.—Arranged and lightened and sent off to Carvajales the great part of the Baggage.—Through Molacillos, and Gallejos to Matilla la Seca,—turned short to the Right, crossed the Ford of Fresno de la Ribera (or Villalazan) which I ascertained two days ago, and Bivouacqued in the Woods upon the Left Bank of the Douro. Wrote to Sir William Beresford merely to say where I am, under cover to Don Carlos d'Espagna. Wrote to Don D. P. at Toro.

I marched upon Toro to conceal my intentions to pass the Ford, for a Battalion of the Garrison, in the opposite Woods might have well stopped my passage.—I have chosen the Left Bank because there I can act upon the communications of Toro and Valladolid, both at once. —Received a letter from Don Julian.—The Fort of Salamanca has fallen on the night of the 27th.—Received 11W. from Sir William Beresford.

June 29. Waited to collect a certain supply of Provisions.—Wrote Sir Wm. Beresford 12W.—I'll move in the night upon Pinhero and Cubo, and then be guided by circumstances. I shall then be close upon the Enemy's line of Communications.—Wrote to Don J.S.

2 o'clock.—The Man whom I despatched from Coreses on the 26th has returned and brought me information. —From Fuente Sauco on the Right to Peñaranda on the Left.—Ponhero and El Cubo will bring me very near to their line of communications as I supposed, indeed nearer than I had hoped.

5 o'clock.—A Division of the French Army reported to be in march upon Toto.—Rode to Boveda del Toro, where the Enemy were said to have passed.—'Tis the 1st Division of Marmont's Army under Foy.—The whole are said to be in retreat.—Either they are going to take up the position of the Douro, which yet I don't think, or they have sent this Division to make Toro sure, to release its Garrison and that of Zamora, and to cover or lead the Retreat of the other Divisions. At any rate I have no choice about what I must do,—I must recross the Douro however reluctantly for the Enemy's coming upon that River, makes the circumstances precisely as they were when my Instructions were framed,—so that I must be upon the Right Bank. Besides,—if the French are retiring, Lord Wellington is pursuing them,—hence there is abundance of Cavalry without me.—I may be of some use on the other side. I can be no longer so on the South.

June 30. I recrossed the Douro at 12 o'clock, and if I had not tried it well, I should have remained there, for the Enemy occupied Fresno with two Battalions, and this would have effectually impeded me.—Moved to Benegiles and Torres.—Wrote to the Conde de Amaranthe, and 15W. to Sir W. Beresford. They contain my reasons for recrossing the River.—Capt. Chapuzet arrived from Sir William Beresford,—brought me 13W.

July 1. Marched by Villaube, Malva, Bustillo, the neighbourhood of Vezdemarban, and bivouacqued in the Woods of San Pedro de Latarce. The Enemy who showed no Cavalry, had two Battalions of Infantry in Avezames, upon which a small Detachment hastily retired from Malva at the sight of our advanced Patroles.—Interview with Don Rodriguez, commanding a Castile Guerilla in the neighbourhood.—Wrote to the Spanish Commandant at Bene-

vente, Don Rodriguez, &c., &c.   Ordered back all the
Forage Beasts to Carvajales for Bread,—the Country is
so exhausted that one can't find a supply of this even for
our numbers.

July 2.   Marched by Belver upon Castronuevo.—
—Quartered the Brigade there.   Forced to do so for Bread.
This Patrole I have made to get acquainted with the
Country generally along the space it has embraced, and to
get acquainted also with the Marching Order, and
Bivouacqing capabilities of the Brigade.—The 1st[1] are
very alert and full of life and vigilance.   The others not
so much so, and anything but practised soldiers, in all that
regards taking care of themselves, though I have no
reason to doubt their perfect good will as to fighting.
Castronuevo will make from its position relatively to the
Esla, Zamora, Toro, and Valladolid, an excellent point of
rest, and refitment and pivot for my movements.   I shall
hope to get my Bread by tomorrow, and to move again.
Perhaps best upon Valladolid.—Must be governed by
circumstances.—I have invited the people to inform me
of the approach of French Detachments of Pillage, and
promised assistance.   I have signified to Don Rodriguez
my wish to co-operate with him.   He has some Infantry,
they may occasionally be of use.—An Officer from Genl.
Santocildes.   The French retreating upon Valladolid burnt
the wooden arch of the Bridge at Toro.   Sent Chapuzet
to the Marshal with the intelligence and wrote him 16W.

Afternoon.—Letter from and wrote to the Conde de

---

[1] See Oman, v, p. 387.

'*D'Urban to Beresford*

'Castro Nuevo, *2nd July*, 1912.

' . . . I can't conclude without saying that I think the 1st Regt. has
reached in every respect a pitch of perfection that I have never seen or
expected to see in any Portuguese Cavalry.'

With this can be compared another letter to Beresford after Salamanca.

'Penaranda, *24th July*, 1812.
Report No. 2.

' . . . I know of no Officer, Non-Commissioned Officer, or Man who
did not do his duty to the uttermost but (as in all actions), some were by
occasion, more prominently placed than others ; and it is my duty to lay
the names of these before your Excellency.   The Lt. Cols. Watson of the
1st, and Domingas Bernardino of the 11th Regts. eminently distinguished
themselves, and after the first of these Officers was unfortunately wounded,
the Regiment was well led by the Lt. Col. João Luiz, all of which makes
the subsequent débâcle of Majalahonda 11th Aug. all the more inexplicable.'

Amaranthe.—Sent an Express to Carvajales to hasten the Biscuit.—Made Commandants responsible for the pillage of the Troops. Wrote to all the Villages in the neighbourhood for Bread.

July 3.   Castronuevo.—Rested Troops.—Got some supplies from the Villages.—Valdez arrived from the Marshal with Orders to report for Lord Wellington upon the Fords of the Douro.—Reported accordingly.—Wrote to Hardinge with it.—Bread for three days arrived from Carvajales, and three days more to follow. Ordered the Brigade to march, and shall get into the Woods near Pedrosa and note before morning this approach to my point.

July 4.   Marched all night.—Bivouacqued the Brigade in the Wood at the Vente de Almaraz early in the morning. —Rode forward and reconnoitred.—Saw the Enemy opposite Pollos and the Allied Advance Guard near that Village on the other side. Wrote the Marshal 18W.— Despatched it by a Peasant from Mota from whence the Alcade is responsible, under cover to Lord Wellington. The Enemy marched from Moraleja.—All in the neighbourhood of Tordesillas.

July 5.   The Enemy's Cavalry accompanied by some Infantry plundered Villages in the Val de Torre, but I'm obliged to be cautious and I must suspend for an instant my moving upon the laternal road to Valladolid, for the whole Army of Marmont is in the neighbourhood of Tordesillas, and if I go to Torre or near Simara he has a shorter road to cut me off than I to retreat, and perhaps, as his Cavalry is not employed he may think it worth while to pinch my Brigade as a little revenge for his own great kicks and disgraces. Made out the Enemy's position enclosed it in 18W.[1] Sent off Valdez to Sir W. Beresford.

July 6.   Reconnoitred.—The Enemy's certainly in movement upon Valladolid. Accounts from Correspondents of confidence, corroborated by Deserters make Marmont at Simancas, or Puente de Douro and the Force at Tordesillas is considerably reduced.

I will move tonight to Castromonte, this brings me upon the plain of Simancas, well advanced,—gives me a road to Valladolid and leaves me a good retreat. Perhaps some occasion will now offer for a blow. Wrote the Marshal

---

[1] D'Urban gives full details of Marmont's movements ' from employees of Don Rodriguez the Guerilla.'

19W. supplying the Intelligence received, under cover to Lord Wellington by a Spaniard of confidence.

July 7. Arrived a little after day-break in the Woods of Castromonte.—Rested.—Received the Intelligence that General Bonnet, with his Division arrived at Valladolid last night and is tonight at Robledillo, Villaan, and Bellize on his way to Tordesillas. Wrote the Marshal and despatched the Letter by a confidential servant of Don Manuel de R.

July 8. Marched at 2 o'clock from the Bivouac, sending the Baggage to Espine.—Passed Peñaflor.—Rested in the woods of the Monte de Torrosa, upon the high road between Valladolid and Medina de Rio Seco.—Marched and continued to within a short league of Valladolid,—turned by the rear of Simancas, passing within a short league of that place (Head Quarters of Marmont) and within the same distance of Tordesillas, passed through Peñaflor and returned over the valley of Torre de Lobaton to the Bivouac.—This Patrole conducted the Brigade into the rear of the Enemy's Left and then along his whole line, at the distance of sometimes a league, sometimes less. I marched in file and raised a long extended cloud of dust. This must have been seen from all his Posts and as he is not well informed of what we are precisely, I have occasioned some inquietude. My expectations of being felt by some of his Cavalry have not been fulfilled,—he either has none to spare for excursions, or he despised us.

Wrote to Sir W. Beresford 20W.—Received back Cornet Amaral bringing me 21W.—Bonnet at Torre de Lobaton and in that Valley.

July 9. Marched at 2,—got into the Woods of the Venta de Almarez at a little after day.—Replied to the 21W. by 22W.—The approach to the Ford (Castro Nuno) not so easy a matter, which they on the other side don't know. However, to do all one can.—Visited Don Antonio Rodriguez at Villavellid.—Sent my Letter to the Marshal by one of his Commissionados.—Bonnet occupied Mota this evening with 1,000 Infantry and 500 Horse,—His Division stretching into all the Villages of the Torre to the front of Tiedra.—Those of Foy in Villalan and thence by Villalonso and Villabendemio to the Tagarabuena and the gate of Toro.—Thus the getting to the Ford, independent of the Force at Cubillos is impracticable or if I do,

I can't well get back again.   I must await a short time for a change.   And this time I shall employ in going to Castronuevo for I have nothing to eat after today, and my Convoy from Carvajales which will arrive at Castronuevo tomorrow can't come any further with safety, therefore I must meet it.

Wrote to Lord Wellington.

July 10.   Put the Brigade in motion upon the Woods of San Pedro at 2 in the morning, remained with the Pickets and Rear Guard and reconnoitred the Enemy in Mota at day-break, found him in Mota.—Followed the Brigade to the Woods of San Pedro, he did not molest or follow me, but I find our march the day afore yesterday has made some sensation.   He has had out two different Columns in search of us without success.—Rested in the Woods of San Pedro.—Marched to Castronuevo.

Wrote to Sir William Beresford 23W.

July 11.   Convoy arrived.—Bread for four days.— Received a letter from Genl. Silveira—wrote him.   Marched in the night and arrived in the Woods of San Pedro de Latarce at day-break.—Communicated with Don Antonio Rodriguez.   The Position of the evening the same.

July 12.   Woods of San Pedro.—Reconnoitred all along in the direction of Torre de Lobaton, Pedrosa and Cubillos.   Enemy very strong there and no possibility of getting to the Ford of Castro Nuno—at least, of getting away again afterwards.

July 13.   Woods of San Pedro Latarce.—Wrote 24W. to Hardinge.—As I had concluded Sepulveda arrived with 25W.—Acknowledged the receipt in a Postscript.

July 14.   Marched in the night, arrived in the Woods of the Venta de Almarez before day-break.   Wrote to Santocildes ; despatched Flangini with my letter and commissioned him to propose an attempt upon Valladolid, or any other thing which would not take me too far from my object.—Rode by the Mota, reconnoitred the Fords of the Badajoz,—ascertained all my directions, roads, and distances upon Pedrosa and Cubillos.—Some French Deserters came in, in the evening, and from the tenor of what they say I suspect the Enemy is going to pass the River somewhere near Tordesillas.—I shall reconnoitre with the whole Brigade and feel his Posts in that direction in the morning.

[*July* 15. The Brigade was forming for the Recon-naissance upon Pedrosa and Cubillos, Tordesillas and Simancas, when at ½ past 4 Chapuzet arrived with 26W. —The Brigade was in march in consequence at ½ past 5, and at 3 I arrived at Castronuevo,—met there my convoy from Carvajales ; made all the arrangements ordered in 26W. ; left the Squadron of Capt. Du Thel, of the 12th Regt. to return to Braganza ; rested everything till 11 o'clock at night ; and marched upon the Ford of Villa-lazen. (*Note.*—Received orders from Wellington to rejoin main army.)

July 16. The Enemy had a Force of two Divisions round Toro, and one Post a league to my left, another not far to my right on the River,—passed without being per-ceived,—crossed everything over the Ford by 5 in the morning,—continued my march to Benialvo,—bivou-acqued the Brigade in the valley.—Directed Chapuzet to prepare for returning to Head Quarters. Reconnoitred round to Toro in front, to Parabinas and Boveda on the right,—returned,—wrote 28W.—despatched Chapuzet for Head Quarters.

In the evening a report of a French Division having crossed at Toro, and proceeded to Boveda. Reconnoitred in the direction of Boveda,—too dark to be certain,— strengthened the Posts on that side and waited the morning

July 17. Reconnoitred Toro, Parabinas, Villa Buenas. —The French repassed the Douro in the night, destroyed the Bridge they had repaired, and moved with everything to their left.—This is more like a concentration for the attack upon our Right than a re-assemblement for retreat,—*nous verrons.*

Received 29W.—Wrote 30W. to Lord W. and the Marshal.

July 18. The French have passed in force at Torde-sillas, and are passing rapidly round our right towards our Rear. Souza arrived at ½ past 6 A.M. with orders to march upon Fuente Sauca,—marched at 7.[1]—At Fuente Sauco met Valdez at 12 with orders to proceed to Fremo de Ribera.—Rested till 2,—marched,—arrived. This has been a Day of Affairs pretty sharp near Castrejon. Went

---

[1] '. . . After conducting a very daring exploration round the rear of Marmont's army,' Sir Charles Oman sums up (vol. v, p. 409) ' almost to the gates of Valladolid.'

to Head Quarters.—Received Lord Wellington's orders to place myself on the Heights in front of Parada de Rubiales in the morning,—to communicate with General Le Marchant whose Brigade of Cavalry is to be there, and to take the orders of General Picton commanding the 3rd Division who is to occupy these heights, to take care of the left of the Army in the first instance and to be brought up as a reserve should it be necessary.—Returned to Parada.—Made all the ordered movements and communications.

July 19. Morning.—Took up the Out-Posts in front of Rubiales in conjunction with General Le Marchant,—all quiet through the day. Evening.—All ordered to march and assemble near Valleza.—Marched.—Arrived in the night.—Bivouacqued near Valleza.   ·

July 20. The morning discovered the whole French Army in march by its left along the heights which extend in a semicircle from behind El Olmo and Castrejon upon Cantalpino. This might be to turn our right and attack, or pass us, and march upon the Fords of the Tormes, and manoeuvre Lord Wellington from the line of that River or cut him off from Ciudad Rodrigo, and his Frontier. Lord Wellington assembled his whole Force in contiguous Columns on the left Bank of the Guarena and watched the movements of the Enemy.—At 6 o'clock A.M. I got orders to move to the extreme right and observe the Enemy's left near Pobeda.—On the march I received a counter order to go to our extreme left and watch some French Cavalry which formed his extreme right behind El Elmo, and also his extreme Rear Guard ; at a ¼ before 8 [1] I reported to Lord Wellington that this Cavalry was in movement and following the March of the rest of his Army. Lord Wellington then marched by his right in three Columns of Lines cotoyering the Enemy, and I remained upon the Guarena between El Olmo and Ribera in observation. Lord Wellington's Army having moved off—that of the Enemy continued to march by its left all day,—and at 5 o'clock I saw at least 20,000 Men of his Army in the Plain of Cantalpino, its Rear near that place, its Front

---

[1] Note no mention in the ' Journal' or enclosed correspondence ' of D'Urban's Portuguese Horse coming in very late from their duty of covering the baggage train' [being] 'mistaken for prowling French cavalry . . . and shelled. . . .' Oman, v, pp. 413–14.

beyond Hornillos leaving that place to its right marching fast, and directing itself upon Villaruella and Babila-fuente. I marched immediately upon Pitiegua and reported what I had observed.

(*July*) 21*st*. The Army marched in the morning in three Columns of Lines (2 Lines and Reserve) upon the Tormes. I received Lord Wellington's Orders to march upon the outward flank of the Right Column of Lines or Left Wing of the Army, to cover and to look out for it. Halted at Monterubia covering the Left,—and bivouacqued in the Plain of San Cristobal by Monterubia. At 5 in the evening got Orders (Pencil Note X from Lord Wellington) to Relieve the Piquets of Genl Anson's Brigade[1] at Morisco and Castellanos with two Squadrons and to march with the remainder upon Cabrerizos. There I got into communication with Genl. Pakenham commanding the 3rd Division, or Reserve of the Army. Learned from him in the night that we were to remain together,—that all the Army had passed the Tormes,—that we were to occupy the Heights behind Villares,—to hold them as long as we could and that we might expect to be attacked by three Divisions coming down the Right Bank in the morning.

BATTLE OF SALAMANCA [2]

July 22. Upon the morning clearing, my Patroles and look-out Officers made out very clearly that the whole of the Enemy had passed the Tormes by the Ford of Machacon near Encinas de Abaixo, and had marched by Machacon upon Calvarassa de Abaixo. This was reported

---

[1] Reproduced in facsimile. [2] It is remarkable that the battle in which D'Urban played such a prominent part should be so summarily dismissed. Two brief reports are appended in which characteristically he did not spare himself in praise of his Portuguese. It was only later, when a brother officer, Colonel Watson (afterwards Sir Henry), appealed to him, after some slighting remarks made by Napier in his fifth volume, that he wrote a long and extensive account, a copy of which is enclosed with his papers.

The reader can do no better than refer to Sir Charles Oman's pages (vol. v, chaps. vi and vii) for a narrative of D'Urban's services . . ., while we may be allowed to quote from a letter from Hardinge who writes, ' Our friend D'Urban led the Brigade on, with the intelligence and bravery that always ensures success,—and he has now added to his merit as a Staff Officer, an executive reputation of conducting Troops in the Field, which was alone wanting to complete his military character.'

to Lord Wellington by Genl. Pakenham at about 10. His
Lordship broke up from the Valley of the Marta where he
had held his Army during the night and morning, and laid
the Troops in position along the Hills which run parallel to
the Heights of Gargavete.

At about 12 o'clock by Lord Wellington's order the
3rd Division with my Brigade crossed the Tormes (the 12th
returned from Piquet being ordered to go to Calzadilla and
guard the Heavy Baggage of the Army) and we took post
in reserve, upon or rather behind the Heights between La
Penilla and Aldea-Tejada.

Marmont was moving all day, there were several sharp
affairs of Cavalry, and a good deal of Cannonade. At
½ past 4 Lord Wellington observed that the Enemy was
determined upon turning his Right and resolved to attack
him. The Reserve (3rd Division) was ordered to attack
the Heights occupied by the Enemy's left. I was directed
by the Commander-in-Chief himself to move in two
Columns of Lines upon the Right, to cover, protect and
co-operate with it.

Note.—Lord Wellington came down from the neighbourhood where he had been examining the Enemy's left,
at a rapid gallop accompanied only by Col. Delancey (but
followed immediately afterward by Col. Sturgeon) and
gave us orders for the attack verbally,—first to me (whom
he had first met with) and then to General Pakenham.

All this was done,—the Battle became general, lasted
for three hours and ended about ½ past 8 o'clock in a
complete Rout and Defeat of the Enemy who lost about
10,000 Men. The Marshal was most unfortunately shot
through the body in making a movement with the 12th
Regt. of Portuguese Infantry which saved the 4th Division.
(See Reports 1 and 2 and Note upon July 22, 1812,
annexed.)

July 23. In the morning Lord Wellington marched in
pursuit of the Enemy, pressed him closely and destroyed a
Rear Guard of 4,000 Infantry between Alba de Tormes and
Peñaranda. I remained all day at Calvarassa de Ariba
collecting Detachments and Stragglers, Horse-shoes, Bread
and Meat. These Detachments were sent to Salamanca
with Prisoners, and left me for the night with about half a
Squadron. Rode into Salamanca to see the Marshal and
to superintend the arrangements for the wounded of my

Brigade whom I recommended to the care and well-known benevolence of Dr. Curtis. (See his Letter annexed.)

July 24. Marched at 2 A.M. upon Peñaranda. Met Lord Wellington there and got orders to wait for further ones.—Marmont has lost his arm. Six Generals badly wounded were brought to this place yesterday and with the Head Quarters marched in the morning for Flores d'Avila.

July 25. Wrote Sir S. Cotton No. 4 Report. The Two Squadrons of the 12th Regt. arrived under the Viscount de Barbacena. Head Quarters at Flores d'Avila. Army closing up.

July 26. Marched and bivouacqued in the Pinar de Arevalo, one mile beyond Vinaderos upon the Arevalo.— Head Quarters at Aldea Seca.

July 27. Head Quarters at Arevalo. In Bivouac upon the Adaja.—Short of Olmedo.

July 28. Head Quarters at Olmedo. Bivouacqued upon the Adaja by Puente de Vallemiguel. Advanced Post towards the Douro. Patrolled to La Seca. Communicated the result to Col. Ponsonby at the Camp of Majorada. Received in the afternoon the order of March for the 29th.

July 29. In readiness to march at ½ past 2 according to the order of last night, but after the Columns were formed got the Memorandum No. 1 from Lord Wellington.[1] —Complied with it.—Despatched a Squadron accordingly. —Marched upon Olmedo.—Saw Lord Wellington.—He goes to Mojados.—I remain at Olmedo with the German Heavy Brigade, my own, one Battalion Light King's German Legion, and Captain Macdonald's Horse Artillery. —Put up the Troops.—Rode to the Front as far as La Nava de Coca.—Enemy in Santa Maria de Nieva and other Cantonments around Segovia where the King (Joseph) is. Sent Lord Wellington by express four different Despatches of Intelligence of the King, and two Deserters from the King's Spanish Guard. These make him out 12,000 Men. Established Communications and Intelligence—pointing the people's attention particularly to the march by the Enemy's right, as suggested in His Lordship's Memorandum No. 1.—Returned to Olmedo.—Visited the Posts.—Gave Pass-Order A.—Received No. 2 from Lord Wellington.

July 30. At day-break at Coca.—Nothing new to be

[1] For this and other letters see *Cambridge Historical Journal*, iii, No. 1, pp. 97 *et seq.*, October 1929.

heard.—Sent out an Officer to La Nava.—Sent back to turn in the Troops.—Despatched His Lordship's Letter to Don Diego.—He is ordered to communicate with me and give me information.—Returned.—Left a small Day Post at Placa de Olmedo.—Wrote Lord Wellington Report No. 1. Received ' X ' from Sir Howard Douglas—state of things in the North.—Lord Wellington moved this morning upon the Douro as he had proposed in No. 2.

The German Brigade of Heavy Cavalry, one Brigade of German Light Infantry and a Troop of Horse Artillery under my charge at Olmedo.

Kept a close watch upon the motions of the King.— Sent an Officer to Cuellar and another to La Nava de Coca, to ensure intelligence, and a Peasant of confidence and intelligence into Segovia. Wrote His Lordship frequently of all that passed.—The Enemy patrolled this evening into La Nava and Coca.—Lord Wellington entered Valladolid at 2 o'clock.—His Head Quarters at Boecillo.

July 31. Rode to Coca and La Nava.—No appearance of a change.—The Peasant returned from Segovia. The King still there, his Troops in the surrounding cantonments as before.

Received Lord Wellington's No. 3 and ordered movements accompanying for Genl. Hope's Division.—Sent him a Squadron of German Heavy Cavalry.—Wrote to Lord W. —At about 10 was aware that the Enemy had withdrawn from Santa Maria de Nieva ; informed His Lordship and of my belief that he was retiring on Segovia and thence to Madrid. Sent him two routes cutting in upon the road from Segovia to Madrid at Otero de Herreros.

Sent the Peasant back to the first Posts of the Enemy. At 2 the Peasant returned.—All in retreat to reassemble at and near Segovia.—Wrote to Lord Wellington.—Received No. 4 from Lord W. Arranged accordingly.—Sent off an Officer of the German Cavalry with his Lordship's Letter for the Governor of Segovia.—Sent an intelligence Officer to Santa Maria and farther on for Intelligence.—Informed Lord Wellington of all this.—In the Evening received No. 5 and the movements for the 1st August.

This of General Hope's is all false Intelligence, and His Lordship will lose the opportunity of cutting off the King, for all bending to the left is ground lost. Wrote Lord Wellington my firm belief that Segovia was the *Point de*

Rassemblement.[1]— Received letters from the German Officer, and from the Correjidor of Cuellar corroborating my opinion in time to enclose.

Aug. 1. At 2 o'clock A.M. got a Report from my Officer gone to the front which proves the Enemy to have all gone to and some past Segovia in the direction of Madrid.— Wrote Lord W.—Marched upon the Eresma with all the Troops in Olmedo according to my Provisional Instructions. Bivouacqued the Troops on the Eresma near Coca. My Officer came in from the Front, and nearly at the same time the German Officer who has been in to the Enemy's advanced Posts. They agree as to his Cantonments,— Segovia, Abados, Espinar, Otero de Herreros, Garcillan, and Anaya.—Wrote to Lord W. all this and at the same time ventured to say that our Horses were fresh from their rest at Olmedo, and fit for any march. Enclosed him the French Officer's receipt for the Letter to the Governor of Segovia. Sent off a Patrole to La Nava, and Santa Maria, and another Peasant from the former into Segovia. —Got No. 6 from Lord W.

Aug. 2. Rode to Santa Maria,—ascertained that all the Enemy had passed the Puerta, that Joseph marched at 4 yesterday morning—that the Head of the French Column of March was past Guadarrama at three o'clock on the 31st July,—that General Espert remained in Segovia with 700 men.—Wrote Lord Wellington all this by an Officer.—Returned to Coca.—Received further Reports all confirming the same.—The French are spiking the Guns, burning the Carriages, throwing Ammunition, &c. into the Castle ditch and enforcing the Contribution ordered by the King. Wrote Lord W. this and enclosed him General Espert's answer to His Lordship's letter sent by the Flag of Truce, which I have got by a Peasant. At ½ past 7 in the evening received No. 7 from Lord W.— Wrote him that it should all be done.

Ordered everything accordingly. Received a Packet of intercepted Correspondence going from General Espert to the King, Marshal Jourdan, and the Minister of War at Madrid. Espert's letter thanks Jourdan for the Regiment of Baden which he received yesterday. Sent them to Lord W.—Marched at ½ past 9 P.M.

Aug. 3. Arrived at the Moros River 1½ league from

[1] Quoted Oman, v, p. 495. Note the date should be July 31.

Segovia at ½ past 5.—Infantry a good deal fagged.—6 leagues of very deep sand.—Bivouacqued the whole in the Pine Wood upon the left bank of the river behind the Bridge of Unez. Rode to the neighbourhood of Segovia, reconnoitred the Enemy's approaches, roads, etc. Communicated with Don Diego de la Feristo the Commandant of Guerillas stationed about the Town. It appears that the Enemy, having received the Regiment of Baden, is about 1,400 Infantry. He remains in the Town all day, and encamps close to it in the night on the Mountain side opening the Road to San Ildefonso. By this Mountain Road he will of course retire; it joins that which the King has taken, behind the Puerto de Guadarrama, at Gallapajar. The Town besides the Castle has its old walls perfect. These are built upon a Rock, formed by the scarped Banks of the Eresma, and a small stream falling into it, which enclose the Town. It is not to be entered without Artillery to breach. To attack it therefore with half the number of the Enemy's Infantry, would certainly fail and I shall lose a great part of my Light Infantry without the least service done. To attack their camp by night (if they continue to come out and encamp) is more feasible, getting first between them and the Town, though there the access is so difficult that success is very problematical.—Wrote Lord Wellington state of things,—ventured to point out to his Lordship that if another Corps would march upon the Town, from which the Enemy would probably retire, as he does not, evidently, intend to remain long, I could place myself (by Roads indicated to his Lordship) so as to intercept him; or that if another Corps would turn him I would march upon the Town.—Asked if His Lordship would have me attack his Camp. I shall have this known in time and without his sanction, I don't know how far his letter No. 7 authorizes me to risk,—he there only says 'feel your way, and learn the intentions of the Enemy,'—I'm afraid I can't make this out an order to attack superior forces, strongly posted. I must have his sanction therefore,—and I simply ask 'would you wish me, if he encamps again, to get in between him and the Town, if that should be feasible?'

Despatched this letter by a well-mounted Officer, and having previously laid Horses on the Road for this purpose, I shall have the answer as soon as it will be possible to do anything.—The Troops must be rested,—and the night of tomorrow will do if His Lordship sanctions the attempt.

Communicated with Don Diego and urged to him strongly the importance of giving me the earliest possible intelligence of the slightest movement of the Enemy. This he promised to do, and he assured me that his people watch him so closely as to prevent the possibility of escape. On the march I can attack him with great advantage.— Not to trust to the Guerillas altogether, I have engaged three Peasants to go into the Town and to come upon any movement. I have returned to Camp at 8 P.M.

Aug. 4, Night of.—Segovia.—Espert has escaped,— and all my precautions have been of no effect. 'Tis vexatious enough.—I have only the consolation that I neglected no care, no pains, no precautions that could be taken or devised. I was this morning at day-break and for an hour afterwards near the town,—all appeared as usual,— tranquil,—I saw no Peasants who had come from the Town, and those at work in the fields supposed the French to be all in *statu quo.* Reconnoitred the road from the Rio Frio,—by Martin Miguel to the right of the Camp on the Moros,—to be prepared for the march proposed to Lord W. in my letter of yesterday.—Returned to Camp at 8 o'clock.—Just afterwards a Courier arrived from the Municipality of Segovia with a Letter. The Enemy marched at midnight, with great haste and silence from his Camp and took the road to San Ildefonso.—My Spies it is clear could not get out of the Town, for Espert locked all the Gates, left guards upon them on the outside till his people had marched, then came out locking the Gate after him, collected the Guards and followed his Corps. But the people in the Town did not dare to force the Gates till day-break when they knew he was gone. Don Diego, however, has been scandalously negligent, for he (it appears) knew of the march by ½ past 2 A.M. and if, as he promised, he had despatched a well-mounted Guerilla to me, I should have had it by 5 or 6, for I left relays to bring Letters to me from the Camp.—Wrote a note to Lord Wellington, at ½ past 8, sent it by a well-mounted Officer, ordered the Horse Artillery, Light Battalion, 11th Dragoons, Baggage and Commissariat to march into the Grove of Lobones two-thirds of the way to Segovia, and there to wait for orders. The 1st and 12th Dragoons to be ready to move with me.

Received Lord Wellington's No. 8.—marched with the two Regiments of Cavalry at ½ past 9, direct upon Rio Frio, the nearest point of the high road to Otero de Herreros, and the straightest line to the other road at San Ildefonso. So much time had elapsed however, that I had no hope of seeing anything of the Enemy. On arriving at Madrona, near Rio Frio, found that Espert's Rear Guard had passed San Ildefonso at 4 A.M. All further following is but to fag the Horses without use. Sent Capt. Abreu's Squadron to patrole to San Ildefonso. Put the Regiments in march for Segovia.—Ordered the Troops there from Lobones.—Went there myself.—The two Regiments of Cavalry in the Town.—Artillery, Light Infantry, 11th Dragoons in the Houses and Groves at its entrance, upon the River, on the Lobones Road.

This Town is impregnable to anything but Regularity and Heavy Guns. If I had attacked Espert here I should have lost all my people, even if I had attacked him in his Camp, that is if he had done his duty. I find that he had 2,500 Men, 600 Cavalry the rest Infantry—Directed Capt. Macdonald to examine the state of the Ordnance and Stores left in the Castle, buried, destroyed, &c.—Wrote to Lord Wellington,—mentioned slightly my disappointment,—the escape of Espert,—my useless and unavailing precautions,—the negligence of Don Diego (who by the way ought to be hanged),—ventured to give my opinion with regard to Segovia, as a Place d'Armes and Depot for the Enemy,—and this because it is incumbent upon me to do so, and because His Lordship leads to the subject in No. 8. and is evidently not aware of the strength of the place, by his asking if I can patrole into it, if I am strong enough to get in, &c.

I have said that the strength of Segovia does not consist exclusively in that of its Castle, though strong, that its walls are perfect, that they are built upon a scarped and impracticable rock, that it may defy everything but Heavy Guns, that its importance to the Enemy is considerable,—a Place d'Armes safe from everything but regular siege, standing upon the junction of the Roads from Madrid and Burgos, at the debouche of the former, —ready to receive and guard everything upon its arrival,

—large enough to hold 30,000 Men,—and finally that I thought it (adverting to His Lordship's Questions) more easily to be occupied than rendered useless to the Enemy (the latter indeed is impossible) but that I thought an Engineer ought to examine and report upon it, and that if His Lordship could spare time I wished him to see it himself,—Enclosed Macdonald's rough sketch of the Guns, &c.

Aug. 5–6. Segovia,—Troops rested waiting Lord Wellington's answer. Received No. 9 from Lord Wellington.—Sent him a Spanish Deserter from Madrid yesterday.—Wrote him that in consequence of his Letter I should march as soon as we had cooked, upon Otero de Herreros, and execute all he had ordered. It will be necessary to get possession very quickly of the Puerto de Guadarrama, —or to drive out the Enemy if he is there, which is likely, as he has occupied the Village of Guadarrama for some days, which is at the foot of the Puerto.—I shall rest at Otero, arrive at the Puerto at day-break and get possession of the pass.—Without securing the Debouche from the Guadarrama I can't get into the Plain of Madrid or patrole towards it.

The German Battalion late in assembling,—could only arrive at Otero at 9 in the evening.

Aug. 7. Arrived at the foot of the Puerto at 6.—Took possession of and occupied it without resistance.—The Enemy had even withdrawn his Piquet which was there last night.—This Post is infinitely strong, and one Division posted in it would require 3 or 4 to drive it out. —The Enemy does not mean to stand at Madrid or he would have defended this pass to begin with.—Posted the Troops.—Reconnoitred the nearest Villages (Molinos, Guadarrama, El Escurial, &c.) in the Valley at the other side,—All quitted by the French at 3 o'clock this morning. —Wrote Lord Wellington.—Sent patroles to Galapajar and Escurial.—The Enemy in Galapajar.—Those from Escurial gone to Valdemo-Villo and Brunete.—Returned to the Camp.—Wrote to Lord W.—mentioned that I intended to move forward in the morning.

10 at night, got No. 10 from Lord W.—of course cannot move in the morning.—Sent him the Intelligence of the Enemy.

Aug. 8. Rode to the Front.—Got upon the Road an

account that the Enemy meant to take up Boadilla,
Mastoles, and Butre to receive Soult from Toledo.—
Wrote Colonel Gordon this.—Received No. 11 from Col.
Gordon.

Aug. 9.   Escurial ultimately quitted.—Galapajar evacuated also.—Patroled to within sight of Las Rosas.—
French there and at Majalahonda.

Received 12 and 13 from Col. Gordon.

Aug. 10.   Marched according to No. 12.—Bivouacqued
in the Park of Moileno.   French retired from Torre
Lodones.—Received Nos. 14, 15, 16, from Col. Gordon.
—Obeyed them.—Received No. 14 at ½ past 3.—Marched
at 5.—Dark when I arrived at Puente de Retamar, upon the
Guadarrama.   Of course halted there for the night and
the rather because, having sent in a Peasant to Las Rosas,
I found the Enemy was there in force with his Cavalry.
—and the Bivouac was convenient and secure.

AFFAIR OF MAJALAHONDA.[1]

Aug. 11.   Reconnoitred Las Rosas at day-break.—Enemy
came out in some force and drove in the Reconnaissance,

[1] Readers may be referred to Sir Charles Oman's narrative, vol. v, p. 508.
It is worth while quoting some sentences from D'Urban's Report :
'In recounting this misfortune,' he generously writes, 'I cannot
justly attribute blame to any Officer of the three regiments of Portuguese
cavalry ; as far as the dust and confusion incident to actions of cavalry
allowed me to observe they all endeavoured by every means in their
power to bring the men on well, and I have only deeply to lament that it
was not seconded by that energy and determination which marked the
conduct of the Brigade at Salamanca of the 22nd of July or by the good
order with which it had in conjunction with the Artillery, driven back
the same enemy. . . .'
He likewise in another connexion refers to the men being so badly
mounted 'that . . . if they rode their horses well into the fight they
could feel no security that they would bring them out of it.'   D'Urban
was naturally much concerned about this affair, but he was entirely
exonerated by his brother officers from Wellington downwards. (See
Wellington's Dispatch, Madrid, Aug. 1.)
Beresford seemed to have suggested some form of punishment of the
Portuguese cavalry, for in a letter of Sept. 8, 1812, Wellington writes
disapproving of such action after having seen and talked with D'Urban.
'As for sending the cavalry to the rear,' he continues, ' that is impossible just at present.   We have still a good deal upon our hands, and we
are worse provided with cavalry than our neighbours ; and a body commanded by such a man as D'Urban, even though they will not fight,
are better than none.   In fact, they behaved infamously, and they must
not be employed again alone, or with our cavalry, who gallop too fast
for them.'

—brought up some Troops,—a few shots from Capt. Macdonald's two Guns and one of the Regiments of Cavalry thrown on his flank drove the Enemy through Las Rosas to Majalahonda.—The German Heavy Brigade at length came up to Las Rosas from the Ron de Torre Lodones, after I had sent repeated messages. The Enemy retreated to the Woods between Boadilla and Mastoles and they to all appearance went clear off.—Lord Wellington arrived, approved of all, and also that the Troops should turn in and get out of the Sun.—The Heavy Germans in Las Rosas with the German Light Infantry, and the Horse Artillery (now joined by the four remaining Guns) at Majala-honda with the Portuguese Brigade of Cavalry.—Patrole to Madrid.—Ditto to follow the Enemy.—All quiet.

4 o'clock P.M.—Enemy advanced with Cavalry and as I knew that Lord Wellington had proposed Majalahonda for one of his Debouches for tomorrow, I determined to hold it and besides, I saw nothing but Cavalry, from whom we ought to hold what we had driven them from. —All occurred, shortly to speak, as in Report Z.—The German support was shamefully late and hence all the loss.—Wrote to Col. Gordon a note at 6.—Sent it by Flangini.—Occupied Las Rosas.—Enemy retired to Majala-honda.—Picquets on the Road to Las Rosas.—Brigade on the Torre Lodones Road.—Received No. 18.—Wrote Col. G.

Aug. 12. Went forward at day-break.—Enemy gone. —Found the three Guns.—Wrote report to Col. Gordon.— Lord Wellington arrived,—if he blames me he abstains from shewing it.—My conscience is quite clear as a Cavalry Officer.—Lord Wellington ordered a Report.—Wrote him Z.—Rested at Majalahonda.—Ordered to march to Madrid ; did so.—Bivouacqued on the Manzanares.

Aug. 13. Wrote the Marshal,—enclosed him my report to Lord Wellington, very little more to add,—told him frankly all and my opinions. Retiro invested.—Lord Wellington's Head Quarters in the Palace.

Aug. 14. In the night Lord Wellington lodged two Battalions in the Gardens of the Retiro, and in the fore-noon all being ready to storm and the Heads of the Columns ordered for that service shewing,—the Commandant sur-rendered himself and the Garrison Prisoners of War, and thus without losing a man Lord Wellington became master of the Great Central Depot of the Enemy, from which he supplied those of the Provinces.—2,400 Infantry (*French*), 200 Pieces of Cannon, 20,000 Musquets, and sets of Accoutrements complete, 14,000 suits of Clothing, 40,000 pairs of Shoes, Provisions for 3,000 Men for six months, and an incalculable quantity of Ammunition and Military Stores.—Thus the Capital and all its resources are in the hands of the Conqueror,—these are the fruits of the Victory of Salamanca,—the 14th August has crowned the work of the 22nd July.

Aug. 15.   The Light Division marched to Valverde.

Aug. 16.   Camp near Madrid.

JOURNAL XIV

1812, *Aug.* 15.   Head Quarters, Madrid.

My Brigade in Camp near the Town in a Meadow on the bank of the Manzanares.

The Retiro having surrendered yesterday, Guadalaxara surrendered to-day.

The Light Division went to Villa Verde on the road to Marjuez, and is there with the Hussars of the 14th Light Dragoons.

Aug. 16–18.   The King (Joseph) continues to proceed towards Valencia.   The Enemy has retired from Toledo. Everything has gone.   Lord Wellington puts the Troops into Quarters of Rest for the Heats.   The Light and 3rd Divisions remains at Madrid with the Commander in Chief. The 1st, 4th, 5th and 7th Divisions to El Escurial.   The Heavy Cavalry to San Ildefonso.   My Brigade to Rio Frio.   Thus they are not only in Summer Quarters, but centrally placed.   If the Reliques of Marmont become troublesome these Divisions can be thrown towards the Douro.   If anything comes from the Southward they can be easily moved towards Madrid.   The 6th and Genl. Anson's Lt. Dragoon Brigade at Cuellar and Rueda are advanced on the one side, on the other the Light, and 3rd. Received an Order to March to the Rio Frio on the 20th.

Aug. 19.   One Brigade of the Lt. Dragoons brought to Madrid.

Aug. 20.   Marched upon the Rio Frio.   Encamped upon the Guadarrama to the left of the Bridge of Ritamar.

Aug. 21.   To the Park of the Monesterio near Guadarrama.

Aug. 22.   To Otero de Herreros.

Aug. 23.   To the Palace of the Rio Frio.—1st Regi-

ment.—Madrona ; 11th Regt.—Ontoria ; 12th Regt.—
Las Navas de Rio Frio. Made Reports. . . .

Aug. 24. Dispatched Reports . . . ; and sent to
establish Letter Parties at Arevalo and Peñaranda to
communicate with Salamanca.

Aug. 25–Sept. 1. The Enemy continues to establish
himself at Valladolid and even beginning to push his
advances to Benavente. Lord Wellington[1] during these
days has thrown forward the 5th Division, Col. Ponsonby's
Brigade of Heavy Cavalry and the Brigades of Pack and
Bradford to Arevalo.

General Maitland has landed at Alicante with a Force
of about 9,000 British and 5 or 6,000 Spaniards.

Sept. 2. At Villacastin, Segovia, by Lord W's desire.
Ill—(Spanish Ague, getting worse in the damp and dreary
old Palace full of Bats and Owls.)

Sept. 3. Lord Wellington moved from Madrid to El
Escurial and put the 7th Div. and 4th Div. in movement
from thence to Arevalo.

Sept. 4. At Arevalo.

Sept. 5. At Almedo.—Enemy has withdrawn the
Garrisons of Astorga, Toro, and Zamora, and quitted
Valladolid. Soult has raised the Siege of Cadiz and is
marching towards Suchet. Abandoned part of his Siege
Train before Cadiz. General Skerrett entered Seville
(August 27th). Stormed the fortified Court.

Sept. 6–9. Lord Wellington moved upon Valladolid—
Anson's Cavalry and Ponsonby's. Upon the 6th it was the
intention to have attacked the Enemy in front of it, but
the Guns of the 5th Division were not up. The Enemy
blew up the Bridge over the Pisuerga and retreated upon
Burgos.

Sept. 10–12. The Marshal having given no Orders with
regard to the Brigade, but writes to me that I shall receive
them from Lord Wellington. He is too busy to think of
writing.—I shall therefore go to him. There is nothing to
be done here, and if the Enemy fight for Burgos I shall be
in time to see the Battle.

Sept. 13. Rode from Segovia to Olmedo.

Sept. 14. Overtook the Head Quarters at Cordovilla

---

[1] Having ' resolved to leave Madrid and return to the Valley of the
Douro, where the movements of Clausel and the French army of Portugal
demanded his attention,' Oman, v, p. 578.

12 leagues from Valladolid on the road to Burgos. The Armies are in presence, the Enemy retreat slowly, and we follow in proportion. Lord Wellington is delayed by the late arrival of the Spaniards, for whom he waits, because without them he is inferior to the Enemy, who has about 24,000 Infantry and 2,000 Cavalry. General Castaños, however, has at length this day arrived at Hd. Qrs. and his Army is to come up on the 16th—given out 11,000.

Determined for the Brigade to remain at least through the Campaign.

Sept. 15. Revilla—Vallejera. Army bivouacqued in front of Villadrigo. Enemy at Pampliega and Villaldemiro.

INVESTMENT OF BURGOS

Sept. 16. Pampliega. Army with its right there. Left upon Villaldemiro. Cavalry with Don Julian, and Bradford's Brigade at Torre Padierhe on the left of the Arlanzon. The Enemy was encamped before Estapar, upon the heights between the Hornaza and the Arlanzon, having two Divisions in advance in two lines, their right upon the Hills of Tamaron, their left upon the Arlanzon at Celada del Camino. A Division of the Heavy Cavalry of Boyer on the left bank of the Arlanzon about Arroyo de Muno. This Ground he held with a determined aspect, and the Spaniards having arrived in the afternoon, Lord Wellington made the following disposition to turn him out of it in the morning. The 6th Division, with Pack and two Squadrons of Cavalry and one Spanish Dragoons, to get into the valley of the Tamaron before day-light and turn the Enemy's right by Hormaza the 1st, 5th, 7th; and Cavalry Divisions to advance in front upon Celada del Camino, Bradford and Don Julian with two Squadrons of Cavalry and one Spanish Dragoons to move by the left bank of the Arlanzon upon Cavia, to show upon the Enemy's left, and to be a real attack in case of necessity and occasion offering. Enemy has 8 Divisions.

Sept. 17. Frandovinez.—The Disposition ordered was made and the Troops placed accordingly, but the Enemy did not wait, he retired in the night. The Army advanced however. in the arranged order. The Enemy's Rear Guard of Cavalry was at Estapar, and his whole Force upon the Heights behind the Arcos with his left upon

Pardajos. This strong ground he gave up without fighting, and fell back upon Burgos. The Army bivouacqued upon the Heights above Buniel. The 6th Division, &c. (Left Corps) on the right of the Arlanzon upon the Heights of Nave de las Calzadas.

Sept. 18. The Enemy again retired. Nothing was seen but his Rear Guard of Cavalry retreating towards Vittoria. Army bivouacqued in front of Villalvilla and above the Hospital del Rey. Lord Wellington rode into Burgos. The Army burned the Suburbs. Lord W. carefully reconnoitrced the Castle; this work which the Enemy has garrisoned with 2,500 Men and a General Officer (du Breton) is strong. Besides the old Castle well-repaired, with its keep, there are two fortified Lines round it and a Horn-work upon the contiguous Hills. The two lines of Defence of the Castle have ditches paled. The Horn-work has a good ditch but the fencing is not complete.

SIEGE OF BURGOS

Sept. 19. Head Quarters.—Villalvilla.—At dusk the Horn-work stormed and carried by Genl. Pack's Portuguese Brigade, and 250 British under Major Cocks' 79th. Place invested. Army bivouacqued round it, Enemy having retired out of sight.

Sept. 20–21. Work going on. Batteries constructing with as much speed as can be expected, for the 3 eighteen-pounder Guns and 6 twenty-four-pounder Howitzers.

Sept. 22. Outer Line . . . assaulted at 12 at night by 400 Men of the 1st Division. The difficulty of the escalade in itself and the great power of fire occasioned its failure. After about $\frac{3}{4}$ of an hour fruitless assault Lord Wellington called off the Troops. Major Lowrie 79th, killed. Capt. Fraser, G. Batt., wounded.

Sept. 23–24. Sap pushing on. Batteries almost ready. Enemy's advance at Pradaños. Lord Wellington reconnoitred and fixed upon a Position (in case of the Enemy's approach to disturb the Siege) upon the Heights of Rio, Bera, and Majaradas. Communications ordered. 3rd encamped above Majaradas. Batteries quite ready, mounted in the Night.

Sept. 25. Ground chosen for a Battery of five Howitzers to throw Spherical Case upon the top of the

Castle to annoy the Enemy at his seven-Gun Battery of 18-pounders (French 16) when our Batteries open.

Sept. 26.	The Bank . . . lined with Sharpshooters and prepared, this not only keeps down the Musketry of the Besieged but covers the Mine which is begun last night to . . . This Mine is intended to open a way at . . . into the inner line . . . while the outer line enfiladed by the Batteries at . . . will be easily carried. The Convent at . . . will be burned by Hot Shot and Fire Arrows, and in the midst of this, a Lodgement made in the Convent ground, which is on a level with the Castle, from thence a Breaching-Battery established, and the Castle wall laid open. Nothing of this is to begin till the whole is ready. The Mine goes on rapidly, and the Sap too. . . .

The Army of Clausel is a good deal dispersed, part on the left bank of the Ebro, part as far as Domijos de la Callada.

Sept. 27.	Sap continued. Mine going on well, one Chamber charged.

Sept. 28.	Proceeding on the Mine, but it does not extend to the inner line and will only breach the lower one.

Sept. 29.	Mine exploded at 12 at night and the outer line breached at . . . but the dispositions of Lord Wellington for carrying it by assault, immediately after the explosion, by some mistake, were not carried into effect.

Sept. 30.	Howitzer Battery at . . . played upon the Breach at . . . to knock away the Palisading in which it succeeded.

Oct. 1.	Battery constructed last night to receive the three 18-Pdrs., to batter the corner of the Breach, so weak that the Men could not work the Guns in it. Obliged to abandon it till night, and the Enemy having got its range knocked off one Trunnion of one Gun, and destroyed the Carriage of another. Guns got out in the night.

Oct. 2.[1]	Two of the 18-Pounders got into the Battery where the 24-Pounder Howitzers were ready. The Mine to the right of the old Breach ready.

Oct. 3.	Powder arrived from Santander. Mine charged.

[1] The day Wellington was informed that the Cortes had nominated him Generalissimo.

Oct. 4.   Battery opened in the morning upon the Breach with great effect. 9-Pounder of the 6th Division and 4 Howitzers firing into the Defences. Enemy, by the account of a Peasant who came out of the Fort, reduced to his Castle stock of Water, that in the Convent exhausted. The 24th Regt. ordered for the assault of the lower line, by the old Breach now becoming practicable, and by one to the right of it which is to be made by the Mine (12 Barrels of Powder). All the Covering and Working Parties in the Trenches to support. Explosion of the Mine to be the signal of the Assault. Mine Exploded at 5 in the afternoon, the effect perfect and the right Breach very good. The 24th rushed to the Breaches with equal impetuosity and good order and they were carried and the lodgement made instantly. It was remarkably well done.[1] Great gallantry and excellent management. Confirms my opinion that *Corps* and not *detachments of Corps* should always be used for services of difficulty or more than ordinary danger. In the former there is a common feeling of honour and shame. The Officers know the Men, the Men obey the Officers. In the latter the very contrary of all this is the case, and the effects correspond with their causes. The 24th rushed in so rapidly that they were covered before the Enemy had well time to open his fire from the second or upper Line, which he could not do till the space between the Lines was cleared of his own fugitives, to the number of 300, flying from the lower, to get shelter in the Upper Line. In this assault the actual Storming Party lost comparatively few Men, but the supports, who were positively ordered not to go to the Breaches, unless their presence was necessary, by the assaulting Regiment being pressed, and who yet did go there, although the necessity did not exist, lost 50 or 60 Men. These were Detachments and less under control. Mem.—Support assaults with a *second Corps*, and not with the Duty of the Trenches.

The Enemy attempted a sortie in the night ; repulsed immediately.

Oct. 5.   At about 5 in the afternoon the Enemy made a Sortie in force, and got possession of the left Breach ; the Queen's Regiment was moved up to support and the Breach was recovered. The work of the last night and

---

[1] See Oman, vi, p. 45, on the cause of the failure of the assaults.

today very trifling. Indeed upon many occasions in this Siege, the work done has not answered expectations or the time given. The Engineers blame the Troops for this. The Troops the Engineers. Great precautions necessary to make all secure in this regard. Much valuable time has been lost by the want of this. Lord Wellington ordered a communication between the two Breaches, which, however important, the Engineers had not made.

Oct. 6. Sap pushed on half-way from the Lower to the Upper Line. The two 18-Pounders began battering the Inner Line in Breach. Two Prisoners report the water short, and that not more than 200 Shells remain.

Oct. 7. Early in the morning one of the 18-Pounders totally disabled; that which lost a Trunnion a few days ago, ordered into the Battery and to be tried. The Breach looks well, considering the time and means that have been given to batter it, but the diminution of the already very small Battering Train is perplexing and vexatious. If however it be possible the Breach is to be rendered practicable and then the Inner Line is to be stormed and the Convent burned at the same time; if however the means of the Battery cannot effect this, then the Siege must become a close Blockade, burning the Convent, and directing all the Howitzers to the throwing shells into the Castle, and thus penning up the Garrison, and rendering it as unquiet and unpleasant to them as possible.

Oct. 8. The Enemy made a Sortie in front at two in the morning, and succeeded in filling up a little of the trench at the head of the Sap. We suffered some loss, and in particular a very heavy one in the person of Major Cocks one of the most promising Officers in the Army. The Breach is much improved.

A Letter of the 5th from Madrid from Sir Rowland Hill to Lord Wellington [1] mentions that the appearance of a Movement upon the part of Soult towards Albacete, has induced him to move forward the 4th Division from the Escurial, and my Brigade from its Cantonments also. —I can't stay to see the end of this interesting Siege therefore.—I set off by Post tonight.[2]

[1] See Oman, v, p. 56.
[2] Sketch plan of Castle of Burgos enclosed with papers.

JOURNAL XV

While D'Urban returned to Madrid to take charge of his Brigade and also to convey important news to Sir Rowland Hill, the siege continued.

1812. *Oct.* 9 to 11. Lord Wellington having informed me that General Hill had put my Brigade in movement to the Front in consequence of a movement of Soult upon Albacete, I set out from Villa Toro (before Burgos) and rode by Segovia to Madrid, where I arrived on the evening of the 11th.—I immediately communicated to Genl. Alten Lord Wellington's Orders that the Retiro should not be given up to the Spaniards, and delivered Castanos' letter to that effect to Don Carlos d'España. Rode in the night to Mastoles where my Brigade is.

Oct. 12. Genl. Hill[1] is at Aranjuez. Therefore wrote him the substance of all that Lord Wellington instructed me to say to him, as in ' R.' Wrote Lord W. also to say what I had done. Gave out ' X ' and ' Z ' to the officers and Men of the Brigade, and returned Lieut. Miranda of the 12th to his Regimental Duty, the Regiment being very weak in Officers.

Oct. 13–14. Inspected each of the three Regiments closely.

Oct. 15–16. Wrote the Marshal the state of the Brigade. Received . . . from Genl. Hill in answer to my letter of the 12th.

Drouet at Albacete. Castle of Chinchilla surrendered by the Spaniards to the Enemy. Ballasteros not arrived at Alcaraz or Barrax. Colonel Skerret will be at Talavera de la Reyna on the 20th with the Cadiz Troops.

Oct. 17. Received . . . from Hardinge. Wrote him . . . and its enclosures.

---

[1] See Oman, vi, pp. 56–7.

Oct. 18.   Nothing.—Marching—order day.   Ordered Baggage to be reduced.   Prepare to march light.

Oct. 19.   Received from Col. Jackson Route . . . and Letter No. 1.

Oct. 20.   Marched to Perales del Rio (3 leagues 12 English Miles) according to . . . There found that the Jarama is impassable, except at the Bridges and a Ferry Boat.   Wrote a note to Jackson to say that I would inspect the River, but that I imagined we must pass at the Barcas of Chinchon.

Oct. 21.   Brigade passed the Jarama at the Barcas of Chinchon (2 leagues from Perales del Rio ; from the Barcas to Arganda 2 leagues.   Marched to Arganda according to . . . One Boat holding 10 horses—40 to 50 an hour,—one trip in 10 minutes.   Of course all day passing.   By Madrid from Mastoles would save two leagues. —So soon as a Boatload or two had passed, rode forward towards the front.   Genl. Elio's Head Quarters at Villarejo de Salvarez.   Rode as far as Villarejo (4 leagues) on the road to Fuenteduena.   Returned to Arganda.   Found No. 2 from Jackson (3 came at 10 at night).   Wrote to him the passage of the Brigade, state of the Boat, Roads and Rivers, capacity of the Towns, and that Elio was at, Villarejo.   Sent in Cypher for our Correspondence.

Oct. 22.   Sent an Officer to compliment Genl. Elio at Villarejo.

Oct. 23.   Sent out two Officers to make Reconnaissances as directed in . . .

Oct. 24.   Received . . . and No. 2 from Jackson. . . . explains the proposed movements in No. 2 and there can be no doubt that Sir Rowland's determination is right. Of course he intends to contest the difficult ground between the Tagus and Henares with a strong and clear Advance Guard and fight behind the latter.

Oct. 25.   Head Quarters removed from Aranjuez to Bayona.   Visited General Hill and Jackson.   At night on my return found No. 3 ordered.   Soult still moving at his right, but he still keeps up a feint on his Left, that's to say he has advanced a part of the Division at Belmonte to Lillo.

Lord Wellington raised the Siege of the Castle of Burgos on the 21st after an ineffectual attempt to storm the Breach in the Inner Line on the night of the 18th.

Army in full march to join this, His Lordship having got Sir Rowland's account of Soult being in movement.

Oct. 27.   Marched to Onruzco.   Examined the Bridges of Carabana and Onruzco.   Good ground for defending either, particularly the former.   But it will be difficult to destroy it expeditiously except by Powder, for it is new and well-built of stone.   That of Onruzco is old and badly built and may be quickly destroyed.   Rode by Estremere to Brea and Driebes and back to Onruzco. All bad Cavalry Country,—scarcely a foot of it in which that Arm can act—Rocks, Mountains, Stony Hills, and the most steep and impracticable Gorges.

Ordered a Squadron to Brea and Driebes according to the Q.M. General's Instructions in . . . to observe to Left and communicate with the 6th at Estremera and Spaniards at Mondejar.   This squadron is a good deal risked so far to the front without support, for Brea is a 2 League to my front, and besides the space, if it is intended to connect the Chain of Out Posts between Estremera and Mondejar, is so great that it will require the Brigade to do the duty.   If it be only to forward Intelligence between these two Posts then half-a-dozen Men will do.   Wrote Jackson all as above.   Begged to know as to the Posts, and whether I should go to Brea with the Brigade.   Mentioned that I would have some Workmen tomorrow and would do what is necessary to the ground near the Bridges.

Oct. 28.   Received 'D'[1] at ½ past one A.M.   Received 'E'[2] at ¼ past 2 A.M. at Onruzco.   All the necessary preparatory steps taken as marked upon . . . The Brigade had orders last night to stand to their Horses at half-an-hour before day-light.   Note to Diggins at ¼ past 5 by a Sergeant of his Regiment.

Executed all prescribed in . . . Patroles upon the Tagus till 2.   Between the Tagus and Tajuna till 4. Destroyed the Bridge at Onruzco and marched upon Alcala at 4¼, having been informed that the Spanish Divisions were already at, or near, that place.   Arrived at Alcala a little before 9 P.M.   Wrote Col. Jackson that I had executed all in . . .

Oct. 29.   Received . . . As I perceived by it that I am

---

[1] Viz. that Sir Rowland Hill had determined to concentrate behind the Jarama on account of the state of the fords upon the Tagus.

[2] *Cf.* Oman, vi, p. 98.

intended as a part of the Cavalry, to cover the Henares, I shall go back to Torres where I would have halted but that the Orders in . . . were precise and positive for Alcala, and where I shall get cover and Forage, neither of which are here.

Observing the Paragraph in . . . which says ' Genl. Victor Alten's, Count Penne Villemur's and your Cavalry should cover the Henares ' I determined to go to Torres,—this is the spirit if not the Letter, of an Order to take care of the Front, and as such I do it without any other direction.

Examined the Country to the front of Torres and Loeches. Took Post at Torres with the 1st and 11th. Placed the 12th at Loeches. Patroles to Onruzco, Carabana, and Perales de la Tajuna. Fixed the Posts and Pickets.

Enemy a small Party to Villarejo de Silvares. Patroles to Arganda.

Oct. 30. All quiet in the night. The Spanish General Don Miguel Freyre with the Cavalry of the 3rd Army, has come into my front at Pozuelo del Rey. Visited him as soon as I had seen the Posts relieved. Agreed for mutual communications. Rode to the Front. [The Orders to destroy the Bridge of Boats at Fuenteduena not having been executed by the 2nd Division before it retired, and the Boats having been drawn over to the Right Bank, the Enemy having found means to pass over[1] two or three Dragoons, easily got the Boats replaced, re-established the Bridge, and last night passed over 4,000 Foot, and 600 Horse, who turned down the River and took the direction of Aranjuez. The King with the Troops at Cuenca has arrived at Santa Cruce de la Zara], therefore his operations are ripe and will immediately commence. On my way back from the front, stopped at Loeches, and dispatched a Sergeant to Col. Jackson with the Intelligence between brackets [ ] in Cypher.

On my return to Torres at 11, found Genl. Victor Alten waiting to communicate with me, and also a letter . . . from Jackson. Upon receiving that letter and comparing it with Genl. Alten's instructions, it is evident that some intermediate Letter has been lost, containing some Order of Movements, for that General is instructed to find me upon his Left. I am instructed to find him upon my Right.

[1] See Oman, vi, p. 99, footnote.

Our present Position is just vice-versa. Dispatched, therefore, an Officer to Jackson, to say all this, and to make
sure of what is intended.

Received . . . from Don M. Freyre at 12 and . . . at
½ past one P.M.—Drew in all the Posts.—Patroles returned.
—Brought up the 12th Regt.—Marched upon Alcala at
3,—arrived at 5,—found Genl. Victor Alten.—Got his
orders to march by the Pardo, leaving Madrid on the left,—
to pass the Bridge of the Pardo, and Bivouac on the Right
Bank   of   the   Manzanares.—Obeyed.—Arrived   and
Bivouacqued at 2½ A.M.

Oct. 31. General Hill's Head Quarters at Alvaraca—
Visited him.—(Got . . . from Jackson after my return.)—
Cause of the Movement explained. These People are
Hydra's Heads,—North and South—Saw Jackson,—
Letter lost as I suspected yesterday.—Received the
General's Orders to pass the Guadarrama and look out to
the Right. Got . . . from Jackson after my return.
Marched at 12.—Calmenarejo for the night.

Nov. 1. The Engineers failed in destroying both Vi-
veros and the Puente Larga on the Jarama. They are
unfortunate in the Bridge way. Marched by Puente de
Guadarrama, and the Fondo de St. Rafael, to Otero de
Herreros, halted and rested ; continued in the evening to
Abados ; communicated with Don Diego de la Fuerte the
Guerilla, he and his people in observation upon the Duero.
Lord Wellington is I fancy at Rueda,—I shall go to San
Garcia tomorrow. In the first instance that position will
ensure me all the intelligence I can want, and nothing can
pass without my being aware of it. Found all the Baggage
of the Army on its March to Villacerta. Directed Col.
MacDonald who has charge of it, to move tomorrow morning to Aldea-Vieja. This is better ;—out of the Line of the
Army's March ; all well placed either for Avila or Arevalo,
3 leagues from the first, 6 leagues from the second. Wrote
to Col. Jackson to mention this arrangement.

Nov. 2. Marched to San Garcia and Herreros.—Sent
an Officer to Col. Gordon Q.M.G. to say where I am if
Lord Wellington should have any commands, wrote Col.
Jackson also.—Fixed Posts.—Rode to Santa Maria de
Nieva and arranged Intelligence from the Upper Douro,—
Tudela, Penafiel, and Roa. Received . . . from Jackson.

JOURNAL XVI

LINE OF THE TORMES OCCUPIED—RETREAT TO THE FRONTIER OF PORTUGAL.

1812, *Nov.* 3. Hetreros.—The bad marching of the Brigade for the last two days made it necessary to give the order. . . .

A French Division entered Madrid last night. They were received by the Authorities and behaved very well to the Inhabitants. The Enemy on the Douro appears to be moving by his Left. Lord Wellington has moved some Troops by his Right towards Almedoi and Tudela. His Head Quarters at Rueda.

Nov. 4. Enemy in force at Villacastin.—Arrived at Otio de Horreros, and entered Segovia in the evening ; I have received no Orders to retire but it is now necessary to do so or I shall be cut off, and besides my staying here is not material in any regard and the Duty for which I came here is finished. I shall march in the morning, cross the Boltoya and await further Orders at Orbita or Espinar, or between those places and the Boltoya.

Nov. 5.[1] Withdrew my Posts and marched at Day-break,—received on the road . . . from Col. Jackson by which it appears that some order for me to use has been lost.

Afternoon.—Reached Villa Nueva de Gomez at 3 o'clock P.M., an hour later and the Brigade would have been cut off. 'Twas luck I moved without Orders.

Evening.—The whole Corps d'Armée Bivouacqued in front of Fontiveros.

Nov. 6. The Army marched at day-break. Ordered by Sir William Erskine to close the Rear of the Light Division. The Army marched into a Position about a League behind the Trabancos with its advances in front of

[1] See Oman, vi, p. 119.

that rivulet and before Muno Sanco. There's a road
branching off from Fontiveros which turns to the Right of
this Position and leads by it upon Peñaranda. Received
order to go to watch it—marched—occupied Juinleon with
a Squadron advanced at Salvadios. Received the
Distribution . . . by which I watch the Right again at
Macotera.

Nov. 7. Giving the Army three hours start—marched
at 9, arrived at Macotera at 12.—Received . . . —Marched
again without dismounting . . . arrived upon the Tormes,
whole Corps d'Armée there. Ordered to pass to the Left
Bank and watch the Fords from the Bridge up the Stream
as far as Sieto Iglesias; these fords are stated to be three.

Nov. 8. Passed the Tormes, in the morning. Brigade
in Martin-Amor, made the Dispositions for watching the
Fords, or rather for Patrolling the Banks of the River, for
working the prescribed space—there are 20 Fords instead
of 3.

Lord Wellington has arrived at Salamanca—called in
to him as in . . .

Reported to the Q.M. Genl. my obedience to the Order
for watching the Fords, and also what I had ascertained
concerning them.

HUERTA

Nov. 9. All quiet at my Posts. Received . . . —
Sent for the Detached Squadrons. —Wrote Jackson to say
this would make the delay of $1\frac{1}{2}$ hour. Sent off the
encumbrances, lame Horses, Sick, &c., to Almeida.

Bivouacqued in the Wood of Machaçon.

Enemy in force opposite Lord Wellington's Position on
the Right Bank of the Tormes at Salamanca, and is
moving a part of this Army up the River towards Alba.
Two Brigades of General Hamilton's and General Howard's
Brigade of the 2nd Division left in Alba,—2 Brigades of
the 2nd in the Wood of Machaçon. One of Genl. Hamilton's
near Palomares, General Slade's, Count Penne Villemur's,
and my Cavalry in the Wood of Machaçon and Genl.
Long's at Palomares.—Pickets on the River.

JUNCTION OF WELLINGTON AND HILL

Nov. 10. The Enemy has a Corps of about 15,000
Infantry and 2,000 Cavalry between Huerta and Alba

and has closed up about 2 Divisions near to the Town.
Third and Fourth Divisions at Calvarissa de Arriba in
support of Genl. Hill's Corps d'Armée. Enemy attacked
the Town of Alba in the evening, with a heavy Cannonade
from three Brigades of Artillery—Repulsed—withdrew
his Troops into the Villages of Garcia Hermandez and its
adjacents, excepting strong detachments of Cavalry which
remained upon the Right Bank from and beyond Alba to
Huerta.

Nov. 11–12. Enemy's Troops [1] in continual movement and he made a careful reconnaissance of the River
from Huerta to Exeme [above Alba]!

Nov. 13. The Enemy moved all his Troops which were
between Huerta and Alba by his Left into the Wood
behind Exeme on the High Road to Avila,—from thence
he can move in that direction or cross the Tormes by the
Fords above the Bridge.

A Spanish Garrison of 300 men put into the Castle of
Alba.

THE CRISIS

Nov. 14. At day-break the Enemy moved down from
the Wood behind Exeme and commenced crossing the
Tormes by the Fords of Ençinas and Galiana and marching
by the Road of St. Pelargo to take possession of the
Heights above Martin-Amor which afford access to the
Roads leading into the Plains of the Arapiles ; at the same
time the remainder of his Force closed up to Alba from the
neighbourhood of Silavança. The 4th Division moved
forward to the Heights of Los Parales, the remainder of
the 2nd and of General Hamilton's Divisions with Genl.
Slade's, Count Penne's and my Cavalry brought into the
skirts of the Wood behind the Heights of Martin-Valero.
Generals Howard and Hamilton withdrew from Alba to the
same Heights leaving advances. General Long's Brigade
also withdrawn to General Cole's Position of the 4th
Division.

Lord Wellington arrived upon the Ground at about
12 at Noon, and at first appeared inclined to attack what
of the Enemy had already passed, with the Divisions and
Cavalry on the spot. The success of this measure appeared
certain and that sure, for while the measure would have

[1] Quoted Oman, vi, p. 130, footnote, and entry for the 15th.

neither risked nor committed anything, would have frustrated all the Enemy's projects. From some Reports from his Left however His Lordship's opinion changed,—they were suffered to continue to pass unmolested,[1]—and as soon as it was dark all the Troops before Alba withdrew, the Infantry to the Arapiles, the Cavalry to Calvarassa de Arriba.

Nov. 15. The Army retreated marching by its Right in four columns, three of Infantry and one of Cavalry, and Bivouacqued upon the Valmuza. Head Quarters Carreiro.

Nov. 16. Head Quarters Aldea de Bireda. The Army marched again in the same order and Bivouacqued upon the Rivers Matilla and La Maha.

Nov. 17. The Army marched again. Bivouacqued upon the Huebra. In passing that River at Sanmunoz the Enemy's advance overtook the Rear. A good deal of Cannonading and some confusion, and the Army had the misfortune to lose Sir Edward Paget who was taken Prisoner.

Nov. 18. The Army marched again and Bivouacqued behind the Yettes and Tenebrosa. Most luckily the Enemy either was not up in force to-day, or did not choose to press—for the greatest confusion prevailed throughout. The principal Column of the Army went astray [2] without any Cavalry to cover it, and 'tis difficult to imagine the extent of the Evil that might, and probably would, have ensued from a vigorous and well-directed attack.

Head Quarters Ciudad Rodrigo.

Nov. 19. The Army Bivouacqued under the Guns of Ciudad Rodrigo. General Hill's Corps d'Armee in the woods between Zamana and Atalaya. My Brigade attached to this Corps again and takes the Outposts in front of it for the night.

Heavy Cavalry crossed the Agueda at the Bridge of Ciudad Rodrigo.

Nov. 20. The Enemy does not follow and I imagine that the Commander in Chief does not think he will, for the Army is cantoned. This Corps d'Armée as in . . . The remainder behind the Agueda.

---

[1] Quoted Oman, vi, p. 133, footnote.
[2] Due to Colonel Gordon, who does not seem ' to have been a success as Quartermaster-General.' (See Oman, vi, p. 138, footnote). A striking contrast to D'Urban.

Head Quarters Ciudad Rodrigo.

[Note to this in Red Ink of later date.]

Atalaya, Villa la Zamana, Sernidilla and other villages on the Right of the Agueda from whence it afterwards marched by Perales upon Coria where it went into Winter Cantonments.

Everything over the Agueda excepting Sir R. Hill's Corps and my Brigade, which are in the Villages on the Right Bank.

During the whole of this Retreat, from the 15th inclusive, the weather has been dreadfully severe, and the Commissariat arrangements having failed, the Troops have been most often 5 or 6 days without issue of Rations, and have suffered the extremity of privation, having lived upon Acorns and some Hogs killed occasionally in the woods. The natural result of which has been great disorder and confusion, and the roads in the Rear of the Columns of March, covered with exhausted stragglers left to the Enemy. In fact by some inconceivable blunders, which the Qr. Mr. General's Department attribute to that of the Commissary General—and the latter to the former —the Supplies of the Army which were adequate to a much larger number, on the morning that it broke up from the Arapiles, were sent down the Tormes by Ladesma upon Almeida, while the Army marched upon Ciudad Rodrigo ; —hinc illae Lachrymae.

'Thus concluded a retreat,' to quote D'Urban's annotation in Jones's "Account," 'exceeding one hundred and fifty miles, made in face of a superior enemy, with the deliberation of an ordinary march, in which consequently the troops suffered nothing from fatigue and the casualties from the sword under 850. The casualties during the previous siege exceeded two thousand.

'This retreat was conducted with singular coolness and ability. Lord Wellington was always master of his movements ; he marched when (and only when) he thought proper, and halted to rest the troops whenever he found it expedient.'

In a further annotation he sums up the campaign as indeed most brilliant, eventful, and important.

---

[1] Cf. Oman, vi, chap. vii. With the Journal is also enclosed D'Urban's memorandum on the Portuguese soldier—a by no means unflattering account. (Quoted in parts, Oman, iii, pp. 173–74).

ARMY IN CANTONMENTS OF REPOSE AND REORGANISATION

1812. *Nov.* 21. Atalaya.—Sir Rowland Hill's Quarters at Robleda.—The Enemy has retired from Tamames.— Sent out Cornet Osorio to observe the Baños Road to Plasencia where 'tis very likely the Enemy will detach.

Head Quarters at Ciudad Rodrigo.

Nov. 22–23. No movements.

Nov. 24–26. [These days D'Urban spent in despatching much needed and important information, viz., that the French were retreating.]

Nov. 27. Wrote[1] . . . to Marshal Beresford together with . . . Reports resulting from the Inspection of his brigade.

Nov. 28. Marched at 8, and arrived at Robleda at 4, found there the Order to Halt tomorrow. . . .—and the Letter[2] from Sir Rowland Hill . . . Answered the Letter by the Dragoon who was waiting to give it me. It becomes a duty to give the Marshal my thoughts upon the Cavalry. Wrote hastily the Confidential Memorandum[3] . . . Sent it to Hardinge to be laid before the Marshal.

Nov. 29. Halted at Robleda.—Sir R. Hill at Moraleja. —Lord Wellington at Fresneda.

Nov. 30. Received from the Quarter Master General . . .—Marched at 12. Arrived at Guinaldo.—Received in the evening the Change of Route. . . .

---

[1] About the Portuguese cavalry being sent to their respective depots (in Portugal) despairing of making them 'fit for service' without 'an English Commanding Officer' and at least 'two English captains . . .'

[2] Trusting 'that Lord Wellington will allow you to remain with me . . . but in case we shall be separated, I cannot refrain from expressing to you how very sensible I am for the assistance and advice . . . I derived from you during the late trying marches. . . .'

[3] There follows D'Urban's report noting 'a material falling off in the interior economy and discipline . . . since the absence of Colonel Watson.'

Dec. 1. The Anglo-Portuguese Army having halted at Ciudad Rodrigo, went into winter quarters (for the next three months).

Dec. 3. At Plascencia. Received circular letter [1] (of Lord Wellington. It is a most necessary injunction, for the discipline of the Army is relaxing to a degree unknown before).

Dec. 4–16. Various entries.

Dec. 17. Queen of Portugal's Birthday,—Feu de Joie.[2]

Dec. 18–31. During all these days the different arrangements were made for bettering the Commissariat, Discipline, Organisation and Drill.[3]

1813. *Jan.* 1–21. During this Month all Depôts and Detachments joined the Brigade by Order of the Marshal; Drills, Riding-School, and strict attention to Grooming and Economy were rigidly enforced (*vide* Orders of the Day) and I succeeded at length in overthrowing the villainy of the Commissariat so far as to effect good subsistence for the Men and Horses.

Made the Reports . . . and . . . to the Marshal upon their respective dates.

Feb. 1–15. In this period [4] all continued as in the Orders of the Day and the discipline and order of the regiments has got on in a way which gratifies me much.

[1] The Memorandum to officers commanding Divisions and Brigades (November 28), see Oman, v, p. 156.

[2] This day D'Urban received a confidential letter from Beresford, who thinks 'the national pride will not allow him to place an English officer in command, and agrees with D'Urban about 'the practicability of forming an effective Light Portuguese cavalry. . . .'

[3] Including letters from Captain Hugh Owen, brother officer of Colonel Watson, on improvements in riding, stable duties, etc., dress equipment, etc., of the Portuguese Cavalry and state of the military chest, all of which tends to show the further intensive training for making the Portuguese soldier efficient.

[4] There are several letters about the Portuguese Cavalry in a much more hopeful tone except that ' the non-arrival of clothing, equipment and money, the Brigade can not get over. . . . If they receive (these) speedily,' D'Urban concludes, ' they will be in April much fitter for service than ever they were before, for the Brigade will be stronger than when it took the field in June and what they have never yet been, the men upon the horses decently broke and which they have been well taught to groom and take care of, ride, and use the sword pretty well and work in squadron readily and correctly. . . .

' This is all I can promise. This I do promise. However when all is done . . . the weapon may have been cleaned but I won't answer for its temper . . .' (D'Urban ever mindful of and probably still smarting under the disaster of Majalahonda of the previous August.)

JOURNAL XVIII

1813. *Feb.–March.* The army still in Cantonments with Wellington, ' after five years successful campaigning in a position such as no British commander had enjoyed since Marlborough,' finally established as Generalissimo of the British, Spanish, and Portuguese armies. The importance of such a unified command need not be stressed in our day !

[The Journal for these dates is comparatively unimportant, except that D'Urban undertook an expedition to the Tras-os-Montes in answer to a call for help from the Spanish General, an action entirely approved by both Wellington and Beresford.]

JOURNAL XIX

1813. *March 11–May 7*

THE FINAL PERIOD OF THE ARMY'S CANTONMENT

(The interest of this Journal lies in the attached correspondence in which D'Urban refers to the decision of Beresford to leave him in command of the Portuguese cavalry, asks for a surgeon, and that his Staff should remain unchanged.)

JOURNAL XX

1813. *May–August*

THE CONCENTRATION OF WELLINGTON'S ARMY FOR THE GREAT ADVANCE—BATTLE OF VITORIA

May 7–30.[1] (D'Urban's brigade on the move, while reports sent to Murray about roads, fords, including one D'Urban himself discovered, and bridges—spade work which no one performed so promptly and effectually as he did.)

May 31. The army not up to cross the Esla. The rains of the day before melting the snow in the mountains made a rise in the river of 2 feet perpendicular increase. The Cavalry therefore could only pass by the ford of Monte Marta. They passed viz. My Brigade and that of the Heavy German cavalry. The advance of the right column passed the ford of Almendra. Threw a bridge over the bark of Manzanal and the troops all continued to pass here. . . .[2]

June 3. Halted to close up the rear division. Whole army ['80,000 sabres and bayonets'] assembled about Toro. Lord Wellington reviewed it.[3]

June 4–13. (The March continued to Burgos which was in its turn abandoned after its works had been blown up.)

---

[1] Beresford, having sufficiently recovered from his wound, writes on May 16 that he has been delayed at Villa Formoso because the pontoons had not arrived from Sabugal. . . . 'This being the anniversary of the Battle of Albuera,' he continues, 'Lord Wellington gives a grand dinner where all the world will be and I wish most sincerely you could possibly be one . . . Bonaparte appears to have left Paris for the army in Germany . . .'

[2] See Oman VI, p. 329.

[3] The first part of his scheme thus accomplished with complete success, the next to transfer ' the base of the British Army from the port of Lisbon to the Bay of Biscay, where he would find stores and ammunition awaiting it and be no longer tied to the long line of communication with Portugal . . . It was an astonishing example,' continues Sir Charles Oman, ' of the strategical use of sea power to which there had hitherto been no parallel in the Napoleonic wars.'

THE BATTLE [1]

June 21. The Enemy strongly posted at Vitoria embracing by Olala, Marguerita, Armnil, Goncelo, Subijana, de Alava and Aimentia. Lord Wellington attacked them as marked on the Map of Alava. The 3rd and 5th Divisions on the Left had some hard fighting as well as Murillo and the Highland Brigade of Sir Rowland Hill's Corps on the Right. The French completely defeated and dispersed, leaving to the Victors 150 Pieces of Cannon, immense quantities of Ammunition, His Military Chest, Equipage, &c., &c. The Troops behaved splendidly; the Ground was not of a nature to admit of the services of the Cavalry, they only served to pursue *d là delà.*

The Hussars and Light Dragoon Brigade respectively attempted what they were not equal to, and were severely punished. My Friend Hardinge unfortunately wounded. Head Quarters Vittoria. Brigade in the Wood of Ylancala. Pursued till dark.

June 22 *and following days.* (The Pursuit.)

June 30. Lord Wellington found the pursuit of Clausel fruitless and returned to Orcayen. . . .

July 2–26. Pamplona blockaded. . . .

The Brigade [D'Urban's] in its cantonments . . . and the 6th Regt. of Dragoons was added to it. Lord W. carried on the siege of San Sebastian, blockaded Pamplona and held the Puertos upon the Pyrenees.

MEMORANDA

Marshal Soult having been dispatched in all possible haste by Bonaparte from Germany so soon as he had intelligence of Lord Wellington's having crossed the Ebro, reached Bayonne on the 13th. Here he commenced with his usual energy the Reorganisation of the Army. Its formation was now altered from The Armies of Portugal,

---

[1] See *Supplementary Dispatches*, viii, p. 3, where in a letter to his brother reporting the battle and after saying that he was well, except for 'the complaint of all old soldiers, the lumbago,' he adds in a postscript, 'It is a curious circumstance that the battle was fought yesterday on the ground called in the country the *English Hills*, on which the Black Prince fought a battle against the French and gained a victory in favour of Don Pedro, called the Cruel . . .'

The North, South, and Centre to The Army of the South
of France.
Consisting of the

Army of the Right—General Reille
Army of the Centre—General Drouet
(Count d'Erlon)
Army of the Left—General Clausel
Reserve—General Vilate.

The whole formed into Nine Divisions. Marshal
Soult Commander in Chief with very full powers. General
Gazan Chief of the Staff.

The Divisions and Corps were all new modelled. Five
New Regiments entire (20 Battalions) added, besides
Recruits to all the Old ones. The whole was new Clothed
and Equipped and every means were taken, by giving it
the appearance of a New Army, to restore the Morale,
and make the Soldiers forget their Disgraces and Misfortunes.

It was natural that the Enemy should build his prospects
of success mainly upon getting ready so rapidly as to find
Lord Wellington unprepared. Having made his Arrangements therefore with unparalleled celerity he put himself
in movement on the 25th, forced the Passes of Roncesvalles and Maya, and pushed forward upon Pamplona.
(1 British, 2 Portuguese.)

The 3rd and 4th Divisions and the Brigades of Generals
Campbell and Byng of Sir Rowland Hill's Corps d'Armée,
retired in good order before this immense superiority of
force disputing the Ground obstinately, and on the 27th
in the evening the Enemy stood at . . . and the Allies
at . . . upon the Map of Navarre, the latter, however,
only reaching to the rear of the Village of Sahauren.

July 27. Lord Wellington arrived having drawn
back Sir Rowland Hill to Lizasso,—left Sir Thos. Graham
keeping the Siege of San Sebastian,—and the Light
Division holding the Communications between Zubieta
and Escuratin.

First Battle of the Pyrenees.

On the morning of the 28th the 6th Division was
brought up and took position upon the Heights above

Eussa and afterwards the 7th upon its Left upon those above Naguilz and Maqueriaim.

At 11 in the morning the Enemy keeping the Army of the Right opposite General Hill, and having those of the Centre and Left at . . ., attacked the 4th Division and the Brigades of Byng and Campbell upon the Heights of Oricain. These Troops amounted to about 9,000 Men, and 30,000 attacked them for several hours, at several points and in every varied method. The Enemy was everywhere repulsed, and driven down in confusion. The British and Portuguese Troops having made at different points 11 Charges with the Bayonet, Marshal Soult found the attempt useless and abandoned it, remaining, however, in his ground at . . .

July 29. Head Quarters Villaba.

Nothing was done on either side, but towards evening the Enemy began to move some Troops towards his Right in front of General Hill, and these were seen at Ostiz. The probability therefore was an Attack upon the Allied Left and all was ready accordingly.

Second Battle of the Pyrenees (Oricain and Lizasso).

July 30. Head Quarters Ostiz.

At Daybreak the Enemy moved his Troops as if to attack again on the Right while he really attacked Sir Rowland Hill in great force on the Left, and about 9 in the Morning began to put himself in movement upon his Left to support the attack on his Right. Upon the instant however, that Lord Wellington perceived this movement commence he himself attacked, bringing up the 3rd Division from Olaz, and turning the Enemy's Left. The 4th Division carried this Attack along with its Right Flank, the Centre remaining in position till the 7th Division had penetrated between Ostiz and Sorama, and the 6th Division were in possession of the latter, then the whole moved on. The Enemy's Right Wing was defeated in an instant leaving 3,000 Prisoners, great numbers of Dead, and having his whole project disconcerted nothing was left for him but a General Retreat which he made in disorder. His three Left Divisions by the Pass of Roncesvalles and the others by Lanz and Donna Maria.

During all this day Sir Rowland Hill maintained

himself with the greatest gallantry against three times his strength.

July 31.   Head Quarters Iruita.

Lord Wellington sent the 6th with the 3rd Division in pursuit of the Roncesvalles Column, following that upon the Lanz Road with the 4th and 7th and the Brigade of Genl. Byng.   The Enemy turned upon Donna Maria and were attacked there and driven upon St. Estevan by Sir Rowland Hill from Lizasso.   Lord Wellington continued to Iruita and took a considerable Convoy at Elizondo.

Aug. 1.   Head Quarters St. Estevan.

Lord Wellington moved from Iruita with the 4th Division, the 7th having fallen into the rear of Sir Rowland Hill, upon St. Estevan.   Sir Rowland Hill turned to the Right, took up his detached Brigade under General Byng, and proceeded to occupy the Puerto de Maya.   The Enemy retreated upon Echalar and occupied the Heights above it, their Rear Guard having made some stand upon the Heights of Sanvilla.   The Light Division moved from Zubieta upon Santa Barbara.

Aug. 2.   The Enemy occupied the Heights of Echalar. Lord Wellington attacked them there and dislodged them. This was performed with an inferiority of at least 1 to 5. Enemy retired into France.   His loss in the Operations since the 25th from 18 to 20,000.   Ours from 5 to 6,000.

Siege of San Sebastian resumed and the Troops took their old line.

Aug. 3.   Head Quarters Lesaca.

Enemy decidedly gone.

Aug. 5.   Returned to my Brigade at Arraiz near Pamplona where it had remained with the other Cavalry when the Army advanced into the Pyrenees.

JOURNAL XXI

1813, *Aug. 6 to the end.* Operations ceased upon the Bidassoa and I returned to my Brigade at Arraiz near Pamplona. Marched on the 11th and quartered the Brigade at Calahorra upon the 13th. Here it remained all August, September and October. The Siege of San Sebastian continued, and on the 30th the town was stormed. Soult at the same time who had made a movement to relieve it, was beaten upon the Bidassoa with the loss of 10,000 men. Blockade of Pamplona continued.

Sept. to the end of Oct. Upon the 6th the Castle of San Sebastian surrendered. Blockade of Pamplona continued. 12th, The Marshal sailed for Lisbon.

Upon the 7th (Oct. i.e. 3 A.M.) Lord Wellington moved the left of the Army over the Bidassoa, and put the advance of his Corps upon the Great La Rhune Mountain above Sare. The left and centre from this time stood upon French ground. 12th—the Marshal returned from Lisbon.[1] Upon the 27th in the morning received 'A.'[2] Got on horseback immediately and reached Erraza, near the Puerto de Mayo in the Pyrenees, on the following day. Found the Marshal in command of three Divisions (3rd, 6th, and Hamilton's) of the centre in the Valley of Bastan. He has sent for me to do the duty of Chief of the Quarter Master General's Department to his Corps during the approaching operations. Lord Wellington intends to attack the Enemy the instant Pamplona falls, and all is in readiness for the purpose, according to 'B.' [viz. a forward movement of the army].

Nov. 1–5. Pamplona surrendered (Oct. 30) from ex-

---

[1] Where he had been to inquire into the scarcity of recruits resulting from 'the venomous libels against Wellington and the British nation at large.' A similar state of affairs in Spain.

[2] Viz. from Hardinge, 'to mount your horse . . . and hasten towards us.'

tremity of hunger.   The weather is so bad and the mountain streams so swelled that it is absolutely necessary to postpone the intended attack till there is a change for the better. The movement waits therefore.

Nov. 6.   The weather so much altered for the better that the proposed movement commences and Sir Rowland Hill moves today into the valley of Bastan near Oricain and tomorrow to the Puerte de Maya.

The attack and forward movement was ordered to take place on the 8th, and the General officers of Corps to meet Lord Wellington at the outposts of the 6th Division on the 7th for final instructions.   The Marshal's Corps for the operation to be the 3rd, 4th, and 7th Divisions.

Nov. 7.   The Commanders of Corps met Lord Wellington at the outposts.   The slopes of the hills were not yet considered practicable, and the attack was delayed till they should be drier.

Nov. 8.   The Marshal moved his Head Quarters to Zugarramurdi and reconnoitreed carefully all the ground embraced by the attack of his Corps of the Army.   The ground much improved, and Lord Wellington fixed the attack for the 10th.

Nov. 9.   The Troops all brought to their respective posts.   The Enemy remained as before.

Nov. 10.   The attack [1] commenced as ordered at daybreak.   The Marshal's Corps of the Army got possession of the advanced redoubts with very little opposition, the Enemy having defended them feebly.   The Divisions reformed rapidly in the valley of Sare, and immediately proceeded to the attack of the Enemy's position, which was covered with redoubts and rendered very strong.   All the Divisions succeeded.   The 7th in the centre, conducted by the Marshal in person, carrying its point first, which facilitated the success of the others.   The whole of the front of the Enemy's position from Sare inclusive to the Nivelle, attacked by the centre Corps of the Army, was in our possession by $10\frac{1}{2}$ A.M.—before 11 the Troops were all formed upon the ground gained, and a report made to Lord Wellington accordingly.   Meanwhile, or very shortly after, the Light Division on the left, and the 6th Division and Sir Rowland Hill's Corps of the Army on the right,

---

[1] The French soldiers received the news of the defeat at Leipsic (October 16–19) on the morning of the Battle of the Nivelle.

respectively, carried their points of attack and before 12 o'clock the Enemy was everywhere completely beaten and in full retreat. The French in this battle have not fought with their former spirit, and hence our loss in forcing them from this formidable position has been less than might have been expected. The centre of the Army followed to the Nivelle at St. Pé, and the 7th, 3rd, and 6th Divisions passed it and got possession of the heights beyond and bivouacked there for the night.

Nov. 11. Movements of the Army and the Enemy had withdrawn part of his force over the Nive ; some Divisions however still remaining on its left bank, but the heavy rains and wind and thickness of the weather prevented any decisive movement against them and the Army remained in position.

Nov. 12. The Army was in position from Biarritz on the left by Arbonne to the rear of Ustaritz and Cambo to the right. The French retired from Bidarte to the front of Bayonne. The 3rd Division took possession of the Barbe Mountain and placed its right upon Arrauntz. Sir John Hope advanced to Bidarte with his posts beyond it, and the Army stood thus :—[Sketch plan enclosed with papers.]

Sir Rowland Hill approached nearer the Nive and cannonaded the Tête du Pont of Cambo.

Nov. 13. The Enemy had everywhere retired beyond the Nive. The Portuguese Troops were put into cantonments. Spanish Army sent back into Spain ; their want of discipline rendering them worse than good for nothing.

Nov. 14. The Enemy filed off through Bayonne and went behind the Adour leaving still however a Division behind the Nive.

Nov. 15. Enemy evacuated the Tête du Pont of Cambo, and blew up the bridge.

Nov. 16. The weather continued very bad and Lord Wellington ordered the Army into cantonments.

Nov. 17. The Army cantoned . . . Lord Wellington went to St. Jean de Luiz. The Marshal to Ustaritz.

Nov. 18–*Dec.* 7. The centre gradually brought up with little loss to within a mile of Bayonne.

The Army of Bonaparte destroyed and dispersed upon the Elbe and Rhine. His arrival in Paris. Speech to the Senate. Demand of 300,000 men in addition to the 300,000 already demanded.

Dec. 9.   (Movement ' Z ' ordered on the 8th.)

Sir Rowland Hill passed the Nive at Cambo with little opposition.   The 6th Division, supported by two Brigades of the 3rd did the same in front of Ustaritz.   The opposite hills were then all got possession of with scarcely any resistance.   The 6th Division advanced to communicate with the high road from St. Jean de Port to Bayonne, along which Sir Rowland Hill advanced with the right Corps.

The Enemy remained in force upon the Ridge of Monguerre of the heights above Villafranque.   The latter heights were carried in the afternoon by the Light Troops of the 6th Division.   The two Brigades of the 3rd returned to their cantonments on the left of the Nive, and the rest of the right and centre remained in position for the night, in the course of which the Enemy withdrew everything from their front, and left the whole of the Villafranque and Monguerre Heights, which were occupied in the following morning.

Dec. 10.   The Enemy who had withdrawn his Troops from the front of the right and centre in the night, and assembled his whole force (55,000 men) in front of Bayonne, attacked Lord Wellington's left upon the high road near Bidarte at about 9 in the morning, and in the hope of finding it weak in consequence of Troops having been thrown to the right bank of the Nive.   He was repulsed by the 5th Division, and the Portuguese Unattached Brigades of Campbell and Bradford upon the high road, and by the left of the Light Division near Arcangues. Two German Regiments entire, with a Brigadier at their head, came over from the Enemy in the afternoon.

The 6th Division returned to its cantonments on the left bank of the Nive in the morning—relieved at Villafranque by the left of the 2nd.

Dec. 11.   The Enemy made demonstrations and a fusillade through the day, and the bridge of boats was moved down the Nive from Ustaritz to Arranta to facilitate the passing supports to Villafranque if required.

Dec. 12.   The Enemy was in movement all day in various directions in front of Bayonne towards Bidarte, and towards evening was evidently moving Troops into the town.   This with the appearance of some of his Cavalry which had been thrown over the Adour, near Hasparren gave reason to apprehend an attack upon Sir Rowland Hill on the right bank of the Nive. The Marshal therefore ordered the 6th Division over the river before daybreak tomorrow. The 7th and 3rd in readiness.

Dec. 13. The 6th Division crossed the river before daybreak, and moved to the support of Sir Rowland Hill.

The Enemy who had (as was apprehended) thrown the greater part of his force through Bayonne in the afternoon and night of yesterday, attacked Sir Rowland Hill between Villafranque and Monguerre but was everywhere repulsed with a loss of from 3 to 4,000 men.

The 6th Division was up in good time to support, but excepting its Caçadores, was not engaged, the Enemy having been beaten by the Troops of the 2nd, and Portuguese Divisions (principally the former) of Sir R. Hill's Corps. The Brigades of the 3rd Division were brought over the Nive by the Marshal's orders when the attack was evident, and the 7th moved to the bridge established opposite Arrantz.

In the afternoon (the Enemy having given over all attack, excepting distant fusillade, by one P.M.) Lord Wellington placed Sir Rowland Hill's Corps from the high road to the extremity of the Monguerre Ridge, and the 6th, and 2 Brigades of the 3rd, from thence to the Nive.

All the Corps engaged this day were particularly distinguished.

Dec. 14. All appearance of renewal of attack on any point having ceased the arrangement was made by Lord Wellington who returned to St. Jean de Luz.

Till 1 *Jan.* Nothing of importance.

1814. *Jan.* 2. In the night reports were received by Sir Stapleton Cotton at Hasparren that the Enemy intended some attempt in the morning, and the Troops of the centre were held in readiness by the Marshal accordingly.

Jan. 3. The Enemy attacked and carried the advanced post of (La) Bastide, passed the Garbouir in some force, and got possession of the Ridge of La Costa. In the doing this they showed 2 Divisions and some Cavalry in front of La Bastide, one Division and some Cavalry near Mendecorde on the high road, thus threatening both the right and left of the 3rd Division. A considerable mass of Troops were seen in support of the Troops advanced against Bastide. The occupation of La Costa made it unsafe for the advanced Divisions to canton in Hasparren for the night. They were withdrawn therefore after dark to the heights behind Hasparren, and the advanced positions in front were held by pickets. This state of things required the arrangement ('7Z').

Lord Wellington came to Ustaritz in the evening 'to talk over the situation with Hill').

Jan. 4. According to (arrangements '7 & 8Z') the Troops moved in the morning of the 3rd, and night between the 2nd and 3rd, and the 3rd Division also took up its old ground in front and to the left of Hasparren this morning. Lord Wellington reconnoitred the Enemy from the front of Briscous on the left. The Enemy remained the same.

Jan. 5. The 7th Division moved early in the morning from L'Orueillon to the junction of the high road with that which leads to Hasparren. Lord Wellington reconnoitred from Hasparren and the front of it, and ordered the attack to dislodge the Enemy from La Costa. The 3rd Division advancing from the left of Hasparren, the 7th holding its ground upon the high road near Mendecorde. The 4th moving to Omattax (where they had replaced the 7th) by the Moulin d'haut, and two Brigades of Sir R. Hill's Corps by the Moulin Bas upon the river Elsery. These movements would make the event sure and inevitably effect the desired end with little opposition and consequent loss. The attack was ordered for 11 A.M. on the 6th.

Jan. 6. When the Elsery having swelled by the rains of the preceding night the 4th Division and Sir R. Hill's Troops could not pass till 1 o'clock, when the waters had a little subsided. The proposed movement was to have been made at 3 P.M. The Enemy abandoned the Ridge of La Costa with scarcely any resistance costing us but one man.

Jan. 7. The whole centre and right of the Army were cantoned as in '9Z.' The weather being extremely bad and the Enemy continuing quiet. The 7th Division thus supports the 3rd, and the advance is more secure.

Jan. 8–9. Nothing new. ('10Z') ordered for the guns of the Light and 4th Divisions.

Jan. 10. Signals ordered, for Sir S. Cotton as by the letter of this date '11Z' (not found).

Jan. 11–31. Nothing new, but the march of one Division of Cavalry and two of Infantry from the Enemy's Army towards Lyons. The Allies under Marshal Blucher and Prince Schwarzenberg advancing upon Paris by Thonville and Longres.

Feb. 1–3. An advance into France will soon take place, and the Cavalry is accordingly bringing up from the valleys of the Ebro and Arga. Mine has been starved by the villainous arrangements of the Commissariat, and I must go to it to get it into such order as may make it disposable.

JOURNAL XXII

1814. *February 4–April 3.*

These months provide the prelude to the last and final encounter. Wellington, after being 'virtually paralysed during the second half of January,' owing to the lack of money and clothing, hampered by the incessant rain and the uncertainty of naval assistance from the coast, with these matters remedied, was at last able to move.

On the 27th D'Urban 'received warning . . . that the Brigade [1] would soon march.'

March 2. Moved the regiments intending to assemble . . . The extreme difficulty of supplies and the Spanish cavalry in our way made this impossible. [Note.— D'Urban not present at the action of Ortheze (Feb. 27).]

March 5. The supplies not up and the halt unavoidable.

March 6. . . . Captain Parão returned from examining the Pass of Roncesvalles. Completely impracticable and blocked up with snow in consequence . . . will arrive at St. Jean de Luz . . . on the 12th, not before, because of the delays occasioned by my precarious mode of supply drawing everything from the country through which I march and without money. . . .

[The next few days the 'Journal' is punctuated with 'obliged to halt.']

D'Urban also notes the arrival on the 17th of Marshal Beresford at Bordeaux, where Wellington had sent him after repeated requests from French Royalists and where he had secured a bloodless surrender of this important seaport.

---

[1] In a further report on the Portuguese cavalry (February 13) he says that 'it will be months before we can recover from the starving regimen to which we have been condemned . . . by commissariat mismanagement . . . the more I trace the cause through all its effects, the more indignant I feel that a strong brigade of cavalry in very excellent condition and not the best in the world, yet the only one Portugal has, should have been unnecessarily reduced to what it is . . .'

There is no further entry of importance till]—

March 28. By a miscalculation of the breadth of the Garonne at Portet the bridge could not be completed and hence, though there was no appearance of opposition, Lord Wellington's well imagined enterprise of passing just above the confluence of the Ariega failed.

[It was not until the 31st that the bridge was completed and the Allies passed over to the attack of Toulouse.]

JOURNAL XXIII

Battle of Toulouse—Armistice

1814. *April 3.* Noé—at night—having informed the Marshal of the Disposal of the Brigade upon the Line of Communications, received his directions to join him.

Lord Wellington, immediately that Sir Rowland Hill had found it impossible to make his way from Cantegabelle to the High Road of Carcassonne at Mon Giscard and so to Toulouse, ordered him back to his former Cantonments and he recrossed the River and returned to them on the 2nd, Lord Wellington having in the mean time chosen a place to pass the River by his Left.

April 4. Rode before Daybreak from Noé, and arrived at 11 at St. Cyprian's upon the Garonne between Grenade on the Left and St. Jory on the Right Bank of it. A Pontoon Bridge had been laid down in the night, and the 3rd, 4th and 6th Divisions each with its Brigade of 9-Pounders passed the River and took Post provisionally at St. Jory. The Hussar Brigades of Lord Edward Somerset, and Colonel Vivian, and the Heavy Brigade of Lord Charles Manners crossed also, and were cantoned between the Garonne at Fenoulhiet by the Front of L'Espinasse, St. Alban's, Castal Genest, Gratertour, Bruyères, and Castelnaudary and Gissolles, along the Front of which Arc ran the Line of Advanced Posts. The Spanish Division of General Freyre had originally been intended to pass today, but this was changed and Lord Wellington ordered over the Baggage of the Divisions which had crossed. The Light Division remained near Seilz, and it is intended, so soon as the Spaniards shall have crossed tomorrow, to shift the Bridge to Seilz when the Light Division can cross and move to the support of the Divisions which have passed, or march to that of Sir Rowland Hill, if there should be occasion. Sir Rowland

Hill moved from his Cantonments, and took the Ground held by the Light 6th and 3rd Divisions opposite the Bridge of the Faubourg of St. Cyprian's upon the Auch Road, watching the Town, and with Instructions to make a diversion in case of observing the Enemy in movement to oppose the Passage of the River on the Left. The Enemy remained quiet and made no movement.

April 5. The River, from the Rains of the night between the 3rd and 4th, has swelled to such a torrent that it has been necessary to remove the Pontoons. The Communication thus remains cut off, but if the Enemy should be aware of this and take advantage of it to fall upon the Troops which have passed with his whole Force, the three Divisions will well hold their own in their Post at St. Jory. Meanwhile the Country within the Patroles will subsist them 'till the River falls. Head Quarters Grenade, Marshal Beresford's at St. Jory.

April 6. The River still prevents the laying down the Bridge. Lord Wellington came over the River, reconnoitred, and ordered an advanced Line of Cantonments to be occupied as more short and affording more cover than that at St. Jory. This Line was from Gagnac on the Right, by L'Espinasse to the Ers Rivulet on the Left. The 3rd Division holds from the High Road to Gagnac and the Garonne. The 4th from the High Road to the Ers. The 6th in advance encamped between St. Jory and L'Espinasse. This tomorrow morning.

April 7. The advanced Line ordered yesterday taken up. The River this morning is falling fast and it is certain that the Bridge may be renewed in the ensuing night.

April 8. Bridge laid down and the Spanish Division crossed and came to L'Espinasse. The 3rd Division moved along the Road from Gagnac beyond Fenoulhiet, and gained the parallel of Campville. The 6th along the High Road to the Post House beyond L'Espinasse. The 4th beyond Campville and then passed the Ers to Launequét, pushing on Light Troops towards the Bridge over the Ers at Croix d'Orade. The 18th Hussars and 1st Hussars attacked a Brigade of French Light Cavalry upon the Road to Alby, drove them through the Town of Croix d'Orade so rapidly that they had no time to destroy the Bridge, and the Light Infantry of the 4th Division got possession of, and held it. Col. Vivian, commanding the Brigade of Hussars and who led this attack with the greatest vigour and good order, was severely wounded. Lord Wellington ordered the Bridge to be shifted this evening to the Light Division which it is proposed shall cross tomorrow morning, and then with 4 Divisions and the Spaniards we shall be in force to attack the French Position upon the Heights of St. Augustin.

April 9. Some delay has been made about the Bridge. The Light Division can't pass before the evening, the Attack therefore is delayed 'till tomorrow, and Officers sent out to reconnoitre the Roads of approach. Enemy blew up the Bridges over the Ers on the Roads of Lanta and Erfeil.

April 10. Easter Sunday—BATTLE OF TOULOUSE.— The Enemy held a Position on the Heights of St. Augustin, North East of Toulouse, between the City and the Ers Rivulet, which runs through the plain at the foot of these Heights, and of which he had blown up two of the Bridges as mentioned last night. He had strengthened the Position by four Redoubts commanding the different Roads of ascent. It was by nature and by Art very strong, and Lord Wellington's original order of Battle for its attack was generally as follows :—

The Attack by the Left.

The 4th Division marching from Launeguét by St. Jean and Balma to cross the Ers by the Bridge on the Lanta Road, and turning the Enemy's Right ascend the heights and carry the Right Redoubt. The Ers is not fordable.

The 6th Division following the 4th (4th and 6th Divisions about 7800 together) through Launeguét to turn to its right, pass the Ers at the Bridge of Croix d'Orade, and then turning to its Left and moving nearly parallel to the Rivulet get possession of, and pass through the Village of Mont Blanc, and ascending the heights by the Erfeil Road attack the two centre Redoubts, and Centre of the Enemy's Position, near the Mont de St. Augustin.

The Spanish Division of General Freyre (10,000) moving from L'Espinasse along the Left Bank of the Ers, and passing through the Village of Croix d'Orade, to turn to its Left, and bringing its Left Flank near the Village of Mont Blanc, be in communication with the 6th Division and forming under cover of the Hill of Borde de la Pugada, ascend the Left of the Enemy's Position and attack his Left Redoubt.

The Light Division moving between the Villages of Campville and Croix d'Orade, to extend through the latter, be in communication with the Spaniards, support them if necessary, making meanwhile a false attack upon the Faubourgs, and taking care of the Road of Alby.

The Third Division upon the Roads of Montauban, and connecting with the Light Division, to make a False Attack upon the Faubourgs along that line, and watch the Debouché from the Town upon the Montauban Roads, and preserve the Bridge on the Garonne. Sir Rowland Hill's Corps of the Army (2nd and Portuguese Divisions) on the Left Bank of the Garonne, to make a false attack on the Faubourgs of St. Cyprian, and if practicable get possession of them and of the Tête du Pont.

Colonel Arentschilde's (late Col. Vivian's) Hussar Brigade to lead the 4th Division. The other Cavalry to act on the Left as Sir Stapleton Cotton might find occasion.

In the evening of yesterday the Road from St. Jean by Balma having been reported impracticable and the Bridge upon the Lanta Road having been blown up, the 4th Division was ordered to assemble at the Bridge of Croix d'Orade and passing the Ers there, precede the 6th Division and passing through Mont Blanc, march along the foot of the heights, gain its original point of attack on the Enemy's Right, and do as before ordered.

Colonel Arentschilde to move by Balma, and finding his way over the Bridge of Montaubran, act on our Left.

At 8 in the morning, the Troops, being assembled at their respective points, debouched according to the previous orders. The 4th and 6th Divisions moving by their Left in three parallel Columns of Lines by Brigades; in the common order of march, Sections of Three in Front. Thus they moved, under a very heavy Cannonade, along the whole Front of the Enemy, till they gained their ordered points where they formed, moved up to the Attack, carried all before them, and took possession of the Right and Centre of the Enemy's Position. At this moment (about 12 at noon) if the Cavalry as had been proposed had been in its allotted place upon the Left Flank the Enemy's confusion was so great that I should incline to think his destruction might have been easily completed, and his retreat into the Town interrupted. Some difficulty of Roads appears to have prevented the Hussar Brigades of Lord Edward Somerset, and the Heavy Brigade of Lord Charles Manners, from having arrived at the Head of the Column as Sir Stapleton Cotton had agreed to do, and this critical and important movement was lost.

The Spaniards meanwhile failed in their attack upon the Left, and Left Redoubt of the Enemy, and were driven back in some confusion. The Left Brigade of the Light Division moved up to the Hill of La Borde de la Pugada in support, checked the Enemy, who retired back to his position, and averted the impending disaster.

The Enemy still held the extreme Left of his Position, the Left Redoubt and a smaller one which was now discovered in its rear, and the 6th Division which had carried the Centre, was ordered to attack that point, supported by the Right Brigade of the 4th. So soon as the Guns could be got up the hill, and get the Enemy's fire a little under— the deep and clayey soil had prevented their getting up in the first instance, and the Centre and Right of the Position had been carried without the assistance of the Artillery. About 5 in the afternoon, the Enemy's fire being a little got under, the 6th Division moved to the attack, and carried the Redoubt in 10 minutes. The Enemy returned into the Town and the Victory was complete.

The Spaniards were made to enter and occupy the two Redoubts thus taken by the 6th Division. The 4th and 6th Divisions held the ground they had carried, and all bivouacqued for the night. Thus was the Battle gained by the two Divisions composing Marshal Beresford's Corps under circumstances of peculiar difficulty, and after a very bloody and obstinate conflict. The loss in proportion to the numbers engaged, is great, but this was in the nature of the thing.

Sir Rowland Hill meanwhile got possession, very gallantly of the Faubourg of St. Cyprian, and the work covering the immediate Tête du Pont. Head Quarters Launéguét.

April 11. The Enemy remained in Toulouse. The Army encamped behind the Heights of St. Augustin. The Bridges of the Ers were repaired, the Cavalry cantoned in the Villages on its Right Bank, and Lord Wellington had it in contemplation to bring over Sir Rowland Hill's Corps across the Garonne (hence the Reconnaissance and Report) leaving a sufficient force to hold the Faubourgs of St. Cyprian, to make it take the ground now held by Marshal Beresford, and then that the latter should cross the Canal, get possession of, and stand upon, the Heights between the Canal and the Garonne. I was directed to examine the Canal and Communications, and I made the Report . . . Marshal Beresford's Head Quarters Balma.

April 12. The Enemy broke up at 11 last night, retreated by the Carcassonne Road, passed the Canal by the Bridge of Baziege, blowing it up after him, as well as all the other Canal Bridges, and he retreated to Villefranche on the High Road to Perpignan.

The Corps of Marshal Beresford moved to La Bastide de Beaupoir. . . . That of Sir Rowland Hill through Toulouse and by the road of Mongiscard to Baziege, where it repaired the Bridge, crossed the Canal and connected with Marshal Beresford's Right.

The Enemy's Rear Guard remained for the night on the Heights of Montguillard. 1 Squadron of the 1st Hussars under Capt. Poten cut to pieces 2 Squadrons of the 15th Chasseurs.

April 13. Major Cook arrived in the afternoon from Paris at Toulouse. Napoleon Bonaparte has abdicated, retires to the Island of Elba with a Pension. Louis the 18th is proclaimed King of France at Paris. Major Cook went to Marshal Soult's Head Quarters. Sir Rowland Hill moved. . . .

April 14. The Marshal went to Toulouse.

April 15–16. Upon these days Marshal Soult shewed considerable reluctance to acknowledge the information sent him by the Provisional Government at Paris or to join in the adhesion to the New Order of things. Lord Wellington therefore appears to have determined not to allow him time to do mischief, and ordered the 6th and 4th Divisions and Col. Arentschilde's Cavalry (the Marshal's Column) to move tomorrow morning to St. Felix (which movement places them ready to debouche upon the Enemy's Flank at Castelnaudary), and the rest of the Army to close up to Villefranche. . . .

April 17. The Army moved and stands prepared for

an offensive movement forward tomorrow.   Head Quarters St. Felix.

Afternoon.—General Gazan, Marshal Soult's Chief of the Staff passed in with a Flag of Truce to Lord Wellington.

April 18.   Count Gazan brought to Lord Wellington a sort of reluctant acquiescence to the New Order of things on the part of Marshal Soult.   An Armistice was therefore concluded.   Hostilities cease, and thus ends our struggle.

April 19.   Memorandum.—Armistice signed at Toulouse by Sir George Murray for Lord Wellington, General Wimpfer for the Spaniards, and General Gazan for Marshal Soult.   These three Officers having full powers for the purpose.

The Department of the Higher Garonne is the Cantonment of the Allied Army.

NOTE.—In the following Post-War Journal (p. 338, § 11) *the explanation will be found for D'Urban's absence from the Waterloo campaign—a grievous disappointment to him after making every preparation, in characteristic fashion, for the departure of the contingent.*

JOURNAL XXV (POST-WAR)

August 1814, *to end of* 1815

INTRODUCTION

WHILE ' Sir William [Beresford] went to England by way of Paris [and] Lord Wellington went to Paris where the King, Louis XVIII, is expected from England,' D'Urban undertook the prosaic task of marching the Portuguese Army of some 28,000 troops back to Portugal (Journal XXIV),[1] accomplished ' without leaving anything behind, with out any instance of disorder or irregularity, and completing six years of unbroken service never having been absent one day from my duty either from sickness, leave of absence or any other cause whatever, having taken part in ten battles and sieges.'

Such services, it is gratifying to note, were adequately recognised, not only by the King of England, who in the following year appointed him a Knight Commander of the Most Honourable Order of the Bath, but also by the Spanish and Portuguese Governments.

For the next three years D'Urban remained in Lisbon, and instead of the rather colourless day-by-day entries, as becomes a soldier, he now unburdens himself in a most outspoken manner in defence of Beresford and his British Officers against the Regents who, in the continued absence of the Royal Family in Brazil, aimed—or so it seemed to D'Urban—at the destruction of the Army Beresford had so laboriously built up and rendered so efficient.

Aug. 30.   Arrived at Lisbon where the Marshal had preceded me from England by a few days.   His reception by the Government pretty well indicated their feeling towards him and the line of conduct they had in view to adopt.   The General who had formed their Army from worse than nothing to be the second in Europe in the scale of Excellence, who had raised their Military Character from the Dust, from something beneath Contempt, to the praise and admiration of the Military World, and had thus

---

[1] Not printed.

place security within the grasp of Portugal by giving her Martial Reputation of Renown ; who had more than once shed his Blood,—who had a hundred times risked his Life, who had sacrificed his fortune and his Health, nay staked his Character as a soldier to serve and save her,—This General,—(will Posterity believe it ?) after Six Campaigns of Glory, returning from the last of these, in which he had led her Triumphant Legions into the Heart of France and left the Terror of her Bayonets under the walls of Toulouse, —This General was suffered to land in the Metropolis of the Country he had thus served, and saved, and lifted into notice, and proceed to his House like an humble individual unhonoured, unvisited, unregarded.

The Plan long meditated by the Government of Lisbon now commenced to develop itself and was pursued with unremitting diligence in the sequel,—

This was

1st to get rid of The Marshal.

2ndly to clear the army of British officers.

I had foreseen that this would be the case, and had predicted it to The Marshal (when he imparted to me his views of remaining at the head of the Portuguese Army), before he left Toulouse to proceed to England.

Reasoning from the Conduct of Portugal towards its defenders in former Wars and from my Knowledge of that Country and its Government, its Nobility and its Gentry, as they are now, I felt certain that such would be the Project adopted by them,—and told the Marshal what the result has proved ; that if he attempted to Hold the Command of the Army after the Peace he would undertake a Task which would subject him to infinite vexation, and which he would in all probability be obliged ultimately to relinquish in Disgust.

I counselled him, if however he was resolved upon Retiral To take Care, not only that He Had the fullest powers from the Prince Regent of Portugal—the fullest and most uncontrolled Powers of acting according to his Judgement,—but also that it should be marked as a measure desired and Supported by the English Government with all its weight as a National [1] Object—in fact,

---

[1] ' Had this been the case, all difficulties would have given way, and it is not easy to imagine what would have been the cause of the luke-warmness of the English Govt. in supporting a Measure the importance of

upon which England had set its mind, and was prepared to carry,—and that both Govts. should be *d'accord* to keep the same number of British officers up in the Service as actually belonged to it.

Even with all this, I said, I thought it but too likely, that the Government of Portugal (although it would not dare or attempt to dismiss or thwart him openly) would contrive by a thousand Acts of which they are so capable to Disgust and traverse him till he could no longer endure his position ;—But that without all doubt that if he returned without This *Carte Blanche*, without this Support and Authority he would be sure to go to the wall ; withal, I begged him to consider whether under any probable circumstances the venture were worth the Risk,—whether he could gain reputation by the Measure and whether he might not lose much.

I suggested to his Consideration The Marshals Schomberg and La Lippe, both treated with ingratitude and driven out in Disgust and I asked if he Ever could leave the Portuguese Army so seasonably for his own renown as at that Period.—When at the Conclusion of a Glorious War, (in which he had formed it against immeasurable odds and in spite of innumerable obstacles,—preserved it, saved the Country with it, led it from Victory to Victory) he would return it to its Country, Covered with Laurels in full Effective Force,—and in the Highest Health Order and Discipline.

This was in His power—Much might be lost hereafter for his Fame and what could be *gained* ?

Most fatally for *us* we are ever sanguine about what we wish,—where we desire strongly, we strongly Hope—The Marshal (God knows why) had such a vehement inclination to Hold his Situation on, that he was incapable of using that Judgement which sees the future in the Past,—and as it were determined to see nothing in the Prospect but Facilities and a Bed of Roses :—

which to her Interests I know the Duke of Wellington was well convinced of and which is too evident to need the dwelling upon.

‘ It is not a little curious that although England continued to lend to Portugal a Commander-in-Chief, several Generals and 150 other officers, making a separate sort of Establishment for them, yet the British Ambassador at Lisbon never received the slightest instruction in case of any question that might arise between the Govt. and these officers & consequently took no part whatever under all the insults which were offered for months to The Marshal, to the Body of offrs. and in consequence (?) to England itself.’

He went to Paris there saw Count Funchal, then to England, and there saw the Ministry and then with an infatuation for which there is no name, without bringing either full Powers from the Prince Regent of Portugal or being even flattered with a Hope of strong support by the Government of England.—He came to Portugal—to fight his own Way, As it were, an Unappraised Adventurer.

What would be the result was evident to the dullest Capacity and it followed with a vengeance—

The Portuguese Government then felt that He was at their Mercy, and kept no occasion of common decency, and set to work without even the affectation of a Mask,—To Thwart, Embarrass, insult and disgust him and to Drive out of the Army at one Blow the British Commander in Chief and the British officers.—

If it be asked what could prompt any Government to throw away the Staff upon which it leaned and chase from its Side those Defenders which had protected and saved it,—I answer—without fear of contradiction (for I know that the reasons I shall give are Historic ones.)—

That,—The Regency of Portugal had long since meditated and resolved that whenever there should be a peace, The Army should be reduced to its former state of wretchedness and Nonentity, as Dangerous to the Power of the Government, and incompatible with it;—which indeed might be the case, for a Respectable Army. By consequence an Army officered by High Spirited and Honourable Gentlemen could never long endure that Its Country should be oppressed by a Government of such baseness and iniquity.

Their Existence then (unless they reformed their System which they are incapable even of imagining) and the Existence of the Army as it returned victorious from the War, were incompatible, and they determined upon its destruction;—The Ruin of their Country which might one day (& that perhaps not very distant) be the consequence, had no weight to deter them from such a treason,—

The nobility of this Country are incapable of aught but Private Motives,—Public Spirit does not exist in Portugal. God forbid I should permit the Suspicion to enter my thoughts that a still more odious and detestable motive, a

still more atrocious description of Treason guided these
men or any of them,—Though one might almost be
warranted in conceiving a desire to exist of delivering the
Kingdom, *Piés et Poings liés*, to be a Province of Spain.—
For this there might be many inducements for men of
their Description.

The Destruction of the Army then being the object
Resolved on by the Government, which there can be no
doubt of, because, they have as good as avowed it,—by
upholding and instructing their *émissaires* to uphold as
principles

1st That Portugal has no need for an army

2nd She is unable to keep one if she had.—

and (still more unfortunately for their Country because
they have avowed it by their actions.—the Destruction of
the army then being their object and their determination,
what were to be the great obstacles to their success in such
a measure ?—

1. A British Commander in Chief who would be sure to
watch over its welfare with a Jealous Eye and if the Power
was left him defeat all their machinations to destroy it—

2. British Officers dispersed among it, many at the
Heads of Regts. those with whom it would be impossible
to tamper, who would faithfully perform the duties they
owed to the Prince, their General and themselves,—and
who besides, with that open Spirit of Liberty, which
characterises soldiers of Freemen, would disseminate
among their Portuguese comrades notions of Right and
Justice—which might easily take Root and be fatal to the
Reign of iniquity and oppression.

These obstacles then were to be removed if possible at
the same time that the vitals of the Army were to be
sapped and its destruction so far prepared by degrees, that
when the time should arrive for their daring to act more
openly the feeble remains of the fabric might fall at a
touch.—

For the Marshal then—as the Prince Regent still con-
strained him and indeed was known to be convinced of
his value,—and as he possessed, still, extensive powers
from His Royal Highness so that they would not order
him off without ceremony—From the instant of his
Arrival, the Government practised Every effort of Intrigue,

detraction, Cabal and aspersion by their Emissaries both in Portugal and the Brazils, to destroy his Popularity with the Nation, and alienate the Favor of the Prince,—while at the same time they need every means that their Power and Ingenuity afforded them to thwart all his measures, Abridge his Powers, interfere with his Legitimate authority and Embarrass him in the discharge of his Duties.—

2. For the British Officers—they raised such a Clamour against them that The Marshal bending to the Storm, thought fit to Yield a point, what in my opinion he never should have done,—he consented to, and made the regular proposals for the Dismission from the Service of Portugal of about a Half of the British Offrs. belonging to it and these officers covered with wounds, and after Six Years labours retired from the Portuguese Army without any mark of approbation—from the Government, the Prince Regent or (to say truth) from the Marshal Himself.—

Many individual Instances of Malignity and meanness were practised by the Government and its emissaries in the prosecution of this General Measure, amongst which the Persecution of General Cox was a very striking one—Nor Did they leave a Stone unturned To Disgust the British Officers with their Position in Portugal, or to irritate the Nation & Army against their endeavour to make them odious and obnoxious.—In the process of this they disseminated the most rancourous defamation of England and everything English,—And by a Strange proneness to Ingratitude which has ever marked the Character of Portugal, These Villainous arts found such a congenial Soil to take root in that in a Short time,—England the Nation which had saved her, which had driven out her oppressors and to do so had sacrificed incalculable Blood and Treasure became to be more hated by the Nobility, Clergy, and Gentry (I don't include the Peasantry for no arts were able to tamper with their good judgement) than France had ever been at the time it invaded, Desolated and Covered the Country with killing.—

Such were the Treasons practised to get rid of The Marshal & his English Officers—and during the same time all care was taken

3. To undermine the Army, to moulder it away, to destroy it Physically & Morally,—To Discharge its best Soldiers to paralyse recruiting, & to ruin the Regts. by

want of Food, Bad Quarters & every kind of Neglect and ill treatment.—

To Undervalue Military Merit, to trample upon the Rights of Officers, to treat them (even of high Ranks) unworthily & with indignity—In fact to Strike a Mortal Blow at the Spirit of the Army.

The Marshal under all this acted with a forbearance and a yielding which throughout I combated in vain & which appeared to me to be pernicious, for the Pusillanimous are ever insolent to those who give way, and at length they Trampled upon him and insulted him and the Army without decency, remorse or Consideration and Forced him to take late a Step which he ought perhaps to have taken more early, go to the Brazils & Personally lay before The Prince the Wretched State of his Army, the Daily Treason of his Regency to it and the Certain loss & downfall of his Kingdom, if he does not return and change the System radically & effectually.

This is a General and Rapid Sketch of what has passed and of the principles of views of this government from the return of the Army to Portugal and of the Marshal from England in the August of 1814,—I have not kept the Events & occurrences in a Daily Journal as I did those of the Campaigns because they have not deserved it,—but The features of things as they passed, as far as my duties of Q.M.G. of the Army in any way brought me into contact with them were as follows.—

1814, *Sept.* 1. Upon my way from the Frontier to the Capital I had taken occasion to inspect such of the Barracks and Quarters of the Troops as lay in my way and found them generally so bad and unfit for their reception, that in the Month of September—I called for Reports from the Different Commanding Officers of the state of their respective Quarters (see A) and upon receiving these I made the report (B) to The Marshal.

Since the End of April the Government had known that the Army would speedily return and yet upon its arrival in August all was unprepared to receive it.[1]

---

[1] Marginal note: This Branch of the Service does not belong to my Department but has been arranged into a separate one 'the Department of Public Works '—under Colonel Fava (?)

2. The Marshal called upon me for a Projét of an Establishment for the Q.M.G.'s Staff and I sent in (C).

3. I also sent in to him The Memorandum (D) with a letter prefixing his acquiescence to its Contents.—
These officers have served the whole war and their claims are very strong.—

4. I sent in the Confidential Report and Memorandum (E) upon the Brigade of Cavalry which I had commanded the last Two Years of the War.

If the recruiting and other points upon which I have suggested in the Report alluded to in the Memorandum be not seriously attended to—there can be no cavalry worth its food.

October, November, December

1. The Marshal by order of the Govt. proposed for dismission & the Govt. dismissed accordingly about one Half of the British officers from the Portuguese Service,— In which the greater part of them had served the Whole War and they have returned without remuneration & several of them without promotion of which the Hope had been held out to them !—This was a fatal Yielding and the Government felt it as a victory & pushed him in other points accordingly.

2. They rejected a proposal to promote Colonel Cox, the late Governor of Almeida—gave the loss of the Place as reason although his Conduct there was well known & had been approved by The Duke of Wellington and the Marshal, and although He had since received the Tower & Sword for his services A Court Martial was ordered upon him.   (E/F.)

3. My report upon the Qrs. sent in by the Marshal to the Government together with a representation,—has produced the Effect of them at least entering into the subject —not however in a Way that will be effectual to ameliorate the Wretched Situation of the Troops, they talk of buildings which will never be carried into effect—and The Minister at War having directed Colonel Fava to go into the subject he addressed certain Questions to the Marshal upon the Nature and proposition of Barracks and Stables for Cavalry and Infantry.

The Marshal ordered me to observe upon these questions which I did in (E).

4. The situation of the Troops in their Quarters being extremely bad, and worse in proportion as the Season advanced—It became necessary that I should frequently call The Marshal's attention to it,—He as often repeated the subject to the Government and at length, (But merely by way of laying the question asleep for a time) they consented that a Commission of Inspection should be appointed to be composed of 12 officers Two for each province, of which the Department of Col. Fava should appoint one and I the other.—

I furnished the necessary Instructions to those who were to go on my part, immediately (G), and when those of Colonel Fava were ready, The whole set out for their destination where as I had foreseen they were studiously delayed in their progress by Col. Fava's Officers,—and the supplementary article (H) which He had represented to the Marshal as necessary and which therefore I had been obliged to add to my Instructions obliged my officers to be dependent upon their Movements so that this Commission was for little or no use, remaining under various pretences for Months in the same place.

5. During the whole of this Time the Troops were passing a very severe Winter, not only in Barracks which for the greater part did not shelter them from the weather, but altogether (in many instances) destitute of Blankets, Mattresses,—or any Article of Barrack Furniture.

My reiterated representations turned over by the Marshal to The Minister at War and Col. Fava produced no effect.

6. In the meanwhile The Government had ordered the Discharge of all those Soldiers who had been Volunteers. These were the Best Soldiers of the Army, and although the greater part of them wished to stay The Government insisted upon their being discharged.—

7. The rations of the Army were Struck off, the Pay reduced, and thus, This Army which had deserved So well of its Country and of Europe was reduced to the most unparalleled misery & distress and the prediction in the conclusion [1] of My Report of September most completely verified.

8. The Means adopted for the last 12 months by the Marshal to procure Horses for the Cavalry had succeeded

[1] Marginal note in last Paragraph of B.

so well that there were abundant to have remounted the Mounted Regts. & to have mounted *de novo* all of the dismounted, but there were no men remaining,—Great Proportion of the Soldiers of the Cavalry had been volunteers, they were discharged therefore and the Regts. reduced to nothing ;—

Under all this the Government rejected all the repeated instances of the Marshal to take any measures for recruiting.—

Thus Closed the year 1814,—and The Government had succeeded in less than Six Months, in getting rid of one half of that Gallant Army, which it dreaded & hated and in breaking the Spirit of the greater part of the other Half.

1815, *January, February, March, and beginning of April*

1. Some of the Cloathing (*sic*) and Equipment for the Infantry having arrived from England & the rest being expected, I commenced the arrangements for Cloathing and Equipping—wrote the circular order (J)—and the officers arriving from the Regts. in March The Issues commenced accordingly.[1] I was called upon to furnish a plan for new Dressing to Cavalry—I dressed a Dragoon (L—M). The plan was adopted in Toto & ordered to be made. The New dress for the Infantry had been already fixed in 1812, and 1813.

During this period Sir John Wilson set on foot in the Minho and Northern Provinces a military present to the Marshal. As soon as this was properly started the whole Army eagerly joined in it in spite of the unworthy and mean practices of the Government to traverse the project. (See 1C.)

This was a real Triumph to the Marshal and the Army and a most galling Mortification to the Government at which they did not attempt to conceal their chagrin.

2. Meanwhile the abuses practised against, and ill treatment of the Troops in Every possible way,—were incessant and the Government proceeded in its Plan (long meditated and digested) of destroying the Army,—It is incredible how rapidly this beautiful Fabric which had taken so much toil and labour to rear fell into decay.—

[1] It is interesting that with the ' Journal ' are enclosed original water-colour drawings of the ' Dress of the Portuguese Troops.' These are based on the uniforms of the British Army.

The Marshal, who all this time had been deceived into a belief that the Prince would return, got into a habit of letting everything lie over in this expectation, ceased to struggle against the tide, and I considered the position of affairs as hopeless.—I even suspended My Suggestions of Representations,—not to fatigue him by Urging what I saw he did not think fit to do,—and although I did not myself believe that the Prince would return,—yet I waitened (*sic*) to see whether he would or not. (During this period all detachments and Escorts through the Kingdom were mostly so irregular & the soldiers suffered so much in consequence that I proposed regular Routes and supplies and gave in the plan accordingly.)[1] When,

Remainder of April, May, June, July, August, to the middle

3. On the 6th of April The Government was electrified by the news of Bonaparte's escape from Elba and learned that Count Palvala had pledged Portugal for a contingent in the common cause of Europe—

4. This News arrived the 6th, on the 7th April,—I sent in to the Marshal the memorandum (N).

5. And upon the 11th April having received the order to call in Militia Returns preparatory to the Cloathing and Equipment of that Body I sent into him (O).

About this time I was called upon to report what I considered the best saddles and arms for the Cavalry—I reported—the Hussar Saddle like the 1st and 4th, but the *Castle* swords like the *last* given to the British Heavy Cavalry, carbines like those of the British Light Dragoons, Pistols ditto—1 *to each man.*

6. Towards the 20th of this month of April—A Demand arrived from the Continent, pledged by Count Palvala,—and the Transports from England began to come into the Tagus.—

7. The Marshal directed me to prepare him a sketch of 12 Regts. of the line 6 Batts. Caçadores—4 Bdes. of Artillery and a Squadron or Two of Cavalry to be assembled for this Service—I gave in the Memorandum (P) accordingly, the Marshal altered it in some measure when it stood as in (Q) and

8. The Regts were warned—completed in all their

[1] Marginal note.

Equipments—and the Routes held in readiness for their immediate March accordingly.

9.   I thought this a favourable Moment particularly as a General Promotion was in meditation to urge once again the claims of my Neglected Officers & accordingly I sent in No. 1 (The annexed Memorandum here alluded to will be found in ——) of (R). The Marshal replied to it in No. 2 and I replied in No. 3.

10.   In the end of April I thought it necessary to send in the Memorandum (S).

11.   The Government having considered of the demand for Troops,—at length after considerable deliberation refused to send any not only to Flanders but for a separate expedition to Bordeaux.—They pleaded their incapability to send Troops out of Portugal without the express Sanction of the Prince and a fear of Spain which was a subterfuge. The Real Objection was their repugnance to any measure which might arrest the downfall of the Army which this Expedition would particularly have stood in the way of.

Preparations therefore upon this score ceased,—and orders having been received from the Brazils to prepare a Corps of 5000 new Cavalry Infantry and Artillery to proceed *there*, this commenced to occupy all the military attention of Government.

12.   For this Corps I was called upon to furnish two Officers and did so accordingly, see (T).

13.   I was called upon to furnish a Detailed plan of the Cloathing and Equipment of the Army and did so accordingly (V).

14.   In the month of June The Hostility of the Government to the Marshal and all his measures became more open and unconcealed, and they rejected his Proposals in a Schedule of General Promotion, for the British Officers,—This brought the affair to a Crisis— and rendered it impossible to proceed.—

He determined therefore to go to the Brazils,—make his plain Statement to the Throne, and then either return with full powers to serve H.R.H. efficiently,—or quit the Service with the British officers altogether.

The Government were most averse to this measure of The Marshal, as may well be imagined—they threw every object in the way of it, refused it their Sanction and, with a littleness worthy of them, objected to His having a Frigate to take him out,—Nay if at this time they had not taken a fit of fear at the apprehended resentment of England, for Several Reasons which gave them cause for such an apprehension, they probably would have prevented any Portuguese ship from taking him.

In July The Marshal called upon me to prepare for him A Code of Standing Orders for the Organisation Discipline [Man]œuvring and Drill of a Regt. of Cavalry, I completed and delivered it to him a few days before he sailed (see W).

I felt it my duty to offer my services to the Marshal to accompany him to Brazil, for I thought his Mission a very likely one to put him in need of council, Consolation and Suggestion,—He either thought I should be of no use to him or thought I could be of use here in his absence and therefore declined my offer and directed me to stay at my Post.—(X).

15. Upon the 10th of August then The Marshal sailed from the Tagus. The Committee of the Whole Army who had been arranging the military present waited upon him the day before to request his acceptance of it, see (Y).

Every officer in and near Lisbon attended him to the Shore and to his Ship and he left Portugal, accompanied by the Affections, respect and Good Wishes of the Army in spite of all the Intrigues and efforts which the Government had so long practised to render him odious.—

16. The Regency had arranged that during the Marshal's absence—The Heads of Departments should take their orders from the Bureau of the Secretary of State so that the actual provisional Cr.-in-chief would supply his place in his absence.—

17. I presented myself to the Secretary of the Secretariat of State for the War Department (Don M. Forjaz) accordingly.

3. On the 28th of August therefore I despatched to all the Corps the Circular (Z) and on the 29th I enclosed a copy of it to D. M. Forjaz together with (AA) being my ordered Report upon the Commission and its Failure.—

4. On the 26th of September I received (BB) from The Minister,—By which I was filled with the greatest apprehensions that the whole Question was disposed of between him and Col. Fava, that nothing whatever would be done for the Troops in consequence of the Report that had

been produced by the Circular of the 28th August, and under this impression and as a last effort I wrote on the 27 Sept. (CC.).

5. I now remained some days without any further notice upon this point so infinitely important to the almost existence of what still remained of the Army ;— Meanwhile I was informed by the Minister that the Commission of Inspection was dissolved and directed to receive any officers accordingly. This of course was done.—

6. On the 17th October I received (DD) and on the 18th waited upon the Minister accordingly.—

I found that at least he had read the Reports in consequence of my letter of the 27th Sept.—

He produced a Report from Col. Fava,—Dressed in Two Columns, one of which contained an Abstract of the Report of each Commanding officer and the other opposite to it, what had been ordered to be done or was already done in consequence.

From the middle of August, September, October

1. My first care after the Marshal's Departure was to make an Effort to get the situation of the Troops in some measure ameliorated, if it should be possible, for The Prospect of Another Winter for them in the same misery of Uninhabitable Barracks and without necessaries as they endured the last was a most painful one.—

On the 25th of August, therefore, I waited upon Don M. Forjaz,—placed before him as strongly as I could the wretchedness of the Troops,—and pressed upon him the actual necessity both in point of Policy and Humanity, to cause some partial remedies to be applied which might at least enable them to live through that Winter.

He desired that I would support what I thought to be feasible, at the same time observing that very little could be done,—I proposed therefore the Commanding officers of Regts. should be immediately called upon to report what was actually and indispensably necessary to enable the Troops to get through the Winter. To this he acceded, —engaged me to send orders to them accordingly, directing them to make their report to Col. Fava, and he assured me that he would give orders to do the utmost possible of whatever the Commanding officer should demand.—

2. At this Interview also I stated to the Minister the absolute inefficacy of the Commission of Inspection of Quarters sent out in the Winter and which neither had done or would do anything,—He directed me to report to him my opinion upon this Commission accordingly.

For the Truth of this Report though Signed by the officer of High Rank and Shewn to be under the authority of the Minister at War, I should be sorry to vouch, but if it be correct—The Sufferings of the Troops will be a little alleviated,—for the Essential Requisites are there reported to be supplied, remedied etc. such as Repairs of Tiling, Windows, Doors, pavements, walls, Cooking Houses, necessaries, Medicines etc.—Supplies of Bedding, Bedsteads, Barracks, Utensils, in fact all the Essentials.

Nothing exactly however was either done or promised for the officers and to my urgent instances of the injustice of this and the Ruin it would bring upon many of them I was shortly but conclusively answered that ' The Government could not afford it and that it was of course *impossible.*'

I pressed upon the Minister also the practical changes of Companies and parts of Corps which were in some cases necessary. He made notes of these and promised that they should be immediately made.

He also informed me that the 5th Caçadores was on its march from Mon Corvo to Lamejo (a change which I had been soliciting for the last 9 months)—and he promised me to move the 3rd Regt. 9th and 8th Caçadores to other quarters also.—I am powerless to do more on this Subject—I trust some little good may have been effected —for this Gallant and Unfortunate Army, which has little merited that these lives which escaped the Fire and Sword of the Enemy in the Battles of Six Years should be extinguished by the hardships and misery to which their own Government so coolly consigns them.

7. In October the Returns for arrangements of Militia Cloathing and Equipment were completed and sent in to the Minister.

8. In the first week of November. The State of the Provisional Depôts in point of arms, ammunition, etc.

The year closed

B. D'URBAN Q.M.G.

Lisbon 31st December 1815

JOURNAL [XXVI][1]

1816, *Jan.* The first week of this month brought Dispatches from The Marshal at the Court of Rio de Janeiro where he had been received beyond his most Sanguine Expectations and where everything went to his wish.—The General Promotions (see B) proposed by him last year including the English officers and the opposition to which was one of the many reasons for his going to the Brazils, has taken place to the general satisfaction of the Army; The Regency, however, are determined to diminish that satisfaction as well as to depreciate the Royal Grace to the utmost of their Power by withholding the promulgation of this Promotion, although they have received Copies of the Court Gazette, under the pretence of a want of official information.—Meanwhile they continue unremittingly every possible means to destroy the Army and crush the Military Spirit of the Country. No imaginable extent of Human folly and imbecility could produce such a series of destructive and mischievous measures as are successively pursued under their administration, and it is impossible not to see that it is all System and regular design.

What can be the views of Regents who put in practice every effort to ruin the Army and their Country ? What but to lay it open to the machinations of Spain and to deprive their sovereign of the finest *appui* to His Throne, of the only means he can have to curb his factious and intriguing Nobility all hostile to him and to his House——and all wishing (If not to make his Kingdom the Province of another) at least to render him A Cypher. One, or other, or both of these is the object of this Government,—acting as it does,—as the Cat's Paw and Instrument of the Fidaljos—and for the Destruction of the Independence of the Prince and of the Nation.

[1] Not numbered.

Towards the 26th of this month,

The Division of 'Royal volunteers of the Prince' embarked.

As this has all along (Even by the admission of the Marshal before he went) been conducted as a separate Army, instead of a Detachment of the Army,—a perfect *Imperium in Imperio*, and its own Chiefs and the Minister at War, and not proceeding by any of the Regular organs of His Royal Highness' Forces,—so I have not been called upon to inspect the Means of Transport or To conduct the Embarkation—and as it is conducted by officers who never saw Troops on board Ship there is but too much reason to apprehend the consequences. So soon as this Expedition was announced, looking forward to the necessity likely to occur, I caused the British Transport Regulations to be translated into Portuguese and gave them to the Marshal that they might prove Standing Orders. I imagine he has forgotten them— and if so the health of This Division must suffer on the voyage.

Feb. Every account concurs to assure me that the Troops of the Division are in such confusion and so badly arranged and organised on board—that I have sent to General Le Cor The Copy of the Transport Regulations and the letter (A). This is all I can do—and I only hope he may hearken to it for the sake of the Troops.[1]

March, April, May, June, July, August

The Marshal—(created in December Marshal General of all the Armies European and American) continues to protract his Stay at the Rio Month after Month and, in the Profession of a Courtier, seems to forget the Army which is the Sole Support of Portugal, and to which he is indebted for all his Fame and all his High Fortunes ; —The Government here meanwhile do not lose a moment to complete their Project of destroying it—and if he delays much longer they will succeed to their Hearts' Content.—

[1] The speech of Canning of April 2 to the Merchants of Lisbon enclosed favourably commented on by D'Urban, saying that it was ' excellently well translated into Portuguese—widely disseminated through the community and produced the best effects.'

(20th of March the Queen of Portugal died and the Prince Regent became King John 6th).

The British Government too who (afraid of the appearance of Expense during the outcry of representations for Economy) are but too much inclined to withdraw the Establishment of British officers,—and have only had the Courtesy and Forbearance to wait his return before taking any decided Step,—but which his Personal Influence in England can alone prevent their ultimately doing,—The British Government, seeing how he himself abandons the object and leaves it to its fate will inevitably become more and more indisposed to make any Sacrifice for his Support in that regard—and more than ever likely to deprive him of His British officers to whom he owes the Existence of the Army and all his success, and without whom All is at an end.—

The Marshal General can no more have a Portuguese Army fit to look at an Enemy without British officers, than an Eagle can fly without wings, they are the Pinions upon which he has Soared, and all his Great and Superior Talents will be unequal to support him without their aid.

(N.B. In the end of August Arbuthnot arrived and it is clear that the British Government mean to give up the Establishment here altogether.)

Not a fortnight not a week has passed without some deadly wound to the Well being of the Army to its discipline, to Its Moral as well as Physical Force, on the part of this Government (see (C)). I am powerless to avert (although wherever I can I never fail to struggle against) the Evil which I so deeply lament,—and in a very short time if the Marshal General do not return and that with the fullest and most uncontrolled Powers, and a fixed determination to use them to the Utmost, I shall, after having watched the Infancy and Full Vigour of this once beautiful and gallant Army, infallibly witness also its total decay and Dissolution.

Sept. 5. The Princesses of Portugal arrived from Rio de Janeiro at Cadiz—given in marriage to Ferdinand and his brother Don Carlos.

Sept. 18. The Marshal General arrived.

He has brought with him Regulations (D) for the organisation and good government of the Army in all its

Branches which are generally excellent and well adapted
to the End in View, but some of them are rather indistinctly
couched and will give rise to cavilling and misinterpre-
tations. However—this is a trifling Evil compared with the
Dispositions of the Government here—These can all remain
in their places—with unchanged Illwill and the same
determination to Resist as ever nor will they do so the less
strenuously (though perhaps they may have the decency
to do it somewhat less openly now that the measures for
the welfare of the Army are the Orders and Decrees of
their Sovereign, than they did when they were only the
wishes and measures of the Commander in Chief.

The Regency have received the Marshal General with
smiles—and decent attention—but I am much mistaken
if they don't soon give him proofs that their Enmity to
the King, to their Country, to him, is as inveterate as
Ever.

If it be so,—he will have gained little in point of reality
by his visit to the foot of the Throne,—nor while it remains
in America do I think he can ever carry its mandates
into Effect.

Oct. As I predicted so it is ;—The Regency commenced
their machinations with the Marshal General's arrival,—
and all is open war again.—They impede the execution
of the Royal orders by every means in their Power,—and
even attempt, by every means in their Power to render
them unpaleatable [*sic*] to the people, and certainly it is
not their fault if there has not been a rebellion.

There is no doubt that the Nobility of Portugal for
the most part is disposed towards the House of Braganza,
—and that they dislike the Reigning sovereign,—the
Government is composed of Imbeciles and dangerous
Theorists. The former at once devoted to the Party
of the Nobility and ruled by the latter,—and the General
Object and End of the whole to deliver Portugal into the
iron yoke of Ferdinand 7th. Hence their Measures
ever since the Return of that Monarch to the Throne,—
Hence The work of sapping and destroying the Army
which they have so unremittingly pursued.—Hence their
desire to get rid of British Commander in Chief and of
British officers—The great obstacles to Treason and its

Consequences—because at once Clear sighted, Loyal and Firm, they can neither be deceived, corrupted nor intimidated and are the finest support of the Sovereign whom they serve. A Representation of theirs that the New System would increase the expenses of the State has been categorically refuted by The Marshal General, (F) (some notes delivered to him in the way of suggestions in returning the Sketch of the Government which he had given me to read) proving that the burdens will be lightened thereby and his Order of the Day (E)—in publishing the Alvacas (D) has quieted the Public Mind and been received by the People and the Army with great satisfaction.

Meanwhile it has been communicated by The Duke of Wellington to The Marshal General that the Supreme Council of Spain had formally proposed to his Catholic Majesty to reject The Princesses (some votes were even for imprisoning them as hostages)—declare war against Portugal and Enter that Kingdom—with the armies already in preparation under the view of South American expeditions—in Andalusia and Catalonia—the Plea of this aggression was the occupation of Monte Video in South America by the Portuguese troops. The King—who loves women and had heard of the Beauty and (?) of the New Queen turned a deaf Ear to this advice—Exclaimed 'Las Bodas y la Paz' (Peace and the Marriages)—and soon after becoming extremely fond of the Queen upon knowing her—dismissed Don Pedro Cevillos—his Prime Minister who had been the most violent against Her Majesty and Portugal.

This move the which although well known to the Regency of Portugal they had studiously concealed from the Marshal General. He, however, soon after he received it addressed a very forcible note to them telling them what he knew and calling upon them under the knowledge of such a feeling upon the Part of Spain to beware how they misused the Responsibility of any longer impeding the executions of His Majesty's orders for the benefit and reorganisation of the Army.

Dec. This note they did not answer officially, but the imbecile part of the Regents took fright at it, and soon after,—upon the Arrival of some intelligence from Madrid, they sent the Sentry of the Government (Don Miguel

Pereira Forjaz) to confer with the Marshal General.—
Don Miguel informed him upon the Part of the Government
that ' Spain was very much exasperated, that the
Lady declared her determination of going to war if it
should turn out that the Portuguese colours had been
hoisted at M[on]te Video.'

That such colours have been hoisted there there is
no manner of doubt so that If Spain keeps the word of
her threat War in a short time is certain.—And she has
Three Armies on foot to support it in 1. Andalusia,
2. Catalonia, 3. Castile, for She has augmented her
armies since the Peace while Portugal has diminished
or rather destroyed her's.   The Regency in making this
communication—admitted that Portugal was too weak
to resist and yet deprecated all attempt at becoming
stronger upon the wretched plea ' that the least appearance
of such an intention would induce Spain to convert her
Threat into Earnest.'

Nay, the Secretary upon The Marshal General's urging
the necessity of at least provisioning the Fortresses of the
first order,—observed that it must be done by Stealth
not to attract suspicion and accelerate the Evil they seemed
so much to dread.   Here then is the whole Enigma Un-
ravelled ! here is the Solution of the Conduct of these
Regents for these Three Years,—The Different acts of
the Piece have followed in rapid succession and this
verges upon the last.   They have gone regularly on in
Destroying the Army Morally and Physically,—in throwing
Everything into disorder and Confusion, in weakening
the Defences of the Kingdom leaving its Fortresses without
Provisions and Ultimately in ruining the Public Credit
and endeavouring to excite discontent and ill will of
Championing The People,—and now—That they have
reduced their Sovereign's Kingdom to a state of Weakness
and as far as in them lay, tied it Hand and foot.—The
Enemy threatens and they cry—' Oh for God's sake don't
think of arming or he will infallibly strike ! '   What must
result then ? and what State was ever saved by crouching ?
—Why Destruction must result and that very shortly—
for If Portugal does not prepare now—what will she do
when Spain (every day strengthening) becomes stronger ?
If she does not now stand at her Arms—The Time will
shortly come when Spain will assume the Right (and what

is worse perhaps will have the Power) to demand that they shall be surrendered.

It is thus that these Regents, the creatures and the Instruments of a wretched and corrupt nobility,—have prepared the downfall of their Country and its reduction to be a province of Spain.   The Marshal General informed Lord Castlereagh and the Duke of Wellington of all this and I pointed out the holding in view the Spanish armies without appearance to the Frontier Governors . . . ?

In the Course of this and the preceding Month as I considered that No. 1 of G. was very inadequate to reward the officers who had served [in] the last War and as I knew that this was the opinion (and justly so) of the Army, I suggested No. 2 to the Marshal Gll. which he was good enough to approve and recommend to His Majesty.

The Government put some questions about Cloathing —which were answered in H.

The Q^r M^r Gl's Dept. being to be established as in the Alvaça of His Majesty in (D) I proposed to make effective by such an organisation as that in (K) and its enclosures.

The Marshal General was pleased to approve and order it to be carried into Execution.—

The Marshal General wished a Reform in the mode of Mounting the Cavalry officers, absolutely necessary as indeed it was.   I laid before him L No. 1—as much of it as is contained in L No. 2 was approved of.

The Prices of compensation and hire fixed—are low but the government will not admit of more—

Upon the 19th of December as reports of Spanish preparations gained ground, and as the Govt. took no measure nor made any public or official communication to the Marshal General beyond what had been made through their Secretary D. M. P. Forjaz verbally and without witnesses (so that it amounted to nothing) I adjured him for the sake of his own Reputation as well as the Good Service of the King—to call upon the Regency to say what they knew, what they apprehended,—and what they intended.—How near was the danger—and how they proposed to meet it.   In order that he might then if it was distant only recommend the fulfilment of the King's Orders,—and in case it was near that he might hasten to fill up the Regts. by Taking from the Militia Regts (53 in number of 1100 men each) as many more as would suffice to give 500 men to each Regt. of the Line and 250 to each Battn. of Caçadores,—thus bringing 16,000 effective men into the Ranks of the Regular Regts while the Militia might be completed from the Ordenanza. This last is the only means to make the Army fit to meet the Enemy—for the measures of the Regency have reduced it so that The Marshal General could not take the field with 15,000 men ' Quanto Mutatus ! '

The Marshal General is good enough to think with me and is preparing a formal Note accordingly,—Be the last what it may—This with His last note will save his reputation ;—and the fright it will throw these wretches into may probably drive them to throw enough power into his hands to save the Kingdom also.—If the Militia Transfer alone is adopted I will answer with My Head to have everything in readiness in Three Weeks to give a feeling lesson to whatever Spanish Armies have set their foot into the Frontier.—So closes 1816—And the rapid decay of all the means and power of this Kingdom which two years ago might have dictated a peace in Madrid and which now—is reduced by its Rulers to be at the feet of Spain, is a fearful proof how soon Imbecility and treason together—in the Executive Government, may Ruin the Nation—and with the overthrow of a Throne however respectable the one—however firm appears the other.

B. D'URBAN.

Lisbon 31st December 1816.

JOURNAL [XXVII] [1]

1817, *January.* A conclusive and most clear and succinct exposition of the defenceless state of the Country in respect to the ineffective State of the Army and the Fortresses, contained in a Note to The Government has apparently produced much effect;—It finished by such an appeal to their Responsability [*sic*] as they could not very well read without being frightened and under the impulse of this fear,—they invited The Marshal to a Conference and assured him of their readiness to do everything he wished.

As a sort of first fruits of their professions they have Permitted the Appointment of The Generals of Division & of Brigade & officers of the Augmented General staff as prescribed by His Majesty's order of the 21st February,—and affect to make some provision for the wants of the Fortresses—This however is all that up to the End of this month has arisen out of their Professions—Nay, they contrive to render even the appointment of the officers null and useless by embarrassing the Financial arrangements,—while at the same time they studiously spread the report that the Marshal is himself the cause of the delayed obedience to the Royal Order in respect to Payments,—and while they withhold all issues as well for present purposes as arrears—they affirm that the Requisite Sums have been placed at his Disposal and thus try to throw the Odium upon him.

Meanwhile, in order to place the Q.M. General's Dept., as far as rests with me upon an efficient footing and to enable it to render those important services to the Army which by the provisions of the late Alvaca have now for the first time [been] made feasible,—I have prepared (*A*)—annexed (upon the footing of the Memoranda never tried in my J[ournal] of last Year). The Marshal has approved and ordered it and it is accordingly carried into effect. By

---

[1] Not numbered.

following these Regulations I imagine that (if any army is
to be left to this devoted Country), an Efficient and Able
Staff, both for Peace and War, may be established and
Maintained.

Feb. 7.   The Marshal General set out a Tour round the
Fortresses of the Alemtejo,—This would be the quarter of
Real and serious attack if Spain should actually continue
in a Hostile disposition, and in thus inspecting Everything
there, he will give all the Spring that rests with him to
give to that part of the Machine for which he is responsible.

Feb. 21.   The Marshal General returned—nothing can
describe the state of Ruin—and neglect into which The
Fortresses and everything military have been suffered to
fall.—It would appear as if the Government had dealt with
the Devil to ruin the Defences of the Country so rapidly.—

The Infantry—what there is of it has maintained its
Discipline decently.—The Cavalry is all ruined as I predicted.   (I made to the M.G. the representations in (*A*).)

March 4.   At length the storm appears ready to Burst
upon this devoted Country.

The Duke of Wellington writes the Marshal General in
substance that Spain has complained to the 4 Great
Powers, England, France, Russia and Prussia, of the
attack of the settlements upon the River Plata—That she
is not satisfied with the way in which they consent to
mediate and that it is very probable, will attack Portugal,
soon—.

This Government at the same time that it has left the
country defenceless,—has continued to alienate the good
will of its only faithful Ally—England—England is not
disposed to help her therefore, and the other Powers take
the same tone.   They may indeed ultimately object to
Spain's retaining Portugal permanently but they will not
object to her being occupied and overrun and plundered
in the mean time.—

To make their blow more sure the Spaniards had even
requested or required of England that the Marshal should
be withdrawn from the Portuguese Service.

The Marshal General demanded an audience of the
Regency and imparted to them his information.

Their Consternation real or affected was extreme, and
they professed the most eager desire to Recruit, to prepare
and do Everything he wished.   With most of them (that

is the Imbecile and comparatively honest) their fears and their professions are Real and Sincere—with the others (or other for I am willing to hope there is but one) that is the T—. They were feigned.

However the Result of the sitting was to permit the Marshal General to take immediately every preparatory step of preparation,—that the means within his reach might afford, and to send to Madrid to desire that Spain would give a categorical Answer as to the Nature and intention of her preparations.

The answer to bring Peace or War.

This is the only way, resistance and preparation how-ever late is the sole Road to Safety, and when once the nation knows with what it is menaced—I am confident that notwithstanding it has been thus tied hand and foot by its Regents, Spain will find the putting on the Yoke a task beyond her Power.

Meanwhile—There are unfortunately No Arms—This most essential want I must endeavour to get supplied from England where I am obliged to go and was to embark in two or three days—to assume the duties of D.Q.M.Gl. of the Army at Home to which I have been long appointed—and which I must go to. The Marshal General, however, writing to the Duke of Wellington that His influence may ensure of my being allowed to come back immediately here, should Spain assemble to attack Portugal,—

If I can expedite the arms there is no service I can render by staying (till the War actually commences) so important as that which I shall do in going.

                                    B. D'URBAN.

After nine years of most meritorious service, then, Sir Benjamin D'Urban returned to England to take up his appoint-ment as Colonel of the Royal Staff Corps and Deputy Quarter-master-General, duties he assumed in preference to the Gov-ernorship of St. Lucia. The following year he was created a Knight Commander of the Royal Guelphic Order; became a Major-General in the British Army in 1819, while in March 1820 he was made Governor of Antigua, Montserrat, and Barbuda.

His subsequent career, including his administration of British Guiana and the Cape of Good Hope, and finally as Commander-in-Chief of the British forces in Canada, where he died in 1849, is to form the subject of another volume.

INDEX

Printed in England at THE BALLANTYNE PRESS
SPOTTISWOODE, BALLANTYNE & CO. LTD.
Colchester, London & Eton